INTO THE OPEN

Other books by Michael H. Shenkman

The Arch and the Path: The Life of Leading Greatly

Leader Mentoring: Find, Cultivate and Inspire Great Leaders

The Strategic Heart: Using the New Science to Lead Growing Organizations

INTO THE Open

MENTORING MYSTIC ASPIRATIONS

Michael H. Shenkman Ph.D.

Audacious Leaders, New Mexico

2015

ISBN: 978-0-9909163-0-7

First Edition

✝

Published by Audacious Leaders
2313 Wagner Avenue, Farmington, NM 87401

www.audaciousleadersedu.com
info@audaciousleadersedu.com

Book and cover design by Robin Wrighton
Text in this book has been set in Perpetua 13/15. Perpetua is a typeface designed by English sculptor and typeface designer Eric Gill (1882-1940). Myriad has also been used as a contrasting font. Myriad is a humanist sans serif typeface designed by Robert Slimbach and Carol Twombly for Adobe Systems.

For information or bulk purchase of this or other books by Michael H. Shenkman, please contact the publisher.

"That part never fixed,
    asleep in us,
        from which will spring

TOMORROW THE MANIFOLD."

              ~ Rene Char[1]

❧

Table of Contents

PART TWO: The Mystic Family

Figures, Tables and Diagrams

Acknowledgements

This book has been in preparation for many years, and many people have contributed, indeed, inspired, its content and intent. It began when Charles Hoffman extended his support to creating, perfecting and expanding upon a program that I called "Leader Mentoring" nearly twenty years ago. Under the auspices of the consulting engagements he sponsored, I met and worked with great people. Some of these are the people whose aspirations I describe, using pseudonyms, in this book.

The work continued and was elaborated by being able to work with many more people who aspired in the mystic figuration. I will not mention names, but I want to acknowledge all of those people who, in the course of our mentoring, encouraged and supported the discussion and exploration of the mystic figuration of their aspirations.

I want to thank the Mentoring Institute of the University of New Mexico, and its director, Nora Dominguez, for opening up a forum to an independent or private researcher in the field of mentoring. By presenting papers at its annual conference, I received valuable commentary and support for this work and the work on mentoring aspirations in general.

I thank the people who have read and edited this manuscript as it evolved from the roughest of drafts to a presentable and publishable text. And then, my thanks to the attentive and engaging editing offered by Kate Victory Hannisian of Blue Pencil Consulting during final editing and preparation of the manuscript.

Finally, I thank my wife and companion Carol. Her abiding faith in this work has never wavered, even when my own faith did.

Dedication

To my wife Carol, my parents and teachers,
and to Ralph Potter, whom I named "Mackie"
and who was my first and finest mentor.

ॐ

Preface

It is not good
To be soulless
With mortal thoughts. But good
Is conversation, and to speak
The heart's conviction, to listen to tales
Of days of love
And deeds once done.

~ Hölderlin, "Remembrance" [1]

It sometimes seems as though the artist, and the philosopher in particular is only a chance in his time… nature, which never makes a leap, has made its own leap in creating them and a leap of joy moreover, for nature then feels that for the first time it has reached its goal — where it realizes it has to unlearn having goals and that it has played the game of life and becoming with too high stakes. This knowledge transfigures nature, and a gentle evening-weariness, that which men call "beauty," reposes upon its face.

~ Nietzsche [2]

Welcome

In the pages that follow I want to foster our ability as mentors to listen to mystic aspirations, understand the lives these potent forces entail and thus be better able to bring their necessary way of envisioning our world into our own decisions, actions and thoughts. If you are picking up this book and deciding whether or not to continue on, I imagine you to be interested in this subject for one or several of the following reasons: You have a deep interest in people who have been called "mystics." Or, I am thinking, only guessing really, that you think of yourself as being a mystic. Or you might know someone close to you who acts in ways that make you think about mystics. Or you might be excited by creative people and want to know more about mystics, or you might even want to work with me in supporting and encouraging the mystic figure's way of bringing new ideas, freshness and restored vitality into our lives. You may even feel that someone you know (or even you yourself) has never quite been heard out, never quite been appreciated, or possesses and offers a kind of wild creativity that just cannot find an audience. Maybe you worry about the loneliness such a person might be experiencing, if not expressing.

I offer this preface in the spirit of helping you decide whether or not to proceed, and to offer some initial orientations to the text that might help you to stay with me and to then feel that you made the right decision in doing so. After all, if we were meeting in person, you would make such an evaluation ever before the conversation commenced; and then you would decide, step by step, how much further into the conversation you wanted to go, how deep you wanted to go, how much longer you wanted to stay, how much attention you wanted to devote. I would be deciding similarly about you. So what follows offers you a chance to make decisions – about me, about this subject, about the course and method of this book – about whether or not to proceed. This book comprises three parts, each of which I consider as being necessary sketches of what constitutes the mystic figuration of aspiration (including what "aspiration" is to begin with): (I) a mindset or constitution of aspirations into a viable and robust psychic/somatic resource; (II) a genealogy of the mystic figuration – which lays out the formation of the only notion of a mystic figuration that we have; and (III) a concentrated description of the process of mentoring a person whose aspirations are taking on mystically figurative characteristics.

I see this book as being of value to the people I described above, and I have written it with four main concentrations of interest in mind. These concentrations, and suggestions for proceeding are:

1. **People who might be experiencing mystic aspirations:** I would read this volume straight through, and consider it as a guide to self-exploration, including Part Three, which might be used as a self-mentoring guide, to some extent.

2. **People who might consider mentoring people with mystic aspirations:** If you consider yourself to be a mentor or consider yourself to be in the process of mentoring someone whom you suspect is affected by the mystic figuration of aspirations, then you would benefit from reading the Preface and Introduction, Chapters One and Two, and then you might consider proceeding to Part Three to survey the salient parameters of the mentoring engagement that I suggest beg for your attention. Using the outline of the mentoring process as a guide, you can then refer to the chapters referenced there with a mind to their imminent application in a mentoring engagement.

3. **People who might be interested in taking up a more formal study of the notions of aspiration and their figurations (roles):** Whether you are an academic or a lay person who pursues notions in depth, this volume implies that there is an approach to considering the creative, transformative, generative and re-valuational dimensions of human engagement that has yet to be explored. You would benefit, I believe, from reading this book cover to cover and also taking side trips in the form of following up on the works suggested in the footnotes.

4. **People with a general interest in, and curiosity about, mystic aspirations and who are considering what kind of attitude, role and pursuit to take up with respect to that interest:** I would read this book from cover to cover, take

your time, move through passages that seem strange or out of reach (come back to them later, since the book is organized iteratively and each of the main concepts is covered several times in different contexts) so as to get a "feel" for this notion of aspirational figuration, in its mystic form.

There is no doubt that within a matter of a few paragraphs, this text will become challenging, especially to lay readers who are not inured to coping with seemingly technically obscure notions. I ask for readers' forgiveness and indulgence and promise I have not made this text difficult in order to bolster an illusion of importance. Rather, in dealing with aspirations in general, and with mystic aspirations in particular, we are venturing into new conceptual space. When it comes to aspirations, not only are new concepts being developed and ventured as these words are being written, but new facets of relations of psychic/somatic energies and organizational capabilities are being discovered. Many of the texts that I cite as guides into this arena of thought became available only as recently as the 1990s – to give you an idea of how recent this research is. And so, the difficulty of the text ensues: you are not likely to be familiar with some of these concepts; we are conceiving of the "mind" or the psychic/somatic system (P/SS) in a new way; we are still forming our ideas about these P/SS resources, and trying to specify how they constellate, consolidate, become articulated and take form – take on a figuration – that robustly enacts aspirational speech (including concepts and ideas), acts and decisions. And so I ask the reader to hang in there with the text. If a concept or idea is not immediately clear, which most certainly reflects my limitations in verbalization, keep moving, for rest assured, the idea will come up again in a different context that might be more clear and will be just as valid an interpretation in that context as it was in the previously incomprehensible one.

With that request in mind, we will now venture into our exploration of mentoring mystic aspirations.

Mentoring the Aspirational Figures

I consider this book to be one part of an extended series of works to support mentoring a certain population of people. I am someone who devotes time and study to support and encourage people I have called "aspirational figures," but who, in more "technical" terms are to be considered people who have taken up their aspirations as matters of devotion and priority, even to the detriment of other aspects (personal relationships, career prospects, financial accumulation), and so are in the position of responding to those aspirations as a kind of focusing concern, even a demand, that their life ways must accommodate, first and foremost. These people thus embody, to the fullest extent that we can encounter and observe, an *aspirational figuration* of a life way. In the life ways of the people I discuss in what follows – the famous and the completely unknown – we see aspiration, this defiantly "creative" and insistently generative psychic energy bounding forth into what might just offer possibilities that are more expansive and more encompassing.

When we feel healthy in our lives, we feel this energy in ourselves. That sense of "feeling alive," of being on the edge, of having our life be opened to learning we had never even before considered as possible, is what these people take as their primary concern. This decision to do so is what makes these people seem "different" from us; and yet, we know enough to make room for just a touch of curiosity, if not admiration, for these people. At first we are likely to reject these people; but perhaps later, when we are at a safer distance from their immediate affects, we find that they have, indeed touched us after all. And then, perhaps, we smile. And so these people I cite here, although "breakout" people, are not strange, untouchable, unapproachable exceptions; they are our managers, our spouses, our writers and confidants, who evoke in us what, in our health, we would most likely choose to nourish and encourage (as we do in raising our children?). And, for mentors, the people I cite here provide examples from which we can learn to recognize how aspirations play in what the people we meet most ardently desire: to feel alive.

What most of us do not appreciate, or do not consider, is that in order to act on those aspirations, people take great risks. These aspirations are not ambitions that have identifiable goals and objectives, products or services that can be explained, proposed or put into a business plan. While aspirations may be approached by classical training and coaching techniques, none of these supporting modalities, which are useful when applied appropriately, will touch *aspirations* directly nor will they be able to countenance, no less address, what aspirations demand of and from people. What is more, those people often do not know what those aspirations will lead to in real practice any more than others do. The breakout creative person is mostly alone with his or her aspirations — unless, that is, a mentor comes onto the scene.

FIGURATIONS OF ASPIRATION. For the purposes of developing mentoring pedagogies I have grouped aspirations into four figurations: leader, artist, prophet and mystic. I regard people as expressing aspirations that fall into these "breakout creative" roles or "aspirational figurations," when, by choice or by acceptance, they shape their lives in such ways as to position at the forefront of their life's decisions acting on those aspirations first and foremost. In accordance with the very structure and substance of aspiration — which we will discuss in detail in Part Three of this book — these decisions take the form of responding, in flesh and blood, to this question: "How do I contribute to making this human endeavor more vital, more *expansively encompassing* of other people, ideas, other creatures, nature and the earth, no matter what they do to put that commitment to work?" The more this question shapes a person's concrete decisions, actions, speech and life ways, the more this person is acting on his or her aspirations. How do they do this? Some of them produce works, great and small, which we get to appreciate and benefit from; others produce in quiet and solitude, or labor out of sight, and never become "known" as "creative" in the conventional sense of the term. What interests me is not the quality of their work, their success or notoriety; what interests me is their *aspiration*: their willingness to shape a way of living, on the slightest of hope and faith, that brings something fresh and vital into all of our lives.

The mentor sees the aspirational figure in a different light than does the trainer, coach, therapist or the lay observer. The mentor comprehends this person's life ways by appreciating just what *aspirations alone* entail, and what happens to people as they pursue their *aspirations*, as opposed to careers, ambitions, or just getting along. We all know about artists' non-conformist carryings on; we know about leaders' "egos," but we do not know much about the overwhelming doubt that besets a "prophet" figure at every turn, and we especially do not know about the continual feelings of rejection and banishment that mystic figures feel. We all know about the effort creative people expend on doing their work, but we only occasionally consider the tremendous amount of effort and energy they must exert in order to resolve the great conflicts and ambiguities their complex psyches impose on their daily living. Many succumb to these demons and fail in their creative pursuits; they suffer in their resignation to conformity, they fall prey to illness and despair. Many succumb to the illnesses of depression, compulsion and addiction that sometimes accompany the creative drives. While mentors cannot address or ameliorate, heal or cure these most severe afflictions, they can work with people who are in pain and help them to find a path and a way to live with the difficulties their life's way imposes on them – before those illnesses take their irreversible tolls.

We are prone to give our attention to the physically, socially or economically "disadvantaged" and less fortunate among us. Indeed, we are made to feel guilty (in most sectors of our society) if we don't do so. The aspiring ones are vulnerable, too. In fact, they are doubly vulnerable. First, their contributions depend on complications and ambiguities in their lives, and second, they exert their efforts in ways that challenge the status quo. Just because many do have great assets going for them (health, lightning-quick intelligence, great capacity for love of life, etc.) does not make them less vulnerable to the defensive aggression of their detractors. Because they are going against the grain, their lives are difficult, financially, socially and interpersonally. So these figures have only their vulnerability to bring into the fray to begin with. The risks they take in doing their work actually put all of their strengths – of personality, of great vitality and optimism, of dedication to their fields of endeavor – in service to the *ambiguities* they use as a creative platform. They risk all that health and energy to make a difference, and this difference emanates from where they are most vulnerable.

Changing Our Worlds

Also implicit in this text is an idea about how our worlds *change*. Since we inhabit a cosmos that clearly changes, we presume that the world we live in here and now also changes. That is hardly a controversial notion. But things start to get touchy when we enter into the discussion of *how* that process occurs, toward what (if any) end such change is gravitating, and what that change process looks (feels) like. In this context we accept that the process so far has not been handled well by humans – if the death toll is anything to go by (and maybe it isn't). It is a guiding premise of this work – the book, the aspiring figures, mentoring – that the human endeavor is distinguished from other aspects of nature by *consciously taking up the decisions (made eons ago) to guide the course of our own becoming more complex, becoming more expansive and more encompassing in the ways we engage occurrences*[3] *to which we are a part.*

The process of change has interested me from my earliest years of being a conscious person. As a "child of the sixties" (the 1960s, that is) I concentrated my academic studies on those thinkers who framed their work in terms of irrepressible change (Hegel, Nietzsche, and Marx, for starters). . As time went on (and several devastating assassinations occurred), I developed the overwhelming sense that we do not do social change well. And yet, as a witness to President Obama's election and other developments that herald inclusion and increased access to choosing one's life ways, I am also gratified to see that change does happen, and in this country, it can happen peacefully, as a result of the skillful use of our institutions. In between these events the country limped and lurched along in years of wrenching sorrows, losses and decline. Most of the ideas presented here have developed during these recent years. I use the current climate, one in which change is actually being undertaken (and fiercely resisted), as posing a good test to these ideas[4].

Key to my conclusions about this process is that the great ideas and visions about "advancing" the human endeavor require long periods (eons, epochs – spanning centuries) of gestation time, which allow for an idea to be discerned, and then still longer periods of gestation, transmission, and transformation. And all of these phases require specific kinds of talents, proclivities and orientations toward human *aspirations*; those specific talents are those that are considered in the mode of the figurations I have delineated, each with a role vis-à-vis the tasks that aspiration has to take up in any given era (including the founding of new figurations). Each of these figures then, each in the context of their own epoch, has a role to play in the drive to construct new ways of living that are more expansive in their comprehensions and more encompassing of diversity.

Things take their time, but that time is lost and dissipates into mere wishes if effective advocates and practitioners do not rise to address those wisps of insight and translate them into robust factors we can engage – words, artifacts, rites and relations and/or institutions. Such messages of the glimmerings of what is offered as a future that is different from grinding on in the same old ways only come by means of humans who express new ideas and do the hard work of putting them into practice. These glimmerings only arise on the soil of what exists at the time these people are honing their expressions, and so these expressions always have a certain form to them, arising in response to specific kinds of conditions that exist and so make these expressions compelling, if not necessary.

And, then, even the most capable and creative of advocates for the new cannot do it all: the idea, the means of expression, the processes for implementation, or the concepts for institutionalizing changes. Rather, through the coursing of time that we call history, the major drive toward what is next is taken up by people with certain proclivities who take mere wisps of notions and render them into viable forms for engagement (competition, conflict, arrangements of order and power). These people, who do the work of generative creativity, must have not only the "internal" constitution to take on the status quo, but they must also have the "materials" at hand, in sufficiently articulated states so as to provide a basis on which to proceed.

Aspiration

While a notion of "change" starts us on our way into the tenor of this material, it does not get us into the heart that drives it or that makes mentoring a distinctive and necessary mode of engagement as my work envisions. To get to that "heart," that beating core that makes it worthwhile to write, read and maybe value this work, it takes *"aspiration."* While notions of change always involve exerting some kind of effort contra the status quo, as does the notion of "transformation," for instance, aspiration puts a spin on change that is at once unexpected and is also exceptional. It takes up doubled movement of change: it contemplates changing the world, so to speak, but it also countenances the changes that will occur to oneself as an engaging being as concomitantly necessarily occurring. Aspiration entails "letting go," not so as to "receive" the "now" – to succumb to "whatever" happens. Rather it actively engages occurrences in ways that intend to make something "new" happen, and also countenances accommodating the changes it will have to accept during the unfolding of the engagement.

Aspiration takes up "change" as a program for seeing with new eyes, as Rilke says, and allows the actions that are to be undertaken to flow from there. Aspiration thus envisions "change" not only of things or even institutions (right away), but *also* envisions that we undertake the work of guiding the psychic, emotional, perceptual, expressive and bodily processes that *enable us to become human in more expansive and more encompassing ways (than we have ever been before).*

23

Aspiration is thus a mode of engaging our world that is decidedly "non-pragmatic," and so may cut across the grain of the action-oriented, production-focused modern mindset. The notion of change that aspiration entails is first to become different human beings, to enact a "re-valuation of all values" in Nietzsche's sense. Toward what, you might ask? (And here is a crucial point for all mentors to appreciate to the fullest:) If a person can answer that question, *they are not speaking of their aspirations any longer*, but are giving you codified responses from a pre-given repertoire of choices that are already comprehensible.

The impetus toward aspiring never gets so far down the road of delineating pragmatic programs of designed interventions. Aspirations lend themselves rather to those states of gathering one's resources in preparation for an undertaking. I have likened it to forming the feelings, intensities, orientations and affirmations that transpires in that breath one takes prior to "jumping in." That precipitative breath is iterated fractally: it occurs (globally and generally) in moments before any notion of an engagement has presented itself; it occurs (with a pang of recognition and clarity) in moments when it is realized that an effort has to be made in regard to a certain situation; and it occurs (specifically and instantaneously) in the moment prior to engaging the scene at hand. This is not yet even "envisioning" the scene, as an athlete or artist might envision the scene of his exertion. It is a moment of constituting a precursor state, a state of anticipation that includes a gathering of one's existent forces, but also accepts and readies for the moment of contact, that those forces will themselves be acted upon and changed by the encounter [5].

Such states are too massively affecting, of course, to be absorbed generally, in toto. And so, in the context of living beings who are encountering a range of somewhat coherent states of affairs, over time, a person comes to give his or her aspiring "anticipatory breath" more of a shape, more of a way of proceeding and boding forth, such that this moment is effective and generative for him or her singularly and personally. The most specific shape in which an aspiration can be constituted is of a figuration and the way a figuration is able to exert itself. And since this figuration precedes any conscious decisions as to a method or a plan, this figuration is not controlled by the aspiring person – rather that person acts as though there were no other way at all. The aspiration thus shapes how it is that any and all actions are envisioned, planned, undertaken and carried through.

THE ASPIRATIONAL *FIGURES*. With that brief overview of the workings of an aspiration, we have just touched upon the way we mentors can craft a narrative around the notion of aspiration: through the sketching and elaborating of aspirational figures: *figurations of life ways that comprise patterns of attributes, characteristics and commitments that are attuned to that aspect of their psychic constitutions that **aspire** above all, that are attuned to those psychic/somatic resources that are dedicated to envisioning more expansive and more encompassing ways of being human, with each other, with other creatures and on the earth.* In this work I name four such figures: leader, artist, prophet and mystic.

This notion of "figuration" then constitutes the "strategy" this book adopts as the way of orienting the mentoring practice aspirations, keeping the mentor's attention fixed on aspiration so as to distinguish this from other orientations to the future (such as goal-setting, ambitions or even "ideals").

Figuration. First, the term "figuration" does not designate those diagnostic realms that are marked out in terms of personality, psychological "type," or profession (such as that of a CEO or an artist). A "figuration" refers to an *orientation to one's life ways that are instigated by aspiration:* an orientation to what does not yet "exist," such that a person prioritizes, organizes and articulates a stance toward certain kinds of activities (that will be introduced below) that take up the task of bringing something new into existence, and do so to the exclusion or de-emphasis of other possible activities. A figuration however, also has more "substance" than being a matter of flailing around in pursuit of wishes or ideals. It also means that in order to act in concert with these aspirations, the person sets out on a course of life ways that can have a chance of catching on, of becoming a viable possibility. And, then, finally, since we live in a context of ways, interpretations, institutions, traditions and practices that have been developing for centuries, the ways that an aspiration will be able to take hold also have a range of engaging that will be more likely than others to bear fruit. A "figuration" of aspiration takes up these ways (consciously or unconsciously, explicitly – such as the life of an artist – or implicitly – such as the life of mystic aspiration), acts under the rubric of these ways (which are more or less valorized by the present situation) because they offer the chance of making the most sense of those aspirations, to others, from day to day.

To say, for instance, that my aspirations take on the shape of a "prophet figuration" does not mean that I proclaim futures or walk around the city in a toga. It means that when I hear about the lives of certain people and when I study the works of certain people, I find that their life ways have some similarities and their aspirations have a certain kind of energy and coherence that makes sense for me, and helps me in making sense of my own work. It means that I find affinity with the ones called "biblical prophets," Greek philosophers as well as the more contemporary figures such Nietzsche or Freud, or philosophers, or others who are devoted to the "life of the idea." I feel a kinship with these people and see a way forward for myself by studying their works and contemplating the courses that their lives took up. It is not the specifics of a biography that I identify with, but the motivations, the feelings these people have as they go about their work, and the way they frame challenges and envision desired outcomes. To say, however, that many people do not take up any of these figurations is not to say that they are devoid of aspiration, only that they have not taken up ways of living that place aspirations in the forefront of their concerns, commitments and ways of life.

The Figures. We readily recognize the names I have assigned to these figurations of aspirational orientation. And we also clearly recognize that each of the figurations so named carries baggage of controversy, of nonconformity and each, in its own way is a center that generates controversy. And yet, for all of the controversy these figures stir, we have to acknowledge that each figure has a role in the historical/evolutionary exploits that have given the human endeavor the diverse and complex shapes and multi-faceted varieties of styles, goals and pursuits it has today. (And in the spirit of foreshadowing, I offer that the "mystic" figure, which we consider in this volume, engages the most complex and unsettling aspirations the human endeavor has ever encountered.)

We know a few of the people who have taken on such figurations, the ones who have made it into the history books; but, and this is a crucial point for all that follows, the people who gain fame, notoriety and have books written about them represent only the extreme-most tip of a much larger and more inclusive iceberg of people who share these orientations and proclivities and who labor, with commitment and passion, in complete obscurity and anonymity. The famous ones, as Newton said of his own accomplishments, ride on the shoulders of giants – most of whom we have never heard. Those shoulders often are those of other unknown and unheralded aspirational figures, whose quiet commitments to their aspirations above all else, filled with heart, spirit, soul, mind and power, drive the human endeavor in every nook and cranny, in every level of organization and in every occupation and profession. The point we make here is that aspirations are shaped into "figurations," and many of us who never achieve fame or "world historical" status share in these aspirational figurations – one of them, or even several.

While these names encompass figurations of aspirations, our work focuses on real living people, people who are making livings, have families and obligations with "real world" demands to grapple with. These figurations operate in the midst of other pressing obligations and demands, and in the midst of other roles that are far more comprehensible and valorized than are those aspirations that mentoring addresses. These figurations thus are ways that these aspirations exert themselves insurgently and disruptively and unsettle people's lives; these figuration thus also

characterize the range of affecting experiences that these people undergo
— even suffer and contend with and/or against — in varying degrees of
intensity and that require of them varying degrees of attention, respon-
siveness and commitment — which at the point of the mentoring
engagement they might not have made decisions about.

"ROLE." Thus, "figuration is not a *personality*, because it pertains not to
one's most repeated and acknowledged behaviors and patterns of speech,
but rather refers (only) to how one envisions gathering oneself (in that
"anticipatory breath" we considered above) to venture into what has yet
to exist at all. A figuration is thus not a *type* because no set of traits or
manners of orientation of one's psycho/physical life have settled into
patterns that can be consciously deployed in order to accomplish one's
declared intentions. At best a figuration has a *"role,"* or what Deleuze
calls an "assemblage of enunciation."[6] That is, one gathers, as best as one
can, in any moment, the constituents of the discernments one has made
into a concrescence of focused concerns, and puts this evanescent experiment out there into the world as an offering, a gift, not of accomplishment, but of becoming, a way for generative co-emergences to
transpire at the site of and in the moment of the offering. When a person
does this time and time again, the role shows itself as having certain
repercussions, and so elicits or demands certain rejoinders and responses
to that endeavor. Helping a person nurture, articulate and form a commitment to an aspiration so that it can become a life way or a "role" is as
far as mentoring can go, and that is as far into concretion and expression
(enunciation) as an aspiration and an aspiring figure can go.

These figurations of aspirations take on the following roles:

The Mystic: A way of life that is committed, without reserve, to
restoring to a state of vitality and liveliness any process of operation has
been rendered mechanical and routine by institutionalized (enforced
and informally conforming) habits. The mystic sets into play "precepts,"
which act as precursors for new and more expansive ways of engaging
the human endeavor.

The Prophet: Sees relations, conceptualizations, orders and hierarchies in new ways and sets out provoking concepts in order to disturb the old settled ways by advancing "provoking concepts" that point to these new ways. This includes discerning new sources, new forces and dynamics in play, and so to conceive of and articulate new possibilities for undertaking the human endeavor.

The Artist: Assembles perceptions, feelings, memories, forms and narratives into novel complexes that make it possible for us to "see with new eyes," and thus devise new manners and modes of engagement with what now makes ***sense (and previously didn't).***

The Leader: Creates a followership and organizes them into an effort that marshals talents, materials and resources (financial, volunteer, informational, etc.) into collaborations that produce products, services, institutions and activities that offer more expansive and more encompassing ways of living our daily lives.

All these figures share an aspirational stance in life: a stance in which engaging the world as it exists from the standpoint of what *can be created,* and therefore *can be brought into existence,* is at stake. Each mode of "creating" has to find its way; and though inspiration flows among the figures, no figure offers the "way" that suffices for what another figure has at stake. What "aspiration" means to the mystic can seem preposterous and an irritant to the leader; what seems "aspiration" to the artist can seem frivolous, if not incomprehensible, to the prophet. All of these figures are necessary in our epoch in order to keep the aspiration-driven impetus alive in the human context. Today we find one figure taking inspiration from like figures or others and we find people combining the actions such figures usually undertake in a concentrated way into their unique stances. The world looks very different to each of these figures. Even when people combine the actions of figures, the contradictions between the underlying psychic/somatic figurations rise to the fore, generating conflicts within the "souls" of these people.

The "Aspiring Mind"

And that brings us to the third aspect of the idea of aspirational figuration: it refers to a specialized assemblage of psycho/somatic – spiritual, physical, emotional, intellectual, expressive – resources that operates on different energies and operates on them in different ways than do the well-documented functions of the conscious "ego." I propose that over the course of the human endeavor we have generated the emergence (or have guided an evolution of) the "Aspiring Mind" as a specific psychic/somatic resource that just might (and it is far from certain) take its place along side of the resources of "reason," if not language, as a viably assertive neuroanatomical assemblage, and thus life-shaping faculty or capability. This "Aspiring Mind" notion or hypothesis envisions the evolutionary/historical (self-organizing) emergence of a sub-conscious or pre-conscious assemblage of capabilities or *faculties* that enable expansive and encompassing discernments and affects (occurring in the course of actively living engagements with one's milieu – other people, creatures, the earth) to transmogrify from being mere wishes or fleeting phantasms of hope into being embodied, articulate and committed life ways. It is that psychic/somatic "transmo-grification" of energy into modes of engaging occurrences and forming distinctive life ways that carries the name "aspiration." This resource thus has aspiration as its sole standard of conduct and as its primary and ultimate concern. [7]

As I intimated, that a "new" psychic/somatic resource might be on its way, might be emerging from a state of loosely and intermittently affecting factors and might be confluently self-organizing so as to attain the standing of being a facultative resource, is not so strange a notion for us to contemplate. After all, humans pride themselves on having developed capabilities of discerning abstract and invisible forces that lay "behind" or "beyond" material factors in an environment, and then developed psychic/somatic capabilities, including that of language, in the form of actual brain functions and regions ("Broca's area") for discerning these forces and expressing them according to "rational" categories, principles, axioms and common sense expressions. By establishing this self-developed resource, humans have been able to devise vast and supremely powerful methods of production and means of acquisition that are unprecedented on the face of the earth. This notion of an aspiring mind resource taking shape follows on that self-organizing logic. The only new twist to this notion is that instead of a resource emerging "behind our backs," or, seemingly as a "gift" of nature or some other force, I envision that the aspiring mind resource is gathering strength based on the exertion of conscious human choice and efficacy.

Neither is it so strange that an impetus so powerful and affecting as aspiration could coalesce into being a distinctive facultative resource, one that is of a kind other than that of the conscious, ego-cogito faculties we employ in our acquiring, knowing and production. We have been living with the idea of there being different faculties, brain and mind regions and specializations for a long time now. For example, for a century now the Freudian unconscious, considered to be a self-contained factor of our psychic life, has been largely accepted, at least as a framework for talking about our psyche. In addition to the "unconscious," Freud's notions of "drives," "libido" and "id" are well-known, and have been critiqued and elaborated upon and largely accepted. We are now accustomed to discerning and articulating several kinds of forces and energies that percolate below the surface of our conscious experiencing and communicating, forces that work "behind" our everyday accomplishments of reason-based, productively active and acquisitive ego-cogito/subject behaviors.

And what is more, we have learned how to articulate and name these forces and to trace the way they generate affects on our minds as they bubble up from their obscure realms into the light of day. So now I am proposing that we can bring into view that resource that gathers the forces of aspiration into a facultative resource that operates on its own terms, and engenders ways of living out those aspirations in the form of figurations that have proven robust enough to make a difference in shaping the course of the human endeavor. In more technical language, that means we can characterize the *machinic*[8] (not mechanistic or mechanical) operations of the psycho/somatic system (P/SS) (if not yet brain regions and psychological processes) that people rely on in order to give their aspirations the force and body of a living way, or figuration.

At this juncture, in the annals of our sober discourses, that is mostly in certain philosophical circles, the notion of there being an "Aspiring Mind" is a figuration, or a "thought image" (in Deleuze's terms). It frames a body of discerning narratives that enable us to gather into a coherent notion how it is that we can guide conscious psychic/somatic engagements in ways that sustain a person's aspirations through all the experiments, ventures and travails that such a life's way entails. That such a capability has been in operation in the course of the human endeavor has been a specific source of wonder, at least since the days of the Greek tragedians who mused, what a strange creature is man. It is this wonder at such "unnatural" perspicacity that the notion of the aspiring mind articulates in an attempt to become an active shaper and guide of that strange energy.

THE DECISION TO ASPIRE. At this point we have to ask, what gave rise to this emergence in the human endeavor? What gave rise to the impetus for a psychic/somatic resource such as the Aspiring Mind to emerge? While I cannot answer that question in depth here,[9] I can say that what has enabled humans to have occasion to consider the emergence of a psychic/somatic resource such as the Aspiring Mind is that, unlike any other creature, over the course of eons, humans coalesced a *decision* to guide the course of our own development. That is, proto-humans and early humans realized that there were many ways to live on this earth. Certainly people can "adapt" by increasing physical prowess or sensory acumen, or increase the density and variety of our signaling abilities in order to co-ordinate and socialize our survival processes. But as humans proliferated over the earth, and did so by accomplishing just such creaturely adaptations, over the course of eons some people noticed all the different ways that human adaptations had taken shape. Some among them were intrigued by this differentiated variety and multiple paths to success. And then some of these people started asking a very specific question: how do we generate new ways, on our own terms, and so have distinctive ways, as a "people," as humans?

Asking this question meant that some people envisioned that humans must have a capability that enables them to move beyond a glorification of our lingual and technical prowess. Then some people made a fatefully epochal *decision*: they decided to take as subject matter that "will" or "drive" that insists on exceeding any status quo state of given ways. In certain regions of the world, in the Fertile Crescent, and then centuries later in Macedonian Greece, this decision took hold and people actually set out to develop new ways of living, discerning, perceiving, writing and behaving, that distinguished this activity in its own right – thus the emergence of the biblical prophets and then the Greek philosophers.

That decision has meant paying attention to operations that cannot be of the same quality as that which enables us to just react to what occurs and deploy habituated actions (and statements) in order to address what is happening. To enact decision entailed developing new discernments, mostly based in language, by which we could first discern more expansive factors being in play at the site of engagement, and then developing ways by which to choose between different options – and to choose options that remained open for further discerning, characterizing and inventing of new ways. The conscious decision to devote the utmost attention and concern to these "generative" impulses (to engage occurrences in ways that are continually more expansive and more encompassing) thus necessitated the formation of new kinds of discourses, new vocabularies and new figurations of the human endeavor itself. In other words, we have been at work engendering an aspiring mind for eons, and now we can start to appreciate what it has rendered by virtue of its own constitution, its own ways, its own figurations of human lives that are dedicated to these operations.

The continued, iterative, insistent and proliferation of this way, the way that stems from this decision to guide our own development, might be coalescing not only into a vague sense of what it is to be human, but might also be coalescing into a distinctive psychic/somatic resource, which, for lack of a better term, I call the Aspiring Mind. Further, I propose (and have written this book as an elaboration of that proposal) that this emerging resource and the aspirations that it specifically engenders and configures, is the proper subject matter of mentoring.

GENERAL CONSIDERATIONS. In order to discern the workings of the Aspiring Mind resource and to begin to work with it, we need terms that orient a discourse that is devoted to it. The Aspiring Mind is a late (current, as we speak) developing resource. It is not merely biological or directly behavior-producing in its orientation to psychic functioning. It is semiotic, linguistic and language-based at its very core.[10] A resource such as what we are calling an "Aspiring Mind" only arose on the basis that language provides. It is because, over eons, symbols, myths and then concepts enabled humans to frame notions and narratives that were exclusively their own (the stories of the people, the word that the people alone use to name events in their lives and worlds), – a psychic/somatic resource devoted to the capability to aspire arose. (It arose, as I said, as a result of a decision to note and give concern to second-level abilities, those that generated *differences* in ways of engaging occurrences, which can only be differentiated by means of high-level significations, narratives and accounts of those differences).

Thus, the Aspiring Mind is a psychic/somatic system that gathers symbols, narratives and portentous orientations, which pertain to complex of states of affairs (in which it is evident that choices are available in order to enact and shape of new ways of living for the people), in order to be able to anticipate the ways in which more expansive and more encompassing manners of engagement are being called for (so as to enable the people to increase their viability and vitality by making new choices henceforth in the face of such complexities).

The guiding terminology of a resource such as an Aspiring Mind is now being developed at several different levels. In its most abstract form, it is diagrammed by the terminology developed by Deleuze and Guattari in their seminal work *Capitalism and Schizophrenia*.[11] Terminology that relates this resource to expressions in philosophy and literature can be found in all the works of Jacques Derrida and Maurice Blanchot (as two exemplars of the "post-structuralist" or "post-modern" genre). The work here is derived and adapted from the study of these thinkers, to which I add the work being done in self-organizing systems and increasing complexity. Terms such as "emergence," "energy" (as in $E=MC^2$), and becoming "more complex" apply here. In the context of contemporary notions of human P/SS development and emergence, I use the term "individuation" to indicate the way that the P/SS of conscious beings (including animals) engages occurrences in its milieu in such a way as to do so, the next time, in a more expansive and more encompassing way. The way this process is felt and experienced in the human context is what the term "aspiration" designates. I will elaborate on this level of terminology for demarcating an Aspiring Mind P/SS resource in the Introduction.

Terms of Mystic Aspiration

In order to provide mentoring support for mystic aspirations, the mentor will need to have access to the terms that will help to clarify, specify and characterize those aspirations. The course of this text is largely devoted to amplifying the emergence of those aspects of mystic figuration to which these terms apply, to validating these terms and then to helping the mentor use these terms while in the midst of a mentoring conversation. And so, while we introduce these terms here, by way of an orienting framework, they will be treated in several contexts throughout all that follows so that a mentor can firm up their pertinence in ways that can become more and more operational.

The Field of Enthusiasm: Mystic aspirations gather in contexts of discourses, disciplines, and endeavors that bear consistencies, constancy, and continued engagement. Rather than approach these "fields" as matters for analysis and further concretization and institutionalized control, the mystic regards these fields as occasions for tapping into the un-reconciled, uncharted, unresolved aspects that exert energy and offer occasions for still-free exploration. It is a field of *enthusiasm* because the mystic does not approach this field in order to have it become an object for technological or economic prowess, but in order for its factors to inspire and ignite new orientations, appreciation and initiative.

Faith-For: "Faith" is a term carried forward from the "religious" and "spiritual" domains because it offers a way to engage occurrences in ways that do not foreclose on its excessive, overwhelming potential for surprising, amazing and moving one to new planes of commitment to the more expansive and more encompassing. In conventional settings, one is encouraged to have faith *in* something or someone. In the case of the mystic's aspirations, there is nothing "there" for a faith to be placed or envisioned "(with) in." What the mystic's aspirations can "hold" and "inscribe" is one's own stance vis-à-vis a field of enthusiasm that holds it out for prospective engagement (articulated in a "precept" – which we will discuss momentarily). The mystic's aspirations therefore take the shape of a faith-*for* what that prospect holds forth.

Fore-giving: This term names the "ethic" of the person who engages aspirations of mystic figuration. What really makes it clear that a mystic aspirational figuration is in play for a person is that they live in a way that directs energy, attention, will and caring toward things that do not exist yet. That means they act into a state of affairs in such a way as to forbid any expectation of an exchange, a return or reciprocity. Most likely, a benevolent response might be one of patient incomprehension; but outright hostility (all the way to being burned at the stake) is not out of the question. The mystic has to give prior to there being even anything or anyone to give to. It is truly an ethic of giving into the "fore" – the fore of before (there is anything, or giving in advance of there being anything or anyone), of giving into the foreground (before there is any ground that provides "sufficiency").

Fore-giving resonates with the common term "forgiving." That latter term refers to a situation in which one "gives" away one's stance of having been acted upon (egregiously, injuriously, usually); that is, one gives "for" the person involved, gives "for" the specific occasion of this giving. In the case of the mystic's form of aspiring, this giving takes place before anything has occurred to another person at all. It is an inceptual giving, one that may even (or will most likely) pass unnoticed and so will not accrue to the "credit" of the giver. It is a giving, therefore, that transpires in a way that is not even a "giving" in the sense that applies to one of established recognition. Thus it is the giving that, prior to any articulation or forming of a field, even one of enthusiasm, sets in place at least a precursor stream or flight of energy on which something more recognizable can occur.

The Precept: Mystic aspirations are expressed and are given the force of an enacted and embodied concern, in the form of a *precept*. The precept expresses a gathering of anticipatory discernments which are ventured forth by the mystic, usually in a saying (or in musical form), as a continually opening line of flight, toward an ever-receding horizon of open prospect, that others might also heed, offer attention, take up and elaborate upon as a way that might offer more expansive and more encompassing ways of engaging. A precept is not a "concept" that one applies to situations that are in play and by which one is directly absorbed at the moment, but is rather a path-breaking *salient* that *clears a path* to something that has not yet been adumbrated or placed into general use. The founding precept of mystic aspiration was, in my opinion, formulated by Meister Eckhart, the fourteenth-century executive of the Dominican order who said, "I pray God, let me be free of God." And maybe the best continuation of that precept, for it is still very much alive as a precept, is what we suggest below: *"Proceed with what exceeds; choose what changes you."* [1] [2]

Teaching: The mystic's work is *teaching*. The precept can be advanced only through patient fore-giving to unsuspecting and unaware people, some of whom might pick up on some of the tenets the expression advances. The work of teaching, as regards mystic aspirations, embraces the continuing efforts that are required in order to keep the precept alive by continually stretching and reaching its parameters and sharpening its articulations so that it can fan out and affect as many as possible, in as potent a way as possible, so that as many as possible can "hear" what is at stake. In the role of teaching the precept, the mystically aspiring figure does not deliver prescribed curricula that will be set into use in economic and technologically productive and power-making settings, but instead patiently lays out pathways on which the precept can be discerned and can be offered as a way someone might want to choose to engage…or not.

Adherents: Each breakout creative figure engenders certain kinds of re-lationships, and only these kinds. Leaders create followers, for instance; artists create audiences, and prophets, disciples. The mystic aspirations create "adherents." The mystic always departs to new and fresh fields where enthusiasm is able to flourish, and so no relationship of devoted constancy is really in the offing for mystic figurations. Instead, the mystic figure's work of teaching leaves each one who is "here" to "hear" on his or her own to decide what kind of response they choose to formulate or commit to.

A Framework for Mentoring

Concluding this preface, I reiterate that this work is offered in the spirit of contributing to fostering the process of mentoring. In the strongest sense I can say that this whole notion of the four "aspirational figures" arose *out* of the mentoring work I have been doing for the past fifteen years; the notion arose *because of* the special drives and concerns, and anguish that was expressed by the people with whom I met. In sum, all of the people I describe in this book are highly competent, highly accomplished, well-respected and complete healthy individuals who execute difficult tasks and assume major responsibilities in and for their organizations. I did not generate a philosophical schema and then test it on willing subjects. The work developed completely in a different direction: Almost each and every person I worked with felt that they had a vision of life to offer that they wanted to act on – and did not know why they felt that way, where that feeling came from or, most especially, what to do with it. The work developed because these successful and competent people floored me as they ardently and passionately expressed that they aspired to some kind of a different way of contributing to their communities than what their jobs offered. I considered it my work as a mentor (and of a prophetic figuration) to form concepts that honored what their aspirations were demanding of them.

My mentoring was pushed and prodded from being a derivative of coaching people to be more confident and competent in their positions as leaders into being an exploration of aspirations that demanded the taking up of even more demanding roles. Thus did it become incumbent on me to devise a way to clarify and demarcate both the commonalities of aspirations that I heard being expressed, as well as the singularity of each person's aspirations. Combining my philosophy education and my decades of coaching, advising and listening skills, along with my own proclivities to conceptualize relationships (as a "prophet"-type figure), the schema of the aspirational figures emerged. It emerged, that is, within the mentoring conversation, in order to clarify and enrich the mentoring experience and to offer outcomes to mentees that fully and without compromise addressed their aspirations.

The intent here then, in introducing the "mystic" figure, is to help you "meet the mystic," as a mentor, as a supporting ally, as one who ponders the question, "whither the human endeavor." I offer you a sense of a particular life's way that offers so much to the vitality of our lives, and that also quite often is in need of a mentor to bring those commitments to their fullest expression and fruition. My hope for you as you read this book is that you will appreciate the creative figure in yourself and that you will either seek out mentoring to nurture those aspirations, or will offer your appreciative mentoring attentiveness to aspiring mentees.

"PICTURING" THE MYSTIC'S ASPIRATIONAL FIGURATION.

In this book, in order to help you triangulate a sense of what it is like to engage mystic aspirations, I offer three different ways of "picturing" the mystic figuration of aspirations: experiential, psycho/somatic, and genealogical. Each can be read independently and in any order. Each section has its purpose in supporting a mentor's engagement with the person who is oriented toward the mystic aspiring figuration.

The experiential section, Part One, is essential in appreciating how someone of mystic proclivities will present him or herself, and what kinds of situations this figuration engenders and so has to face, often repeatedly. This section will allow mentors to ask about and probe for the transpiring of these situations (dominance of female influence growing up, constant expulsion from settings, an urge to leave, a sense of urgency as to what people are missing out on, etc.), and then to *affirm* that it is precisely these difficulties that constitute the mystic's way, given what his or her aspirations are. And so the issue is not to "fix" these, compensate for them, develop contrasting and complimentary "life skills," but to take these situations up as what constitutes the necessary learning that will transform mystic aspirations into a mystic figure's style, role and life's way.

The schematic diagram of the aspiring figuration of the mystic's P/SS concludes Part One. It is intended to provide the mentor with an appropriately complex but specific diagram of how mystic aspirations take shape and become as robust as they can be as a P/SS resource – given that they remain matters of aspiration, figuration, style and role. The "device" I employ here is to posit the operation of a psycho/somatic systematic (P/SS) resource I call the "Aspiring Mind" (see Chapter Three). This section provides the mentor with a schematic template on which to analyze the mentee's statements in terms of the operations toward concretizing aspirations, and thus be able to investigate what operations are more developed and capable and which ones (important to the mystic's aspirational figuration in particular, with emphases on one assemblage/operation or another quite different in each of the figurations) need further elaboration and so can become a "project" in the mentoring context.

The genealogical section presented in Part Two provides the mentor with the only substantiation of the specifically mystic figuration that can be offered. The mystic's aspirations arose because certain ways of life, for certain kinds of aspiring people, became intolerable. It arose in specific circumstance, encountered specific modes of resistance (burning at the stake, imprisonment, banishment and excommunication, to name a few) and so the P/SS resources that took up these aspiring urges also developed and took shape in certain ways. It has been very helpful to me to be able to point to these (few) historical people and their struggles to make the point that what the mentee is experiencing is right in line, is right in the thick of what the mystic figuration of aspiration does encounter. And since we usually only take on one figuration, one role, these situations can be anticipated and so the work involved in developing a role for this aspiration entails taking these kinds of responses to heart. They are not defects of a personality, they are not inadequacies of competence, and they cannot be avoided.

No mentoring engagement will follow a set course. Only the two of you – mentor and mentee – are at the table. Still, in concluding this volume, in Part Three, I offer a guide as an example of how the accounts I provide in the earlier sections might be deployed in order to address certain aspects, stages, phases and concerns that the mentoring conversation entails.

A Different Mentoring

In closing this Preface, I feel an obligation to explicitly respond to what readers may already be sensing, and that may, for some, stir resistance: "This notion of 'mentoring' that you introduce here," a reader might protest, "seems to be of a different kind than how I have conceived it in the past: mentoring as an informal and collegial imparting of one's concern for another person." I know that such a concern is real, since it was once acted out in very definitive terms during the course of one of my leader mentoring training sessions.

I had recruited a very capable, accomplished and articulate candidate to be a mentor in my "professional leader mentoring program" (see: www.leadermentoring.com). The day after this exercise, he angrily informed me, by email, that he was dropping out. His explanation went something like this: "I thought you recruited me to be a mentor because of my experience and knowledge, and then I have to sit through a day of *training* in order to be a mentor in your program. I feel insulted." Some readers may feel that this book is making just such an imposition on them. It is a common notion in our culture that "mentoring" refers to a process in which a person offers his or her gained wisdom, and with no further ado, "transmits" and "transfers" this knowledge to a chosen protégé, with the intent of shepherding this person along and through a difficult passage to the success the mentor personifies (and for which the mentor anticipates granted acknowledgement – preferably in some explicit statement of veneration). I am saying, that in order to mentor the creative aspirations, here of mystic figuration, a person has to *prepare*, learn, *think differently* and so his or her course of career, professional or "life" success does not suffice in this engagement. I do make just such a claim. But in so doing I am by no means demeaning either the prospective mentor or his or her life accomplishments.

In fact, to be clear about my valorization and appreciation of mentors who address aspirations, I am saying that in order for you to choose to be a mentor of aspirational figurations, you must already recognize and appreciate that the generative or creative urge has a character of its own, that it is fragile and so it needs caring attention on its own terms; and finally, you want to provide such caring. To even recognize that aspirations are distinctive psychic and emotional states of being, and to realize that they merit some attention in their own rights, indicates that you are already open to an orientation that this "different" mentoring I am outlining here requires. You have self-selected as being at least curious, and are even hopeful that it can offer you something that will be worthwhile. You already want to meet, talk to, engage and support people who exhibit the aspirational impulse; and so, you already value it. I am adding nothing to your willingness or ability to impart those gifts.

I will be blunt here: what I am saying, in offering this preparatory "course," is that these *figurations* in which aspirations take on specific shapes (mystic, prophet, artist, leader – in my referential framework), they are historically developed, and have specific courses through which they (are permitted to) unfold in our culture. Accordingly I propose that if we as mentors are to fully serve our mentees' expansive and encompassing sensibilities as *aspirations*, and not other modalities of striving (ambition, careerism, increased competitive prowess and skill), we need to be clear in our own minds and in our own approaches, as to what that mentoring support entails for that aspiring mentee. There is no doubt that some readers are and have been able to arrive at such clarity without my assistance. But I cannot help but feel this as well: the whole notion of aspiration as being a psychic/somatic state of being in its own right is new, and so it (also) is fragile. The notion of aspiration contends with, and is usually overwhelmed at every turn by notions such as ambition, goal setting and prowess of skill that can be immediately deployed in the pragmatic and materialistic orientations of socioeconomic acquisition, production and success.

The notion of aspiration does not preclude that at some point in the course of engaging with others an aspiring person will have to learn the ways of ambition and careerism; but it is a notion that is set apart from those productive processes, as a "source" or an "inspiration," for instance, without which production is merely reproduction and success is merely increased accumulation of appropriated materials. We pay dutiful homage to the lone inventor, the solitary thinker or the genius who stood alone (before being "discovered"). And so at some level we acknowledge that in the moment of aspiration there is no recognition, valorization, no prospect of success to be had. We in this mentoring endeavor are supporting those who choose to take up aspiration as a life's way, and do not rest content with having once had a single moment of "inspiration" that is subsequently left behind in the pursuit of success and happiness it can bring (as attested to in TED talks, for instance). We are working with people for whom that solitary state of aspiring is a constant state of being. And so, any time and effort we make in clarifying and making more robust what *aspiration* entails, for ourselves and for others, benefits everyone involved: you, the mentee and, I might say, the human endeavor itself.

I also want to be clear that because this notion of there being an "aspiring mind" (as I lay out in Chapter Three) is so new, and because I have not seen it treated as a psychic/somatic resource in its own right anywhere in the literature, you readers are sharing with me an adventure of sorts, accompanying me on a journey of a kind – and I appreciate that sincerely and totally. As I have tried to show by means of a fairly rigorous footnote thread throughout the text, all the tenets of my experiment are developed in resonance with ongoing and significant philosophical and some outlying psychological research and thought. Nietzsche, Deleuze, Derrida, Nancy, and Heidegger are not philosophical lightweights; paradigmatically, Kauffman and Gel-Man are not easily dismissed; and finally, psychologically Thelen and Smith, Kelso, Csikszentmihalyi and Damasio are not slackers or pretenders either. While they may not specifically endorse my interpretation of their works, or might not apply it as I have to aspirational figures and mentoring, I am confident that this work reflects what their work is capacious enough to accommodate.

Still, the application of these notions to (1) a distinct formulation of aspiration as a self-asserting psychic/somatic assemblage is my contribution; and (2) the application of this notion to a mentoring pedagogy is new, experimental, and to the best of my knowledge advanced uniquely here. And so, as you decide about going further in this text, I want to assure you that in the scores of cases in which I have applied and developed this pedagogy in the service of mentoring mystic aspirations, never once has there (yet) been an occasion where the mentee was disappointed. [13] Of course, I increase the chances of having the conversation being a constructive one by screening and envisioning the figuration that is in play here (or that there is, in fact, no aspiration involved at all). But just the fact that there can be a screening and assigning process to this work indicates that something that does entail a figuration, a selection of a way, a preference and an orientation to expressing aspirations at least does merit our sober, considered, serious attention. This book offers a way to guide, constrain and clarify that attention. I do not claim for it that this work pretends to be finished, complete and/or a definitive authority on the subject, but it does offer a way for you to begin to flesh out the notion of aspirational figurations, and for us to converse about this possibility of mentoring people who take them up, in their own terms, in their own rights, and for the sake of those aspirations themselves.

Further, and in conclusion to this commentary, I believe and have suggested elsewhere [14] that amid the welter and clamor of developmental services, *only mentoring hears the call that aspirations evoke in others and only mentoring is devoted to helping the aspiring person translate that call into a life's way, on its own terms, as aspiration and nothing else.* We are thus not only practitioners of a pedagogy as mentors of aspirations, but we are first and foremost, experimenters, explorers, an advance team that sets out to hone a new way of engaging each other, of speaking to each other — a way that is worthy of and is in attunement with emergent aspirations.

We mentors of aspirations are paying attention to a whole sense of the emerging dynamism in our midst and we are certainly just beginning to appreciate what ways we humans have to act on what is there disclosed. Of this, in this spirit, I cite, for your contemplation, one of the more lyrical thinkers in this work, Jean-Luc Nancy:

> From the crystal to logic, there is an ordering and an organization for which no design can account but whose very tension — crystalline, organic, living, thinking — tightens toward our attention: not in order to resolve it, but in order to come to meet it, in order to experience it. This is what we call "thinking." [15]

And, for me, this "thinking" begins in aspiration, and is first given in words as the precepts offered by those of mystic aspiration.

And so, to those who choose to proceed, the work awaits. Let us proceed. And once again, welcome. *Salut.*

The Mystic: Introduction

Whenever I find myself growing grim about the mouth; whenever it is a damp, drizzly November in my soul; whenever I find myself involuntarily pausing before coffin warehouses, and bringing up the rear of every funeral I meet; and especially whenever my hypos get such an upper hand of me, that it requires a strong moral principle to prevent me from deliberately stepping into the street and methodically knocking people's hats off – then, I account it high time to get to the sea as soon as I can.

~ Ishmael (from Moby Dick) [1]

Nin coerceru maxunim contineri minimo divinum est.

(Not to be confined by the greatest, yet, to be contained within the smallest, is divine.)

~ Hölderlin [2]

…We are experiments: let us also *want* to be them!

~ Hölderlin [3]

"Mystic," You Say?

"Mystic."

The word vibrates. It conjures up images of strange things being said and done by strange people. Its etymology refers to mystery, the hidden which cannot, intrinsically, by its own nature, be revealed. To hurl the descriptor "Mystic" we signify we are encountering a phenomenon to which we don't quite know how to relate: a kind of person, no doubt; but a person we cannot clearly comprehend.

In this work, all people who carry their aspirations on their sleeves, the people of mystic, artist, prophet and leader aspirations, are each strange in their own ways. But of all the people who take up these roles, the one who bears mystic aspirations is the one who is thought to be most strange. While, as we will show, this preconception is largely untrue, there are good reasons behind the notion. For one thing, the mystic figure, in the West, is relatively new. The leader, artist and prophet roles appeared much earlier in the unfolding drama of the human endeavor. Over eons the leader, then the artist and then the prophet established places for themselves in Western culture, and evolved institutions to validate their contributions. Mystics are the latest eruption of the generatively aspiring type, and though they have been granted sanctuary in various institutions (e.g., cloisters, monasteries) for varying periods of time, mystic aspirations are neither established as a constructively creative figuration, nor do they have institutions in which they consolidate their function, identity or contribution.

Secondly, this role, unlike the other roles, is still actively in the process of being configured. We truly don't know what "form" mystic aspirations will take on as we go forward, we truly don't know what will happen as a result of mystic precepts taking hold in our world. And because the mystic precepts affect all the other figures, we don't really know what "creativity" will entail as the mystic way takes hold – if indeed it does. We still don't know how to relate to people who strongly exhibit mystic aspirations – quite often their pronouncements of precepts leave us at a loss for words. And, lastly, people with mystic aspirations can seem strange to us because they are largely invisible, and when one asserts himself or herself, we are taken aback.

So, mystics have a role in our world, we are saying. People who aspire as they do live, work, play and love among us; they play important roles in the organizations that affect our lives. But what role, exactly, do mystic aspirations enact? How viable can that role be? If they work so solipsistically, so alone, can we ever hope to find them, no less benefit from their work? They are among us, you say? Maybe a friend of ours is a mystic, or an employee or a relative is a mystic, you say?

These are not rhetorical questions. These questions frame all that follows. We are offering a description of mystic aspirations as affecting the life ways and life choices of people right in our midst, people alongside of us, with whom we work and play. And we are offering a way to fully appreciate what they have to offer and then be able to offer mentoring support so that these aspirations can be more robustly asserted by these people.

And then we are going one step further: if the human endeavor is to continue (and this is an open issue), we have to learn completely new ways of living and being in our world with each other and with nature – and it is those who do the hard work of articulating their mystically figured aspirations, who form precepts that can be comprehended (if only for rejection), who do the work of teaching, who will open a way forward. *I propose that in order to fully grasp the import of the process that refreshes and revitalizes the human endeavor, that renders it sustainable, and ultimately creative, mystic aspirations have to be embodied and enacted by people who take up this role, and then we have to carry this work on by taking it up in our own generative ways.*

FEW, BUT AMONG US. There are few mystics, compared with other vocations, and even in comparison to the number of people in the other aspiring roles; but mystics do live and work, love and die, among us. And they mostly fit in quite well, for a time, anyway, and are even among those we count as some of our most successful corporate officers. But we only live alongside these people by not taking too seriously how different they are from us; and as they live among us they are often working hard to fit in and to not express how truly differently from us they feel about what is important in their lives. Part of our work then is to notice them as embodying and enacting *mystic aspirations* rather than as the executives or scholars, philosophers, writers or poets or painters, world-historical visionaries that we now are able to recognize. Then, once recognized, we have to help them to fully recognize themselves: to see in themselves the mystic energies and psychic dispositions that drive (and exhaust) their talents. Then, the mystic work, the mystic evocation of that refreshed humanity, can take on its properly generative role among us.

Let me tell you about someone whom I consider to be enacting mystic aspirations. I'll call him Dan. He occupied a high position in a company, a chief financial officer, reported directly to the company's CEO, and had more than 50 people in his department. He dealt each and every day with investors and analysts, and drew up reports that had to pass government-sanctioned audits. He is joyful, and brims with energy and optimism. Employees throughout the company sought him out, regarding him as one of those executives in the company who would listen to new ideas and even bring some of them to fruition – and not take credit for the idea, either. He has a wife and two children. He has said to me, "If it weren't for them, I'd curl up in a ball and never leave bed." He isn't an avid reader, but he is an eager learner, having achieved this position while still in his thirties. After a few years on the job, and having achieved important milestones for the company, he announced he was leaving. When he left, he really had no definite plans. He hadn't received another, more lucrative offer. He really didn't know what he wanted to do. He was just feeling that this assignment was over. He just felt that he had to move on.

His "dream thing." "I can't explain this to anyone else," he said to me, "but I think you'll understand. I just need to pay attention to my 'dream thing.' " This "dream thing," he had explained to me in one of our mentoring sessions, was not a specific dream or goal or even a vision. It was like a different place in his psyche. As long as he had this dream thing, a sense of being able to move, to change, that his life could be full every day, he was happy. Once, when he could not have it, when he had to toe the line and put his dreams on hold, maybe indefinitely, he felt nauseous, depressed, like a robot. Before he left the company, he told me that he was beginning to feel that way again. If he was going to have his "dream thing" back, he was going to have to just cut loose, take his chances, do something different.

Here's what I want you to notice about this story: He worked in a high-level, "normal" job, with joy and competence. He achieved excellence and was universally appreciated. He had no untoward "experiences" or revelations. He was a CFO, a chief *financial* officer, for heaven's sake! He was not religious. And, note this, *he had to move on.* He had his "dream thing," and this was more important than any title, position or even income level. That is my point: mystics are among us. And, we have to get to know them quickly, for they move on.

Like Dan, all of the mystically aspiring people we will meet in this book work in organizations that were well-heeled enough to hire me and my firm as mentors to their senior executives. All of the people we meet are therefore accomplished achievers in their lines of work and in their careers/professions.

Lest that seem strange, and maybe an abuse of the term, let me remind my readers who are already familiar with this subject that the apotheosis of the medieval mystic, Meister Eckhart, was a highly placed Dominican administrator who was moved by his order from place to place like a modern-day turnaround specialist. From what is known of him, he had no untoward experiences that placed him in a union with God, and he disdained such things in his writings. He was condemned by the Church, not for his failures as an administrator, but for his writings and preaching (in the vernacular, accessible to anyone who was interested) that laid out the tenets of a new Western vision of a full life. Teresa of Avila, also a revered classical mystic, revitalized and greatly expanded her own Carmelite Order. Gandhi, a recent mystic of world-historic stature, was a lawyer and a politician who founded a great movement.

Our Surprising Mystics: Faith-For and Fore-Giving.

So, here is one of our necessary counterintuitive tenets: people who take on mystic aspirations as a life way are high-achieving, extremely competent participants in the ongoing organizational life of our productive world. They don't distinguish themselves as mystics by overtly strange behavior in their daily affairs, but even in those pressured corporate settings they do exhibit an open flow with life's most free and unrealized possibilities – the best and most exciting ideas that are circulating in the halls and lunchrooms of the organization. They don't distinguish themselves by virtue of having rapturous, so-called "mystic experiences." To the contrary, their aspirations are rather expressed by their propensities for unending questioning of what is given, and by affirming what else might be possible, in light of all that they feel and sense around them. They don't distinguish themselves by their opaqueness and incomprehensibility, but by their unrelenting creativity and ability to see beyond the ordinary, the oppressive routing of an already organized life, and the power structures that enforce this. They are not revolutionary destroyers or subversive connivers seeking power; instead, they articulate their notion, do all that they can to advance and organize it, and then, either when the idea is in operation, or when it has been implacably frustrated, they leave that place, vacate it, and move out into a new open field, a new circle of light, one that others may not even see.

PATTERNS OF THOUGHT. I identify mystic aspirations, as we will see later, by discerning certain patterns. The "dream thing" Dan talked about is one such pattern. Another is being constantly called "creative" and yet (or for that very reason) not necessarily being welcomed with open arms into the inner circles of power. In one way or another, a person who takes up and acts on her mystic aspirations will inevitably not fit in comfortably in the established order. In some cases, for instance, their demeanors might seem a bit aloof – they are not fully on the team, not believers – or, in another case, their enthusiasms might feel insufferably naïve or irrepressible; and yet, once again, their contributions are so vital, they cannot be discounted or denied. So, these people are sent out into the field, to do things that others don't seem to be able to figure out.

People who are feeling the press of mystic aspirations often display "edginess" to their temperaments. They can be "prickly" and argumentative. We relate to mystics as we would to a strange uncle, nice to visit, but we don't want to linger for too long at his residence, or be there alone. Mystic aspirations impel people to do things that seem peculiar. One such person I mentored was constantly moved from one job to another within the corporation. She was just "strange" – intrepidly creative, insistently rebellious, obliviously individualistic and too restless to stay in any one place for long. She was too kind, creative, attentive and supremely competent, wherever she landed, to let go, but the executives in the company constantly asked, "What can we do with her next?"

THE ASPIRING TEMPERAMENT: FAITH-FOR. This much is true: mystic aspirations do impel people to live differently from those who restrict their ways to the mainstream. Yet, I have met mystics in the most prosaic of places and in very significant leadership roles in the organizations in which they work. These include a former marketing executive, now unemployed and becoming a consultant; a chief financial officer in a corporation; another person initiating and running global projects for a government agency; and a vice president in charge of major operations in a communications company. They are in these roles, but are not defined by them, I find. When conversations with these people scratch just below the surface, I cannot help but notice something different about them: they would each leave any role they take on in a heartbeat in order to pursue something larger and of greater impact and significance. And that larger significance is always in front of them: it is palpable, it calls to them and beckons them out of whatever position they are now in. And of the mystics I have met, I can certainly say, wherever they work or serve, whether from their writings, their projects or other works, they move us; and they do not rest until they have made a difference. They move us to new perspectives, and they revitalize our old ideas. These mystics I have met are first and foremost teachers; and so, from these mystics we learn something.

One way to sum up this difference is that the mystics I have met in my mentoring practice are people who live in a state of being, who live out an ethic I call *"faith-for."* They live in *a way that is devoted to bringing about the new, the fresh, and the most vital aspects of what the human endeavor holds in store for us.* And I do not mean new gizmos that will soon be on the market. No — *the "new" in the aspiring mind of the mystic comprises the utterly unforeseen and still unrecognized and not yet conceived.* They take their lives out into an *open space,* an undefined landscape, marked only by an incandescence of energy and light. Others may see this space and think nothing of it, pass right by it, or walk right through it and see only empty ground and desert. But mystics see and feel, sense and tingle with vivacious energies that are set free in play, and that they choose to play in and with. They are the supreme teachers of the vastness of the energies of which life partakes and which humans can enjoy in unlimited variety, if they would only do so.

FORE-GIVING: THE MYSTIC ETHIC. Mystic aspirations play out in ways that it is hard for us to conceive, and the way they play out is even hard for mystics to conceive, even though they experience this way every day. Mystic aspirations do not come with a price tag, or even a means of valuing them. What mystic aspirations offer us is given before (prior to and in the face of) any proposition being in play that can account for them or offer something in exchange or in compensation for them. The simplest of examples might help us understand this: A young woman, just graduated from college, is about to start work in a city far away from her parents and although she needs a car, she can hardly afford one. The mystically inclined parent immediately blurts out, "Take this car of ours, we'll get another one." The other parent, more inclined to take the costs of such an offer more into account, is taken aback. "We'll figure it out," says the mystically inclined parent.

This kind of offer is made by parents every day. And when it is, the way that this offer stands out from the flow of exchanges and earned rewards never ceases to amaze those involved. Now consider such an offer that has this kind of structure, this giving without any anticipation of return, on a larger scale: offering one's time and effort, offering a lifetime of service, offering to stand out in front of the group so that an experiment might proceed or a risk might be taken. This is the logic of the mystic's aspirational ethic: to give with no expectation of return, or in some cases, with no expectation of even getting a response.

How can it be otherwise? Since we are saying that the mystic's aspirations set in motion the kinds of realizations, the kinds of awareness, the activating ideas and concepts that open futures beyond anything imagined so far, how can they act in any other way? While that is an easy idea to articulate in terms of logic, it is quite another matter to enact in real life when livelihoods and reputations (and even life itself) are on the line. Mystics do this. If not for mystics, I aver, there would be no such thing as a "future" that would be anything but a repeated reproduction of the same old ways.

Why We Care

Historically speaking, mystics have always had a tough go of it, as we shall see in Part Two of this book. Some of their travails are of their own making. Mystics have a way of behaving in which they willfully defy our help – not just decline our help, but put themselves in opposition to any help that we might envision offering them. They don't ask for our help either; they don't ask for favors; and they don't ask you to give them what you have or ask what you can give them. They don't ask for our advice or have any intention of taking it if it is offered. They are often not the kind of people who fit the profile of what we think of as needing help from others. Mystics just don't fit into the normal ways in which we think about giving care, or what care even entails.

I think back to that moment in history when the mystics established a role for themselves in the thirteenth century in the Low Countries of Europe. The earliest avatars of the mystic figure were people, mostly women, who left their homes, even their families, in order to *teach new ways and new ideas* (an important point as we go forward) to whoever would listen to them. In those times, when the new commercial centers of Europe were just taking shape, great social upheavals were taking place. Cracks opened up amid the established regimes of feudal authority and orthodox beliefs. Medieval social organization and church dogma that had been dominant for centuries were being outstripped by pressures from rising populations, the influx of new modes of learning (brought by the Muslims during their conquest of the Iberian peninsula), and from new modes of production, trade and commerce. These forces broke down barriers of land ownership, power distribution and in the very way value and worth were determined. In the newly arising cities, new ways of making a living opened up and alternatives to the pastoral and peasant life made their appearances. In this new and fresh regime of society, women also took up the cause for change by breaking free from the social constraints of pastoral isolation and peasant servitude. Significant numbers of them wandered into the newly burgeoning urban centers; some of them were literate and even well educated, all of them were adventurous. They all answered a call to stand up for a new and more expansive realization of the human endeavor that few of their peers could see, that entrenched powers defended to the hilt, but that these women *felt* powerfully as being worthy of their devotion. This call (of aspiration, in our terminology) commanded their decisions to move on, into the unknown, the foreign and unwelcoming. These women were called "Beguines."

No one cared about these women, either. Their husbands were enraged that their wives had shunned them. Church authorities were threatened by their vernacular and individual proclamations of contact with a new rendering of the passion of the Christ – a relationship with that spiritual life without intermediary, translator or anointed authority figure. A new source of labor was arising that threatened guild and artisan production. And then, whole new modes of communities were created – Beguinages – in which participation was completely voluntary and self-selected. Finally, women were coming together and binding with each other, forging a force that simple sexual domination or social ostracism could not contain. It is this energy, which the Beguines grasped immediately as a basis for action and organization, expression and knowledge, which initiated the modern age, the mystic age, which is still unfolding to this day.

KEEPING FAITH-FOR. And so the mystics that I have met in my mentoring work, unknowingly and completely without any intention of walking in their forebears' shoes, continue to strike out on their own, seek out their own ways and seek out adherents who can hear and who they can teach of the vast openness that awaits our initiative. Today's mystics are still the ones who leave everything of this world behind in order to *keep the faith* for new and more encompassing possibilities for humanity and other living beings (known and not yet happened upon). We do not mean that mystics advocate a "faith," in the sense of a delineated religion that prescribes beliefs, rituals, modes of penance, and paths to salvation. Religions have appropriated that word, to our lasting detriment, in order to glorify their fantastic myths and icons as properties of specialists of the "spiritual." Mystics do just the opposite: they give their lives over to what is not yet in existence, so as to welcome *all* into a vitalizing, energizing, expanding and opening endeavor. Their faith is that such an endeavor is the essence of life and humanity itself. They find repugnant the priests and demagogues who distort and reduce this potency to matters of possession or mechanism. This is *"faith for"* (rather than faith "in").

Mystic aspirations require that one keep true to this "faith-for" in every way possible, and, even more, against all odds, keep it alive. They must swallow their fears. They also quite often have to forego temptations of status, power and security. They have to be able to respond, to engage, and to activate with enthusiasm and rigor when a step is taken into a more expansive and encompassing possibility. They keep the faith-for even as scorn, incredulity and punishment are heaped on them. And, they keep the faith-for by carefully cultivating each and every minute and tenuous seed of possibility that comes their way.

Why Do We Need Mystics?

"So," you might ask, "mystics live in an ethic of 'faith- for' a future of openness to new worlds and possibilities, and they 'fore-give' of themselves with no expectations of return or compensating exchange. But as long as I am making a living and supporting my family, company and country, why should I be concerned with such things? Why should I care about mystic aspirations or that there are people who enact these aspirations among us?" We need mystic aspirations because we need our fellow humans to venture into experimental and provisional ways so that we can learn about what is possible for this endeavor of ours, this endeavor of being human. We need other humans to "show us" what it looks like to hold a faith-for what we might be able to do and become as a noble species on this good earth. We need other humans to give voice to or act out how yesterday actually brought something new to us, something that we may have overlooked, but now don't have to. Where else will such a vision come from? We need people among us who speak our language, who also live in our societies, take jobs like ours, raise families, but who *also* live out this faith-for and aspire to envision ways of living we have not yet allowed ourselves to even dream of.

Why do we care about whether or not some people do the hard work (of forming and fore-giving precepts, and then teaching) that mystic as-pirations entail? Because humans learn in no other way but to observe, note and let themselves be affected by what other humans do. Learning for humans is no small matter. It brims with paradox. We feel most alive when we are learning, and yet we resist learning the very new ways of being that will help us be more alive (some get thrills from drugs instead, for instance). We feel that opening our lives to more expansive and more encompassing comprehensions of our worlds and of others is a good thing, but we cower in fear when we face the strange, the stranger and the greater good, and so we congregate in enclaves that repeat the formulas that enshrine and glorify our conformity. Before the time when there were texts, before the time when there were schools, before the time when there were cultures and societies that kept peoples' "ways" alive, humans had to observe how it was that some succeeded where others perished. And then we observed the people who survived, learned what they did, and accepted their new ways (if we didn't kill them first).

And then, at some point, maybe 5,000 years ago, we realized that at some level, like it or not, this learning was a good thing, and a distinctively human thing at that. So we set out to learn how to learn; we set out to become a species that would learn how to transform itself and its ways of being. The mystic figure arose much later, to remind us of this commitment to learning and to set out new ways of learning that were equal to the tasks of modernity, knowledge, trade, production and freedom. In each epoch, in my narration of the human endeavor, a kind of figure arose who bore forward the aspiration for learning that was necessary for a transformation of ways to take place that would be equal to the increasing complexities of emerging human efficacies such as language, technology (metallurgy and agriculture), lawful societies and then conceptualizing reason itself. The figure of aspiration that has arisen in our age (a mere 800 years ago) is that of the mystic.

So, who should care for and about mystics? *Whoever cares to feel that life is worth living and wants to foster the conditions for a vitally fresh and alive existence in the midst of a vibrant and flourishing natural world, needs to care about and care for the mystics among us.*

MYSTICS NEED US. And here is the other part of the equation: People who adopt the life ways of mystic aspirations need *mentors*. What can mentors do? They need a mentor's attention, first and foremost. We have already acknowledged that mystics envision and stand up for worlds we have not yet seen. We have already demarcated their strangeness, their abstract and disruptively demanding ways. How can they need mentors? What can they need from us? They need *mentoring*. If not mentoring from a single provider, then they need to obtain bits and moments of the care that mentoring offers from many people. It may be no more than a gaze, a look or even an engaged silence in which the mystic's words, vibrancy, and power are held, intact, having landed in a place which allows them to remain whole. Maybe it's a slight nod, or soft word, that says, "and...? go on." Or the mentor may even venture this to the mystic utterance, "Tell me more; and help me understand..." Just taking the time to offer the occasion to listen to a person's mystic aspirations will have powerful effects on making those aspirations come alive.

Mystic Aspirations Appearing in the Human Fold

As I intimated above, mystic aspirations were not always active among us. In the Western/European context, they arose as a way to break through and break out of the medieval world that was locked in by oppressive social laws and rigid spiritual and religious practices. Before then, the earliest precursors of the Western form of the role appeared in the context of the decline of the Roman Empire – in the Middle East, most notably Saint Paul, and then throughout the Greco-Roman world in sparse and rare numbers. Their message was dizzying in its breadth and scope: nothing less than a complete re-centering of the human endeavor, a complete resituating of human life in the cosmos itself, could overcome the thoroughgoing legalistic enclosures of Roman law and Pharisaic Judaism. Paul and Pseudo-Dionysus, Pythagoras and Plotinus seeded the ground for just such a re-centering.

But these avatars only prepared the field for what others would later sow. It took another millennium for those seeds to take root. This took place during the thirteenth century, to which I have already alluded, when the

Beguine mystics surged onto the declining feudal scene. As I implied above, we now live in the age made possible by mystic envisioning. Along with that notion I will add this: in our schema of the breakout creative roles, the mystic role is relatively new, in comparison to the other roles and certainly in comparison to the history of humanity and its Western forms.

Since their firm establishment in our culture, in the thirteenth century, *today's* mystic aspirations have evolved. In the face of the complete hegemony of human production – from every item of use and consumption being rendered into the empty commodity form to the whole earth's climate changing in response to human activity – there is no longer a firm and centered institution or image that can act as a unifying force for aspirations. Aspirations are now multiple, "molecular," concentrated at one of the sites of human engagement that begs for some kind of vital and enlivening connection to wider contexts, intensities, events and concepts. Today's mystic aspirations have thus departed from their initial intuitional settings of unity and transcendent oneness, and now, in the form of "anamystics," bring forth their realizations out of pure multiplicity, locality, surprise, difference and fleeting surges of occurrence. [4]

What is important for us is that as long as energy streams into us and onto our planet, from the sun and the wider universe, as long as $E=MC^2$ holds, and energy underlies all that we take to be "solid" or in any way "present," mystic aspirations will play a decisive and defining role in the processes that vitalize and freshen our living.

What It Takes to Be a Mystic

And so who among us qualifies as being one who enacts specifically *mystic* aspirations? Much of the literature on this subject I find to be unhelpful or downright misleading. For instance, Kaehner [5] cites the evocation of "mystic experiences" by drugs, or through being enraptured by nature, or by achieving yogic equanimity, and disqualifies them all.

The only "real" mystic in his eye is the theist who feels and responds to the presence of a separate, personal deity. The traditional commentator J. Marechal[6] actually uses words such as "approved" mystic, referring to the seal of approval put on some mystics by Catholic authorities. Obviously the parameters of even these ecclesiastical authorities change, since mystics were once condemned, and in the case of Marguerite Porete, burned at the stake. Meister Eckhart died before he could be so condemned, while San Juan de la Cruz (Saint John of the Cross) was so abused that he died shortly after escaping his imprisonment. Notions such as these highlight the ways that our discomfort with and around mystics is revealed, and they offer no help at all to someone who wants to support mystic aspirations by mentoring.

Let me alert the reader to the hard and fast premise of this work: *I do not give any weight or credence to the notion of "mystical experience" or "mystic union" in our understanding of the mystic temperament, in our comprehension of what the mystic life entails, or in our appreciation of the mystic aspirations, and I do not think the use of drugs or hallucinogenics is a part of any regimen for a mystic life way.* (In fact, the use of drugs is, in my estimation, a way to avoid coming to terms with what these aspirations entail, or are self-medicating measures taken because of the pain caused by suppressing these aspirations.)

But, you might protest, what about the fact that mystics (Hölderlin, Nietzsche, Celan) have gone mad, or that some do have frenzied "experiences" as recorded by the likes of Teresa of Avila or San Juan de la Cruz? Or what about the fact that even you acknowledge (later in the book) that many people who have mystic propensities also suffer from depression? So, inevitably, we are brought to the conjunction between the mystic and madness.[7] Indeed, I'll gladly say, all the breakout creative figures have a stroke of "madness" in the portraits painted of them. We love to think of mystics as wild ecstatics rolling around the floor exclaiming their rapture at being touched by God. There is no doubt that a favorite theme of people clinically diagnosed as schizophrenics and psychotics is hearing messages from God. What distinguishes these people from the likes of the female mystics Hadewijch or Mechthild of Magdeburg, who we exalt in Part Two, who vividly depict their own amorous encounter with God?

So, how do I regard mystic aspirations such that these extremes do not pertain? Here are some of the criteria I use:

1. Mystic aspirations induce and stir, first and foremost, a great and overwhelming love of and for the human endeavor, the earth and its creatures. They are, after all, *keepers of the faith toward what can be brought forth, indeed in bringing forth itself, which we call "fore-giving."*

2. Mystic aspirations, when nurtured and supported, enable a person to be more amenable to absorbing more raw and copious flows (overflows) of energy, and even suffering. The whole impetus of this aspirational figuration is to enact and embody *the human ability to expand the boundaries realization that living beings can engage.*

3. *And that means sober, disciplined, intensely concentrated work to make a vision come alive and give it its place in the commerce of the world.* No one of mystic orientation, none of the figures we bring into the genealogy we offer (in Part Two), deems him or herself elected or elevated out of the human fray or family or chooses to opt out. All of their efforts are directed to speak in the language of the worlds in which they live, and bring to the people who use such language and subscribe to the conventions and institutions of their worlds, a new and fresh sense of living as a human and not merely as a part in the system, a tool in its mechanism. They seem to the rest of us to articulate the power of another psychic dimension, another "register" of openness to vital energies that have not yet, and may never be, amenable to ordinary, functional, purposeful "meaning." But, to the mystic, they only articulate what has emerged as worthy for them in the course of their

study, learning, and immersion in the profound depths of an as yet unexplored "way."

4. People of mystic aspiring survive their demanding way because they are remarkably strong and resilient. They exude such remarkable amounts of energy, they exhibit such grand *enthusiasm*, that it is nearly incomprehensible to me what it must feel like to be them. I want to spend some more time on this notion of the mystic's energy. Nietzsche imagined something he called a "dynamometer," that measures the pure "life force" a person absorbed and emitted as a living being. I will imagine such a meter exists for our purposes as well. Let's say that to get through the normal modern, urban day, it takes an energy level of four on a scale of ten. At level four, it is possible to do one's job, manage a family, deal with social irritations, multitask at times, and have enough energy to watch some TV at night before collapsing into bed. And, with this amount of energy, we are not expecting any consistent creativity or originality, just good, solid, reliable, satisfying performance in our daily, morally regularized and approved existences, with maybe some flashes of creative urges popping through. People who devote their lives to realizing their aspirations, whose lives deal with more experiential ambiguity, whose urges to be creative and of service have no guidelines to fall back on and so have to be self-generated, require a seven or eight level of energy. First, they need more energy just to figure things out. Then, they need more energy than the norm because the tasks they set for themselves – new expressions, new artworks, new sciences or concepts – all require great amounts of energy to execute. On this "dynamometric" scale, the mystic has an energy reading that is *off the charts*. Why? First, their psychic filtering and constellating or consolidating mechanisms are very weak. Everything requires figuring out, deciding about, ordering and prioritizing – and that is before a single word is uttered or action is initiated. Then, mystics

continually drive themselves out of the set and familiar — even the most artistic or conceptually difficult — into territories where they are in the open, completely exposed, completely dependent on their own energies to make their ways. And they do it, they survive all of that, and even more: many of them succeed in bringing forth the most amazing, original, break-the-barrier kind of expressions. That level of energy is simply amazing to contemplate.

5. Mystics experience their lives in ways that are *both different from the way we do in the mainstream of life, and in ways different even from the other aspirational figures.* Where we and the other aspirational figures are able to live what we think, create out of what occurs to us pretty well directly and forthrightly, the mystics live out of *another* world that they construct, in more or less complete form, in their psyches. And it is by comparing, contrasting, judging and interacting with *both worlds,* in juxtaposition, that the mystic lives and acts. This is the primary and driving conception we have of the mystic life. We call it the mystic's "Field of Enthusiasm." We discuss this idea in detail in Chapter Three.

6. *Mystics only know how to give.* That is their answer to the conundrums that beset them. *Give more, give more of their emotional involvement, and give more of their time, energy, and knowledge. Give. They give it away.* I call this mystic *"fore-giving."* But they are not the easiest people to give to. It is not that they evaluate a gift coming to them. Rather, they take such as gift as a new element they must incorporate into their worlds, and that requires them to give and exert even more energy.

7. *These mystics live very open lives.* Their boundaries are far more fluid than those of others. It is hard to land in some certainty; and when they do, it is only for a limited duration. If "ecstasy" means being out of stasis, out of a condition of being settled, then those mystically inclined are most often in just such a state.

They can be fierce friends and totally unreliable at the same time. They can be incredibly articulate about a state of affairs and this ambiguity, but confused at the same time. They take on the greatest levels of responsibility and challenge they can envision, and suffer the whole time they execute against their commitments.

The watchword for mystics is indeed, "open." It is into the open that they step; it is to "open up" closed and rigidly stratified worlds that they labor; it is the criterion of being "open" to living at its most raw and unformed that they adopt as their standard (for themselves and others).

8. Mystic aspirations require that experiences of their own emotional vicissitudes and the fluctuations of an unstable outside world be taken to heart. Each and every moment for these people is a learning experience. *They know how to construct worlds that don't yet exist* (as we will see in Chapter Three). And so they yearn to *teach* what they have learned as well. Living is for learning, not vice versa.

9. And this learning is devoted to one way of being: that of *being alive,* in touch, vital, creative and generative. There is no way these people can reside in duplication and repetition; no bureaucracy can contain them. And so they thrust themselves out into the world again, as wanderer, as individual contributor, as teacher, often with long periods of withdrawal into seclusion along the way. These are not the people who create cults or seek any kind of following. These are the people that you must seek out, must go to in intimate conversation, must meet in a state of mutual giving and learning. And then they go their own way.

We ask you, who but a mystic could imagine life this way:

To possess no advantage, neither better food nor purer air nor a more joyful spirit – but to give away, to give back to communicate, to grow poorer! To be able to be humble, so as to be accessible to many and humiliating to none! To have much injustice done him, and to have crept through the worm-holes of errors of every kind, so as to be able to reach many hidden souls on their secret paths! Forever in a kind of selfishness and self-enjoyment! To be in possession of a dominion and at the same time concealed and renouncing! To lie continually in the sunshine and gentleness of grace, yet to know that the paths that rise up to the sublime are close by! — That would be a life! That would be a reason for a long life!...[8]

This is the way of *fore-giving,* the mystic ethic.

PART ONE

The Basics of Mystic Aspirations

Chapter One

Meeting the Mystic:
Energies of Pure Vitality

From time to time, one sufficiently remembers and makes clear that fact that the absolute must not be sought outside the absolute, and especially that we would certainly never grasp the absolute, if we did not even live and conduct it.

~ J. G. Fichte, *The Science of Knowing* [1]

It should also be mentioned here that the meaning of the speculative is to be understood as being the same as what used in earlier times to be called "mystical," especially with regard to the religious consciousness and its content. . When we speak of the "mystical" nowadays, it is taken as a rule to be synonymous with what is mysterious and incomprehensible; and, depending on the ways their culture and mentality vary in other respects, some people treat the mysterious and incomprehensible as what is authentic and genuine, while others regard it as belonging to the domain of superstition and deception.

~ Hegel, *The Encyclopedia Logic* [2]

...[It] sometimes happens that it is precisely he, perhaps, who bears within himself the heart of the whole, while the other people of his epoch have all for some reason been torn away from it for a time by some kind of flooding wind.

~ Dostoyevsky, Brothers Karamazov [3]

Meeting a Mystic

Bradley had been a friend of mine for several years. He had great success in business, but his dominant characteristic was great discomfort with all that such accomplishment brought. His real love was generating big, re-forming and transforming ideas around business, technology, science and society. He tended to get quite depressed by the state of the wider world.

He responded to his concern by creating a whole new way of bringing technological innovations out of the laboratory research stages into commercial production. His idea for this "tech transfer" process involved completely new relationships among all the players – scientists, investors, supporting institutions, and employees. In his head, his idea was fully developed, completely laid out and explained. . His vision provided for an explosion of innovation: extricating technological breakthroughs from labs and universities, and releasing them into commercial production, into exciting projects for employees, good chances of reasonable returns for investors, and rewards for the inventors. As he saw it, his plan seemed to meet all the criteria for capitalist innovation: good ideas, a receptive culture for innovation and the availability of capital, the returns from its investment sufficiently rewarding the risk.

He set out to find backers and prospects to put his plan in motion and get really great, new and innovative products to market. His quest proved to be a quixotic one that spanned several years. He met with moments of great success and in some quarters he was heralded as a "genius," a "model entrepreneur" whose vision could be trusted to lead others to their own commercial and financial successes. But his proposals were also met with scorn, especially in banking, investment and venture

71

capital circles. His idea required one step that seemed out of reach for his prospective clients: it required that they share the riches. This seemed to be beyond the pale of many who allocated capital to promising technical ventures; it thinned out the returns, diluted the shares and skewed the risk/reward ratio. The idea wound its way through many revisions until it started to resemble a standard business deal. But eventually, after scores of ups and downs, after one prospect after another dropped away, my friend lost interest, and walked away from the venture entirely

His personal life was not much more satisfying. A broken marriage, several failed romances and side trips marked the way. His response to all of this disappointment was to retreat. He spent several months mostly by himself, reading and stewing in the feelings of sadness that seemed to surround him. A psychologist with whom he consulted just rehashed the obvious kinds of observations about self-defeating behaviors, fear of success and other pop psych diagnoses. Friends were unsure whether to offer him solace, encouragement, or a swift kick to the butt.

My conversations with him had a different intent. I wanted to talk to him about the mystically figured aspiring energies I suspected were at work in him, and help him explore this psychic/somatic dynamic. I did *not* intend to "*make* him" into a mystic, or even "bring out" the mystic that I suspected was "in" him. After all, no one aspires to become a mystic, or more properly speaking, no one chooses the way he or she aspires at all, no less to aspire in the ways of a mystic figuration. The conversation was just intended to alert him to the notion, for his consideration, that his aspirations had a shape, a tone and even outcomes that aligned with stories of Western mystics who also strived to set new ideas in motion, and met with mixed reactions at best. My intent was to diffuse the judgment (his own and that of others) that he "failed," and to help him keep that aspiring way alive in him.

While there are few pure mystics in the world (or pure prophets, artists or leaders, for that matter), many of us harbor those energies of aspiration that make it hard to accommodate "real life." And none of us harbor energies that place us at a greater distance from the quotidian than do mystic aspirations. So when suggest that my friend is susceptible to mystic aspirations, I am suggesting that his "disposition" toward a certain role in life puts him at a certain kind of disadvantage in terms of everyday functioning, that is, in meeting others' expectations or in accepting what is given, at hand, and what is understood as "common sense." These "givens" just won't do for the restless, idea-generating aspirations that take on mystic figuration. Now, the mystic's dissatisfactions hardly render them non-functional. Bradley and others of mystic inclination I have met are highly functional, often rising to the pinnacles of their fields. Still, I see that mystic propensities, in some significant, but not disabling way, make it harder, if not impossible, for Bradley and others of the same proclivities (for no mystic is like any other) to "be like everyone else."

As a mentor, my intent is to help Bradley find a way to name his aspirations' figuration (in this case, that of the mystic), give them substance that can be nurtured and developed, and set on a firm, joyful path. As a mentor, I can help him to tap into the dynamism of those energies that surge through as his creative spirit. By providing an occasion to identify, explore, articulate and map out practices that strengthen those energies – channel those same vague feelings, urges, up-surges that propel him out of conformity to the ordinary into a sense of not just a project, but of defining a *role* for him – I can help him to sustain those aspirations and keep them alive through all the trials and tribulations that await him on this path.

Mystics Appear

HOW I MEET MYSTICS. When a person bearing mystic aspirations comes into my life, it is neither because I have sought one out nor because someone who considers him or herself to be a mystic has sought me out for my mentoring services. I meet these people in the course of mentoring corporate executives about the life of leader aspirations. These people lead organizations of all kinds, usually under the challenging circumstances of starting up, growing rapidly or undergoing massive strategic and cultural transitions. The leaders I have met in these contexts are highly placed, very "successful." I do not go into those contexts hoping to find a trove of mystic-minded people. It might seem strange that I find mystics placed as hierarchically high-level executives in the corporate world. It might seem contradictory that a "mystic" – such a strange and otherworldly figure – would have a role to play in the bustle and mechanistically leveled functions of our most conformist modes of commercial life.

But, as I have come to realize, encountering a mystic in corporate settings, while rare, is, paradoxically, actually quite likely to occur. From my research into mystics of the past, and in my continuing study of them now, I find that the stereotype of the mystic as a solitary, brooding, mountaintop figure who thrives on the wisdom of the winds is a self-serving lie of the uncomprehending. Instead, mystics are such high-functioning, highly comprehending and highly involving and giving people that the most creative organizations, the ones that see their mission as transforming more expansive and encompassing possibilities into realities (be they in the religious, political, service or commercial spheres) seek them out, want badly to retain them, and promote them to high level, strategy-making roles.

HOW CONVERSATIONS DISCLOSE MYSTICS. No one comes to me or is assigned to work with me because they express mystic aspirations. There is no designated role for mystics in our secular business-driven, corporately modeled culture.[4] There is no position "VP of Mystic Realization" in our corporate hierarchies. When I do encounter a mystic, I realize this happens only because the meeting with this person is somehow different in tenor and intensity from meetings with other executives. When I mentor leaders, for instance, I am prepared for the "normal" exchanges of facts, ideas, impressions and opinions. For the "typical" executive, the world is "normally" divided between subject (the leader) and objects (the goal, the organization, the technical issues). The conversation in these situations focuses on helping that leader see how his or her life is worthy of leading in such challenging situations.

But the energy of mystic aspiring figuration quickly changes the trajectory, tone, pace and complexity of the conversation. This highly creative, generous, energetic, articulate, impassioned person seems to be a little different (in ways we'll explore) from even the most effective of the leaders in the company. She is not different in the ways you might think that the mystic would exhibit – fuzzy in her thinking, longing for solitude and withdrawal so as to be left alone with her great thoughts. No, this person most emphatically wants to lead. But her idea of "leading" is different. She isn't that interested in producing a new widget on time, under budget; to her, "leading" means putting something really important, big and life-changing into the world. Then, maybe because of this extra "push" she gives to the "big idea," she isn't easily fitting into the organization's culture, even though she is devoted to it. She throws herself into the company's mission whole-heartedly, to her full capability, which is immense. Yet, for validation, she doesn't really look too far beyond her own sense of the world and what she wants to accomplish in it. Promotions, more money, "employee of the month" awards don't cut it for her. She always weighs and tests her commitment to the organization against her own comprehensive and vitally connected standard. These standards she articulates clearly – although such standards as she holds seem abstract, grand and almost embarrassing to express. And it is precisely these "standards," these terms of her peculiar motivational ori-entation, that set her at odds with her peers.

And this difference is not a matter of degree. Surely, any leader will have good ideas and is willing to sacrifice or at least defer a big payout if she is going to guide the organization's efforts in a viable way. But in the case of our mystically aspiring exemplar, she always makes clear, "I *choose* to do this; I don't *need* to do it; I don't *need* this in my life. I could move on to something else in a heartbeat." She always asserts, "If this situation starts to diminish what I truly care about, no less violate my principles, I am out of here." The force of her commitment to this standard is palpable: it radiates in her eyes, it stiffens and expands her bodily presence.

NEXT STEPS OF QUALIFYING. Slowly, I start to assess whether the quality of her creative drive departs in significant ways from what I commonly see as the leader's orientation.

To move into a mentoring conversation that has mystic aspirations as its focus requires that a mentor's suspicions or hypotheses undergo serious examination. We will consider this "diagnostic process" in depth in Part Three, but here I want to keep the expressions of mystic aspirations as the focus of the text. In the context of my professional mentoring work, such opportunities for extended exploration and examination do arise. Because I meet with people eight times over the course of several months, I get to listen to a person's language and thought patterns, study temperament profiles, and hear of a person's dreams for a better world – all in great detail and filled with personal and emotional investment. Over time I test out whether my mentee's orientation is aspirational in the ways that accord with that of the mystic figuration. I listen to the mentee in order to discern if this person's creative drive is not so much directed immediately to the impetus to act, but instead is predominantly directed in order to envision new ways of living, to express those ideas cogently and powerfully, to give of oneself in order to provide an exemplar of those ideas, and to abide with those ideas and their adherents through adversity. I see if this person is constant in directing her attention and efforts to creating a space, a logical and emotional order of things that reflects what is ultimate, in need of treasuring and protecting if their lives are to be lived with their inherent "power" being actualized. What they are protecting, defending and abiding by is not a "transcendent" power that ordains a course of action from on high, but rather is a sense of there being something more alive, right in the midst of things, that people can fully embrace as being intimately a part of their single, mortal, socially committed and engaged lives, if, that is, they have the courage to do things a bit differently.

Instead of exchanging information in the course of our meetings – information about the competitive situation or the company's politics, or even one's own life situation – the mystic exchanges something else. Her wellspring of raw emotion breaks to the surface, often accompanied by tears. It is not that this person is emotionally fragile, out of control, or touching on some deeply seated and concealed wound – mentoring is not psychoanalysis, after all. Indeed, after a life of working hard to "make it" and "get along," the mystic has a deep store of "rationality" to draw upon, and is more often than not tough as nails. But as the conversation proceeds, and I probe about the experience of putting a new idea into the world, the mystic's defenses are breached. *The emotion of living* both within and outside of the world, the tension of not being able to accept what is given, the anxiety of constantly encountering disappointment – these all take prominence over any kind of mission at hand and come to the fore. And the emotion itself, more than the project, is what is at stake in the conversation, more than the faults of the world or the brilliance of conceiving of a particular solution. The emotion springs from that feeling of release, of not having to hide, and of being heard, without judgment or defensiveness, by me, the mentor.

The emotion that comes to the fore is almost that of a celebration: that in this moment of the mentor's hearing, the mystic's aspirations are being given credence. The emotion celebrates the aspiration, not her despair or discouragement. I can paraphrase one such exclamation of potentially mystic energy that occurred recently. This person – Racine, we'll call her – just started to talk in a stream of expressed self-reflection: "Why do I feel this way? Why can't I be happy with what is at hand, like others are? And I certainly don't have the answers, so what am I doing to myself, feeling this way? I don't feel like any kind of a leader at all, frankly. I feel like something else, but I don't know what that is."

THE PRESS OF AN *ALTERNATE* WORLD. Mystic aspirations generate a feeling that "something" is kicking around in her heart and mind that continually unsettles, disrupts and disconnects her psyche from a contented interchange with the things, facts, opinions and accepted verities of the given, commonly held world. Mystic aspirations fully envision a more vitally lively world, teeming with diversity, chances and opportunities. The feeling – and it is the feeling that is the issue here – that the real world she lives in just doesn't jibe with its potential is more than most people are willing to allow themselves to admit, no less allow to happen. And, let me say, this is no mere intellectual proposition or idealist wish that is expressed. I hear and feel from Racine, for instance, that *she* is testing *me*, and that she is offering just a sampling of the energy she really feels. Still, her whole demeanor hits me like a high-voltage shock of energy that arcs across the chasm between us, between her and the world she is living in, between what she feels as alive and vital in her as it collides with a deadened and solidified world.

Touchstones of the Mystic Life: Faith-For, Fore-giving and Your Health

In this section, I will summarize the seven touchstones that characterize a mystic's aspirations: abundance, faith-for, fore-giving, health, questioning, teaching and solitude. We can generally characterize these touchstones under the heading of *exuberance offered* from start to finish. For people who are inclined toward the mystic life, the constricted and constrained ways of experiencing that is ordained by conventions, professions and social pressure, those categorical separations and restrictive rationalist causal validities, are not sufficiently vivacious and generative to stem the streaming into their lives of powerful, unconscious and uprooting energies. Mystics take their measure of life from sustained, exuberant, powerful and powering flows of energy that sometimes defy logic, but always are willing to give more, in ways that sometimes fly in the face of common sense, but always suggest ways that offer more to the human endeavor, other creatures and the earth. It is not that there are just different ways of doing things, or that some technological or social innovation seems to be the answer for the mystic – although once committed to an action, they, like everyone else, have to buckle down and wrestle with concrete issues. It is rather that different things are actually at stake for mystic aspirations. It is the life of aspiring, over all and above all, that they stand for and exemplify. Here are the ways this aspiring life looks to the mystic, the echoes and refrains of which (as we will see in Part Two) resound through their pronouncements, projects and precepts.

TOUCHSTONE 1 – ABUNDANCE: FLOWING AND OUT. In the mainstream of daily interaction and commerce, we value "objectivity." Analyzing impressions and placing them in logically connected relationships provides us with the comfort of having our experiences validated through accepted processes and concepts, that are themselves validated and interconnected with other objectively validated processes. Mystics use and rely on those processes in their everyday lives as well, of course. Those who work in high-level corporate roles, or who take on other commercial responsibilities, are as adept as any in using these methodologies of rationally industrialized productivity.

But somewhere in their ruminations about life and the big picture, mystics are susceptible to raw experiencing itself, to that dynamic and unpredictable flow of vital engagement that put our senses into the stream of living occurrence, and they do not or cannot suppress this streaming vitality. These mystically inclined people have to let the undefined and undecided have its way, since no psyche pre-occupied with everyday goings-on can analyze or contain such a flow. They have to accept the power of this vital flow in all its uniqueness and strangeness since it can be neither denied nor suppressed.

TOUCHSTONE 2 – FAITH-FOR. While their analytic powers are no match for the overflowing life energies they encounter, their willingness to absorb those energies, without qualification, are capacious to the hilt; and so this torrent of abundant and overflowing life hardly disables them.

79

Because the mystic's own flow of life (great mitochondrial energy production in the nuclei of their cells?) is so strong, they match life's energies with their own. The result is a super-abundant creatively generative process that meets this overflowing of energies with their own ability to open and expand their sense of their own lives. the mystic embodies nothing less than an outlook on life that I call "faith-for," taking delight in letting go of their own preconceptions, prejudices and judgments and releasing their aspirations and anticipations into the flow of what lies beyond the horizon.

It is a *"faith for"* (rather than faith *in* something in particular) because they adopt a stance of faith that is neither prescriptive nor predictive, but instead suggests that a more expansive and more encompassing grasp of events will bear fruit. Their categories of comprehension, in other words, unsettle rather than explain. Their own surging energies propel them out to the perimeters of how learning and deciding take place, and some even stretch out beyond that erstwhile boundary to what they cannot grasp by any schooled means.

From the standpoint of their faith-for, mystic aspirations put them in the position of having to greet their experiences with gritty passivity, enforced gentleness and a knowledgeable naiveté. That is, they experience what goes on in their lives as harboring a powerful paradox: On the one hand, they feel they are *subjected to* the experience, and are grabbed onto by the experience; and on the other hand, this surging flow is met at every moment with decided discernment, lucid attention and awaiting comprehension. And so, faced with this complex way of living, mystic aspirations engender appropriately complex responses: some people who experience these complexities remain silent, while some others are driven to speak and/or write.

The mystic lives with a propensity to savor those moments and has a tendency to let these moments go on for a while. And, this is the critical part: the mystic has developed the ability to compose a new sense of herself and her world on the basis of what that experience brings forth.

While the mystic may be momentarily "at a loss" to jump into the conversation or argument (situations mystics avoid when possible), her great store of personal energy encompasses this "lack of filtering and processing" with great powers of free-floating imagination. Instead of facts ready to use, the mystic's psyche *generates* worlds that make sense, that cohere, and that are complete in themselves. To mystic aspirations, this generated world is just as real and as productive as is the already processed world of everyday commerce. For the mystic there are now two worlds, one existing alongside of the other; one has a newness that propels, energizes and excites, while the other has an effectiveness that produces in blithely content profligacy.

Whether they are silent or actively expressive, the people who experience these aspirations work so as to elucidate, contextualize and free up the experiences in ways that are "truthful" to the full power of their communicative abilities – and are always working to stretch these abilities in order to "honor" the occasion. The mystic's ultimate and driving question is not, "What's in it for me?" It is not, "Will this succeed?" Instead, the mystic engages the existing world from these questions: "What can I give to make things different? How can I make this *be*? How can I make it *all* come to *life*?"

TOUCHSTONE 3 – FORE-GIVING. This term names the mystic's ethic. If the mystic is going to act in a way that accords with her innermost driving and shaping aspirations, she must, like it or not, *proceed with what exceeds*. The mystic gives credence to that which exceeds what is given as being real and true. Mystics revel in the excess of experience over knowledge, and in the ultimate triumph of the unknown over what we are so convinced of; they bask in the excess of emotion over the words for the emotion. [5] As such their way of living is hardly restricted to the terms of the adequate exchange. The mystic has to proceed, like it or not, into situations in which they have to give and cannot expect any kind of return, recognition or recompense – and often, not even a response.

The mystic lives *out* of the personally vested and powered realizations of her faith-for. She has no "choice" but to articulate this sense of the more expansive and more encompassing prospects without reservation, *right into* the heart, right into the teeth of the conventional world. What can she expect from this peculiar initiative? Will she be understood? Will people welcome the risks she proposes need to be accepted? Will people share her propensity to put personal gain aside? For those tending toward the mystic life's way, fore-giving is both a relief and a sorrow. It is a relief to know that this giving with no expectation of return is not foolish; and it is a sorrow to know that, over and over again, this giving out, with no expectation of return, is once again in the offing: there is still more to give.

TOUCHSTONE 4 – HALE AND HEALTHY. Anyone who has lived the mystically aspiring way for any length of time realizes that *health* is an issue, and, perhaps, health is the first and foremost issue. In the absence of keeping oneself fit, mystic aspirations require so much energy to absorb, and are so unsettling of "normal" goings-on, that, in the absence of health, such a person is prone to slip into depression, even to the point of considering suicide. From what has gone before, that cannot be a surprise. To live out the life of fore-giving and to offer, unsolicited, the rigors of a faith-for, the mystic has no other source of bodily strength than her own habits and practices – diet, exercise and sleep.

At this juncture, it might be a good time to take up the notions that surround the idea of mystic experiences, raptures, ecstasies or even madness. The mystically aspiring people I have met and mentored would have no interest in such things. From the characteristics I have offered so far, we can see that mystic aspirations propel people into living in highly charged ways, into engaging experiences that are overcharged with vibrancy and energy. These people do not need raptures or ecstasies to feel the way they do. Rather, maybe it is we, inured to the quotidian humdrum, who hear their true enthusiasm and aspiring way, such that the ecstasy is in our eyes.

This whole line of thinking that connects mystic aspirations to raptures and ecstasies doesn't help the *mentees*; rather it generates a protective net around us. It harbors us within a force field of protection that gives us permission to keep mystic aspirations at bay. This mechanism works by discrediting every aspect of what mystic aspirations demand of us by making these demands the results of a kind of "madness," one that we are sober and sane enough to evade. First, we use this notion of the mystic's ecstasies to buttress our dismissals. For someone to be a mystic, they must exhibit these experiences; and because they exhibit these experiences – these missives from the beyond, swathed in emotion and paroxysm – their utterances can be dismissed. Then, from the other side, when the people of mystically figured aspirations *do* present their *precepts,* those demanding utterances that embody their faiths-for, these are discredited – no matter how thoroughgoing the research, experience and viability of the person's work may be. By means of this double inoculation – by highlighting how strange a mystic experience is and by rejecting the unsettling and disrupting precepts actual mystics offer because they lack the ecstatic imprimatur, the creative contributions mystics offer are kept at a safe distance, out of sight, beyond the pale of validation, and thusly our psychic armor is not dented. [6]

In my mentoring work, I see mentees reject any hint of these kinds of experiences. Notions such as "raptures" or "ecstasies" do not provide the mystics I have met with the standards, measures or validations that constitute mystic life ways. Instead, the people I work with are mystics because of the way they dedicate themselves so fully and without reservation to their aspirations and the way they bring their best and most valued vitalities to them. Their strangeness comes from the depth of their dedication to what can only be *envisioned* as possible and that they seek to set into motion what can only, at the present time, be expressed as precept. All of this is done with the gentleness of a seeker, the vulnerability of a creature in motion, the humility of a cultivator and with the free giving of a child.

83

TOUCHSTONE 5 – QUESTIONING BEYOND THE PROBLEM AT HAND. "Okay," you might grant, "people you have met who exhibit mystic aspirations are bright and powerful people. But is there something else that you are saying about these people besides pointing to their precociousness?" I certainly am. There are many people who are bright and energetic, who are able to manipulate a lot of data and who are able to formulate very appealing statements along the way. And certainly, to act on any of the figurations of aspirations that are described in this schema (artists, prophets and leaders as well), requires a healthy dose of precociousness. But we are considering a particular slant or orientation or "drive" that characterizes mystic aspirations in their singularity; that is, mystics raise questions of a certain kind. The questions they raise are not analytical questions that take common notions apart and show how their logic is faulty or contradictory, or even that their presuppositions are groundless. And they aren't legalistic questions that seek common sense justifications of the way things are. Instead, the mystics' questions take what is given and push beyond it. They ask questions of the kind that were described by Robert Kennedy (quoting George Bernard Shaw): "Some see what is and ask why; I see what is not yet and ask, why not." As one of my clients put it, "I want you all to see your limitless destinies." The mystic talent is to see the prevailing and constraining concepts at work and then, while not eliminating or discrediting them, to *always ask, how we act so as to get beyond them, to break them open, to see what they hide.*

Historically, or genealogically (as we will see in Part Two), this mode of questioning first stretches the way we use or deploy concepts, especially the most important ones, like God and the laws of the cosmos. The first mystics deployed their "apophatic" speech, or speaking in denials and negations about the nature of God in order to keep that notion out of the hands of commercial and technological adjudications – to keep God holy. Then, in the contemporary philosophical scene, the work of mystic aspirations becomes a matter of showing how any conceptual exploration worthy of the name (which excludes positivist philosophical analysis, for instance), breaks off from certainty and apodictic clarity and stretches out to "archi-traces" that engender nothing but differences that escape conceptualizing. This "deconstructive" approach places the mystic aspiration right in the heart of our literature and science, in works of the likes of Joyce and Blanchot, and in the works of Gödel and the quantum (and sub-quantum) spectrum of cosmological astrophysics. This mystic questioning instigates the founding of still another paradigm for addressing the nature of our living in this universe, and that is the notion of self-organization and increasing complexity, which specifically guides this work.

TOUCHSTONE 6 – TEACHING AND THE PRECEPT. And so, what do mystics *do,* when all is said and done? Mystics *teach.* I would go so far as to say that the Western notion of teaching, and the situating of education as a necessary factor in becoming a competent and functional human being who participates in our socioeconomic processes comes to fruition simultaneously with the rise of the mystic. Further, those founding mystics – the Beguines of the thirteenth century Low Countries – validated teaching and education as a socially necessary practice. That said, with education being reduced to producing job-ready functionaries, mystic teaching keeps itself apart.

Mystic teaching offers neither instruction nor training nor apprenticeship in the technologies of the present day. The mystics teach what their lifetimes of investigation, questioning, research and probing of their own aspirations have led them to: a *precept.* A precept is an expression of what aspirations have at stake if they are to take shape and affect people's lives such that they too can aspire and engage their lives in ways that are more expansive and more encompassing. They are not commands, in the sense of "do" or "don't do" this or that; and they are not adjudications as to what is "best" or even "feasible" for humans as a whole. They are indications of ways forward that have yet to be proven, but that only can be undertaken at all by doing so in a spirit of living in ways that are more expansive and more encompassing. I offer as an example what I consider to be at the heart of every mystic precept (of aspiration) that I have ever heard: *proceed with what exceeds.*

TOUCHSTONE 7 – SOLITUDE AND MOVING ON. Then there is the absolute requirement for *solitude*. Some people who are inclined to have a conceptual or questioning approach to life need to do so in the marketplace, in the company of others. Not so with mystics. Socrates' love of his solitude, the reverie he could attain in that solitude (and maybe embarrassment about what is thought to be his epilepsy) always overrode any need to be with others. Nietzsche and Bataille craved long periods of solitude, even though they maintained lifelong friendships. But all mystics esteem most the time and the locales of their solitudes.

That is not to say that mystics live solipsistically; however, it is to say, most emphatically, that after a time in one place or in one social or organizational setting, those whose lives are shaped by mystic aspirations will *move on*. They do not live or want to live all of their time alone. As we have said, mystics are organizationally engaged. They take their imagining into disciplines, discourses and practices that demand their engagement. They continually want to enrich their imaginings with learning: about the inner workings of what they see, about the connecting principles and flowing transformations that are so palpably real to them. Learning is their way to turn the roaring river of their imaginings into real-life power generators. While the institutionalized world doesn't measure up to what they envision, they measure their own lives against what they can bring that world up to, in terms of releasing new vitality and opening its ways to expanding efficacy.

This rhythm of alternating solitude and engagement is the wellspring of a trait often cited when talking about mystics: their love of travel, their propensity to move on, their innate restlessness. Some travel geographically over wide expanses, some remain nearly itinerant within the confines of their own locales – Socrates comes to mind. Some retreat to a favorite getaway – Nietzsche loved the Italian Alps, for instance. Some stay, do their work and then move on. I think of the great medieval and Renaissance mystics, Meister Eckhart and Teresa of Avilla, respectively, who did the high-level work of creating orders and then moved on to new locations to repeat this work elsewhere.

Mystics are wanderers. Their need to wander replicates the dance and free play of energies they experience in and from that field. At the risk of seeming childlike they maintain in themselves a diminished and bruised sense of innocence (a play of forces in multiplicity). This propensity to leave, and mystics do leave, thus comes from the mystic's need to keep in step with this rhythm between solitude (or at least a situation where their thoughts and ways have free reign) and engagement (when it is time to take their experiencing into the fray).

Part of leaving also has to do with the fact that their precepts not only rarely come to complete fruition, but also that what mystics set out to do often fails outright. Mystics take their organizational failures in strange ways. Bradley was just heartbroken, embarrassed and has largely withdrawn from the scene. Alice was sent into a headlong tailspin for a long period of time. She wanted to radically reset, rather than return to the corporate fold, but reset into what, that was not as clear. Fran believed so strongly in her mission that she absorbed all kinds of rejection and non-comprehending responses from her peers in order to advance that mission – at the tremendous cost of near burnout. Jen reacted to not being well-comprehended by her peers by throwing herself headfirst into a nearly suicidal project at which no one else in the company had succeeded and ended up burning out. Dan just walked away (from seemingly sparkling success).

One theme ran consistently through all of these responses from potential mystics: deep personal hurt. Their pain was not about their egos being bruised. There was very little anger and defensiveness in their response. There was little of the kind of "picking up my marbles and going to a new game" need for self-validation. What was felt, it seemed to me, was a matter of being dislocated. They were thrown out of the Garden, so to speak. What was lost was not just their position or authority, but the possibility that something they knew could make a difference wouldn't happen there. The world closed up on them, leaving them and their dreams on the outside. It was not as though a project had failed, but rather something that they offered had been refused (or at least not comprehended or understood by others).

I found these responses an occasion for reflection. Leaders do take the failures of their aspirations personally, for instance, but they almost take such failures as a badge of their own determination; their way of self-trust impels them seek out a place to lead again — to lead something else somewhere else. With mystic aspirations, this was not the response I was seeing. So this picture occurred to me: these people had freely, without qualification, wanted to give the world something of what they had experienced and realized as vital. They gave it in (their) good faith (faith-for), and with no small amount of personal vulnerability. They gave freely, of themselves, with no expectation of great return, but in the hopes that something important could be accomplished by their venturing their gift. It was this giving that was rejected. And it was a gift that came before there was any expectation of exchange or return.

What the mystics put out there was what I came to call their fore-giving, which we described above. We'll have much more to say about this phenomenon as our reflection on the mystic continues, but here, the point is that mystic aspirations presented me with a different response. While they moved on from the immediate site of their failure, their aspirations remained intact, and they sought out new territories, new soil on which to gather and make sensible the same aspirations, those same vast and untapped energies that revitalize life, but they also give of that energy before there is any certainty that it will have a chance to germinate. To the extent that they keep their aspirations alive, they seek out a new venue that might enable those aspirations to flourish for just a bit longer, to be heeded by a few more people, that might give those aspirations some strength to take root on their own accord. They seek fresh grounds on which they can once again give in advance, out of abundance, out of that excess that permeates their lives; and then they squander it freely, for all to partake of. That is what "fore-giving" needs and offers.

So Who is Learning Here?

When we speak of mentoring we certainly envision an asymmetrical relationship in which the mentor imparts something to the mentee. What is clear is that mentoring aspirations in general, and mentoring mystic aspirations in particular, disrupts that flow of imparting and receiving. I think there is no aspiring way I have met that demands more of my willingness to let go of my preconceptions, my certainties and common sense prescriptions about what life holds in store for us. When I mentor aspirations of this kind, I realize that when it comes to living more expansively and more encompassingly, we mentors have to learn from our mystic mentees. Further, maybe we cannot mentor at all, that is we cannot really competently address aspirations as our concern, if we have not engaged mystic aspirations in all their grandeur, expansiveness, risk-taking courage and fore-giving generosity.

And so, if we are to mentor aspirations, we first we have to recognize those among us who live this way, or live parts of their lives this way. We have to value their ways, and learn how they take shape, how they came to be and how in the course of our Western ways, we have learned to accommodate these energies, at least to some extent. Not that we adopt their way; but we need to valorize their aspiring way so that our mentees value this way as their own lives are shaped by these aspirations, and instead of fearing these awesome energies, learn to heed them, nurture them and do the work that they entail.

Thus we have to learn to listen to these aspirations in a different way. Instead of listening for how we can help this person "adjust" to what is at hand and perform in ways that will help them accomplish their ambitions and worldly goals, we need to hear how these people's aspirations are seeking support and nurturance, how these people are willing to give their aspirations their due, if only doing so offers them a way forward. We need to help them keep their aspirations alive, which, in the case of the mystic ones means giving clarity to notions such as faith-for, fore-giving, the precept and teaching.

Mystics are those who had the faith-for such an undertaking and live in this opening way. By their enacting faith-for, they help us find the right way to affirm each tentative foray that we dare into that new endeavor. "We must find, for each thing in turn, the special means by which it is affirmed, by which it ceases to be negative," says Deleuze. Later he continues, "Innocence is the game of existence, of force and of will. Existence affirmed and appreciated, force not separated, the will not divided in two – this is the first approximation to innocence."[7] These are descriptions of Nietzsche's mystic imperative. When I meet mystics, I get to see these same great energies right before my eyes, right across the table from me. And these mystics are our friends, neighbors and co-workers. As I realized, it is *we* who have been blind to them, while *they* have seen us clearly all this time.

Chapter Two

Opening to The Mystic Mind

…Only becoming-active has being…Only becoming-active has a being which is the being of the whole of becoming…everything is affirmed in a single moment… affirmation changes nuance and becomes more and more profound…

But the complete formula of affirmation is: the whole, yes, universal being, yes, but universal being ought to belong to a single becoming, the whole ought to belong to a single moment.

~ Gilles Deleuze [1]

The new life, which had to dissolve and did dissolve, is not truly possible…; dissolution is necessary and holds its peculiar character between being and non-being. In the state between being and non-being, however, the possible becomes real everywhere, and the real becomes ideal, and in the free imitation of art this is a frightful yet divine dream.

~ Hölderlin [2]

But the spirit is not the life that shrinks from death and keeps itself pure from devastation, but rather the life that endures it and maintains itself in it. . It wins its truth only when, in utter dismemberment, it finds itself…[Spirit] is this power only by looking the negative in the face, and tarrying with it. This tarrying with the negative is the magical power that converts it into being.

~ Hegel [3]

Encountering The Mystic Way

From my veranda in the foothills of the Sandia Mountains in Albuquerque, New Mexico, I see the valley below in all its expansive glory, reaching out to the horizon. Mountains a hundred miles distant are visible. . There are times when clouds fill the sky and darken the ground below. Sometimes, a beam of sunlight streams through the clouds and splashes to the ground; the light illuminates a small sector within the whole panorama. In the midst of the darkened valley stands this one illuminated area. In my imagination, this ground is illuminated as though being favored by the celestial light. If we suspend disbelief for a moment, the image of this concentrated, earthward-bound, streaming light can also serve as a metaphor of the mindset that a mystic's aspirations set into motion: that of a will to open and illuminate, to explore, to emerge from any surrounding darkness, as a force that is fresh and unnamed. In the mystic, I encounter a person whose seeing can take in vast expanses, stretching to a far-off horizon. Other senses are keen as well. This is a person on whom the ordinary markers of conventional life have far less of a claim, seeming more like distractions, noise, or "sense candy" – just so many intrusions, interruptions, obstructions. These things of our given life that give direction and purpose to most of us serve only to add so much clutter and noise to the mystic's way.

While these people do not think of themselves as mystics – no such category of "personhood" can be said to be offered in the normal course of things – at some level of their self-awareness they also realize that they are more capable than others in founding or understanding new, cutting-edge notions; they discern opportunities and dynamics that are just not apparent to others. They feel their feet to be firmly on the ground, and they feel just as surely the aliveness of that ground; and they bring the two, their feet and the ground, into dynamic contact. While it may not be at all clear what the way forward will entail, there is nothing uncertain about the liveliness of anticipation and prospect that they feel. One person I mentored described to me how, as she was climbing a mountain, the loose gravel beneath her feet gave way. She said that in that moment she had a strange sensation – not that the ground gave way because she was stepping on it, but because the ground had its own way of holding and giving way. She did not feel that there was anything uncertain about the locating of her feet on that ground, the ground just moved.

Our question is, what kind of a "way" is it that mystic aspirations put into play? What kind of creative and generative urge is it that yields such an expansion of what would seem to be the simplest occurrence? After all, people with mystic aspirations experience the same factors of matter, sense and energy that we do. They go to work, sit in traffic, have meals, and raise children. How is it that the same world, the same activities that we all perform, end up having different significances for mystics? How do their psyches work such that these differences in perspective, in priorities and life decisions come to the fore?

Answering this question is no easy matter. Of course, there are matters of brain chemistry and brain "wiring" – and we will not neglect these differences (see Chapter Three). Then there are factors of experience, memory and child development. Our analytical capabilities cower in the face of such "deep" factors. And, undaunted, we will actually venture into these thickets soon enough. But, what we might not consider, and what also frames the orientation of the mentoring conversation (as opposed to the therapeutic or coaching ones), is that a history and a pathway of learning, expression and practices have shaped the mystically aspiring mindset, and have provided very faint, hardly perceived, yet still affecting ways that the mystic shapes her aspirations into a life way.

Whether the mystically aspiring person knows it or not (and the mentor needs to help her come to know it), the expressions she finds herself thrown into have been set into motion by very concrete and specific people and incidents that have occurred in Western European history. She may not step into that history knowingly, but through reading, through listening to life stories, or through appreciation of certain precedents, she can tap into a deep stream of behavior, thought and mindset patterns that has pulsed through our (Western) culture for nearly a millennium. Mystic figuration of aspirations arises because our way of living presents certain kinds of dissatisfactions as well as certain avenues on which to challenge and open up its constrictions. Only by at least *understanding* that the mystic has parameters of expression, a continuity and ways of living that have proven to be suited specifically to these proclivities can the mystic's energies be consolidated, and made intelligible and viable as a life's way for this person. First the mentor has to cultivate that understanding, in at least a rudimentary way, and then the mentor can appreciate what is at stake in the work that lies ahead.

Clearly, when we say of someone that they live or "live in" a "mystic way," we are not making a judgment based on body type or sartorial preferences. Mystics may dress differently than others do. But when I work with mystics in the business world, they are attired in the same "business casual" wear, or the same dark suits (men's and women's) as are the others in the business. So when we make such a distinction we are referring to patterns of speech, or different emotional casts they express, or the different range and scope that their values enact. All of these put together become a noticeably different "way" of engaging their worlds.

But, those signals are unreliable. However much we judge a person's temperament to be "mystic," no one comes with an identification tag that says "mystic" on it. What we encounter are the glimmers of the ways that certain saliently affecting expressions of aspirations have percolated to the surface. These are the effervescences by means of which aspirations appear at all, and this is certainly the case with the aspirations that give rise to mystic proclivities. Those effervescences are surrounded and constrained by and narrowly channeled through an acculturated, deeply schooled, highly competent and indifferently generalized milieu of socialization. No mentee I have worked with is "purely" mystic or behaves as a mystic in every aspect of her life. She enacts specifically mystically aspiring proclivities in certain areas, disciplines, interests or passions in her life, while, in the meantime, other parts of her life appear to be completely "normal." It is that "effervescence," that rising to the surface of her mystic "way," that breaking through the hardened and containing shell of convention that the mentor addresses. That is, the mentor addresses the "aspiring mind," or the mystic bent or slant of mind that she aspires to bring to her concerns, pursuits and commitments.

To fully appreciate this mystic way, we must ask ourselves (as mentors): What is happening in those moments of the meeting when this mindset exerts its impetus and asserts itself in this person's speech, actions and decisions? What does her world look like? What do her words really mean? Why is she expressing these feelings and not others? To be fruitful in this meeting, we must be able to fully listen to the mystic, hear the resonances that he or she bears forward into the encounter. Then we have to help the mystic access these resonances, echoes and evocations so while possibly still tormenting for the mystic, this torment is taken as subject matter, and not as a "judgment from on high" that some kind of trespass or transgression is afoot. For that reason, we have to take an excursion into this mystic's mind "coming into being" as she engages that "world" that, so far, only she fully discerns.

THE MYSTIC FIGURATION OF THE ASPIRING MIND. Mystics respond to their life situations as they do because their aspiring minds are "constructed" in a certain way. Everything they aspire toward, in other words, has a peculiar nuance, tenor and "feel" to it — one that makes that aspiration distinctive in terms of its perceptions, emotions, orientations and intentions. These aspirations, prior to any awareness of their influence being available, pre-sage, pre-form and ever so subtly and in the most delicate of nuances, influence the way that this person will assemble, gather and form how she makes sense of what is occurring in her living engagements. We mentors are "listening" for indications of how this non-conscious shaping of sense-making is taking place so that we can discern if and/or how these aspirations have a mystic figuration.

The Mystic Figure and The Story of the "Aspiring Mind"

Let's begin our appreciation of the mystically aspiring figure by appreciating how deeply ensconced mystic figuration is in our Western (European-based) culture – a capitalist economy, Judeo-Christian/Platonic/Enlightenment intellectual heritage, republican governance and large-scale bureaucratic organization of production. The figuration that mystic aspirations took on in the West developed in specific ways that are quite distinctive. While such orientations in the Orient and India appear to be similar to those of the West, once the surfaces of the great Eastern traditions are broken through and their presumptions, values and outlooks are appreciated, we see all the ways that Eastern practices and figurations are not the same as what we describe as being the case of our Western mystic. While some of the expressions used in Eastern traditions help Western mystics express some aspects of their discernments, the difference remains.[4] The Western mystics' ways develop along pathways that are distinct in the world and so, by definition and as a direct outcome of that history, necessarily distinguish themselves from our own everyday goings-on.

$E=MC^2$. We are familiar with how dependent our bodies are on our environment – if from no other signals than the effect of carcinogens in that environment, or the peril of global climate change to human life as we know it. We are also aware that we are truly made from the dust of the earth, because of the vitamins and minerals we need, and because non-processed vegetables and grains are what nourish us most. We are also aware of how our "minds" are shaped by our larger social milieu. Just as when we see a unique path of development for the religions, the art, the governance and economics of our culture, we see how these factors impart to our individual "selves" a "Western" character. From the mystic's perspective, "mind" is just one more way among others (albeit a pretty exciting one) that great cosmic powers constellate into entities. For instance, if our descriptions of mind start with Einstein's formula of $E=MC^2$, then every single thing – entity, being, object, occurrence, event – is a quotient of energy in one state or another of acceleration. Energies that are still streaming onward, we find, actually constitute some 90 percent or more of the universe's "stuff." Some energies have slowed, stabilized, gathered, coalesced, and then more or less (complexly) organized into some kind of "material." In this view or in paradigms that extrapolate from this view, life captures flowing energy and directs its momentum into a centripetal vortex that organizes into discrete and active beings. [5]

When I work with my mentee's aspirations, and particularly when I work with mystic aspirations, I rely on the fundamental picture of our cosmos and life, and the mind that the formula $E=MC^2$ sets into play. Viewed on that energy-to-matter continuum, a "mind" can be thought of as being a highly mobile energy gatherer that is organized with great complexity and nuance into individual living ways of engaging environments and (then) worlds, and as an organ that does so in ways that allow it (within a range of parameters) to change and expand its modes of operation in response to the increasingly complex states of affairs it encounters. Getting the right picture of this expansive, "individuating" action is important in what follows.

This notion differs from the conventional notions we have of the relation between our "minds" and the environment. We customarily think of minds as being separate and autonomous processing devices that operate upon the inert material given to us (as nature or society or other facts) in our experiencing – that ever-mysterious way we "contact" our environments and worlds. Most accounts of mind concentrate on one of its dimensions, that of its ability to perform a variety of functions from sensing to rational conceiving, from emotional charging to cool judging. But to understand aspiration, and the figurations of the aspiring mind, we need to restore to our conceptions the "connected," "collective" and "communal" and dynamically "emergent" notion of the mind.

ASPIRATION RISING. And now, with abruptness and shocking speed, we will turn our attention to a "story" about how aspirations came to play such an eminent role in human affairs. What humans have accomplished as a species during the past 20 millennia or so is utterly astounding. No species has developed such far-reaching changes in its way of being in the world as humans have. How did this happen? The typical account of this process of change (some call it "progress") is that great "world historical individuals" founded new ideas or institutions. Cyrus founded empires, Abraham founded monotheism, Thales founded philosophy, etc. The "genius" theory of how the human endeavor has evolved (which is not to say "progressed") has currency as shorthand for identifying moments of inflection and shifting of a historical trajectory. But the "great man" (and mostly it is men) theory covers over a far more complex situation. In our view, the ability to guide the course of the human endeavor and engage the psychic/somatic structures that such changes entail has more to do with that "connectedness" *between* minds that we have so painstakingly described. Great transformations in the human saga have happened because humans developed the means to get back in contact with the larger vastness of our generative milieu and broke out of the confines of whatever individual minds imagined, foresaw and dreamed of. The figures (and there were many at any given time or place) that broke out arose in their epochs and established the ways of transformative creativity we speak of here. The mystic is not exceptional because he or she is a "genius" or because of some way in which they are regarded as "exceptional." No. Mystic aspirations are important to us because of their commitment to connecting to the world, other people, other creatures and the earth. It is their faith-for and their fore-giving that merit the devoted attention of a mentor.

That is, our aspirations, practices and life ways are determined by how we orient our *attention* — the way we direct our *focus* in this vast complex of diverse natural, social and intellectual formations of our culturally defined world (a mind's exo-memory as it is congealed, combined, structured and lived in by minds' outputs being massively collected).

Object-focused orientations take the produced culture-world as fact, as what exists, and also take it as material for use. *Culture-focused* orientations apply consciously recalled and cultivated Mind energies to the culture-world and innovate, produce, and administer within acceptable parameters of engagement. *Aspirationally-focused* orientations undertake to bring mind and culture-world together in an exchange of mutually affecting engagements, the results of which engender more expansive and more encompassing ways to conduct our lives. This "fused engagement" of our minds and culture-world is what we call *"aspiration."* The mystic feels the need for this "fusion" and feels the need to intensely activate and engage her aspirations generally (in the mode of "faith for"), and allows them to have the greatest affect possible, the greatest effects she can bear, on her psyche, and offers (fore-gives) this as living proof of the possibility of the kind of transformations that are possible to undertake in the culture-world (which she expresses in her "precepts"). Mystics show us this orientation to living in its purest form; they show us what aspiration looks like, feels like and does when in action. [6] Mystics adopt a certain relationship between their own psychic processing and this great store of human cultural production. They keep it all in a state of highly energized relating, over wide areas of what the mind encompasses.

The people who aspire in the way we call "mystic" arose in order to directly address, to protest and counter certain conditions in their worlds that impeded the ability of people to expand and extend their reach into vibrant, generative living. These realizations didn't happen all at once and came to fruition only because of the amazing efforts that individuals and communities exerted by coming together to make new and important insights about human living available to as many people as possible. [7]

If human beings (among other constituents of the earth) are, at their most basic level, constellations of energy, and if those constellations can *change* from one epoch to another, there must be in force a dynamic that generates such change. For there to be such categorical differences between epochs – and therefore the goals, aspirations, world views and mindsets of the people in those epochs – that transforming dynamic has to be overwhelmingly powerful. It has to overcome deeply engrained forms of bodies and processes of living; in the human arena it has to overcome powerful habits of engagement and plow over utterly dominating institutions of government.

Clearly, such a dynamic is at work. After all, we know that through the course of the earth's history species of organisms go extinct (in the case of dinosaurs, after ruling the planet for 140 million years), while new ones appear. We know that among all the lines of development species exhibited through the eons, there were also occasions in which species appeared that had capabilities that completely outstripped those of existing species. We also know that species changed one characteristic or another as the milieu in which they lived changed (and this occurred, according to our story above, in a manner of flowing connections amid all streams of formation and constellation in that milieu), and then suddenly qualitative shifts suddenly took place, and a new species emerged. This process is called "punctuated equilibrium" as described by Steven Jay Gould.

Mystic aspirations are specifically concerned with those aspects of the human engagement that are *necessary to consider* if our own epoch is to open up to greater vitality and engage our worlds in manners that are more expansive and more encompassing. So, when we encounter the mind-set we call "mystic," we are encountering a person for whom a new epoch is already underway. The mystic has appreciation, respect and even deference for much of what the older epochs have to offer. This is no demolition-bent revolutionary. It is usually the ruling elites of the existing regimes who destroy the "insurgents" – those representing the new epoch, but also those who would drag a society or nation back to an old form – with impunity. The mystic is dedicated to what is coming, what is underway.

The mystically aspiring figure is not putting out there a utopian vision of human heaven on earth. Those eschatological ideas are usually in play when an epoch has crumbled in terms of being a robust ordering principle, and the new epoch has not yet taken shape. We saw this take place when the Roman Empire was in decline and "end of the world," ideas ran rampant. Christianity arose on this soil. We saw it again in the twentieth century as utopian totalitarianism took root. Communism and Fascism are its secular, Self-based forms, while atavistic theocracies take up the most elemental and infantile forms of governance that is appropriate to earlier, nay, ancient epochs.

Instead of propounding atavistic throwbacks to mythical glory days, the mystic's aspirations offer this vision: a new epoch is underway and awaits our rising to the occasion. In spite of being scant on details (but taken up with equal dedication and competence in their own ways by other breakout creatives), the mystic articulates and lives the life that the aspiration to a new epoch invites. [8]

THE DEVASTATION. To appreciate the mystic's aspirations it is helpful to think of just how much effort it takes for the mystic just to compose, no less comprehend, what occurs around her. I choose, somewhat dramatically, but necessarily so, to call this characterization of what the mystic mind-set sees around her as "devastation." The old structures are breaking down, exhausted and caving in under their own weight; a symmetry break has occurred, and certainly all of these eventuations do not proceed by any design, at least by any design any one person, institution, force or power could conceive of, no less execute. The changing occurs because of how inexorable and irrepressible are all the myriad forces that express themselves and exert efforts in order to take their places in the mix of things. All the aspirations that are in play in living milieus generate not only changes among the existent factors in play, but also accumulate into forces that induce changes that are expansive and milieu changing. Mystic aspirations are attuned to how those energies are exerting forces that are in play right now, and people who aspire in this way feel that in many ways the changes have already occurred – it is just a matter of time before the affecting potencies of these forces show up as new states of affairs. One might say that the "zombie" view of the world expresses how mystic aspirations characterize *this* world – a world that has already passed, that is already a living dead, that is passing on to a new level of living ways.[9]

The term "devastation" thus has a particular meaning for mystics: a once-great vastness, a once-great expanse of vista on which action and creativity could form, is wiped away, yielding to the vastness hurtling out before it. Mystic aspirations come to the fore, rise to our awareness when the floodgates of change, or the utter devastation of war, the rising tides and fires of climate change, or the sterility and rigidity of ideologies turn the old to ash. In the classic eras, times of calamitous devastation happened periodically.

As our genealogy of the mystic way will show, in our own cybernetic, hyper-productive, free-flowing capital times, one could say that devastation at some level happens continually, by compulsive necessity and non-conscious design,. We live amid the rush to turn over, to plan in the obsolescence that permits a "creative destruction," as the emblem of the efficacy of our economic might. And so, I suggest for your consideration, we live in mystic times: times initiated by mystic opening of rigid dogma and cosmology, and times that demand of us that we continually deploy mystic re-envisioning of the course and content of our lives (though now, admittedly for decidedly non-mystic, institutionally advantageous purposes – and hence the advent of the anamystic, as we will see below).

The Life of Aspiration

Mystic aspirations do not envision or prescribe that a particular outcome or result needs to happen in order to fulfill their efforts. Mystic figures, unlike religious figures or representatives of a specific "faith," do not even necessarily use the mechanisms of their own accepted institutions (including their corporate institutions) to do their work. Their visions are not "teleological" in the sense of requiring either a "first cause," a "final outcome" or utopia (except, in the case of today's "anamystic" of truly appealing to aspirations that open out onto *no* place[10]).

Mystically aspiring people have only *precepts*, not prescriptions, in view as they do their work, and so have no interest in precipitating destruction or even in devising local "replacements." Such ends and purposes are more typical of politicians or entrepreneurs (and, certainly some of these ends can be quite positive, life-enhancing and progressive – or ends of this nature can be used to promote larger, less commodious ends). The mystic espies the devastation with sorrow; she flows out of the void left in the wake of destroyed institutions and life ways and into the unformed open of what just might now be possible in this newly opened "margin" of possibility. She illuminates the new "open," opened by the symmetry break. The devastation provides the occasion when mystic energies expand, with less resistance, and therefore with greater "staying power" and also with concrete avenues of both negative and generative instances, events, and objects.

The mystic aspirational mind doesn't just think in an abstract way, seeing her world as a collection of concepts or a conjunction of forces. She sees the larger, invisible but formative dynamics that are in play, but she also sees an underlying logic that offers certain outcomes that are generative and life-engendering to the core. The founding Beguine mystics, especially Marguerite Porete, foresaw the utter collapse of "the little church" if it did not change its ways (two hundred years before it actually happened). Nietzsche foresaw a cataclysm on its way in Europe. But they also saw the vital and pulsing possibilities for a new epoch, right there at the heart of the devastation.

LISTEN. Take a moment with this passage from Hölderlin's fragment, "Becoming in Dissolution" and capture from it the sense of the emergence of new life out of dissolution, if not a precise analysis of its psychic mechanisms. [11] In Hölderlin's work, the term "idealistic" stands in for what we here are calling the precept: [12]

> This idealistic dissolution [the aspiring mind that ventures
> beyond the merely given] is fearless. The beginning and
> endpoint is already posited, found, secured; and hence

this dissolution is also more secure, more relentless and more bold, and as such it therefore presents itself as a reproductive act by means of which life runs through all its moments, and in order to achieve the total sum, stands at none, but dissolves in everyone so as to constitute itself in the next; except that the dissolution becomes more ideal to the extent that it moves away from the beginning point where as the production becomes more real to the extent that finally, out of the sum these sentiments of decline becoming which are infinitely experienced in one moment, there emerges by way of recollection…a complete sentiment of existence…There emerges from this union and adequation of the particular of the past and the infinite of the present the actual new state, the next step that shall follow the past one. [13]

So mystics, despite and over and above their poignant evocation of devastation, are those among us who are most affirming, who truly live as the *faith-for* what comes as the generative: they truly give everything they have to offer, they truly live in order to affirm a new epoch that is underway. Mystics have no illusions that this epoch will fulfill the utopian promises of suffering being relieved and complete freedom or democracy being established here on earth. They see that this new epoch will open to more expansive and more encompassing ways for humans to bring forth those raw and un-tamed energies into a vital life (as opposed to a depleting, zero-sum way that devastates people, creatures and the earth). Indeed, even in our own troubled times we can palpably feel that "a new birth" of freedom is in the offing: political freedom, economic expansiveness and liberation from the toxic addiction to fossil fuel energy. Every mystic I have worked with, even those mystics I have met who are working in the bowels of the U.S. defense establishment, have nothing less than their commitment to their faith-for and their aspirational vision in mind.

Part of what this work is about, therefore, is for those of us who are not mystics to be able to first hear, heed and hearken to the mystic precept – the unsurpassed faith-for what comes only in the open. And then comes the demanding call to us: grow into a mindset, a generative one, in which we are willing to let our ego-based fears go at least long enough to hear, at least what we can hear, of the mystic's vision. That is most likely a demand too large, a leap too far. And that is why we have posited the necessity of there being among us other figures who translate such visions, through processes of specification and psychic entraining, into what we can comprehend (artists and prophets do this) so that we can act on it (by the force of the efficacy of our creative leaders).

Summary and Transition

Mystic aspirations pose a difficult proposition to the mentor. To perceive mystic aspirations we have to form our ideas about our world differently than we do in the course of our everyday doings. In a way, we seem to be saying one has to *be mystical* in order to discern the mystic way. "After all," the everyman in us might protest, "what is all this talk of E=MC^2 and consciousness as the sea in which we swim, if not mystical blather?"

What is true about such a protest is that the mystic cannot be perceived or grasped by the most trivialized and clutching of the consumerist mentality (or in religious piety or in blind ideological rigidity); but, in the moments of our lives wherein we feel most alive and most in search for our connection to living vitality, something approaching the intent of these notion does arise. And so, yes, it is in these moments when we might exert the effort to grasp the mystic mindset, and then just possibly we might be moved by it.

But let's condense what we have said down into a graspable nugget, to give us the best chance of opening ourselves to the mystic mindset.

THE TIME AND PLACE OF MYSTICS. Mystic aspirational figures arose among us at a certain point in history because the thirteenth century world had become sclerotic, exploitative, and mendacious to the core. Mystics did not arise before these conditions arose, and to me that says something about the human spirit: there is nothing that mandates such an appearance, after all. If mystics are among us, foregiving precepts that take us into the open, there also must be conditions present that provoke their concerns. The issue is when will we learn how to listen to them? Mentors here provide the catalyst: they keep the mystic's aspirations alive so they can do their work, and so they can do their work of teaching. Without the health that mentors help mystics maintain, they and their precepts will once again be eclipsed (as was the case for 200 years in Europe, beginning with the so-called Enlightenment and extending until the Idealists kicked up the dust and raised the ghosts of their erased ancestors, such as Meister Eckhart). We will be left buried in the detritus of our exquisite productivity and technically innovated ingenuity.

Mystically aspiring figures tell us: Humans too easily become objects: static entities inured to their "human nature." This is the negative side of their message. And then these people take up the causes, the disciplines, the precepts that want to bring another way of living first to our attention and then into practice. They want to remind us that first and foremost, and never able to be altered, we are constellated, congealed, organized energy – a momentary dissipative system that reverses entropy for a time. We are this, all together – with other humans, other creatures and the earth in its cosmos. Is this a strange message? Yes. But is it a mere fantasy, a mere myth to chuckle at and disregard? No. As I noted above, this is a firmly, convincingly validated notion that guides our most structured and earnest of efforts at situating ourselves in nature and in the cosmos. Mystics are trying to help us prevent these observations from being captured, trivialized and expounded to death as arcane academic notions; they want these notions to act on us as platforms for launching into vitality by sensing the faith-for given therein. They are trying to show what a life of bringing energy into bodies and inspiring bodies with energy can bring forth.

THE MYSTIC ETHIC: FOREGIVING. The mystic is showing us a different way, a way other than that of making ourselves into objects. What is that way mystic aspirations are showing us? It is the life of aspiration, we say. But what are the specific actions that show us such a thing? Something rises to our attention when it is acted out and observed in its moment-by-moment unfolding; something becomes a "way" only by being constantly guided into the course of events that our living comprises; and something becomes a way only by actively bringing forth the energy of living so that finds its place, or gives itself to making a place for those energies to take shape (and not merely pass through).

We call such conduct so dedicated to a "way" an "ethic." This comes from the *"ethos"* which indicates a person's "character," the role and manner, the sensible accommodation of a temperament to the world lived in. The mystic figure's ethic is that of "fore-giving." This is a living immediately before, in front of you, a living right at you, right into the very teeth, heart and core of what matters to you in a way that gives to you freely, without anticipation of return, in complete excess of any expectation of you, of that aspiration. It is a free giving of what only is freely given and gives freely. It is a giving that always comes before, prior to any prescribed occurrence can marshal itself. It is from out of the blue, out of nowhere, before any thing, before any time that anyone can muster in a socialized encounter. It is thus "fore-given."

Mystics arose among us to remind us that we are pulsing, coursing, streaming energies that coalesce for a moment – and so we can undertake not only the world as a project, but ourselves. We are *aspiring* beings, their precepts declare.

As Hölderlin, the founding mystic poet says,

> For from the abyss we
> Began and have walked like
> The lion...[14]

Chapter Three

The Mystic's Aspiring Mind

We sought pure being itself...[We] want to grasp it in its primordial appearance...

Posit pure immanent being as the absolute, substance, God, as indeed it really is and posit appearance, that is grasped here in its highest point as the absolute's internal genetic construction, as the revelation and manifestation of God, then the latter is understood as absolutely essential and grounded in the essence of the absolute itself. . I assert that this insight into absolute inward necessity is a distinguishing mark of the science of knowing as against all other systems.

~ J. G. Fichte [1]

In the fields with which we are concerned, knowledge comes only in lightning flashes. The text is the long roll of thunder that follows.

~ Walter Benjamin [2]

The Priority of Aspiration

In mentees who tend toward the mystic figuration, we encounter people who are *aspiring* toward a way of life that is so expansive and more encompassing of the vitality and diversity around us that the generality, intensity and vehemence of their expressions make us uncomfortable. The faith-for character of mystic aspiring – a faith *for* what the human endeavor can embrace – seems at once fantastic, and yet, as this person articulates and embodies this very "impossibility," her energy, vitality and insistence on taking her seriously. And then the clarity of her expression transforms this outlying notion right before our eyes. Her words transform what was, moments ago, an outlier, into being something we just might consider to be "possible," if not exactly inevitable. Here, in the flesh, is a person who in so many ways is already living in that different life way, already embodying a different way to be human.

Most of us have aspirations and appreciate the aspirations of others, to a degree; but some people live and breathe those aspirations, some people dedicate their lives to them, and, at whatever price, bear that dedication. These people do not regard taking up a role in order to advance their aspirations as being a sacrifice, or as something that cashes in comfort in exchange for some noble ideal. Even to the casual observer it is obvious that the dedication engendered by mystic aspirations goes deeper than do the wishes or ambitions we can casually nod at and then brush aside. People with mystically figured aspirations seem to live on a different plane of a paradoxical expansive intensity. They react to ordinary things diffidently, in a detached way, sometimes with exasperation and impatience, and often disdain the ready-to-hand and prescribed relations that constitute our everyday existence. It is not any particular *thing* that is at stake, but the *quality* of the feelings, images and sensations that rises to the level of concern while she engages those things. It is not to solve a problem here and there that the mystic mind is dedicated. On hearing of a problem that piques her concern, the person with mystic aspirations is *all in,* so as to exert a force, a power that both acts and is acted upon, so that the *world* changes – at least just a bit. It is to have the quality of that engagement be alive to insight, energy and adventure that mystic aspirations value. And also, despite this apparent detachment from everyday concerns, I have yet to meet a person with mystic-figured aspirations who is uncaring, nonchalant or callous toward these verities and entities we hold so dear; to the contrary, their way of engaging is often intensely caring (as in fore-giving). As their co-workers and bosses have found out, it is just that their way of engaging and caring in no way countenances blind loyalty or dedication to the things of this world.

THE MENTORING CHALLENGES. For all those reasons, working with a mentee who expresses mystic aspirations presents unique challenges to the mentor. For one thing, a person who is fully engaged in the mystic figuration, or who is facing the difficulties incited by this role, is likely to be in an age range between the mid-forties and early fifties.[3] These people will not be amenable to nostrums about life balance and "spirits." The role engendered by mystic aspiration is one that consolidates later in life (as opposed to the roles of leader and artist that take shape relatively early). It is likely that a person with mystic aspirations will already have achieved high-level and responsible positions in business, government or other institutions, or may have already made significant inroads in the world of art and literature. In the figuration of mystic aspirations, the mentor is working with a person who is at least every bit as experienced, accomplished, thoughtful and articulate as he or she is. Second, the mentee hasn't engaged a mentor in order to get counseling on how to conduct her day or organize her closets. The mentor is being asked to help this person become more robust and capable in her *mystically aspiring* life ways. The question continually arises: How do I keep my attention focused on this rarified and diffuse "aspiration" of hers? How do I arrive at questions, articulations, concepts and examples that resonate with her mindset?

And so, let's be clear: quicker than anyone, a mentee with such aspirations will walk away from a dead-end conversation that falls back on the same old stuff about motivation, goals and skills, or that great nostrum, "life balance." To keep the conversation going, and indeed to keep it moving along on a constructive trajectory, the mentor cannot get stuck in the specifics of situational problems, or the hindrances of achieving career ambitions and goals. Somehow the mentor has to get to that sense of fore-giving and wide-open faith-for that the mystically aspiring mentee is struggling to express. And once these near-side factors have been bracketed or put out of play, the mentor cannot get lost in this disorienting expanse; he has to be able to navigate this expanse, one that has precious few of the markers of conventional discourse to aid in that orienting.

A FRAMEWORK FOR MENTORING CONSTANCY. We have so far clarified certain salient and apparent aspects of the demeanor that mystic aspirations engender. Mentors have to ask themselves, do these expressions pertain to "real" aspirations, in the sense of being actual organizing and organized structures for this person? We certainly cannot answer this question without having some frame of reference that enables us to regard these expressions on their own terms, and not judge them against the dictates of "normality." For the remainder of this book we will be establishing referential frameworks that pertain to aspirations alone, and to mystic aspirations in particular.

We begin by sketching a schema of what we might envision as being an "aspiring mind:" a psychic/somatic resource that is dedicated solely to sustaining, enhancing and making robust the aspirations that enable us to engage occurrences in ways that are continually more expansive and more encompassing. We concentrate here on those assemblages that contribute most directly to the forming of mystic aspirations.[4] By sketching out a schema of the psychic/somatic structure of the mystic's aspiring mind, I hope to offer mentors a rich set of considerations that might keep the conversation on a course that the mystic will appreciate and benefit from. The idea here is that the workings of aspiration are different, are set apart, and employ a different set of machinic operations than do the mechanically representing and reproducing faculties of the ego and the cognitive operations of the cogito.

In Part Two, we continue our work of carving out a distinctive framework for what constitutes mystic aspirations by considering this figuration's genealogy, from its founding moments up until the present time. This second approach will help the mentor to "practice" the conceptual variations that mystic aspirations engender, and will also provide more evidence that mystic aspirations are indeed at work in our current state of affairs, and that this mentee with whom we are engaged is part of something larger, something important and someone we need to learn to hear (and whom mentors can help to learn to speak – her precepts – more effectively).

And now we venture into the aspiring mind in its mystic figuration.

Introducing the "Aspiring Mind"

"SNAPSHOTS" OF THE MIND. To keep the conversation on track, and to hear our mentee in ways that approach what she is trying to express, the mentor benefits from having in mind a "snapshot" of the "mental processes" that mystic aspirations entail. In the next few pages I offer a diagram, a sketch, so to speak, of the mystic's "aspiring mind," or those operations by which a person's individual psycho/somatic system (P/SS) takes raw energies and inexplicable urges and proclivities to act and speak and decide in certain ways (that seem completely "natural") and forms them into behaviors that are invested with faith-for, commitment and dedication – in this case, of mystic figuration. I hope that by being able to refer to this diagram the mentor can ask pointed questions, ones that the mystically aspiring mentee is interested in exploring and from which mystic aspirations are likely to benefit.

We are quite accustomed to using these "snapshots." We combine terms and images into diagrams that distinguish our many facultative P/SS resources. Each of these snapshot diagrams sorts out the specific processes, among the many that the mind generates, in order to explain the behaviors that we are currently considering. For instance, when we are working with a child, we operate on the basis of our notions of a "child psychology;" or when we work with athletes, we offer advice based on observations about "peak performance;" in philosophy, the school of "phenomenology" developed a schematic model of how we come to "know" things in ways that offer scientific validity; and when we work with people in mental or emotional distress we rely on images of the mind gone awry as depicted by "abnormal psychology." And we do this, not just in academic discussions, but also in our everyday interactions. For instance, when we speak with a child we do our best to hear, appreciate and then "get into" the logic of connection and experiential realizations the child has access to by pushing into the background all the ways that adults process things through social, economic or technical filters.

Similarly, the mentor has to approach the behavioral and attitudinal orientation of aspiration by performing similar acts of selective schematizing, filtering and re-prioritizing from among facultative capabilities. In listening to and for the way aspirations shape lives, the mentor needs to elevate these factors into prominence and truly de-emphasize the presumed importance we assign to our everyday or technical-scientific mentalities.[5] To reorder our attention, we benefit from having some idea about just what a mind in the throes of aspiring consists of. Just as Freud developed a schema that depicts the "mind" that psychoanalysis treats, mentors too need a schema that provides a map of the aspiring mind. That is just what I propose to do now — in an abbreviated form focused on mystic aspirations.[6]

I am proposing that the mentor use a snapshot of the "aspiring mind" in order to keep within the parameters of a conversation that is appropriate for particular needs of mystic aspirations (and, in other cases, for aspiring leaders, artists and prophets, and all kinds of combinations of these aspirational mindsets as well). As soon as the mentor begins the conversation that intends to cultivate mystic aspirations, even when offering some kind of relaxing, acclimatizing small talk, I suggest that the mentor put aside whatever values and models he uses in his daily routines and clear a "space" so that he can listen with energetic and exclusive attunement to these workings of the mystic mentee's "aspiring mind" alone.

LOCATING THE ASPIRING MIND: ON THE EDGE. In the snapshots we commonly use for picturing psychic processes, we make the casual distinction between the conscious mind and the unconscious. Since this schema is relatively well known, I will use it here to "situate" the aspiring mind in our own psychic map.

When we talk to people about what they are doing with their lives, we always assume that we are talking about factors about which they are conscious. But when we probe beneath the surface a bit, as mentors do, we find that factors that are not conscious at all are at play as well. Freud used the term "unconscious" in a technical way, to demarcate organic and physical factors that affect the conscious ego without ever themselves becoming conscious. These included memories – real, repressed and even mythic (of the Jungian order, or even of historical derivation, such as the great patricide as recounted in *Totem and Taboo*). In the Freudian therapeutic model, these unconscious factors do affect conscious impressions, often profoundly so; and they continually affect the psyche and facultative functions without a person even knowing it. In the Freudian model, the more that conscious operations (of the Ego and Superego) are unable to master (censor) the upsurges of unconscious psychic energies, the more "symptomatic" our waking behaviors and speech become.

In the mapping operation we are undertaking, we insert the P/SS resource of the aspiring mind on the borderlines *between* the unconscious sector that Freud describes, and our conscious processes. The "aspiring mind" resource constitutes an *in between* zone, between what we do not cognize and what we are aware of. And we have to add this quality to our depiction of this resource: the aspiring mind is not a static residue of energies that have been siphoned off and rendered inert. This resource constitutes a zone of *unresolved energies* that cannot become fully conscious (as yet) and yet are coherent enough to remain *in transit* to conscious articulations (in actions, speech and decisions).

It is no wonder that aspirations have remained untreated by our materialist sciences: they are energies that as far as the mind is concerned are ambiguous, fuzzy, neither here nor there, and yet cannot be denied their affecting properties. The aspiring mind comprises energies that, while still unformed are still *"feeling their ways"toward* some viable and encompassing and comprehending expression. The P/SS resource will not accomplish the completion of that expression, but it organizes energies such that this search, reaching out beyond the already given, is kept active, in play and affecting whatever else the P/SS's faculties accomplish. The intent of the aspiring mind resource is to imbue other psychic/somatic capabilities, such as muscle movement, speech or cognitive awareness, with an unresolved, still reaching quality. We can consider the aspiring mind as that resource that impels us to "take a deep breath," and allow time and space to re-collect ourselves, to gather our capabilities into a new config-uration, one that anticipates and accommodates more expansive and more encompassing aspects of our engaging.

LIFE AT THE EDGE: WHAT THE ASPIRING MIND CAN DO. The "in between" location of the aspiring mind enables it to participate in reciprocal exchanges of affecting and being affected in ways that are not hardened and prescribed. Both our conscious and unconscious faculties have recourse to the aspiring mind when certain situations arise. It is summoned by the cognitive resources of the mind whenever a suspicion takes hold that something is occurring that has not been adequately taken into account; and it is referred to by the unconscious when something that has been "repressed" or has gone unaccounted for asserts itself in order to be noticed or taken into account by those conscious machinations.

Since the unconscious and conscious faculties are far more robust than the aspiring mind, they affect this emerging resource far more potently than it affects them. The aspiring mind is affected by unconscious "wishes" or senses of energies that are not yet completely appropriated, tamed, and honed to conscious purposes. However, the aspiring mind is *also* conscious enough, and is, I would say, more vitally and energetically conscious, so as to want to *take up a direct and engaging relationship with those unconscious factors, rather than dominate, repress or subjugate them to conscious intentions.* It allows those unconscious and "wishful" energies to have a modulating effect on the ego-cogito's drive to make things conform to the conscious programming that attains certainty; and yet, while valorizing these "wishes," it does so without losing sight of all that those conscious processes make possible. It allows those energies latitude to work on those conscious process in order to arrive at conclusions or hypotheses that might offer more expansive and more encompassing ways to go about our living. [7]

There are structural and operational consequences for taking up a position so close to the edge of the intelligible, while, at the same time being so exposed to the incessantly and irrepressibly chaotic and unsettling energies that fester in the unconscious. For one thing, since it resides so close to that unconscious wildness, the aspiring mind is not able to fully integrate with the more habituated and well-trained psychic resources that yield practical and moral knowledge and certainty for us. Snagged, as it is, between two incompatible psychic dynamics, the aspiring mind is regarded as the "stranger within" – as that pesky little voice that protests against submission and resignation. Then, as it develops its own machinic operations, at the behest of the figurations we trace in our work, this stranger is pushed further and further out and away from our "adult" mind functions; it is pushed further and further away from the functional competencies that have getting things done as their mandate. The less amenable this resource is to being assimilated in the dominant conduct of logical, technical and socialized affairs, the more self-standing it becomes, and the more its machinic processes develop in their own idiosyncratic ways.

The direction of our narrative is certainly clear. I am suggesting that for the aspirational figures we consider here, the aspiring psychic resource is certainly pushed out of the mainstream of P/SS operations, but instead of being ignored, repressed or derided, its potencies are accorded attention, are valued and worked on in order to provide them with clarity, communicability and the force of veracity ("the ring of truth," so to speak), if not certainty. These figures turn their conscious resources of language and conceiving onto them; and these affirming operations directed at the aspiring resource are so constant and are referred to with such frequency and are assigned such importance in these people's lives that these operations are regarded "as though" they had formed their own psychic space. At some point (and this moment arrives later in life for mystics and prophets), the aspiring mind becomes distinctively competent enough in an individual's life (and then as a living factor in the human endeavor) so that it is able to stand on its own, apart and at a distance from ever being absorbed into habituated everyday life. For some people, such as the mystically oriented aspiring ones, it is even able to become a focal point for ways of living that elevate these aspirations to being of primary concern. This is likely to be the case with the person across the table from the mentor. And that is why it becomes important to be able to envision a notion of P/SS workings that operate specifically on those concerns. [8]

The "Infrastructure" of the Mystic's Aspiring Mind

SPANNING OPERATION. To say that we have "located" the "aspiring mind" is a figure of speech, of course. There is no "location" of such a resource in the brain; there is no dedicated location that can be mapped by an electronic scan the way that the Broca's region of the brain that specializes in language has been mapped. However, such a "center" might well develop in the coming eons, just as did the center for language. But for now, we have to be content that our schema is useful at least for consolidating a picture of the way our mentee's mind organizes those aspects of experience that she cares about most: her aspirations.

To schematize such an operation as transpiring in a coordinated and productive way is neither a strange nor disreputable procedure when it comes to envisioning our psychic engagements with occurrences. From the earliest days of formulating our reflections on the human spirit, we have employed metaphors and figures to describe psychic activities: from Plato's chariot of the soul, to Freud's schema of Id-Ego-Superego, to the myriad renderings of the "mind" as fire, water, air or other mythic figurations that poets have provided. Here we are using figurations in order to concentrate our attentions onto the machinations that turn mere wisps of wishes into life ways that are dedicated to aspiration. By conceptually grouping specific psychic operations into coherent "assemblages," we can deepen our inquiries into what psychic energies are being marshaled to the fore so as to engender a dedicated commitment to aspirations. And, no less importantly, we provide our mentoring initiative with a means of keeping on track with the aspirational aspects of what the conversation is yielding. [9]

So far we have "located" the resources of the aspiring mind at the boundary between the unconscious and the more deliberate operations of psychic life. We have also specified that having arisen precisely at this juncture between conscious and unconscious engaging, the aspiring mind actively performs special operations that *span* and *bridge* between seemingly incompatible and even conflicting kinds of psychic energies — the unassimilated and rejected or excluded, banished and exiled energies that are relegated to the unconscious, versus the functioning, composed and assimilated energies of the conscious mind. The machinic iterations of the aspiring resource not only bring these seemingly incompatible energies into proximity, but out of these incompatible and conflictual energies, this resource develops *patterns* that coalesce profoundly incompatible energies into a viable, if not unified or identified, psychic force. This resource is never able to (and never attempts to) complete, crystallize or solidify these coalesced energies into "things" or "objects," but it does go so far as to meld these energies into the robustly acting creative impulses we call aspirations. By continually, iteratively and insistently taking account of the affecting agencies of these "hybrid" energies, the aspiring mind ends up distinguishing and distancing its operations from other psychic processes. We now turn our attention to those specialized, aspiring operations.

"INFRASTRUCTURE." As certain people refer to their aspirations more and more, and as these aspirations are called upon to underpin actual behaviors, these spanning energies are driven to become more and more constant and functional as processes that are more and more iteratively reliable. That is, as people refer to the upsurges of aspirations more and more and articulate what these energies bring forth as notions and articulated possibilities, the energies that have been relied upon for these articulations form into more constant and stable "infrastructures" or "machinic assemblages" (as we call them, following Deleuze / Guattari[10]). By "infrastructure" I mean that the processes performed by this "in between" resource are iteratively, repeatedly, "machinically" (not mechanically) generated such that a P/SS resource or specialization that coheres in what we can call "the aspiring mind" operates in a distinctive and robust way. By keeping these infrastructural components in mind, the mentor (and the aspiring mentee) will be able to concentrate on what the aspirations are demanding for psychic competence and fulfillment, as opposed to what the other (also necessary, and also very actively producing) psychic processes entail. To be clear, the factors and processes of this infrastructure, while not "brain functions," are, I would argue, completely affective of very important and highly valued behaviors – and ones that for any aspiring-motivated mentee become all-consuming and ultimately important. These assemblages are, at a minimum, clusters of organized impressions and conceptualized articulations that can be (at least philosophically) figured, valorized and shown to be effective in arriving at propositions, motivations, actions and writings that are then evaluated for their pertinence to other, more routine, life practices. [11]

As we proceed to describe the infrastructure of assemblages of the aspiring mind, it would be helpful to bear this in mind: once a person has given preference in attention and care to the generative impetus of aspiration (the resources we are describing under the rubric of an "aspiring mind"), these operations are elevated to prominence and priority. For the figures we are considering in the context of mentoring, these operations have been accorded so much weight and importance that they permeate every aspect of their life ways as they set out to engage their respective worlds.

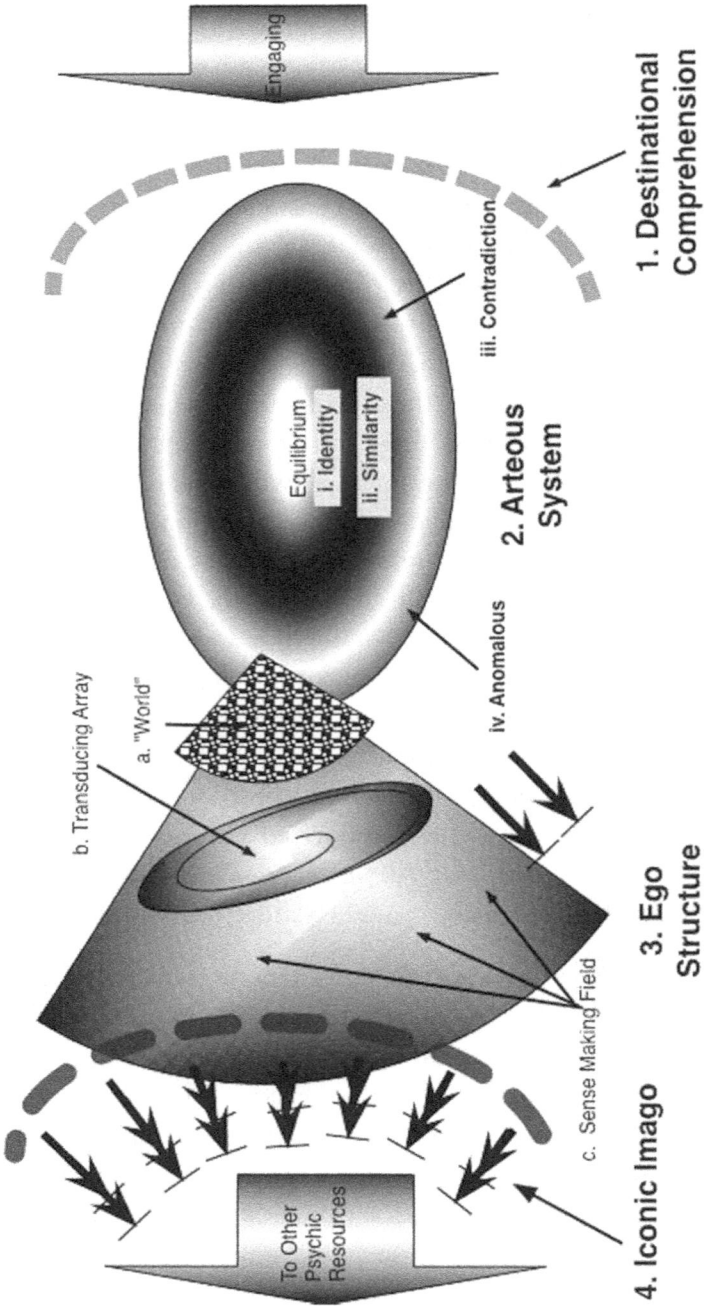

Assemblages of the Aspiring Mind

Engaging

1. Destinational Comprehension

iii. Contradiction

Equilibrium
i. Identity
ii. Similarity

2. Arteous System

b. Transducing Array

a. "World"

iv. Anomalous

3. Ego Structure

c. Sense Making Field

To Other Psychic Resources

4. Iconic Imago

Figure 3.1

Figure 3.1
Assemblages of the Aspiring Mind

The Aspiring Mind has four macro-assemblages: (1) the Destinational Comprehension (DC), (2) the Arteous System, (3) the Ego Structure, and (4) the Iconic Imago.

*The **DC** encounters the energies at the site of engagement in their most raw form and establishes the "stance" of the Aspiring Mind's orientation to the engagement as accommodating or resisting, as introverted (asserting existent formations), or extroverted (yielding to the site's efficacies).*

*The **Arteous System** constellates the energies from the DC into an orbital arrangement around an attractor of energies (as memories, monuments or memo-rializations) that have settled into nearly static equilibrium. Around this "heavy" attractor, these energies form into orbits based on how close they are to being able to achieve equilibrium and so be constellated into categorically synthesized relations — (i) identity, (ii) affinity / similarity, (iii) opposition / contradiction; and (iv) anomalous (energies that are not able to be categorically arranged on a continuum and remain "wild").*

*The **Ego Structure** forms the sense that orients aspiration / individuation to what is possible, available and at stake at the site. It has three sub-assemblages (each of which also has more specialized components): (a) the "World" assemblage, (b) the Egoic Transducing Array (ETA), and (c) the Sense-Making Field (S-MF). The Sense-Making field actually comprises three "Self-Streams" that combine with "Soundings" (precursors to word-forms) in order to coalesce energies and saturating phenomena from the "World" sub-assemblage into engageable factors. These streams are Desiring, Imagining and Conceiving (and constitute the focusing concern of prophetic aspirations).*

*The **Iconic Imago** (the "Open" for the mystic's aspiring mind) provides a moment / space for gathering resources into an affecting complex of sense-making, what we might call a "proclivity," or "talent," or in Jungian terms, a "temperament."*

Source: Michael H. Shenkman (2014). Albuquerque, NM.

121

OVERVIEW. To appreciate the complexity of the resource of the aspiring mind, we have only to ask ourselves one question: What does the "aspiring mind" accomplish? As we have said throughout our narrative so far, the aspiring impetus takes what, in infinitesimally fleeting moments, pops into a mind as a "wish" or a "fantastic idea" and enables it to become sufficiently robust so as to become a fully invested, embodied life's way. In that simple exchange we have all we need to prepare ourselves for an excursion into increasing and expanding the complexity that our P/SS faculties and capabilities are able to accommodate and act upon. In other words, to do what the aspiring resource must accomplish is no simple matter; it is a highly complex and thus highly "evolved" P/SS as-semblage. (In fact, our account of the development of this resource envisions its emergence as the specifically human response to the increasing complexities of our ways of life through the ages; and so only a resource that is itself complex would be capable of providing capabilities that would be equal to those states of affairs.)

The *aspiring* mind is thus a specialized psychic/somatic assemblage that concentrates *one* aspect of our engagements with what is occurring among others. The aspiring mind resource concentrates psychically formative processes on the moments of an engagement with occurrences wherein a *range* (variety, and therefore offering choice) of responses is available in that state of affairs. It acts in the way of a "peripherally" sensing acumen. Whereas the ego and cognitive functions and faculties of the P/SS are concentrating on what can be recognized (as), identified (with) and tied to known and certain verities (for immediate action), the aspiring mind cleaves to those aspects of the occurrence that are deemed "outside" of the norm, and that are relegated to other-than-conscious repositories in the mind. Some aspects of that envelope of usable material garnered from (or skimmed off the surface of) an occurrence are certainly buried deep in an "unconscious" of the Freudian type. But others, aspects of the occurrence that are more amenable (available or marginally intelligible – at some psychic/somatic level) are taken up by (diverted to) the resources of the still non-conscious aspiring mind.

The only role that the aspiring mind has within the complex assemblage of the P/SS is to allow for more expansive and more encompassing modes of facultative engagement to be *generated in ways that can be chosen and acted upon — in defiance of any habitually automatic reaction*. It concentrates on and then keeps open the P/SS capability to defer, delay and thus open up new horizons of responses, rather than immediately shunt off engaging energies into prescribed, species-based or socially sanctioned behaviors. Once it concentrates on this purely generative moment, it then takes the unprecedented step of forming into forceful urges or proclivities that (beneath our conscious decisions) actually tilt our behaviors or responses in new directions. They actually impel one to take actions (utter statements and make decisions) that have never been envisioned before, or at least have never been taken up as species- or so-cial-level ways of engagement with occurrences.

"INFANTIC." We can perhaps be assisted in our grasping of this strange state of P/SS engagement by coining a term. Because it is situated in this "unresolved" zone and operates in this "between" state, there is a quality to the aspiring mind resource that I call *"infantic."* I coin that term in order to at once refer to the way we observe infants reaching out into what must seem like a veritable void, in order to take its place and function in a situation. The aspiring mind calls to the fore our "infantic" capabilities in which our reaching, groping, searching and freshly orienting action is able to constitute our sense of place and viability in a state of affairs. For infants, everything that is encountered qualifies as requiring these initiatives of striving; adults encounter fewer situations that meet these criteria and that elicit the resources for such activities. [12] But in the case of the aspiring figures, and in the case of the mystic figuration most particularly, these yearnings are kept active, are thrust to the forefront of whatever is occurring, and by virtue of being continually acknowledged and heeded, strengthen the aspiring mind resource. In figures such as these, the aspiring mind can be put on a trajectory to become thereby a viable facultative resource that can affect any engagement that these adults take on and so render any occurrence as being a "legitimate" matter for aspiring discernment.

Of course, the aspiring mind is not that of an infant. Indeed, sustaining the "infantic" impetus in the P/SS of an adult – to sustain a capability that continually stands for the process of searching and groping amid evermore skillfully articulated certainties – requires that this aspiring resource be more complex, by at least a factor of "x," than the constructions of those certainties comprise. The steps that enable complex organisms to have a range of choices in their way of engaging occurrences is thus necessarily complex, and the aspiring mind resource has emerged as a specialization *not* of being able to generate more complicated and sophisticated algorithms of knowledge and production, but rather as a specialization that allows the P/SS to extend its *own* complexity, and do so in advance of any practical "need" to do so. The aspiring mind is not just complex, therefore; it generates further complexity, first for its own capabilities, and then of the objects, relations and comprehensions it offers to conscious mechanisms.

"MACHINIC" VERSUS "MECHANISTIC." Accordingly, as in any complex system, there are many different operations that are involved in generating a coherent effect. Complexity, after all, emerges on the basis of dynamic and proliferating combinations between and among simple operations. In the case of the aspiring mind, it constitutes another regime of specialization of the P/SS, which the process of "self-consciousness" and reflective determining can factor into its considerations as the P/SS moves from experiencing to decisions, actions and speech. And so, just as our "conventionally" conscious and acting mind requires several different kinds of relatively *mechanically* repetitious operations to perform its work – sensory, emotive, perceptual and linguistic P/SS specializations – so too does the aspiring mind emerge in the form of as-semblages that are specialized in their *"machinic"* operations. [13] The aspiring mind uses exclusively machinic operations, while conventionalizing P/SS operations, once established (in normal "development" of psychological processes) are mechanically repetitious.

Machinic operations are strictly and solely generative operations that allow for emergent processes to take shape (some of which are then taken up by mechanical repetition). Machinic processes are ones that "iterate," or "make a thing" out of multiple encounters, or extended engaging of an encounter over several psychically distinguished moments. Machinics are required when one such moment or iteration is taken to be not quite the same as the last, but that between the moments there can be granted enough continuity, from iterative moment to the next iteration, so that a connection or bridge can be sustained between the moments. Machinic operations, starting at the infinitesimally small and fast, thus span between the moments and allow these moments, in their character as bridged affiliations, to continue on.

These machinic spanning operations never repeat, in the sense of being exact reenactments of what went on before, but when either situations or occurrences of engagement are sufficiently stable, to some extent, or when the machinically iterating process is robust and expansive enough, the differences between all of these spannings can scale up by means of a *supplementing* process. That is, these spannings do not *cause* one another in the classical sense. In the machinically iterating process, one moment does not "relate" to another in any "causal" way. Rather, continually spanning, bridging and re-forming machinic iterations of amenable similitude or resonance sustain one another each other for a time (while the too-wild and anomalous spanning operations dissipate) and this sustained resonating allows the operations to continue on through succeeding iterations. As the iterating process happens upon resonances that reinforce the sustaining power of the machinic operation, it gathers strength and can even generate affects of its own (feelings, charges of intuition, etc.). When a spanning operation scales up to generate its own effects (feelings, sparks of "intuition," for example), an assemblage that performs such iterations can establish operations that are enduring and affecting in their own rights. [14]

MACHINIC ASSEMBLAGE. An assemblage consists of nothing but a scaling-up of infinitesimally minute autocatalytic iterations (and micro-symmetry breaks) that have accumulated to the point of exerting a distinctive "force" in its own right. An assemblage is thus distinguished by *the nature of the relation* or spanning operation between machinic iterations that it has accommodated and allowed to accumulate.[15] It is because attention is directed at these machinic operations that the iterations have reached some level of amplitude, mass and persistence (or maybe just an "insistence" at this point), and that these machinics are then given their own credence such that psychic "space" is devoted to them, or that neuroanatomical resources are expanded (or modified) in order to accommodate these myriad of infinitesimal machinic iterations. Having such spannings take place in psychic operations is not peculiar to the human endeavor. Indeed, all creatures that depend on "conscious" operations can be said to have such spanning operations, at least to the point that their next actions are based on "decisions." Rather it is specifically the turning of attention to these spanning machinic operations that engenders an aspiring resource such as we describe now.

When the iterations become overwhelmed by the demands to accommodate complexities that are beyond its scope, the assemblage might blow apart (in a fit of rage or breakdown), but it might also break off an amplitude or mode of iterative machinics and form a new assemblage, which then might or might not be able to establish itself as a viable P/SS resource alongside of, in addition to and supplementary to, the already established assemblages. Such is the case with the increasing complexity of the differentiated machinic assemblages we envision as constituting the aspiring mind.

The aspiring mind comprises four macro (fractally scaled, machinic) assemblages, (1) the Destinational Comprehension, (2) the Arteous System, (3) the Ego Structure and (4) the Iconic Imago (see Figure 3.1). Each of these assemblages specializes in one operation that is required to establish our aspiring and individuating mode of engaging occurrences (while other P/SS resources specialize in other capabilities that enable "conscious" or — an especially dubious term — "intelligent" modes of engaging occurrences). Each of these contributes a specialized machinic operation that is required in order to enable the gathering, translating and transmitting of the energies in play at a site of occurrence and render them as psychic material for our further disposition and use. While this whole apparatus is considered in detail elsewhere,[16] we will concentrate our attention on a sub-assemblage of the Ego Structure, the "World" assemblage, and on the Iconic Imago macro-assemblage. While all the other assemblages certainly have their role to play in forming mystic-type aspirations, the "World" assemblage and the Iconic Imago assemblage are most dominant in constituting the mystic figuration.[17]

The "World" (Sub-) Assemblage (of the Ego Structure)

When the aspiring mind takes up the energies that it can accommodate from the occurrence it is engaging, these energies are immediately treated differently than they are in the contexts of the other productive resources of the P/SS, such as the ego or the cogito. In those more stabilizing P/SS structures, energies are ensnared and scooped up not in order to put them to use, or to lock them away and keep them from doing further "harm" to our good functioning. The aspiring mind performs a diametrically opposing operation on these energies: it treats these energies as though they were wild pups, infants and seedlings whose very wildness and unformed states are valued above all. They are treated like precious foundlings and are provided with the space, time, opportunity and appropriate machinic operations that supplement and enrich them, they are afforded more time and (psychic) "space" to circulate and diversify their proximities and affiliations. By offering this space (in the acts of faith-for and fore-giving) these energies, hopefully, someday, will be able to generate potentially new ways of engaging the occurrences of our lives. This psychic space and machinic operation constitutes what I call the *"World"* sub-assemblage of the Ego Structure.[18] The "World" assemblage thus comprises energies that are saturated with as much of still-affecting potencies at the site of engagement as it is possible for this person's P/SS aspiring mind resource to accommodate.[19]

"Saturating Phenomena": Factors of Relationship. We have noted that the concerns generated by mystic aspirations comprise ideas, notions, teeming relations and dynamic movements of what are not yet generally available to "normal" sensorial operations. These "soft" or "fuzzy" factors in our engagements take shape, are given time to enrich and strengthen themselves, in the "World" assemblage. In that realm their character shifts from being that of pure surges of intent to being more encompassing and diverse in their dimensions and in their nuances of affecting potency. In that nurturing and expansively welcoming assemblage then, these raw energies loosen up, relax and release their isomorphic tensions. Instead of being "particles" of information, they become *"saturating phenomena"* [20] or elemental and indissolvable, purely *relational and affecting powers*. It is these saturating phenomena that continually and most especially move, motivate, energize and enervate the aspiring mind of the mystic.[21]

These saturating phenomena constitute the "World" of an aspiring mind. To the aspiring mind, the "World" assemblage comprises, above all, factors of *relationship*. When aspiring is active, nothing in its purview sits "out there" inertly as a thing or object. Rather, when the most vibrant and variable aspects of an occurrence are taken up into the sweeping embrace of aspiration, they are *presumed* to have the ability to *generate affects;* and the aspiring mind is a psychic recourse that *seeks out specifically these affects above all others and elevates them to being matters of primary concern.* These affecting factors, factors that render one's experience as having power to change one's life in some measure, are deemed to be what is most salient and valued in the engagement, and are given priority of attention and power *even over one's own existing state of being.*

The Site of Changing Ways. The aspiring mind, as a specialized P/SS resource, has as its primary and concerning "World" these "saturating phenomena," which only compel responses that can be accommodated only by the P/SS *giving way to their affecting powers.* That is, this "World" does *not* comprise these phenomena in the way the enterprise of science detects, names, analyzes and measures causes, effects, forces, matter, elements and particles. In the "World" assemblage, these saturating phenomena actively generate open and as yet undecided or undetermined states of being that the aspiring mind sets out to accommodate (by giving way to them) and then turn around and set to work shaping what the P/SS has at its disposal for its (most generative and vibrant) impelling influences. These phenomena do not make absolute claims of priority and solidified "thingness" on the aspiring mind; *rather, they issue calls for sober and sincere openness to the point of mutually affecting one another.* The aim of the machinic of the aspiring mind is to achieve a dynamic state of interplay, continuing communication and mutual formation.

When we say that the "World" of mystic aspirations comprises "saturating phenomena," we mean that everything "in" that "world" flows, indeed, overflows, with the forces that affect whatever it is that that is at stake for the aspiring mind, and possibly for other P/SS resources. This "World" is alive with certain factors that insist on being related to, of being accounted for in the form of changing one's orientations to the (larger) occurrence, happenstance and experience in general. In the aspiring mind, these generative factors are given not only credence, but they are granted utmost priority and their transformative powers are set free – to some extent – to do their work. These are the "facts" that mentors listen for and abet in their struggles to gain a foothold in someone's life.

I have identified six such saturating phenomena:

- ***Completeness:*** the sense that what is at hand is what there is, the way it is, and is *all* that there is.

- ***Coming Toward:*** the irrepressible sense that a change is afoot and the person need to address this imminent change, forthwith.

- ***Threshold:*** the phenomenon affects this person's very core, it changes the person's goals, and his or her sense of self the more it approaches and becomes "real."

- ***Face, Flesh, and Voice:*** the phenomenon affects the aspiring mind personally, with specificity and a sense of its own vitality, "a life of its own," and so the aspiration feels real, alive, as though it were beckoning to be taken up as a life's way.

- ***Otherness:*** it is not his goal or idea, but is "out there," beyond whatever is already comprehended of the situation.

- ***Excess:*** the "World" of the aspiration is always greater than what one person is about, it always exceeds what can be grasped or known and it always is greater in scope, magnitude, intensity and amplitude than anything the aspiring mind can accommodate. The aspiration is humble.

RELATING TO SATURATING PHENOMENA. The relationships demanded by saturating phenomena have no externally determining criteria available for their being comprehended; therefore, they are taken up in the most idiosyncratic of ways. Still, these "ways" do cluster or gravitate around certain patterns (historically and maybe genetically set on certain trajectories of expression, in the manner of self-organizing fractals gathering around an attractor) that we can note. These patterns form "ways" or life ways that each of the breakout creative figures will tend to put into circulation (and then further specify them according to their own individually devised ways of engagement and expression). Table 3.1 maps out this first-level translation. It is up to the mentor, however, to do the next level of translation and understand how the mentee's terms come into play as expressions of their aspiring mind's "World."

Table 3.1: "World" Saturating Phenomena in Mystic's Aspiring Mind			
"World" Saturated Phenomenon	Mentoring Factor	Aspiring Factor	The Precipitated Behavior that Responds to the Saturating Phenomenon
Complete	The concern that is aroused for under-taking an aspiring engagement.	Vision	The mystic feels the immediacy and pressing "reality" of her mission. It is imbued with all the logical and experiential completeness of both a dreamed vision **and also** the logical completeness that the "waking mind's" resources bring to bear.
Coming Toward	The stance that is taken up in advance of the exigencies of the concern.	Teaching	There is no other way to express this sense of immediacy, since it does not "exist" than to do all the work of bringing it into the rubrics of expression and evidence that is required by the "waking" world. Teaching expresses not the urge to proclaim or pronounce, but rather to express the feeling of being pressed upon by the power of the aspiration's virtual "world" affects.
Threshold	The locus of engagement that will have to be met by learning.	Precept	The task is to articulate what the aspiration promises, what its completeness and coming towards – what all its saturating phenomena – will, in the future, if taken up will open out to and allow to come into play. That is, what this aspiration will open as a terrain within which to work, as a set of capabilities that can be developed, as a means of discernment that can be facultatively gathered. All of this will take time. The precept thus marks out the possibilities of what an epoch or era might hold.

Table 3.1: Continued **"World" Saturating Phenomena in Mystic's Aspiring Mind**			
Flesh, Face, Voice	Focus of commitment as a compelling, ongoing, experiential engagement.	Faith For	This is not an all or nothing proposition; but it is palpably real and has real bodily effects. As such, there is offered a welcoming for the whole of it, while not prescribing any totality or presumption of universality. It is the embodied wholeness, the palpable "realness" (even though it is not yet "real," that is), that is avowed by the mystic's precept.
Otherness	The force of resistance and its character, way of emergence.	The Open, Field of Enthusiasm	The affects in play have their own character that cannot be evaded, and any exertion of egoistic power is an attack on the aspiration, its body, itself. And, it just might be that such an attack, in future operations, will be necessary. While the mystic is completely aware that such events may transpire, she does not avow any such actions. She stands for the aspiration.
Excess	The opening to and the necessity of forging an *ethic* of constancy in engaging the occurrence.	Fore Giving	The mystic gives whatever the vision, open, faith for and precept require for fruition. That also means the mystic fore-gives to whomever she senses is of a disposition or bent to *hear* and be *here* (to be an ad-here- ad-hear- ant) with the precept. That includes storming over and through her own ego formations and needs so as to enact and embody this giving. It seems, therefore, that the mystic has a "weak" ego, one that is easily swayed by others' exertions either on her behalf or in opposition to her. Actually, it is true that she does not act, primarily on the basis of the needs of her "waking" ego, she is actually hyper-strong in terms of being able to summon energies and ways of being such that giving, pure and unmitigated, occurs.

Table 3.1:

"World" Saturating Phenomena in
Mystic's Aspiring Mind

Table 3.1 summarizes how saturating phenomena generate the essential expressions of mystic aspirational figuration. In the context of mystic aspirations, these saturating phenomena stand out as the flow of an occurrence washes over this person's P/SS. These saturating phenomena "color" every nuance of an occurrence – and especially for situations for which the mentee has the responsibility for articulating and devising intentional responses to what is happening there. The mentor's take away from this table's descriptions is how different from the usual way of getting along the mystically aspiring mentee's orientation is. She has at stake a wholly different set of parameters. The mentor can also see how it might be that such a person will feel at a loss, will feel inadequate in the face of these aspirations. The mentor's response cannot be one of helping her "feel better," but rather will be valued to the extent that the mentor connects these feelings to the real dynamics of the aspirations that are engendering those feelings, and then shows the mentee their immeasurable worth, to all of us.

Because of the prominence of saturating phenomena, mystic aspirations put the mentee in a "compromised" stance, one might say, vis-à-vis the hardened, quick and certain verities of everyday life, and even as regards other aspiring figurations. Compare this stance to that of a leader. In that role, a person concretely envisions the next actions that will be ventured and articulates them clearly for followers. In contrast to this, a mystically aspiring figure begins her work in a state of near "speechlessness," a state of being purposefully inarticulate (called "apophasis") that expresses, not certainty and dominance over the state of affairs, but rather expresses reciprocation to the saturating phenomena. She avows, "I, as an individuating and aspiring being, will find within my own being a way to respond to these phenomena and set them into play in my life as best as I can."

Source: Michael H. Shenkman (2014). Albuquerque, NM.

Striving. *Striving* is never absent from the responses one can offer to the "World" assemblage's effects. The response seems to always generate as much of a distance between person and the demand as it closes that gap — or else, of course, some phenomenon or another would be put out of play, and this is not at all what aspiration intends. The mystically aspiring person, after all, is acting as a single, living being (or creature), which, before it can offer anything in the way of a response to these phenomena, has to find and then take her own place in the milieu where her experiencing is occurring.

For example, the saturating phenomenon of Face, Flesh and Voice sets up a sense of the palpability and "reality" of this aspiration, such that it engenders that aura of urgency we see in the mystic mentee's demeanor. This saturating phenomenon palpably engenders the sense that these "possibilities" she senses have heft and can generate effects and can even be heeded, in the sense of being "heard." This engenders her global orientation of "faith-for": she takes up the responsibility for welcoming and affirming this eventuation into being. Or, the aspiration is so excessively abundant and overflowing that there is no other way to "respond" but as a "fore-giving" right into that flow, both as a gesture of opening to the "otherness" of the aspiration and as an act of "giving way" to something that is on its way to having profound effects on one's way of being. And so we see how the "World" in the mystic's aspiring mind appears as a supremely vibrant and generative occasion: one that is already giving of itself so as to affect whatever encounters it; and since she is encountering it, the responsibility for its continuance and viability is also hers.

The saturating phenomena comprised by the "World" assemblage are thus never fully realized in anyone's waking actions, no less in those of mystically oriented aspirations. If a person claims to know how to achieve what is being strived for, what is at stake for this person is no longer aspiration at all.

Not an "Attribute." Saturating phenomena do not necessarily attach to a specific thing (though they can), and they carry energies into the psyche that are not cleanly separated such that they can be treated, analyzed, or stabilized into something like a "material" object. In the operations of the aspiring mind, any specific object is thus not a matter of certified knowing that is amenable to technical manipulation, but registers as a matter that conveys its own peculiarly and singularly appropriate and articulate *emotive response.* So, those unsettling factors that are engendered by saturating phenomena never contain their "solutions," and do not have their projected applications implied by their "appearances" or even their "essences," as conventional logic would have it. Saturating phenomena always bear traces of other, incipient, still-to-come states of being, for which the existing psyche is unprepared, except for aspiration's insistence on being ready to give way. It is incumbent on the aspiring mind to continually, iteratively and machinically (not mechanically) attune and re-attune its resources to what, in its experiencing, one must *anticipate* of one's "World."

The aspiring mind labors to form *constancies of flows* among the emotive factors that are in play, affecting and arousing responses from moment to moment in that person's whole psyche. Instead of forming a mechanism that (metaphorically speaking) physically hardwires a thing to an action and an outcome, the aspiring mind creates a "program" that flexibly opens and closes those mechanical (or electronic) switches, thereby redirecting flows into coherent relations, and all the while remaining agnostic to the specific ends any relation, switch-complex (application) accomplishes. It operates "algorithmically" and not mechanically on the factors in its "world." (We say this with the qualifying proviso that this "algorithm" is also constantly in play under the affecting powers of saturating phenomena and is far from being a rigid or final "program" for carrying out prescribed actions. At best, it is a "guide" for making some immediate choices so one can "move on" in the aspiring life way.)

Aspiring actions then, are not, as I have said, directed right at objects, directed with a clear path to have one's hands or instruments alter the place, material, context or composition of what has been designated in advance as a "thing" or "object." Aspiring actions, which are organized by the Iconic Imago (II), are directed at shaping *responses* to saturating phenomena – to factors of experiencing that are demanding their due as calls for a *relationship*. As such, the II always takes the aspiring person into a *mood*, an *attitude*, a *perspective* and/or a *stance* with respect to the larger "atmospherics" (the moral condition, socioeconomic forces, social assumptions and logics in play) of the state of affairs.[22] The aspiring mind discerns and assigns added weight to these particular feelings, and these feelings are even moved to the forefront of the way the state of affairs is engaged in general. Other feelings, such as fear, the need to belong or conform, or the need to be "right," are displaced. When the aspiration is raised to prominence in this way, the mystically aspiring person (in this case) responds, not to what is already there, but to what is coming, what is most affecting and transforming, what requires a stance of fore-giving. The aspiring person envisions not a task to be checked off and completed, but a role entered into and sustained as a life's way.

The Mystic Iconic Imago: The Field of Enthusiasm

In Figure 3.1, I have depicted that the aspiring mind coalesces into being an effective life way by first gathering together and assembling its sense-making energies (in the "Sense-Making Field) and then uses the "materials" generated there to construct another assemblage that I call the "Iconic Imago" (II). In this assemblage, the aspiring mind sweeps up the "in-coming" (coming towards) energies (as does a switch) into a composition and turns them around into a "dis-position" that is directed "outward," and so is prepared to undertake actions that are oriented and guided by what it has assembled there. (With this "internally" oriented guide to action, the aspiring mind can at best venture an action, experiment, offer and/or, in the case of the mystic figure, fore-give.)

The Iconic Imago is the assemblage of the aspiring mind that sets the whole field of aspirations in play as a distinctive and recognizable mood, temperament and character of the person, to the extent that this person takes up aspirations as a primary concern, that is. When a person does elevate aspirations to such a level, as do our aspirational figures, every "material" thing is surrounded with an aura of what the saturating phenomena render and "transform" an object into. The so-called "substantial" aspects that are "contained in" the state of affairs (the "things," the "causes," the facts that are used in the sciences, or the "values" that are assigned to a commodity for the purpose of enacting exchanges) only appear as pale constructions of expediency. All the rest of what the occurrence issues and offers up to the engaging person is what concerns the aspiring mind and constitutes the factors that the II relates to. Each figuration of aspiration engenders a formation of an iconic assemblage that is able to activate, incarnate and enact its mode of aspiring (the leader figuration, an arch; the artist figuration, an amphitheater/arena; and the prophet figuration, a labyrinth).

FIELD OF ENTHUSIASM. The mystic figuration of aspirations generates an energized and illuminated open space that actively awaits what comes next – in the aspirant's engaging. I call this icon of mystic figuration the "Field of Enthusiasm" (F/E). In this field, saturating phenomena are set loose, and their energized surges are limited only by the "horizon" of the person's current life ways.[23]

There is no other way to describe how mystic aspirations are coalesced into being a force for speech, action and decision than as this open and continually opening *"Field of Enthusiasm"* (F/E). Is this a "dream world," comprising fantasies and wistful desires? Certainly, to someone who is ensconced in the "real world," it appears to be; but this is not the case for the mystically aspiring person. And, admittedly, consisting as it does of what saturating phenomena deliver to her aspirations, the mystic F/E comprises factors that do not have any "existence" attributable to them. This factor alone leaves mystically aspiring people vulnerable to the charge of being dreamers who do not have a plan. The mystic figuration is unique in this regard, even among the other aspirational figures – after all, the artist has images and impressions from experiences to open up and reconfigure; the prophet has at least a world of ideas (the newest of which articulate mystic precepts) to use as co-ordinates for his meanders. But what do mystic aspirations have to grab hold of? In essence, she only has the effects of what saturating phenomena are delivering to her from moment to moment.

And so while the F/E is "open" and extends onward in all dimensions, without defined features, reaching and groping to what are also unmarked horizons, it is not an "empty" expanse that constitutes just an abyssal "nothing." This F/E purposefully circumscribes an area that is marked off and differentiated from the "material world" precisely to the extent that it responds to saturating phenomena and then, rather than immediately crushing them into objects at hand, and to the extent that it *allows them the room to play around.* It is a concentrated space that even encourages these phenomena to form affiliations of all different kinds and so engender ventures and experiments of behaviors. These affiliations comprise energies of all kinds, some of which are known, others that might be knowable, and others that remain completely unknowable despite exerting affects and influences on the mystic's psyche.[24] These still surging and drifting confluences may gather for a moment, or may break off or be cut off so as to exert distinctive "moments" of coalescing. While these coalescences may be amenable neither to being named or forming into larger structures, they do have "feels," they do have "characteristics" that engender unique effects, which do pique distinctive psychic events. Mystic aspirations thus do literally "inhabit" this field, and shape the life ways of those who do. And so, still, we must persist with our question: How do aspirations and their F/E become so "real" for the mystically aspiring ones among us?

Here are the ways that I have seen this "incarnation" of mystic aspirations take place:

Pays Attention. Start with the fact that in the first place that this person pays attention to these aspirations, in whatever state of being formed or unformed they might be found. Why she does so is another question that is certainly interesting, and one that is no less intriguing than how anyone gets to be the person that they are; but the mentoring conversation is not able to approach these developmental conundrums with any competence. And so, once again, why does this field command her attention? For another reason then, the F/E *is,* after all, a *"field."* This term designates an area that can be marked off from or within a larger milieu because it has some character and exhibits constancy of persistence of that character. The actions that mystic aspirations intend do as little translating of saturating phenomena as possible, and keep them at a distance from relating to the material factors that constitute our facts, certainties and assumptions as possible.

Active Constructing. And here is the other factor that makes the F/E something more than merely a dreamland: in order to assemble these diffuse and purely affecting phenomena into the coherence of a field, the mystically aspiring figure is actively *constructing* it. She is doing so against all the forces that convention, reason, knowing and producing can bring down on such a contrarian effort. Let's give the mystic her due: it takes tremendous effort to go up against the formidable resources of the knowing and constructing ego – with all of its technical, socioeconomic, legal and linguistic resources – and keep aspirations open and flowing with whatever range of "freedom" and untethered affiliations can be had. The F/E is thus a construction that defies logic and the inertial massing of psychically conforming (belonging) forces.[25] The tool she uses to do this construction is, of course, language. And the work of mystic aspiration is to deploy language in such a way as to gather into being a force to be reckoned with these energies. And so mystic aspirations are expressed in their *precepts*: the commands uttered so that a new way of experiencing what occurs for us is sketched out as a possible course of action (see Table 3.2).

Table 3.2
"World" Saturated Phenomena in the Speech of Aspiring Roles

"World" Saturated Phenomenon	Mentoring Factor	Leader	Artist	Prophet	Mystic
Complete	The concern that is aroused for undertaking an aspiring engagement.	Followers, Dialogue, Narrative	Idea	Word, Law, Concept	Vision
Coming Toward	The stance that is taken up in advance of the exigencies of the concern.	Drive (Energy and Will); Strategy, Flow	Passion	Proclamation	Teaching
Threshold	The locus of engagement that will have to be met by learning.	Self Trust, Brand, Signature Behavior	Mythos: Self as Medium	Exile, Diaspora	Precept
Flesh, Face, Voice	Focus of commitment as a compelling, ongoing, experiential engagement.	Self Awareness, Moral Learning	Material, Tools	The Spirit, People, Community	Faith For
Otherness	The force of resistance and its character, way of emergence.	Practical Insight, Moral Imagination	Challenge, Contender in the Arena	Marketplace, Bazaar, Labyrinth	The Open
Excess	The opening to and the necessity of forging an ethic of constancy in engaging the occurrence.	Attentive Responsibility	Enduration	Pathos	Fore Giving

Source: Michael H. Shenkman (2014). Albuquerque, NM.

Use of Language. Thus a mystic figuration, even more than the other figures, "assembles" an II in a highly "original" (if not originary) manner. The "building blocks" of the mystic's II are *nearly* purely constructs, *nearly* purely confluences of saturating phenomena and *words.* This construction of the mystic's F/E is thus what is expressed by the *precept,* which we will describe in the next chapter. And so, rather than purely dispersing, the aspiring energies that have so laboriously worked their way through the assemblages of the aspiring mind become entangled in the sticky and viscous material of established words/signs/non-verbal or tonal resoundings that are able to linger in the mind, can be repeated and echoed or even represented (in a writing or a scribble or a tone or refrain). These factors of expression can then accumulate and so thicken the field, making that locale a holding place wherein these energies linger or resonate for a while, engendering combined patterns and even larger complexes – which can become, at least precepts.

The mystic figuration of the II, the F/E, is thus a matter of what these *words,* these new words, these utterly inadequate words point to and point at us to be heard. In the mystic F/E these words are not dead letters on a page, but constitute utterances of active, generative formation of what anticipations we must in prepare ourselves in order to meet and take up what increasing complexity is demanding of us. The F/E is thus the field that awaits us, and it is opened to us by mystic aspirations, first and foremost.

Concluding Thoughts

And so this F/E becomes a factor in the human endeavor as the texts, the word and precepts of what, up until the interventions of mystic aspirations, had been relegated to the netherworlds of our unconscious, or had been ignored or even shunned. This field comprises the kinds of feelings that some of us are ashamed to acknowledge, no less articulate. And yet, in the works and precepts of mystically aspiring figures, they become true visions, eternal truths, of what the human endeavor has set out to accomplish.

The way of mystic aspirations is opened by our attunement to what language offers us as a power of envisioning anew. To take up language in this way is that of the vocation of teaching. In Part Two we will listen to the great mystic teachers. Our intent in doing so, as mentors, is to learn how to listen to these aspirations, to get some practice and to test whether or not we can so attune our own listening to this greatest of aspirational ways.

Chapter Four

The Development and Expression of Mystic Aspiration

And the youth, the river, ran out into the plain,
Sadly glad, as the heart overflowing with itself
Perishing with love,
Plunges into the torrents of time.

Sources you had given, and given cool shadows
To the fugitive one, whilst the banks looked on
After him, and their lovely
Trembling image rose from the waves.

~ Hölderlin [1]

This liberation, this embodiment of cosmic memory in creative emotions, undoubtedly only takes place in privileged souls. It leaps from one soul to another, "every now and then," crossing closed deserts. But to each member of a closed society, if he opens himself to it, it communicates a kind of reminiscence, an excitement that allows him to follow...And from soul to soul, it traces the design of an open society, a society of creators, where we pass from one genius to another, through the intermediary of disciples or spectators or hearers...

Thus the great souls — to a greater extent than philosophers — are those of artists and mystics...At the limit it is the mystic who plays with the whole of creation, who invents an expression of it whose adequacy increases with it dynamism. Servant of an open and infinite God... the mystical soul actively plays the whole of the universe, and reproduces the opening of a Whole in which there is nothing to see or to contemplate...Undoubtedly philosophy can only consider the mystical soul from the outside and from the point of view of its lines of probability. But it is precisely the existence of mysticism that gives a higher probability to this final transmutation into certainty, and also gives, as it were, an envelope or a limit to all the aspects of method.

~ Deleuze[2]

...[Life] goes beyond the limits that knowledge fixes for it, but thought goes beyond the limits that life fixes for it...The thinker thus expresses the noble affinity of thought and life: life making thought active, thought making life affirmative.

~ Deleuze[3]

We propose to define mysticism as this reciprocity between existence and thought: to think of being as Releasement one must first of all have a released existence. This appears to be a more satisfactory approach to the phenomenon of mysticism than all definitions that derive the mystical experience from the arrival in consciousness of an all-encompassing being that submerges us.

~ Schürmann[4]

Surprise! You Aspire the Way a Mystic Does!

At this stage in the human endeavor, here in the opening decades of the second millennium AD, one no more "becomes" a mystic than one "becomes" left-handed or gay. No one I know of sets out to "become a mystic." There is no such "vocation" as "the mystic" (as there is a vocation of becoming an artist or a leader, for instance). In fact, when mystic aspirations assert their ways in a life, the affected person is perplexed by the kinds of feelings, orientations and longings that beset her. The strangeness of the "onset" of the mystic figuration of aspirations, at this point in time, can be understood by the application of this idea: "ontogeny recapitulates phylogeny."[5] By way of analogy, I translate this statement to the case of mystic aspirations as allowing the thought that the coalescing of aspirations into a mystic figuration comes late in life, just as the appearance of the mystic figure emerged late in the course of the human endeavor (in the Western/European context).

How do we appreciate this late emergence of the mystic figuration so as to help the mentee to relax into what is transpiring and to orient our mentoring to the state of this emergence in the case of the mentee?

CHILDHOOD PRECURSORS. Of course, as a child is developing, no one suspects that a mystic bent might be forming.[6] The child goes to the schools chosen by his parents, enters into the expectations of career and material accomplishment, and maybe, love and family. People who take up mystic aspirations as adults started out in life being taught the same language used by their parents and communities, and they are taught the same manners and customs that make them "good" people. They are inculcated with the same civic lessons intended to make them "good" citizens; they learn the rubrics of the same economic structures that habituate them to the behaviors that make them "good" workers and "responsible" consumers. All the usual automatic presumptions of life are heaped up, strung out, a tunnel with convenient markers and touchstones all along the way.

Then, at some time later in life (and also later than those of the other aspirational figures), those who are prone to mystically inclined aspirations start to feel their effects. Is there some "trigger" that sets off an inclination to being affected in this way? We have cited a few factors that seem to show up frequently in those who tend toward mystic figuration. Those factors include a strong presence of female influence and authority in the child's home. The father might be absent from the scene for reasons pertaining to work or illness; or the father might have died when the child was young. In some households, the mother (or other females) just exhibit overwhelming influence even when the "man of the house" is around. Other factors include a propensity for solitude, or being an only child, and having a natural curiosity and imaginative precocity. These factors are not predictive of the emergence of a mystic figuration of aspirations precisely because any coalescing of aspiration is always a delicate and tentative affair that is easily crushed by a child's circumstances. And so there is one final element that might allow for the emergence of a mystic figuration: good fortune as to socioeconomic circumstances (including access to attentive and competent educators and a wide variety of resources that encourage, nourish and nurture learning). The child might well exhibit extreme frustration and impatience with a constricted or superficial curriculum geared to the lowest common denominator and will need wider resources to strike out on his or her own. Having equally precocious, bright, articulate, curious and sensitive peers helps to keep these aspirations alive through the torments of childhood and adolescence.

Some of those whose childhoods map onto those parameters discover, later in life, that many of the formulas for assimilating and fitting into the given socioeconomic, cultural and career frameworks in which they were brought up, and that seem to work adequately for others, don't work very well for them. Of course many of us go through a sorting out process in order to find "where we belong," and so give ourselves permission to put aside certain aspects of everyday life that just don't work for us. But that isn't the kind of process I observe in the case of mystic figurations diverging from the status quo. What makes the case of mystic aspirations different from what most of us experience is that for the mystically inclined, as time goes by, so many, if not most, of those formulas don't work, and they don't work on so many different levels, that a feeling of hopelessness wells up (especially when the person is tired) and a sense of isolation and radical "difference" seeps in to the person's self-conception.

ADULT ONSET. It takes a long time (and, usually a mentor) for a person who is prone to the mystic figuration of her aspirations to realize, and accept, that this figuration might be asserting its sway. The one who faces these concerns as an adult often hears stories that as a child she seemed to often live in a dreamy state, shy, amenable to solitude and filling the time with self-generated fantasies. Others hear that they expressed problems with anger; many didn't particularly fare well in regular classrooms, and for that were branded with the stigma of failure. She was told how her behavior was so perplexing to even the well-meaning adults in her life: why does she refuse to do this work, since she is also undeniably bright, quick to speak, observant, easily affected by what was going on around her, and is so acutely capable on many different levels?

Once the articulation begins and others react to those pronouncements and behaviors, it becomes clear to this person that "something" is going on. The gap between the life's way promulgated by mystic aspirations and the life that is predominantly guided by conventions becomes wider; the discomforts have persisted for so long and have persisted so intensely that the mystically affected person feels the need to refuse and stand outside, and, if necessary, precipitate a break, and put some distance between her ways and the ways around her. For most this break is hardly therapeutic: relief is neither offered nor is it in the offing by taking this step; this feeling of rejecting the existing state of affairs goes unnamed, and these drives to arrive at a different way to express and experience what occurs in her life cause distress and sometimes stir up silent desperation.

There comes a point when the mystically aspiring person finally accepts that she is not going to "fit" in the usual ways that one makes a niche for oneself – in a career or job, in a suburban-housed family, marching in lockstep to socioeconomic and cultural norms. Many do make the decision to acquiesce to and with that difference, but not without a struggle or feelings of regret. One mystic mentee, as she came into greater awareness of her stance, said that the previous fifty years of her life had been wasted. By no means, I immediately responded. This process of the unfolding of a mystic way, and the discovery that it has been at work – like it or not – takes a long time. For the mystically aspiring person who is facing this realization, there is even some embarrassment. This realization arrives so late in life, at a time when such "childish" things are supposed to have been put aside (if not necessarily dealt with). Crises of this sort just aren't supposed to happen.

Expressing regret is in line with another aspect of the development and realization process: from the beginning, the process has been filled with so much doubt, all along the way, its realization does not just burst out in a reverie of fulfilled confidence. Living in our technologically mastering world, in this age of Google, we expect any doubt or question will soon break onto a solution, an answer – a formula, product or program – reinforcing our mastery once again. Having a question in the technologically mastered world is just a special time, a time of piqued attention; and it ends, in a solution – likely a compromise, but at least a proposition or course of action that releases one from the question. Mystic aspirations however, pose questions and engender senses of what is occurring that are as likely to vanish as soon as a word, no less a solution approaches. Then, when having that formulation is accepted, when the person's Field of Enthusiasm (the mystic figuration's Iconic Imago) is no longer in play or is no longer prioritized, the energies are consigned to other psychic resources and are even handed over to other aspiring figurations or even to existing social institutions. Thus the so-called "solution" (what every pragmatic colleague will demand of her) ends up feeling more like a death than a satisfying accomplishment.

Encountering Aspiration

Lest this sound as though this person dwells in a perennial swoon, remember the impetus that drives this person into the open: *aspiration.* The mystically aspiring person is most fully *alive* (and that is the criterion, rather than "happiness," for instance) when *aspiring* is holding sway. We are speaking of someone who dwells – with competence, commitment and an ability to expand her capabilities – in a Field of *Enthusiasm.* We are speaking of a person whose faith-for willingly opens to the generative seeds of possibility; we are speaking of a person whose judgment expands and extends in order to encompass freshly and newly opening dimensions. What may appear as "pain" and a persistent "seriousness" – especially against a social backdrop that valorizes gratification, pleasure, entertainment, celebrity, screaming distraction, etc. – is also a disposition toward a "World" that is vibrantly open to affirming anticipations. And the mystic is full of those.

The way of mystic aspiration is not that of discouragement. She may, at times, be overwhelmed by perplexity or the seeming impossibility of her vision; and this realization may indeed induce frustration, and even exhaustion; but it won't induce her resignation. Mystic aspirations require a gathering of one's psychic/somatic resources into a complex of firmness that will not be dis-couraged: the courage of engaging with what is not yet at hand is not taken away or cancelled *as long as,* being *in a state of health and strength,* the mystically guided aspiring one can act with faith-for and fore-giving. When the mystically aspiring person is tired, the summoning of the strength of the stream that opens (in faith-for) and expands (by fore-giving) is not equal to the demands at hand and she can become despondent, even depressed. This happens. But that propensity, in the hale and healthy heart that aspires, simply awaits its resurgence.

Mystic aspirations often drive people toward more abstract endeavors such as religiously or philosophically oriented studies, or matters of theory, or even speculation in scientific and technical matters. Some find a home in abstract arts, such as poetry writing (I think of Mallarme or Celan, for instance) or composing music (Beethoven and Messiaen come to mind). If they land in a corporate setting, they seek out positions that enable them to exert influence at the level of strategy, marketing, organizational transformation and culture. Because of their "feminine" ability to see things whole and to articulate the wider contexts and connections among events and people in their organizations, the mystically inclined often rise quickly to positions of authority. It is a paradox that mystically aspiring people, those most prone to move out of any given hierarchical (male-dominated) structure, become denizens of large-scale organizations (the Catholic Church, universities or other kinds of spiritual institutions) for a time in their lives. But of course, for many, this paradox cannot be sustained. Even as they rise "successfully" through the ranks of the hierarchy, those who are rising on the levitation of their mystic energies often struggle with the strictures of high organizational roles. They appreciate the responsibility and the impact they can have on people by being in such positions; but they also chafe under the demands to conform, compromise and contend with difficult, conservative personalities. Some survive for a long time while others don't. In my own experiences, the mystics I have met were executives in companies and subsequently left, were fired or were moved out of administrative roles into more "creative" slots.

The magnitude of the ruptures precipitated by mystic aspirations will depend on many things; but that there is a watershed moment in this journey seems to me to be inescapable. All of my mentees of mystic figuration tell of their experiences of *rupture* with the authorities, the institutional status quo. In the absence of that kind of run-in, others simply leave their present (even successful and rewarding) circumstances. Simply, as the mystic grows and as her psyche forms more firmly in its very openness and expansiveness, the given "world" of patterns and byways becomes too small — way too small. The "smallness" of the world, in fact, becomes the object of the mystic's concern. The smallness refers to the narrow goals of businesses, the dominance of popular opinion and its leveling of culture, the restriction of what people value in each other as colleagues, employees or companions.

150

THE ANGUISH OF BEING CAST OUT OF SMALLNESS. To the mystically aspiring psyche, this smallness strikes a blow right at the heart of her ongoing assimilation to a situation; it evokes in her all the feelings of "failing." The smallness certainly feels bad internally, but there is more to it than that. To the ever-expanding and encompassing psyche of the mystic, this smallness doesn't come close to accommodating or encompassing living vitally. The mystic feels a sense of injustice in all of this. Every mystic I have met expresses amazement at how the actions, decisions and beliefs of those around her, especially those in positions of power, if not "authority," disappoint her. Of course, if a mystic is working in an organization at the time, this censuring of the very people the mystic had once granted authority becomes evident. Maybe it shows in a facial expression during a meeting, in a memo that the mystic knows is suicidal but feels compelled to write, in a world-shaking sermon that has to be delivered, or maybe it shows in the mystic's being driven to organize a protest of an injustice that is utterly intolerable. One way or another, the mystic's propensity to defy deadness, closure and smug worldly certainty will out. And so, one way or another, the mystic is asked to leave.

Long before she is actually fired, banished or condemned, the rupture has already occurred in the psyche of the mystically aspiring figure. You might recall from the Introduction the description of Dan, the CFO who left a good job in order to pursue his "dream thing." Dan left this company because it had lost its allure of excitement. What did people at Dan's company think when he announced that he was leaving his CFO role and going to…nothing? Did they think he really had a big corporate job in his pocket? (After several trial situations, Dan eventually settled into a role as CFO of a promising, chaotic, just-forming start-up). [7]

Make no mistake: this rupture is a painful moment for the mystically aspiring ones. What had once seemed exciting has become intolerably dull; what once formed a goal to strive for has now become a lowly and unworthy pursuit. It is here that the mystics often speak of "anguish." A feeling of irreparable loss with no way envisioned for recovering what has gone. At this point the full realization of the mystic endeavor is presented, and forever and anon becomes the touchstone of the mystic life. This rupture is as irrevocable as it is inevitable. Always, the one impelled by mystic aspirations will leave in order to set out once again. Whether it is the image of the wandering Taoist or Nietzsche's (and Teresa's) need for solitude or Eckhart's detachment, the world will never give to the mystically aspiring ones what they need. Once they accept the fact that a chasm yawns between their vision of the world and what is out there, there is no turning back. Once departed, they move onward, with greater decisiveness. In an open, secular and pluralistic society (which in some ways, at least in terms of entrepreneurialism, ours is) the next steps taken by the mystically aspiring one are likely to be constructive, creative and even generative, if given half a chance, that is.

THAT STEEL IN THE SOUL. In my opinion, it comes down to this: the mystically aspiring ones, those who do keep their aspirations alive, are able to marshal, nurture and use their vital, bodily, physical energy resources in fore-giving ways in service to their Fields of Enthusiasm that feed and nourish their faiths-for. A mystic needs a vast store of energy to be able to emerge from this night and carry on this life way; if they do not have this energy, and if they are not able to readily and knowingly summon that energy to the fore, the travails of the "broken mystic" await. [8] The people I meet as a mentor have usually found ways to cope with that abundance, but not necessarily thrive with it. The mentor's job, which we'll detail in the next chapter, is to help these survivors to the way of living in which they *do* thrive.

Frankly, I never get to meet the ones who do not have those flows of energy that are insufficient for sustaining their aspirations, mystically figured or otherwise. Neither will any mentor, most likely. The ones who emerge with their aspirations alive have "steel" in their souls, says a colleague of mine. For me, that "steel" is forged by the sheer force that mystic aspirations exert as they surge forth from the mentees' Fields of

Enthusiasm. They need this steel in their souls, since rupturing happens constantly; it is not a matter of getting through this dark night once and for all or growing out of it as one does an adolescent crisis. This is not some developmental phenomenon of the surging limbic system we are talking about here, or the overflowing of hormones. *This rupturing is a way of living for ones who aspire in the mystic way.* It has the character of crisis as a way of being, not as a situation marked by exceptionality and circumstance. The mystic's need for being able to draw on a forceful stream of overflowing energy and the corresponding ability to continually gather it from the abundance she senses around her never abates.

GOING IT ALONE. Even in their "down" moments, mystically figured people will often decline any help that is offered. They wait, alone, for their energies to kick back in; they know (in private solitude and silence) that the virtualities and qualia in their field will come alive once again when they get some sleep and get some good food in their systems. But, even in their disinclination to accept help, they also know the disquiet awaits them. What the mystically aspiring mentee seeks, for herself, on that deeply personal level (and this is the chief motivation for seeking out a mentor), to construct a way, a series of affirming steps that she can reliably take in order to break the cycle of feelings of failure, convalescence and a restored sense of competence.

HEALTH. What breaks the cycle? This question lies at the very core of any mentoring that we undertake with these figures. The question must be addressed: What is it that *for this person* will break the cycle and will enable her to stay more constantly on an affirming course? The answer is *not* medication. It is a matter of *health.* A good night's sleep, a long walk in the woods or along the streets of a beloved city, good (non-processed) food, maybe meditation and yoga, will do the trick. For others, a more systematic approach is needed: she needs to circumscribe the range, the domain of her faith, and so knowing how to identify the more "digestible" qualia she is able to encompass. Here it is a matter of taking on smaller, less encompassing precepts, but ones that still convey the force of the mystic's demand. For others, being systematic means keeping the domain large, but finding a plateau, a level of exploration that sorts out the interstices at which connection and clarity need to be forged. And learning which of these, or what combination of these concentrations will be psychically/somatically viable for the living being of the one who aspires mystically. For this we need to consider that course of learning that pertains specifically to those aspirations.

MAKING HER WAY TO MENTORING. We can briefly summarize the most common (if such a word can be applied here) moments of this course of learning as follows: When the one who comes under the sway of mystic aspirations is young, her lack of comfort is met with an abundance of energy, curiosity, a drive to hit the road and explore, and a sense that an adventure always lies over the next horizon. This "wild" energy also seems to flourish in households in which the father is somehow absent (deceased, diminished in a capacity to exert himself, or estranged from the family unit), or at least the feminine influence dominates.[9] However, as the mystic ages into the mid-thirties and forties, that naturally wanes. At the excess of youthful energies wane, the proclivities that the aspiring resource offers may be able rise to greater prominence. That is, if that person has been fortunate enough to pursue that life of adventure and learning, all that experiencing has simply fed her mystic proclivities, has enriched them with new ways to generate ever more nuanced and even more pointed comprehended expressions of her aspirations (well-supported by conceptual, imaginative and textual supports) as they move out in their trajectories toward more expansive and more encompassing ways to engage her life's gifts and challenges. However, if the person does not have such opportunities to nourish, nurture and cultivate her aspiring ways, she will likely just submit to that "normal" life – career, family and hobbies can do the trick for some. But, to the extent that some vestiges of the aspiring resource are still active (and that is usually the case), there will be a price pay for that sub-mission: paying this price is often manifested in forms such as depression, compulsive self-medicating (alcoholism) or profound cynicism.

But some *don't give in.* By virtue of some inexplicable and unaccountable accident of nature, their energy rebounds and takes flight once again. For some unknown and unknowable reason, these people rise out of states of discouragement and set out to keep trying to bring those aspirations to life. A price is paid here as well. Often, their employers (or spouses) tell them, "it isn't working out," and they are expelled. At that moment, or as those moments accumulate, either by "choice" or by some "stroke" of realization, their mystic aspiring saga begins. Thus expelled, like it or not, the mystically aspiring ones are thrown into the open. Now it becomes a matter of navigating in a new milieu: now, no longer blithely accepting of the conventions of the habituated life, she must learn to respond to the power and demands of her own "World" assemblage's energies. Her task becomes one of *doing the work:* digging deep into what her concern is, giving it shape and bringing it to expression. And while this is going on, giving great time and attention to the cultivation and strengthening of her innate energies. It is on the vitality and integrity of these energies that the mystic's life depends.[10]

THE MENTOR'S CURRICULUM. That work entails two main elements in my estimation, both of which are addressed in subsequent chapters in this book. The first (addressed in Part Two) is to learn the *genealogy* of mystic aspirations. Every mystically aspiring mentee I have encountered is painfully aware of her growing "outcasting" from one mainstream activity and convention after another. In one form or another, certain questions always come up: "Where do I belong?" and "Who are my people, my peers?" My answer is that while there are many mystically aspiring people among us, and their aspirations take on innumerable varieties of interests, intentions and expressions, this figuration of aspirations emerges from a genealogy that comprises the known works of the avatars, authors and pioneers of this way. I strongly urge my mentees to become familiar, in some way, somehow, with the well-known figures whose works have come down to us. The mystic figuration, in its Western incarnation, only emerges as it does because these people, who also once walked among us, wrote works of such persuasive

155

potency that they have persisted even though they have hardly been countenanced, no less comprehended. In order to assist the mentor and mentee in this part of the curriculum of mentoring mystic aspirations, Part Two provides an itinerary of texts and sources with which such a study can begin.

The other element in developing a robust mystic figuration is mentoring, with the mystically aspiring person finding and working a mentor who is capable of comprehending those aspirations on their own terms. There is no other way than through mentoring for affirming mystic aspirations. Every mentee of mystic figuration I have talked with has had some influence in their lives — a parent, a teacher, a book — that has provided that kind of supportive moment of recognition, that space that allows for a "feeling" to be iterated and taken up as a possible "way." Or, to put it in the terms that we developed in the last chapter: people who take up mystic aspirations benefit from a moment in which the saturating phenomena of a vibrant world are provided the dignity of being gathered into a viably functioning (facultative) assemblage — the forming of a viably aspiring P/SS resource, which we call the "aspiring mind."

The next question that the mentor will ask, of course, is what does this learning and the mentoring process accomplish for this person? Of course we have talked about providing emotional support for a challenging life's way. Mentors will want to help that person also establish the practices that express mystic aspirations and put them into play. It is to these aspects of practice that we now turn. In sum, the mentor will endeavor to make clear how specifically mystic aspirations are expressed, as the *precept* and will elevate to prominence and stature the role of *teaching.*

Expression: The Precept

Only by doing the work of formulating the *precept* can one coalesce those diffuse and unsettling aspiring energies and enthusiasms into its mystic figuration. Prior to this formulation, people may have vague feelings about their lives or what their "personalities" entail as a lifestyle.

They may even, at times, happen upon figures with which they "resonate," and may find that some consider that person to be a "mystic," or some other kind of figure. But these are fleeting moments. As we know, many people with many orientations have this quality and abundance of energy and perspicacity, and most of those are not likely to configure their aspirations in mystic ways. To have those energies coalesce into any "figuration," such as we speak of in the context of this book, requires that the mentee undertake to make the conscious or implicit commitment – comprising a turning of attention and dedication of practices – to making certain things happen in the world.[11] And, accordingly, the mystic figuration of aspiration of energies coalesces in the form of articulating a precept, or it is not a mystic figuration. As such, I can also say that any mentoring engagement centered around mystic aspiration must culminate in at least a conclusion as to whether this person wants to do this work of articulating the precept, or not (which is a legitimate outcome, to the extent that it is an informed decision).

To sketch out the notion of the role that the precept plays in the development and articulation of mystic aspirations, you can begin by thinking of someone you know who has an abundance of energy, is optimistic about life despite obstacles and setbacks, and sparkles in terms of articulation, wit and comprehension of what is going on about them. Think of this person as also exhibiting a hunger to dive right into the thick of things and even assume responsibility (which may or may not mean "leadership") in what is transpiring there. Then, these people might regard the conventions and conformities that most people abide by with some level of disdain, if not derision. If I was meeting with such a person, I would immediately have preliminary suspicions that mystic aspirations were in play. Still, I would reserve any judgment and I would refrain from embarking on a course of mentoring this person in anticipation of a mystic figuration until I had more evidence (Keirsey Sorter scores, biographical information, other patterns of speech, etc.[12]) To be sure, there are many ways that such people express their concerns and find good "outlets" for expressing their energetic proclivities other than a mystic figuration of aspirations. To be clear, caution is justified here since few people, compared to even the other figures, configure their aspirations in the mystic way. And so, what is it that might signal to the mentor that this person may be in the process of forming a mystic figuration of aspirations and that this course of investigation is worth pursuing at all?

QUALIFIED ENERGIES. For one thing, we know from what we discussed in the last chapter that the energies of aspiration, while abundant and forceful, are neither brutish nor do they project profusions of power. The energies of aspiration are already characterized as saturating phenomena, and constitute what we have called the "World" assemblage. As phenomena these energies, in their ways of engendering spurs and goads that presage states of *relation,* are already affecting P/SS operations in ways that immerse aspiration in contexts and concerns that elicit the sense that change is afoot, is on its way, in the flesh. And then as abundant energies, that as yet have no actuality or claims on behaviors or decisions in everyday activities, these phenomena permeate aspirational orientations with an urgency, a pull into states of concern that cannot be evaded by the aspiring ones, and especially cannot be evaded by those with mystically inclined aspirations, for whom the "World" assemblage is so prominent.

Language(s): The Key. To appreciate the mystically figured response to the roiling energies of saturating phenomena, we have to go back to the basics of our premise that the mystic figuration of aspirations arose as a way of deploying *language* as a means of prying open all ways into which everyday life practices have hardened into facts, certainties, ideologies and institutionalized practices. In our age, the term "language" covers a lot of ground. It covers all the ways that communicative means have been gathered into constituting an affecting and effecting domain (comprising objects, contexts and meanings)[13] that stands in its own right such that it can be worked on, changed, controlled, can inspire or depress or conjure images in its own or other syntaxes (a line of poetry can inspire a musical piece or painting or vice versa). In order to remind us of the plurality of language forms that aspirations marshal to the occasions of engaging, I will append "(s)" to the term.

In the case of mystic aspirations in particular, we need to appreciate this notion of the independence of a domain of language(s) in a very strong, bi-directional sense. On the one hand, the mystic figuration arises at all *because language(s) are effective and are capable of generating affects on people's lives,* in excess of and in addition to any "natural" force, such as a sunny day or a blizzard might affect people's lives. On the other hand, mystic aspirations specifically revert to language(s) as a way to affect the very things that language has made possible in the first place – everything from religion to law to science and art – and do so by deploying language in order to unsettle whatever has so far been accomplished thereby. This conscious and deliberate, considered and intentionally aggressive deployment of the resources of language(s) indicates that mystic aspirations might be at issue for this person. That is because the specifically mystic expression of aspiration takes up the role of consciously and concertedly directing language so as to render orientation to her chosen concerns.[14]

Language and Abundant Energy. A mystic figuration thus, at a minimum, exhibits a strong attraction to language(s). And this is not all. Once again, many people are attracted to language, and many of these people use it flaccidly, as verbal manipulation, or use it carelessly in a lazy manner, or use it cynically as a tool to obfuscate, confuse, deflect and mendaciously misrepresent situations. In contrast to this casual or even professional attraction to language, mystic aspirations deploy language(s) in ways that set their articulations apart. That is, mystic aspirations place language(s) *in service* to all the abundantly expansive energies of the "World" assemblage's saturating phenomena. Mystic as-pirations seek to bring to expression not "what this thing is," or "what" is this thing's "essence," as would a philosophical account; rather, mystic aspiring seeks to express how it is that an occurrence has qualities of "coming towards," of constituting a "threshold" of state changes, that the occurrence has a "voice" and exerts affects as does the "flesh," etc. We can refer to Table 3.1 to refresh our memories as to the ways saturating phenomena give rise to the tendency toward certain words, at least in the context of mystic aspiration.

One mentee expressed this as his unwavering attraction to "beginnings," as occasions that energize him: situations that consist of suspicions, expressed in hypotheses or speculations, that can be pursued and further articulated into a course of action, or at least a "plan." And then, there is Dan, whom we cited as one who pursues his "dream thing," which includes the latitude to form new expressions of what might occur in ways that envision future actions of others.

In the fold of mystic aspirations, language(s) are not envisioned as being enumerations of existing names or identities. Instead, language(s) are thought of as ways that strive, struggle and reach out into the recesses of words and syntax in order to express how one viscerally and bodily seeks to encompass saturating phenomena and does so in ways that keep them alive and able to generate relations that are more expansive and more encompassing. Thus, the confluence of language(s) and "World" energies constitute an Iconic Imago of a Field of Enthusiasm, rather than a set of hard identities, hierarchies and formal grammars – which are amenable to the construction of "things," facts, procedures (methods) and certainties. In this Field, language(s) are completely absorbed in the flows that saturate them that this field (only) serves to offer a firmness in positing expansiveness and openings to new vistas that enrich the human endeavor and that intend to offer more choices for it as it seeks to guide its way onward (but it does offer a sense of firmness, coherence and continuity, if not identity and objective certainty).

Persistent Affirmation. Attitudes that others might express about such tentative and speculative formulations might engender cynicism, or despair and deprecation of possibilities – especially in the boardrooms and conference rooms of our productive institutions. But in mystically aspiring expression, these attitudes are not so much excluded or eliminated (at the outset, until the moment when the precept encounters its inevitable opposition) as they are just not in the mix of language(s) and aspiring energies at all. This is not a matter of naïveté or innocence either. This confluence of language(s) and saturating phenomena does not come out of thin air, or ex nihilo. The occurrences that mystic aspirations engage are already deeply marked (scarred, contaminated, mechanized, deprecated and stifled) by what the conventional ways of our daily living do to them. And so the confluence of language(s) and saturating phenomena in the Field of Enthusiasm arises to *begin with* in the face of what already degrades the human endeavor, and so what others would claim to be "the reality," of the situation.

But we must recall our premise: aspiration in general does its work, seeks within those margins and envelopes of what exists for chances for expansion and further connection that fosters increasing complexity. Because this impetus drives the formation of such a thing as aspiration, and for no other reason, mystic aspirations regard these same occurrences in different ways than what others might accept. In the mystic figuration of aspirations, these same occurrences also bear their saturating phenomena that bode forth in excess and presage an encompassing engagement that expands possibilities rather than shrinks them, or has the P/SS shrink from them. It is just that mystic aspirations take these insults of the quotidian in a different way: as an occasion for aspiration. This occurrence is not dead in one's hands, is not fully grasped or comprehended, and would, in actuality, welcome a different expression. This same occurrence is ready to accommodate a new *precept*.

A New Force. In a mystic figuration, these two factors – (1) abundantly enthusiastic energy of saturating phenomena and (2) language(s) – come together, combine into becoming a force in its own right in the mystic expression of the precept. The mentor's work is to help the mystically aspiring mentee form that expression. To do this requires, of course, that the mentor instigate a shift in perspective about the mentee's "self" and/or "personality." The shift entails transfiguring the mentee's sense of self from being a person who has a personality that is blessed with great energy and perspicuity, to being a person who encompasses and embraces this energy as an expression of her aspiring mind's Field of Enthusiasm, as a concrete and comprehendible P/SS assemblage that has the sole function of reaching out into and for more expansive and more encompassing ways of being human, as the enacting of faith-for by acts of fore-giving.

It is a matter of effecting a shift from a state of mind in which a person acknowledges that she "has" an abundance of energy to one of taking responsibility for caring for that energy and taking up what that abundance of energy can mean *for others*. The mentor helps a mentee shift her orientation such that she no longer only says, "I have a lot of energy in order to do my job," but she also says, "I exert energies so that this work can become more energetic, more expansive and more encompassing, and for no other reason." She is able to take up the role of mystic figuration so as to promulgate and articulate a precept.

Precept in Action. By now I am sure you want to get a better grasp of what such a "precept" entails. A recent incident condenses the working of the expression of the precept into the fewest words and into a concise snapshot of the way mystic aspirations (if not yet specifically mystically figured intent) are expressed in precepts. A highly energetic woman, who exemplifies to a tee all the qualities we described above, was being considered as a likely candidate for a promotion into a senior executive role in a very large, innovative and technical organization. She made her reservations about taking on this "director" position very clear. The question that she asked the person who was encouraging her to take on such a position (as relayed to me by this sponsor) was, "So what work does a director do that is *important?*"

A simple enough question, and it is a question we all can understand. But by looking at this question a bit more carefully, we can detect its "perceptual" character. We can all agree that is the question is spurred by aspiration, rather than by ambition or careerism, and it is a question of demanding an articulation of worth, value and vitality – of being in a position to act generatively and in ways that are more expansively affecting – that befits the mystic orientation (and is certainly not exclusive to that orientation, but that would absolutely be present in a mystically aspiring one). This person was taking responsibility for her "World" concerns such that she was questioning whether a position that is paid more and so carries higher organizational prestige is actually one that *contributes to what her aspiring energies, her Field of Enthusiasm, impels her to care about.* Her deployment of language in this simple and direct question is an example of the "precept" in action.[15]

At some point then, as aspirations take shape, they might veer into a confluence of language and expansive energy that (through iterative operations) forms into being a vigorous assemblage (an Iconic Imago) that intends to pry open hardened presumptions so as to become amenable to more expansive and more encompassing engagements. When such a confluence is enacted, a figuration of aspirations has coalesced. It is the coalescing of the Field of Enthusiasm and language(s) that specifically *establishes* the mystic figuration as a viable role and life's way. All the affects of energies and tendencies toward language that are exhibited prior to that coalescence occurring is a matter of learning or constitutes a tendency that might or might not take shape as mystic figuration of aspirations.[16] With evidence that this confluence is in play, the mentor can have a high degree of confidence that this person's aspirations have also become *figurations* in a *role* that we can call "mystic." By noting or by encouraging the arrival at this point of convergence, mentors can acknowledge that mystic aspirations have become matters of awareness and concern for the mentee. At this point, the mentor can acknowledge that mystically figured aspirations are what this mentee can decide to use and deploy in various forms so that she will be able to generate *precepts* that intend to offer more expansive and more encompassing ways of engaging the human endeavor.

The Precept, Properly Understood. Accordingly, when we speak of the notion of the "precept" in the context of mentoring aspirations, and their mystic figurations, we mean just this: the *precept articulates in words, syntax and behaviors the confluence of aspiring energies that have found their expression in a language so as to take effect as a viably engaging role in the context of human affairs.*

In light of the factors in its emergence, the precept then bears two characteristics in its articulation. On the one hand, as it pertains to the energetic component of the confluence, the precept is an expression of the expansive dimensions of occurrences that are available and in play. And then, in addition (in the logic of supplementation), the precept concentrates its deployment into language into a saying that immediately takes its place in the very context that it intends to disrupt and expand and so has these four consequences:

1. The statement entails undertaking an action.

2. The action entails moving out from static, established states of being and acting.

3. The action thus "unsays" what any statement can actually "say;" and dislocates the statement from any given state of affairs, and most especially from the states of affairs in which the statement is uttered.

4. The action entails a shift in the usual patterns and orientations we take with respect to our engaging what occurs, and points to options that are more expansive and more encompassing.

This deployment of language, that the precept always intends, is an operation that is called "apophasis." We will see examples of this deployment when we take up our consideration of the genealogy of the mystically aspiring figuration in Part Two. For now we can absorb the primary notion that the mystic figuration exists, lives and does her work in the forming, articulation, clarifying and promulgation of the viability of her precept. She does this by taking up the role, doing the work of teaching. In this role, in adopting the role of *teaching,* one reaches the full expression of the way of mystic aspiration.

For instance, we all can grasp what the statement, "Proceed with what exceeds" means; every word is clear and completely within our most common abilities to grasp. And yet, to engage that statement entails encountering our experiencing as what it is that is precisely under scrutiny and being subjected to an expansive intervention. In the most profound way that the mystically aspiring speaker can articulate, the precept performs all of the operations we have cited. One cannot take up that statement as an intention without re-orienting one's engagements, however one does so at the present time. The statement is perceptual in that it always points to there being a different way, another possibility, and thus another decision that has to be taken. The statement is clear and concise and "unsays" the validity and habituated ways by which we look at what is about to ensue.

By the way, the same mentee who asked her supervisor that challenging question also described her approach to being in a new situation this way: "As I go out the door, I say to myself, 'Be ready for the adventure.'" Once again, this decidedly mystically aspiring person speaks, even to herself, in ways that enunciate her precept.

The Energy of Elucidation: The Role of Teaching

TEACHING AS A VOCATION THAT COMBINES FORE-GIVING, FAITH-FOR AND THE PRECEPT. Continuing to trace our narrative of the development of aspirations into mystic figuration and expression, we now ask this question: now that the mentee's mystic aspirations are coalesced into the expressible force of the precept, what does a person do with it? One might suspect, for instance, that forming and avowing the precept might evoke demagogic behavior that a person might believe that he or she is "right," over, above and against the claims of anyone and everyone else. But this would be a gross misreading (and misapplication) of the tenor of mystic aspirations. As we have already described it, the mystic way is that of fore-giving and faith-For. And so how do these ways jibe with forming the precept?

The impetus of mystic aspirations, now coalesced in the forceful and affecting expression of the precept, directs the person's energies at making possible what can become more expansive and more encompassing. The intent of the precept is never prescriptive, in terms of laying out the "right" way, as in a managerial directive. The precept, rather, and in opposition to any such prescriptions, presents a declaration that stands for those aspects of occurrences that refuse confinement and codification and that offer the "adherent" (whom we shall discuss momentarily) the sense of a way onward that is irrepressibly vital, alive, uncertain and that permeates an occurrence with its excessive (as this saturating phenomenon) potencies. Thus the precept, maybe the ultimate one is that of Meister Eckhart, who says, "I pray to God to be free from God."

Neither does the precept espouse all the qualifications that undermine an emerging potency. In the spirit of faith-for, the precept articulates an envisionable way of engaging states of affairs such that those tentative, wisp-like filaments of emergence are given their due. That is, the striving to connect that all-saturating phenomena in the "World" of the aspiring mind is valorized in its own right. Without a qualifying, delimiting or prejudicing reduction of this emergence, the precept articulates a way to proceed in ways that are strictly that of faith-for; and that means the precept articulates what can come into shared engaging only by acts of fore-giving. It articulates, as we have shown, what can come into play in general circulation of language and action only by undertaking a bi-directional labor: a labor that *both* envisions something more expansive and more encompassing *and also* undertakes a giving oneself over to making room and making way for the expansive and dimension-altering sway and affecting powers exerted by saturating phenomena. The formal term for this kind of an act is that of "e-ducation:" leading oneself outward and onward; and the operation that enacts education is *teaching*.

Indeed, in the development of the mystic figuration of aspirations, taking up the role of teaching is what comes next. We have said that the "precept" is necessary so that mystic aspirations can affect others. Indeed, the mystically aspiring person is no solitary. Even those great historical avatars of mystic figuration who retreat from the world for a time, as did Nietzsche or the Beguines of the Middle Ages, did so in order to honor and do their intensive and demanding work of formulating the precept so that its expression would strike maximal and optimal resonances in their surroundings. The focus of working with a precept is not to polish a tile and make it shine (to use the Buddhist image of futility), but rather to figure out where to place that tile so that it will do the work it was intended to do. *The work that follows on from formulating the precept is to closely consider the ways we humans take up and act on what occurs in all of our lives so as to encourage aspiration, engender generativity and institute practices that are more expansive and more encompassing right at the site of their emergence.* Their work is to bring forward what has appeared to them, and has necessitated for them the forming of a precept; it is to provide accounts that others can relate to that can also evoke in them, the listeners, a vision of how to extricate themselves from all-absorbing social mandates.

To use the terminology we have developed in this study in describing the work that follows on from the formation of the precept, we would say, the work that takes up the injunction of the precept constitutes *activating* an articulation of the impelling impetus of saturating phenomena to expand and intensify the reach of their engagements so as to foster ways of living that are generative, more expansive and more encompassing. Mystic aspirations are devoted to discerning and articulating the power of saturating energies that portend increasing complexity and expansiveness. The energies of saturating phenomena, as we have said, disrupt and even devastate the status quo. The way of mystic aspiring is to accommodate those energies and give them safe harbor such that they can find their affinities and means of being sustained by the forming of language bridges that span from the inertial state to a generative one.

ENTERING THE *ROLE* (VOCATION) OF TEACHING. Thus the work of mystic aspiring is not complete when the precept has been formulated. The precept itself has to be linked to actions that seek to expand their compass of affecting. The work that the precept enjoins mystic aspirations to undertake is to activate ways out of the static and toward the generative so that moments of increasing complexity (ephemeral and tentative as they are) have a chance to withstand the forces around them. Some of those opposing forces would consume, suppress and doom them back into the night of stasis, while others would blow those potentially generative moments apart with outrageous overreaches of claims and demands. Mystic aspirations, using the precept to navigate these treacherous waters, probe and grope amid all the energies of the existent state of affair in order to propose, and teach ways that sustain at least whatever generative energies this state of affairs can accommodate. There is no substitute for this comprehending and discerning groping and searching out – impelled by the precept and nourished by the aspirational concern for what can become more expansive and more encompassing.

To take up the *role* entailed by mystic figuration as expressed in the precept, means that there is work to be done. Precepts must be sketched and ventured in experiments; new connections must be forged and their contexts must be defined; the contrasts, conflicts and contradictions the precept engenders must be identified, elevated to the breaking point and contended with. The precept must be shaped so that it can withstand challenges – of being co-opted, compromised or demolished – and it must be worded so that it retains its affirming and inviting demeanor through repeated expressions. In this work, the effects of saturating phenomena emerge as penumbras of expanding energies, – the excess and overflowing of what is required by any single existent (once it is established), the coming into the open. The role of mystic figuration is to project what the confluences in the Field of Enthusiasm, the open, bring to light, to "elucidate" them, or to teach them. This work does not envision its end or the attaining of its goal; it envisions living along in a way, in a role, in a vocation or calling that we call teaching.

Teaching is thus the specific act that embodies faith-for and calls for, and possibly evokes or elicits fore-giving, for the teacher and for those who "hear." The teacher elucidates the connections offered by the precept and then explicates these elements of the precept into curricula and pedagogies: the new and strange is articulated in terms of what is in play, in terms of what exists, and makes them strange once again. The teaching of mystic aspirations strives to open up, amid the familiar and settled, those elements that portend "more," and offer a chance to undertake initiatives that can change the state of affairs in ways that render it, henceforward, more expansive and more encompassing.

Teaching is thus the defining role of the mystic. Teaching is not a matter of presenting the subject matter of articulating a field that is freshly opened and thus welcomes, indeed that invites, initiative. Teaching sets the precept into play. And, as we have seen, it is not verities that the precept comprises, but they set into place trajectories that envision destinations that have yet to be enunciated or charted.

What actions do the mystically aspiring teachers that I have met take up in their role and vocation? One person I met in my mentoring literally traveled around the world convening forums of leaders of nations to devise new institutions in their countries that ameliorated conflicts with neighboring nations. Another worked in third world countries to establish public health resources, while another worked with individuals in order to reframe their life experience in ways that opened onto new and expansive expressions of their talents. Others, of course, write and place into circulation new visions of engaging life's ways in attunement with expansive and generative energies, saturating phenomena, which permeate generative occurrences. We will review the teachings that crystallized the mystic figuration in Part Two.

In sum, the work of mystic aspiration is, by means of the precept, to suggest a way, a path (a staircase, or a passage into deeper interiors) such that new constellations of occurrence can take their places and form anew a human endeavor. The work is painstaking, it is personal, it is risky and it is an act of giving. In the mystically figured teaching role one has to translate what is potently alive and tentatively offered, as something that is also really demanded, and then can also be envisioned as compellingly possible — not just optional, but not mandated, but instead as what for the sake of a more expansive and encompassing human endeavor we must open ourselves toward. The role entails continually forming new bridges that span from the tried and true to the tentative (bridges to nowhere, for sure), and so make the passages envisioned both promising and threatening. All of this is offered in an atmosphere of skepticism, fear and, sometimes, homicidal animus. To teach the precept (and what is sure and known as another's precept) takes monumental courage.

ADHERENTS. It is thus clear that mystic aspirations do not promise definitive methods, no less assured outcomes. Thus, the mystic role does not generate relationships that ascribe to a way or that even generate collectives of common approaches. Mystic aspirations, when taught in the most faithful way, to their uncertainty and perceptual initiative, can generate only "adherents" — people who are present, "here" with the aspirations expressed by the precept, and as such "hear" what is being said as an event in and of itself. These are ad-"here"- ants or ad-"hear"-ants because the open thus illuminated occurred only at the site, at the sound put into play by the precept's *efficacy*.

Onward in Mystic Aspiring

If there is to be any continuing development of the aspiring mind with mystic orientations, it is in doing the hard work of becoming more and more proficient at the teaching of the precept. In concluding this chapter, consider this: *the mystic precept comes to us as a diamond-hard, incisively cut work of articulation.* It is the result of great labor and day-by-day disciplined discovery that continually unfolds in the course of living the role of teaching. It is no loosey-goosey, air-headed dismissal of life. It is a hard-driving, totally educated and competent foray into the heart and depths of what this living can bring forth. If we cannot take the time and make the effort to grasp the mystics' efforts, made solely for our benefit, that is our loss, not their deficiency. And this situation — *ignore*-ance, befuddlement, fear and defensive retrenchment — is exactly what mystic aspirations face, except for the generosity of their adherents. Yet the mystic aspiration brings new worlds (small "w", no quotes — *our worlds*) to us.

And we now move to consider the genealogy of the mystic role, the way that these aspirations have been given shape and robust figuration in our Western/Anglo-European context. Because the work of these people did, in fact, shape new worlds for us, this way has been proven as viable, effective and indispensible. We will trace an emergence of a new way of engaging the human endeavor, from its vehement eruption as impassioned appeals to those exceeding energies to their most unexcelled articulations. To be sure, these initial forays into mystic expression may seem to have failed: the world is still very much with us, as the poet would say. But, as we will also show, the precepts of these figures, their teachings on what humans *can conceive as being possible for them,* did indeed engender more expansive and more encompassing ways. We can rightly ask, what is our "modern" world, after all, if not putting into practice what a precept showed us as being at least possible?

PART TWO

The Mystic Family

Chapter Five

The Mystic Awakening:
The Beguines and Meister Eckhart

Lead us up beyond unknowing and light,
    Up to the farthest, highest peak
      Of mystic scripture,

  Where the mysteries of God's Word
    Lie simple, absolute and unchangeable
      In the brilliant darkness of a hidden silence.

Amid the deepest shadow
  They pour overwhelming light
    On what is most manifest.

Amid the wholly unsensed and unseen
  They completely fill our sightless minds
    with treasures beyond all beauty.

~ Pseudo-Dionysus [1]

...For I am a free human creature, and also pure as to one part, and I can desire freely with my will, and I can will as highly as I wish, and seize and receive from God all that he is without objection or anger on his part – what no saint can do.

~ Hadewijch [2]

If I am to be consoled in proportion to my nobility,
God's breath must draw me effortlessly into itself,
For the sparkling sun of the living Godhead
Shines through the bright water of cheerful humanity
And the sweet pleasure of the Holy Spirit
Who proceeds from them both
Has taken from me everything
That dwells beneath the Godhead.
Nothing tastes good to me but God alone.
I am wondrously dead.

~ Mechthild [3]

Such a Soul, says Love is in the greatest perfection of
being and she is closest to the Farnearness, when she no
longer takes Holy Church as exemplar in her life. The
Soul is thus under the work of Humility, and so is beyond
the work of Poverty and above the work of Charity [the
approved Virtues]. She is so far from the work of the
Virtues that she cannot understand their language. But
the works of the Virtues, who obey the Soul without
contradiction are completely enclosed within such a soul,
and because of this enclosure, Holy Church does not
know how to understand her. Holy Church singularly
praises Fear of God for saintly Fear of God is one of the
gifts of the Holy Spirit. Still, Fear of God would destroy
the being of freeness, if she could penetrate such being.
But perfect freeness possesses no why.

~ Porete [4]

The upsurge of the mystic figuration of aspirations, while not arising instantaneously and ex nihilo, did have a grand entrance onto the stage of

Western European life. The mystic figuration was thrust into the heart of Western life in the thirteenth century by a succession of extraordinarily talented women poets and dramatists who put their Fields of Enthusiasm into play in such a forceful manner that they could not be ignored. Considering that what they were expressing had never before been thought, or at least had certainly never before, ever, anywhere, been articulated so completely and eloquently, homage must be paid. As one reader of this material commented, their vision of what life consisted of was so modern, so passionately expressed and so defiantly put forward that it astounds us, even today, to read their works. This chapter, long in order to present this genealogy, is included not only because of the excellence of the works cited, but because the expression of the mystic figuration has never been surpassed and has never strayed from the core of faith-for and the life of fore-giving that these mystics, properly so called (because they gave their whole lives over this figuration of aspirations).

This chapter in no way qualifies as a "history" of the mystic figure in the West (and I know of no such history being in existence – although starting a search on the topic by entering the names "Bernard McGinn" and "Michel DeCerteau" will provide a good start). I include this material for two equally important reasons. First, a mentor is advised to spend time not only with this chapter, but also to delve into the primary texts themselves as another way to become familiar, if not comfortable, with what mystic aspirations envision, encompass, stand for and express. And second, the overall premise of this work on aspirational figurations is that these figures emerge historically, as ways that embody psychic/somatic expressions of how people in the Western tradition, and in Europe in particular, expanded their facultative capabilities in light of the increasing complexity of life around them, in order to engage these in ways more amenable to comprehending and being active with regard to those complexities. There is thus no "natural" way that mystic aspirations are configured (the latest of the figurations we consider in this project); the only figuration that we have and that we are able to appreciate, no less take up, is what the avatars of this life way set in motion. The subject matter they describe did not exist in the way they expounded it before they did their work; and the way we might envision to engage that material did not exist before they ventured their own experiments. Again, homage is due.

As important as any aspect of this genealogical citation is the fact that the founding mystics we cite are women. As I briefly intimated in Chapter Four, the mystic figuration arises out of a predominantly feminine nurturance. I can say, and I would defend the proposition, that the mystic emergence marked a resurgence of a feminine figuration of aspiration in the face of male-dominant figurations that have gone before them (leader, artist, prophet). The feminine "passion" here is not incidental, it is constituent of the mystic figuration of aspiration in general. This holds even as we take up the vaulting figure of Meister Eckhart. A paragon of Catholic philosophical prowess, to the point of assuming the chair of honor previously occupied by the better known Saint Thomas Aquinas, Eckhart's mystic vocation began in earnest when he took up a position in Paris. There he was assigned to deal with the uprising of the mystics who were unsettling the people with their strange notions. So while Eckhart masterfully and without peer – ever – placed mystic insights in a philosophically (and doctrinally) grounded discourse, he never surpassed the *thinking* that the founding women mystics set in play.

The Precursors: Plato, Paul, Plotinus, Pseudo-Dionysus

PLATO. Our genealogy has to create a branch outside of the Christian fold before we can fully depict the family tree. We have to make that side trip to ancient Greece (prior to John's era) we promised above. The mystics we feel most akin to in our genealogy have traces of what is called "Neo-Platonism" in them. This appellation refers to Plato, the great fifth-century BC Greek philosopher and maybe proto-mystic. In my opinion, whatever else can be said about the "truth" or "applicability" or "morality" of Plato's work, it is undeniable that Western thought was set onto its distinct course by this philosopher. All serious discussion of the dominant concepts in our culture and/or science pass through Plato's force field.

One of Plato's most important contributions to our genealogy is that of the "Ideas." Briefly, and with great injustice to the orthodox exegesis of this seminal conception, this doctrine states that the ultimate reality is not what we see and sense here on earth. After all, everything that occurs here passes, degenerates, intermixes and falls further and further away from the perfect, true and eternal. The "true" therefore can only be grasped by an act of the intellect (reason) in which the "Ideas" make their presence known. This notion paves the way for innovations such as processes for determining "truth," for notions of "justice" that transcend an eye for an eye. And, in the Christian fold, this notion is translated into (not at all mystic) fancies of a truly separate, independently and autonomously existent God set afar from us in an otherworldly Heaven. This leads to a further (neither mystic nor particularly constructively generative) development in which each segment of social life and bodily reality are isolated and then some aspect of its "essence" is projected into the eternal, infinite beyond.

PAUL. I would offer that the first stirrings of western/Christian mysticism take place in the writings of Paul. In the first century AD, earthly (Roman) law reigned throughout the regions in which Saul the rug merchant roved. In the eastern fringes of this empire, however, other notions of what constituted legitimate law also were in play. On the fringes of Roman legalistic rigidity, the combined Hebraic and Platonic formulations forged a One out of the Many and challenged the notions that declared and enforced the laws of commerce and allegiance to the Roman pantheon or (especially) the legitimacy of Caesar as being the supreme arbiters of the real, the valuable and the eternal.

For Paul it was by means of entering a "mystery" that people achieved a fullness of life. The codified Hebraic law loses its efficacy because through the Christ story, God's own way, transcendent and eternally creative, has made its entrance. According to Alain Badiou, Paul inaugurates a "fourth discourse" that directly bears on all the work in the breakout creative project. First, with regard to the mystic figure, Paul insisted that the Christ event could be grasped neither in the everyday discourse of commerce (that he, Saul the rug trader, knew well), nor in the Hebraic manner of the book and the law, nor in the Greek model of the Logos, the logical, comprehensible whole their wisdom accommodated. So he inaugurated a fourth language, that of the Christ event itself. Badiou explains:

> Let us note in passing that Paul delineates, as if in shadowy outline, a fourth possible discourse, besides the Greek..., the Jew, and the Christian...It is the discourse of the ineffable, the discourse of nondiscourse. It is the subject as silent and mystical intimacy, inhabited by "things that cannot be told," which would be better translated as "unutterable utterances," only experienced by the subject who has been visited by miracle.[5]

Using Badiou's insight, Paul's precept can be translated as a cornerstone of the mystic endeavor: the true power of the fresh, living and generative does not lie within the province of what the authorized knowledge and practice permits. It comes only in an event of faith-for, that unspeakable power that cannot be appropriated by these or any powers. The Platonic model that abstractly and mythically depicts the power to behold the truth, the uncovered saying of the One, and the Aristotelian blueprint that lays out its logical parameters, limits and connectedness, now has in addition a path to transmuting this power of mind into a living way. By means of Paul's Christological cosmogony, people now have a precept (in contrast to the prescriptions that are inadequate for such an accomplishment) that does enable each and every one of them to appropriate divinity for him or her self.

PLOTINUS. Plotinus (204/5 – 270 AD) lived in a world that was undergoing epochal transitions. Plato set out to demolish the polytheistic and mythological world with one divined through reasoned intellection. Plotinus lived in a world where the nature of a Universe, which is commanded by a One, was being adumbrated and elaborated through all the permutations that the reasoning intelligence devised. We must understand that at this time, none of the separations of psychic functioning that we now take for granted had been identified or accomplished. No separation of self, intellect, and experience existed. So whatever the reasoning intellect divined, all that was given was thus true and commanding for the determination of life. All their realizations were considered to be fully metaphysical and philosophically universalistic, and therefore totally efficacious.

With a soaring intellection and a great power for expression, Plotinus sets out a dynamic frame of cosmic realization. He sets out a post-mythic creation story of tremendous scope and viability. Essentially, the idea boils down to this notion: the Godhead has "dimension." In the mythic account, a god with human-like or monstrous attributes exerts a power such that events transpire. Plotinus describes, not a "dimension" in the sense of a surface or range of space that can be measured, but rather he attests to there being a completely different mode, state or status of occurrence in the universe, one that is not amenable to the accomplishments of our categorial understanding. Plotinus thus, paradoxically, refers to a spaceless and timeless "dimension," one that we might call an *imaginary* dimension. It is analogous to the geometric point or line, which does not have any "real" counterpart in the natural world, but nevertheless has a functional "reality" that actively shapes the extensions proceeding from it, that comprise it, but, at the same time, only have the shape of the extensions that it does because of these "non-existent" factors. At their core, all creatures therefore bear an element of the godhead in their nature. All existents thus also bear a quality of the "unborn" and eternal in them: there is a residuum of what always as yet has not "existence" in their cores. And it is from this infinitesimal trace of the divinely emanative energy that the mystic realization also has its truth. All of existence emerges, burgeons forth from what is eternally inscrutable and is completely other – is thus "saturated" with this aspect of its arising (as a phenomenon).

PSEUDO-DIONYSUS: THE PRACTICE OF *APOPHASIS*. In the fourth century AD another remarkable figure in the mystic family made his appearance. This mysterious figure has no given name that we know of, but comes down to us with the appellations Dionysus the Aeropagite and Pseudo-Dionysus. He directly builds on, reinforces and concentrates the most mystical inferences from Paul and John into the seminal mystic expressive practice (described in the previous chapter), *"apophasis."* Apophasis is a process that is part of the forming of a precept in which the author "unsays" [6] just as much in the statement as he or she has just said. For instance we could imagine saying, on a clear day here in New Mexico, "The sky was so deep blue that it wasn't blue at all." We say something is blue but isn't. We could say, of course that the sky was some other color, and name it. But that is not the intent of the sentence. Instead we are expressing a relationship to the sky that exceeds any of our accustomed classifications. By making the statement we did, we are drawing attention away from the act of classifying and naming and putting the reader into our situation: one of experiencing something that we purposely do not want to be reduced to this mundane world.

In an essay of a few pages, Pseudo-Dionysus inscribes this practice into the mystic oeuvre:

> Trinity!!! Higher than any being,
> > Any divinity, any goodness!
> > Guide of Christians
> > > In the wisdom of heaven!
>
> Lead us up beyond unknowing and light,
> > Up to the farthest, highest peak
> > > Of mystic scripture,
> > Where the mysteries of God's Word
> > > Lie simple, absolute and unchangeable
> > > In the brilliant darkness of a hidden silence.

Amid the deepest shadow
> They pour overwhelming light
> On what is most manifest.

Amid the wholly unsensed and unseen
> They completely fill our sightless minds
> with treasures beyond all beauty [7]

The Mystic Arises

The great upsurge that gave rise to the full-blown (incarnate and living among us) mystic figure (or the mystic figuration of the aspiring mind) happens in the West, during the thirteenth and fourteenth centuries in what are referred to as the Low Countries of Europe (primarily the Germanic realm, but also in the Burgundy region of France, Flanders and the Netherlands). Mixing profound devotion to the life of the spirit with medieval notions of chivalry and romantic love, and an inveterate and irrepressible drive to express a new way of being human, mystics explode onto the scene. These people are women: educated, articulate, most of the landed noble classes, some abandoning their pastoral isolation for the newly burgeoning urban centers. Some, like Hadewijch and Mechthild of Magdeburg are irrepressibly sensual; others, like Marguerite Porete, are profoundly psychical and spiritual; all of them are consummately physically courageous (Porete, for example, was burned at the stake on June 1, 1310).

In this new mystic upsurge, two toweringly new realizations are brought into the mystic genealogy that literally reorganize the West's psychic structure — body and mind, intellect and emotions, one and all. This realization takes one's vision of the human situation beyond what any naïve theistic notions can accommodate. These epochal figures, whom we are about to introduce as the founders of the mystic genealogy, set the human endeavor on a journey on which we are only now fully embarked. Their mystic realization entails a radical, whole-psyche engagement with all that a single person's faith-for can embrace, opening out onto the inescapable precept that forbids being content with what is merely at hand in the institutionalized, conventional world of commerce, law and communication.

THE LATE MEDIEVAL WORLD: THE TWELFTH–THIRTEENTH CENTURIES. What are the forces that made this era so amenable to the "flowering" of mysticism?[8] That is the question that guides our all-too-brief survey of this exciting epoch in the human endeavor. Like all such eras in history, this is one in which emerging life forces contend with vestigial forms (in all their vibrant, horrible, and ecstatic manifestations) and generate a cauldron of unrest. One force was population growth in the newly forming urban centers. Between 1374 and 1482, Brussels saw its population increase from 20,000 to 33,000. Antwerp's population grew from 15,000 to 55,000 between 1437 and 1526.[9] Those may not sound like huge numbers to us, but we are used to large migrations and population increases. This was a new phenomenon to the residents and authorities in late Medieval times. And it was no isolated occurrence: the great urbanization movement that marks the modern era had begun in earnest in late medieval Europe.

Along with this came the rise of the bourgeois, burgher, or commercial class and its use of money. This is no small eventuation in the course of Western development. While trade, commerce, metallurgy and other activities of local production had been going on for eons, in the European urban context, the demands for speedy production, the creation of novel products, the easy processes of exchange (thus the rise of money, credit, banking) accumulated to form a distinctive way of life. One of its most distinctive features is that the search was set on its way to express abstract notions such as social credit, economic value and their active circulation in concrete specie (coin, notes, IOUs) in ways that were constructive and allowed for growth and larger-scale increases of wealth. This new way of life accordingly strengthened the need for establishing new cultural institutions and making their services available to ever-larger segments of the population (more and more of whom were needed to meet the expanding demands of these new ways). One of those cultural necessities was education. To feed this newly skilled group of artisans, merchants, traders, and money managers (bankers, lenders, insurers), the demand for education surged. As Simons reports:

> Starting in the twelfth century, merchants and other powerful groups in the main urban centers successfully challenged the Church, which since the early Middle Ages had controlled all educational institutions, and established secular schools that offered elementary instruction in reading, writing, and arithmetic. ...[Cities] subsidized elementary education for children of poor families. But in the fifteenth century, the larger cities also organized 'higher' or Latin schools comparable to those of the Church...New initiatives in schooling carried out from the late fifteenth century onward under the guidance of the *Devotio Moderna* and humanist scholars offered educational opportunities to an even greater number of children so that travelers to the Low Countries in the mid-sixteenth century noted with admiration that everyone could read and write, and there was a general interest in learning. [10]

Such a disruption signaled a new imperative: if one's sense of personal worth and status could benefit from learning new ways by means of education, such worth and status must be tied to the powers unleashed in one's spirit, in one's soul, in one's ability to aspire overall. And if this is the case in the commercial sphere, there must be an analogue of this valorization in the spiritual, religious world. While this burst in an educated "middle" class (between a landed aristocracy and a class of economic outcasts) was inevitable and necessary if a burgher class was to emerge, its unintended consequences were immense for the reigning orthodox church structure. Ideas about religious perfection proliferated. And these were not naïve, peasant-like sentiments, or fantastic chivalric simplicities. Some of these ideas were extremely sophisticated. New dualisms, new paths to perfection, new conceptions of the Christ story and its import were promulgated. Notions of how good and evil were manifested proliferated. These were dramatically enshrined in codes of conduct, ways of life, that anyone who so chose could participate in. The lines of the Reformation can clearly be seen here. But that is still far off.

The contest between the church and alternate forms of the religious path takes on new vigor. In this case, that provided a fertile milieu in which alternative and minority forms of religious expression were accorded a level of attention. These new ways of expression resonated with the search for new economic relations, and could not be easily dismissed. As they resonated and became more sophisticated in expression and incisive in their critiques of old, static, hierarchical ways, they started to impinge on habituated devotion to the more tired and ever-more vacuous forms of church, chivalry and aristocratic exclusiveness. Two other consequences flow from this that will be of immense importance in our story of the rising of the mystic: vernacular religion broke through the exclusivity of priestly intervention between people and their God. Our mystics all wrote in the languages of their people. Preaching was taken up by many, and eclipsed what the Latin-trained clergy could dish up on any given day. The latter were simply out-numbered. And second, women were educated in ever-greater numbers. And from these emerged a new stance for women, and then for the human endeavor: the Beguine Mystic.

The Beguine Women's Movement and the Founding of Western Mysticism

THE RESURGENT "FEMININE." Historically, or in terms of our epochs (in Western history), we note the following: the rise of western religion and philosophy is also marked by the rise and solidification of patriarchy and male hegemony. With the mystic insurgency, marked by the rise of the Beguine mystics in the thirteenth century, the forces of the feminine were reinstated in the process. The feminine passion for bodies being able to gestate and nurture new life, for a current arrangement of affairs to act as the bridging state of affairs for a new emergence, suddenly had a voice. And the Western world has never been the same. Set in motion, never to be stemmed, was the realization that the universe gave rise to, in a manner of "birthing" (increasing complexity), to all that is. [11] It is the feminine character of the universe itself that becomes the threshold of what human efficacy has access to at all; it is the feminine character of allowing ourselves to open to increasing complexity that fosters the drive toward modern notions of democracy and justice. The feminine is primary, originating, birthing and "beyond." This way of the mystic that we are learning to countenance in our attention, logic and encounters with our own aspirations takes the form it does because it expresses precisely and exactly the reassertion of the feminine.

FAITH-FOR AND FORE-GIVING: GENERATING SPACE. From out of this desert of recognition and oppression of women (except as objects of heraldic love exploits of quixotic males), came women who insisted on bringing their story of the life of the spirit, their way of living in a vastly changing world, into being. No account of the Beguine life underestimates the tremendous risk, scorn, derision, and oppression (including, in many accounts, violence and rape) these women faced as they embarked on this journey. And still, through variations and permutations, this movement lasted as an identifiable part of European life for five hundred years. [12]

The women of the Beguine movement carved out a distinctive niche within the cutting-edge social innovations of their day. On a personal level, women who were willing to strike out on these original paths rejected the outright social and sexual practices that were mired in misogynistic traditions of subjection and submission, while also evading any claims to priestly or scholarly exceptionalism that males were likely to defend to the death (the death of those women, that is). And then, to counterbalance their rather striking refusal of their assigned roles, they also offered the growing bourgeoisie something that was always in short supply – a source of cheap labor – mostly in the production of textiles (weavers). And some of these women, being educated and literate nobles, also provided utterly invaluable services to the new urban environments – becoming teachers of the new ways to the children of the rising bourgeoisie. And finally, since these burgher city-folk were preoccupied with their busy lives of money-making, they had little time to devote to developing a viable public sector. The Beguine women also provided services to the poor and outcast, education and other supports to the growing commercial sectors. For the social-climbing bourgeoisie, the invaluable services the Beguines provided were well worth the constrained independence these women demanded in return.

Another contributing factor to their success, and another controversial focal point in the scholarship, is the ties many of these women had to the aristocratic and growing wealthy burgher classes. According to later studies (Simons, Murk-Jansen, as opposed to Grundmann, for example), the early Beguines came largely from well-to-do families. Many were educated (as evidenced by the extreme literary breadth and depth of the Beguine mystics we will peruse below), and many came with wealth sufficient to establish themselves either in the community at large or as owners of private dwellings within court or convent Beguinages. As the movement matured, it attracted women of lesser means. Eventually, one of the factors contributing to the erosion of the communities, and their eventual disappearance, is that the Beguinages were victims of their own success, attracting more poor and indigent women than there were resources that could provide for them.

As with all women's movements, of course, this one encountered vicious and virulent assaults from the institutional authorities. Suspicion and derision started coming their way almost at the first appearance of these strange "new" women amid the throngs of the already disruptive urban populations. Even "Beguine" was intended as a term of derision.[13] It is easy to imagine scorn being heaped on these women for daring to defy convention and to totally dismiss the misogyny on which shallow male egos perpetuated their social, religious and economic hegemony. The condemnations sound strikingly similar to what we hear today about women's rightful place being in the home and in the role of child bearer and childcare giver.[14] But one charge is especially important for our narrative: the charge of rendering sacred texts and religious teaching in the vernacular, i.e., in the language of the common people. One of the most persistent critics of the Beguines, Guibert of Tournai, a Franciscan master of theology at Paris, in 1274 (the very height of the Beguine movement) put it this way:

> There are in our lands women called Beguines, and some of them are famous for their subtleties and enjoy speculating about novelties. They have interpreted the mysteries of Scripture and translated them in the common vernacular, although the best experts in Scripture can hardly comprehend them. They read these texts in common, without due respect, boldly in their little convents and in their workshops or even in public places...[15]

I love this passage for its completely uncomprehending acuity (if I can employ such an oxymoron) and condescending innuendo that echoes the bombast we hear even today. It points directly to the mystics we will be discussing shortly. For, as he says, their speculations about novelties *are* subtle, and they *are* difficult to comprehend. And they are so even today. They point to realizations of a way of living that certainly were breathtaking in their day, even as they are edgy today. Our point in all this is that it is from the hard and pioneering *lives* of these women that a mystic awakening of immense import ensues. We can look back at this time and into the lives (such as we have them) of the Beguine mystics and see in its entirety the course of the mystic life. The Beguines created with their very lives the "outside" of the mystic universe from which they spoke of new realizations about the human endeavor. At least one great person of that age, Meister Eckhart, realized the import of their work and made its impact undeniably felt even in the most cloistered and protected of institutional settings.[16]

But first, the great "trio of literary Beguines" as Barbara Newman calls them.[17]

THE BEGUINE MYSTIC TRIO

HADEWIJCH'S FIELD OF ENTHUSIASM. Hadewijch lived in the Low Country and wrote in the mid-thirteenth century. Little is known about her life, and since there were more than 111 pious women named Hadewijch throughout the twelfth and thirteenth centuries, there is little we can hope to learn about her. She either headed or founded a group of Beguines, and she was a literary master of highest merit. Clearly from the suppleness of her writing and its erudition, she was a well-educated woman. Bernard McGinn says of Hadewijch that not only is she the most difficult of the "literary trio" of the Beguine mystics to summarize, but also her "literary mastery surpasses that of any other medieval woman mystic..."[18] It is sad that this is all we know of her, and a symptom of the misogyny of the times. How much writing of prating male church bureaucrats do we have?[19]

Hadewijch's works comprise visions, poems and letters. In the work of Hadewijch, and for the succeeding Beguine mystics, "love" is assigned a new significance. From being a mysterious force acting between people to propel them together, love becomes a "place" of transformation in which it is realized that the truth of existence is union and community in the divine. This is not a static location in which people mill around in a daze, however. It is a place, a self-generated and self-constituted site, that could not have been precipitated by any human efficacy (the un-precipitated appearance of such a site is called "grace" in the religious context). In this site, dynamic and powerful forces are localized and concentrated. Think of a hurricane as a place amid the vast atmosphere of earth. No forces of earthly and mundane convention and/or constraint can survive here.

Hadewijch's journey to her Field of Enthusiasm is envisioned as one a troubadour would sing of as a journey of the heart, one that beloveds take toward each other. But the beloved she speaks of is Love, love itself — a "state" and condition viewed metaphorically as though it were a being. But this Love is not a beloved man she longed for in the flesh, but brings to a full-blown image the way her whole psyche concentrated Love into a manner and way of being, And this way is what we now can appreciate as the devotion to her faith-for that is enacted in her free acts of fore-giving. Look at the Poem in Stanzas #17, "Under the Blow":

1

When the season is renewed,
Although mountain and valley
Are everywhere dark and colorless,
    The hazelnut tree is already in bloom:
While the lover of Love has a sad lot,
    He too shall grow in every way.

2

What use are joy or springtime to him
Who gladly took delight in Love
And never finds in the wide world
    One whom he can trust or rest in—
To whom he can freely say: "Beloved it is you
    Who can utterly satisfy me!"

3

What joy can surround
Him whom Love has thrown into close confinement,
When he wishes to journey through Love's immensity

And enjoy it as a free man in all security?
More multitudinous than the stars of heaven
    Are the griefs of love.

4

The number of my griefs must be unuttered,
My cruel burdens must remain unweighed:
Nothing can be compared to them,
    So it is best to give up the attempt.
Though my share of griefs is small, I have borne it;
    I shudder that I exist.

. . .

6

O proud souls who stand as if on Love's side
And live freely under her protection,
Pity one who is disowned, whom love overwhelms
    And pursues in a despairing exile!
Alas! Let whoever can observe reason live free with
reason:
    My hear lives in despair.

7

For I saw a shining cloud rise
Over all the dark sky; and its form seemed so beautiful,
I fancied I would soon with full happiness
    Play freely in the sunlight;
But my joy was only a fancy!
    If I should die of it, who would blame me?

. . .

10

Fortunate is he who can wait
Until Love give him all in exchange for his all.
O God! What is patience to me?
     To wait, on the contrary, gives me greater joy,
For I have abandoned myself wholly to Love
     But woe has treated me all too harshly.

11

This is all too hard for the lover;
To stray after Love without knowing where,
Be it in darkness or in daylight,
     In wrath or in lovingness; Were Love
To give her true consolation unmistakably,
     This would satisfy the exiled soul.

. . .

13

Oh, what I mean had have long meant
God has indeed shown to noble souls,
To whom he has allotted the torments of love
     To give them fruition of Love's nature;
Before the All unites itself to the all,
     Sour bitterness must be tasted.

Love comes and consoles us; she goes away and knocks us
     down
     This initiates our adventure.
But how one grasps the All with the all,
     Alien rustics will never know. [20]

When my mentees with mystic aspirations read this material, they immediately recognize this quality of feeling. Her depiction of the Field of Enthusiasm is alive, vibrating with life-generating energy: *fruition,* she calls it. And this notion of *fruition* is her true bequeathal to the genealogy of the mystic. The notion is a variant on "love," on the insistence of free giving, of Fore-giving that characterizes the mystic ethic. And, consistent with its Beguine context, it breaks the momentum of misogyny that had enshrouded mysticism, and still entrances philosophers.

Why is this place one of "love" rather than Hell if it is so destructive of the everyday? Because in Hadewijch's way, "Love" is the name given to her immense and pulsing Field of Enthusiasm. Within it whole new realizations, whole new possibilities of living, gestate and are born. And, for the mystic, this coming into life within this field becomes the guiding salient of their lives. They do not so much "have love" or experience "love," as they feel themselves to be utterly created by the love, the generation and fruition this place makes into an irrevocable necessity.

MECHTHILD OF MAGDEBURG: THE OVERFLOWING, VITAL LIFE OF FAITH-FOR

> I do not know how to write, nor can I, unless I see with the eyes of my soul and hear with the ears of my eternal spirit and feel in all the parts of my body the power of the Holy Spirit.
>
> ~ *The Flowing Light of the Godhead* (IV, 13)

Everything about Mechthild (1210 - 1297) is a matter of *overflowing.* First, just her incredibly long life overflows the usual boundaries of medieval life, by a factor of two! Her way of living completely overflowed the strictures of the life allowed for a medieval woman. Not only was she a Beguine from an early age – she received her first calling at the age of twelve – but she did not become part of any established

Beguine community until she was in her sixties, when she was too infirm, and of too poor eyesight, to withstand the persecutions to which she and her sisters were subjugated. Then, when she joined a community, it was the one at Cistercian Helfta, already known for its excellence in producing pious literature; there she mentored other outstanding woman mystics including The Abbess, Gertrude the Great and Mechthild of Hackeborn. Finally, her writings. These works broke out of the strictures of convention by being presented in the vernacular, not the accredited Latin of institutional texts; and overflowed in their willingness to advocate for the Beguine life in defiance of male conventional and institutional condemnation. A life of overflowing, indeed.

Mechthild's opus itself was written over a lifetime. Comprising seven books, it seems to have a chronological feel. In the early volumes, one is more likely to see the images of erotic overflowing than one does in the later volume. Book VII in particular seems like a retrospective on a mystic journey from a vantage point of great maturity. The outline of Mechthild's work and realization of her mystic life is contained in this oath:

> Genuine pure love of God has four things about it that never rest. The first is growing desire, the second is flowing suffering, the third: burning sensation in soul and body, the fourth: constant union bound to great vigilance.
> (IV, 15)

Overflowing. While Mechthild's faith-for is expressed as her love and her bridal relation to God, what is most striking to me is the way the relation is *affective* for her. She writes not to portray the vision and its consequences so much as to express how a life feels when such a relation is not only possible, but also necessary.

> O you pouring God in your gift!
> O you flowing God in your love!
> O you burning God in your desire!
> O you melting God in the union with your beloved!

> O you resting God on my breasts!
> Without you I cannot exist. (I, 17)

Immediately we sense the flowing, unstructured nature of her experiencing – its completely open faith-for way. The words "pouring…flowing… burning…melting…resting" convey an all- or-nothing psychic stance. No fine distinctions of psychic differentiation into internal or external, analytic or relational are made here. And what are the relations into which these psychic energies flow: "gift…, love…, desire…, union…, my breasts." All of these are notions of unrestrained passage, unconstrained feeling, a dissolving of object and boundary. A few passages later on, she says: "Under this immense force she loses herself…In this pure clarity she is both dead and living." (I, 22) Oh, the power that is burgeoning forth here.

What could be clearer? This is a psyche so soft, so cloudlike in its effervescence, that union with all the powers and energies that pour into the living world seems as natural and easy as a stream flowing over a rock. While others with firm psyches and functional dispositions and preferences would have to crash and shatter their way through to some glimmer of light, to Mechthild it is simply a matter of flow, of allowing the wetness of the undifferentiated surrounding to surge forth as faith-for what (as a saturating phenomenon) comes. Her answer presages Porete: abandon the will:

HOW A PERSON WHO LOVES TRUTH SHOULD PRAY

The person who loves truth likes to pray thus: "Ah, dear Lord grant me and help me that I always seek you in a holy manner with all my five sense in all things, for I have chosen you in preference to all lords and all sovereigns as Bridegroom of my soul. Grant me also Lord, that I might find you with all my longing burning or spent though it be. I desire also that I may enjoy you with the flowing love of all your gifts.

> Give me Lord abundantly your outflowing, that it fill my heart and mind so that pain, scorn, and bitterness may ever feel pleasant to me. Grant me that it may ever turn out that way for me though your favor, generous God; now grant me this.
>
> Help me also, Lord to keep you by giving up completely my one will according to your desire. Then I would ever, ever lose that love that never ceases to burn. Amen."
> (VII, 15)

Life from this vantage point is one of total humility: of a realization of living in which horizons extend out and out over a teeming ocean (to use a Nietzschean metaphor), a vastness for which one can only abide in a spirit of faith-for. One "returns" to the carnal world as if sinking, as if one's ardor is being cooled, as if one's pressing efficacy is slowed by immersion in molasses. One is totally alive with the energies of that field, but utterly constrained by the tiny threads of habit and language into which the social being, the role-taker and perceived and adjudged individual must abide.

> The soul, rich in love sinks downward under the pull of profound humility and constantly retreats from what God does to her out of love...The body too, sinks far down when it serves its enemy, obeys without complaint, and avoids its friends to God's honor. The soul sinks deeper still because she has more strength than the body. She sinks with great zeal to the lowest place that God holds in his power. Oh, how dare I name this place for those who know nothing of sinking humility.

And for Mechthild, this is the ethic that she can know: for all of this living in the desert, for all of this wrenching from out of contentment into a state of endless pursuit of this love and continuity of flowing energy in the field of enthusiasm, one praises it. Either one takes up the life of faith-for, or there is no life — from the perspective of the mystic's aspirations, that is.

"When our human understanding grows dark, / with the lament in our heart we awaken divine love." (VII, 31) ""Give me everything that is yours," says Mechthild's Lord, "and I shall give you everything that is mine." (VII, 55).

MARGUERITE PORETE AND THE ETHIC OF FORE-GIVING [21]
[These quotations are from a dialogue between characters in Porete's book:]

> **The Soul by Faith:** And we see [the glorified humanity] by the virtue of Faith, in contradicting the reason of our mind, which sees nothing there but bread, nor anything else not felt or tasted or smelled. But our faith contradicts all these for it believes firmly, without doubt, that there is neither whiteness, or odor, nor taste, but it is the true precious body of Jesus Christ who is true God and true man. *Thus we see it by faith.* [Brackets in the text; italics mine — MHS].

> **Courtesy of the Goodness of Love:** …for I can tell you surely, without being blamed, that no one can arrive at a profound depth nor to a high edification, if he does not arrive there through the subtlety of a great natural sense and through the sharpness of the Light of Intellect of the Spirit. And this one cannot know very much in petitioning the divine will. For Intellect, which gives light, shows to the soul what she loves by her nature. And the Soul receives the approach and the juncture through Light of Intellect and through Concord of Union in Fertile Love, she receives the being toward which she tends in order to have her rest and repose.

> ~ from Chapter 15, *The Mirror of Simple Souls*

Marguerite Porete exemplifies the ethic of the classical, mystic aspiring in its mode of fore-giving. With her we enter another dimension of the mystic genealogy where living according to the dynamics of this ethic is no longer a tentative matter that has to be vindicated and validated, as it is still with her precursor sisters. The vividness of her mystic personhood lives on in her work and her legend. We know practically nothing of her life, but can glean some clues from her writing. She was clearly an educated woman. She was clearly knowledgeable about the religious literature of her day. She was an outsider even among the outsider Beguine community, as her soul's song (Chapter 132) belies. She must have presented a remarkable force of personhood to her times and community. The power of her certitude in presenting her mystic life brooks no compromise. I am sure she behaved the same way: no compromise, and no little disdain for those who were uncomprehending of her way. For her pains she was derided as a *"pseudo mulier,"* an imposter of a woman, and burned at the stake.

In 1310 she was condemned as a heretic. Her crime was alleged to be a matter of the content of her work, of course, but her execution seems to have stemmed from something else, from that *behavior* we spoke of, the ethic to which she held fast, without compromise. At the time of her trial, she had sent out her book to noted ecclesiastic authorities, who gave it their seal of approval. So the accusation that her book constituted a heretical writing was, at best, tenuous. But what sealed her fate is that she refused to respond, honor, or acknowledge the legitimacy of her accusers. She answered their pointed accusations with complete silence. And this defiance, as you can imagine, was too much for the august body of the self-proclaimed righteous to endure. The inquisitors gave her three chances to answer their charges, and still she refused to respond. On June 1, 1310, she was burned at the stake. Her persecution marks the beginning of the institutional oppression of the Beguines.

Her little book was supposed to have been banished and likewise destroyed. But, the censure was not executed perfectly. In one instance, maybe the most significant, the work came under the scrutiny of Meister Eckhart. One year after her execution, the great Eckhart was summoned to oversee the same Paris Dominican order that had issued the sentence. [22] Rather than merely repeat the sterile theologies of his peers, this great mystic heard the voice of Porete and heeded its resonances with his own generative mysticism. It is thought that his great Sermon 58, on the poverty of the soul (in which he prays to God to be free of God), written when he was under investigation, was a devotion to her. Such is the legend.

Her work circulated anonymously for centuries, having influence on many of the great seventeenth-century mystics, including Juan de la Cruz (also condemned, and eventually exonerated). It was only in 1946 that this text was connected with Porete, fully restoring her to her rightful place in the mystic genealogy. That feat alone validates the truth of the legend.

The Book. *The Mirror of Simple Souls* comprises a dialogue among several characters who share a stake in the mystic life. The dialogue form has the advantage of dispensing with a lot of narrative and getting right to the points the imagined characters want to make. The book springs out at the reader with this kind of bold directness. The characters are engaged in a militant conversation: establishing the rightful pre-eminence, attitude and ethic of the mystic life. They are not equivocating with each other. Dame Love, the driving force of the dialogue, has her disciple, The Soul, to testify to the effects of her power. They both speak directly to (male) Reason, who as we see from the opening epigram is vanquished to his death (even though he reappears mysteriously several chapters after he proclaims his own passing). Other speakers drop in and make their comments and then disappear, indicating that Porete has no concern for dramatic consistency. In the life of the mystic, voices and presences are merely fleeting phenomena.

There is one other significant character, named "FarNearness." This (male) character is referred to but does not speak. There are many ways to think of this character: as an Eckhartian "Godhead;" as a member of the Trinity, an august Father, so to speak; or as a direct apparition of God's quality of being both near enough for one to experience momentarily, but also always vanishing, distant and ungraspable in any way. In the dialogue the character acts as a paradoxical vanishing point – a character who has a definite voice and "personality" that generates the energies experienced by the other characters and yet is always at a distance – and this at the same time: both palpable and sensed and ever becoming distant, both invoking the sense of a relation being offered and then having that offer pull one's reach into an ever-receding oblivion. [23] FarNearness is first mentioned (in Chapter 58) as "a spark in the manner of an aperture and quick closure" in the advancing life of the mystic (Porete's Fifth and Sixth stages, of seven stages), "as long as His work remains and endures."

I can begin to appreciate what the notion of FarNearness sets in motion when I take it as being a (fictionalized, imaginative) personification of the Field of Enthusiasm itself: so utterly beyond any "place" to which we can physically travel, yet immanently generative of the mystic sense of (what constitutes the most important) place at all. It is so expressive that it takes on personality, a quality of reaching out and having an effect. This is no mere dramatic device either. We will see how Meister Eckhart grasps his field of enthusiasm also as a living force, a "Godhead" beyond God. This "ground" is a place of teeming generativity, a generativity that Porete anticipates with the full vitality that such a psychic resource requires of us.

Lastly, the book is about the final two stages of a seven-stage process of coming to mystic communion with God (for us, coming to live freely and fully with and within the energies at play in the field of enthusiasm).

Annihilation of the Soul. Marguerite Porete is best known for her theme of the "annihilation of the soul" as the way to God. Attendant with that is her startling declaration of how this soul, so annihilated, has no use for the virtues. She makes no attempt to hide what the premise of her mystic work is. In Chapter Five, three pages into her narrative, she declares it:

OF THE LIFE WHICH IS CALLED THE PEACE OF CHARITY IN THE ANNIHILATED LIFE.

Love: Thus there is another life, which we call the peace of charity in the annihilated life. Of this life, says Love we wish to speak, in asking what one could find:

1. A Soul

2. who is saved by faith without works

3. who is only in love

4. who does nothing for God

5. who leaves nothing to do for God

6. To whom nothing can be taught

7. From whom nothing can be taken

8. Nor given

9. And who possesses no will.

Now, can we read anything that is clearer? This is the purest act of fore-giving. Its propositions are numbered in case you tend to flake out in reading long paragraphs. And, the consequences of the proposition are astounding – worthy of the stake to some.

First, "annihilation of the soul" means just that: all the holier than thou notions of virtuous desire, of blessed grace from God, of meritorious deeds or pious contemplation as ways to God are dispensed with, by the time of the seventh and final stage that promises the fulfillment of the mystically aspiring life – achieving the ethic of fore-giving.

"The best that I can tell you is that if you understand perfectly your nothingness you will do nothing, and this nothingness will give you everything...As God has transformed you into Himself, so also you must not forget your nothingness." (Ch. 34) And again, "What is its rule? It is that she is dissolved by annihilation into that prior existence where Love has received her..." (Chapter 137)

The virtues are useless and a distraction. "So this soul has gained and learned so much with the Virtues that she is now superior to the Virtues, for she has within her all that the Virtues know how to teach and more, without comparison. This Soul has within her the mistress of the Virtues, whom one calls Divine Love, who has transformed her completely into herself, is united to her, and which is why this Soul belongs neither to herself nor to the Virtues." (Ch. 21) The virtues, after all, have nothing to do with God, but with merit and safety on earth.

Thus we cannot "petition" God for that which we would even know how to petition. (Chapter 106) – a startling conclusion. Think of all the prayers to win football games, hit home runs, win wars...How completely foolish and egotistical these petty petitions are, pressing one's own needs above those of others. Is this a worthy vision of one's God? Porete dispatches such feeble pretenses with disdain.

What is required is a free giving away of one's self-named, self-serving, even self-determined desires:

> **Soul:** You see how He has freely given me my free will...He has given me nothing more...For insofar as He has given me free will by His pure goodness, He has given me all things, if my will wills. He does not withhold otherwise, of this I am certain.
>
> **Fear:** And how, for God's sake, Lady Soul, has He given you all things, says fear?
>
> **Soul:** In this, says the Soul, that I have freely given him

my will, nakedly, without holding anything back, for the sake of His goodness and for the sake of His will alone, in the same way He gave it to me by His divine will for the sake of my profit, by His divine goodness..." (Ch. 104)

Without a Why. Then there is "life without a why" – the way of foregiving. This is a revolutionary notion in the context of growing urbanism, mercantilism and money culture. In such a setting all life is validated according to its purpose. Certainly we see that in our own "pragmatic" culture, where people search for what "purpose" God intends them, or mollify their hurt feelings with the old saw, "Everything has a purpose." In this pedestrian line of conception, God himself has a purpose, or several purposes: Creator, Judge, Granter of victories for the petitioners.

Porete regards such pseudo piety with disdain:

> Such a Soul, says Love is in the greatest perfection of being and she is closest to the Farnearness, when she no longer takes Holy Church as exemplar in her life. The Soul is thus under the work of Humility, and so is beyond the work of Poverty and above the work of Charity [*the approvedVirtues*]. She is so far from the work of the Virtues that she cannot understand their language. But the works of the Virtues, who obey the Soul without contradiction are completely enclosed within such a soul, and because of this enclosure, Holy Church does not know how to understand her. Holy Church singularly praises Fear of God for saintly Fear of God is one of the gifts of the Holy Spirit. Still, Fear of God would destroy the being of freeness, if she could penetrate such being. But perfect freeness possesses no why. (Chapter 134)

No virtues, no why, no purpose: what are we left with? I think this is the set of questions that frightens the authorities the most, now and then. The fear that such a person evades their grasp, sets up a logic that clarifies a sense of living that lies beyond the claims on which their authority depends, and, thereby sets up an alternative regime of sense and meaning (and a strangely generative power). What can they hold over her head as threat or lure? And then, of course, her actual behavior in the court of inquisition vindicates all their fears. "And the One in whom she is does His work through her, for the sake of which she is entirely freed by the witness of God Himself, says Love who is the worker of this work to the profit of this Soul who no longer has within her any work." (Chapter 41) What employer could hear that and not recoil in horror?

Eckhart

> While I stood in my first cause, I had no God, and I was my own. I willed not, I wanted not, for I was conditionless being, the knower of myself in divine thought; then I wanted myself and I wanted nothing else; what I willed I was and what I was I willed. I was free from God and all things. But when I escaped from my free will to take on my created nature, then I got me a god; fore before creatures were, God was not God: he was that he was… Wherefore we pray we may be quit of God…[24]

> Why I pray God to rid me of God is because conditionless being is above God and above distinction: it was therein I was myself, therein I willed myself and knew myself to make this man and in this sense I am my own cause, both of my nature which is eternal and of my nature which is temporal. For this am I born, and as to my birth which is eternal I can never die. In my eternal mode of birth I have always been and now and shall eternally remain. That which I am in time shall die and come to naught, for it is of the day and passes with the day. In my birth all things were born, and I was the cause of mine own self and all

things, and had I willed it I had never been nor any thing and if I had not been then God had not been either.

...I flowed out of God then all things said, There is a God. [25]

In Eckhart the classical mystic figure is consolidated, elevated and completed. By fully enacting the inheritances of the Beguine mystics and the dynamic aspects of the speculative mystic tradition, he comprehends the field of enthusiasm as a self-generating effusion of generative creativity. With Eckhart, faith-for is legitimated by the full array of cultural, religious and intellectual rigors that can be mustered to the cause. The world opens, for the first time in Western history, as its own generative condition, without a why, in infinite, concrete and actual play as the locus of the best of human transformative efficacy. In terms that take this efficacy to its maximal expression, and in marshaling the conceptual tools available to him at the time, in order to the bring faith-for to the fore, he is unsurpassed.

ECKHART AND THE BEGUINES. Eckhart's mysticism was inspired by the Beguines. His own "simple soul" was aroused by their mystic ways, as his sermon "The Good Housewife" attested. He concluded this sermon with this invocation:

'She had no fear for the winter with her household doubly clad,' as the scripture tell of her. She was clothed with strength to withstand imperfection and was adorned with the truth. To all appearance, this woman was rich and had the world at her feet, but in secret she knelt at the shrine of true poverty. And when her outward comforts failed she fled to him to whom all creatures flee, setting at naught the world and self. In this way she transcended self, despising men's despisery and not minding it, for all she had in mind was the tending of the sick and the cleansing of the foul, which she managed by dint of her

> pure heart. Even so let us look to the ways of our house
> and not eat the bread of idleness. [26] (Pfeiffer, LII, "The
> Good Housewife")

In this passage I see a reflection of the way the Beguines responded to the force of urbanization, by carving out a new form of life for women. First, he saw certain forms of living coming to nothing, being dissolved and abandoned. He saw all that is, all "being" disrupted by a great, larger-than-life event. What did this say of a "natural order" for the human endeavor? It said there was never such an order. Then he saw people creating new ways of life, new forms of production, commerce and, in the Beguines, new conceptions of human relations. What did this say of the generative capability of humans, viewed individually and collectively? It said this: somehow humans are completely capable of generating new ways of living *ex nihilo,* from nothing. Finally, he saw new varieties of spirituality coming into being: Beguine spirituality, to be sure, but also a proliferation of other modes of spiritual realization as well. This spirituality at once celebrated the power of the human spirit, and also placed it in greater proximity to and dependence on God.

Eckhart asks: "What are we to make of God when we see so many grand, significant, liberating changes all around us – none of which were prayed for, none of which were foretold in institutionally interpreted scripture? What are we to make of such a colossal reorientation of all the significant relations one had thought God held dear?" This level, scale and intensity of change disclosed to Eckhart nothing less than *generativity without source:* a generatively creative force unleashed by the human endeavor that was without precedent. So Eckhart's God was different from the one that was merely a distant and remote personified "creator" who is jealous for his kingdom. The world is not made up of static entities such as man, nature, and God (and his tripling progeny) were conceived of. Unnamable forces of tremendous power continually change man and uproot nature. And God? What must a God be such that this occurs? Certainly not one who is satisfied with creation and then enforces its stasis. Certainly not one who would kill his own son merely to have his superiority over this suffering world made manifest. Certainly not one who is preoccupied with the "sins" that people commit in their soon-to-be-surpassed circumstances. None of those formulations made sense any longer. And so Eckhart *reconceived God* so as to account for the true generativity he saw in evidence all around him.

While the Beguines attested to the new facts on the ground, Eckhart intuited the need to *think anew*. When, since Plato, had this proposition been put before a court of peers? In Eckhart's hands, a project of Nietzschean scale, of a revaluation of all values, is proposed. I see Eckhart's realization as this: if all relations between man and nature can be so completely overturned, then there are no "rules" from on high by which human life is bound. And if God is of such a nature that these rules are not of his nature, what must that nature be? And, of course, what must this God be? Indeed, our notions of change, of nature and of God all stand in need of transformation. Surely God cannot be satisfied with a one-time "creation" and then set rules and moralities in place that enforce this world in an everlasting stasis. The conclusion from this line of thought is far-reaching and radical: This God must be of a different nature than one of a conserving, obedience-demanding Father, who, by the way, is willing to sacrifice his Son to commend his own glory. Eckhart thus dares to speak of a God that is nothing, creates nothing, founds nothing, but instead presents what can only be a God of generative potencies.

Eckhart thus opened the mystic way, removed any interim barrier, and cleared the open all the way to the edge. This clearing, devoid of any false or partial attachments, entails a different ethic, a different way of undertaking the human endeavor: only fore-giving what one must hold in one's faith-for will do. This is the edge that faith-for continually drives onward, beyond what has a name or can be possessed or even strived for and so can only be undertaken in a life that courageously fore-gives. The mysticism of Eckhart is where we begin to contemplate this faith-for as a concrete life's way, and fore-giving as a viable, even necessary, ethic.

He is the figure who lays out a living ethic that each mystic person can take up in his or her way. With Eckhart's work, the mystic way is set as a course of its own and utterly breaks out to a new realization of the human endeavor.

ECKHART'S "GROUND": SELF-CREATING WHOLENESS. To a degree never before attained, Eckhart explicated the notion of the mystic *open* — his work fully explored the utterly free play of energies that have no given form and cannot be assigned any prescribed attribute. While this notion has its predecessors in Plato (the light in which nothing is seen, beheld by the escapee from the cave, for instance), Eckhart, following on and elaborating the work of the Beguine trio, among others, transforms this excessively brilliant realm into a *field* that is no longer a remote beyond, but instead constitutes a "beyond" that resides right in the very core of the human soul itself. We call this "beyond" our aspiration and aspiring mind. But, of course, Eckhart had no access to such a formulation. The terms he had available were theological, were matters taken up by the Christology of his time and by the conceptualizations of God's cosmic powers that demarcated the human realm versus that of the heavenly and divine. Eckhart broached those boundaries,[27] for the most daring and distinctly human devotion and effort. All modern and contemporary notions about human knowledge as an endeavor that actually engages with the total and real "truth" of the cosmos require this momentous shift in how this great cosmic power is to be regarded and valued. It is not that we are equal or adequate to these forces or the "Godhead," by any means. However, in the place of the mythic formulations that leave the human endeavor cowering before its might, the mystic Eckhart sets out the demand that we stride into that energy, headlong. And, by means of the other factors in Eckhart's vision that we will enumerate shortly, he expresses how the means to do so are also parts of our human efficacy.

These ways, to be sure, are mystic: we encompass this great power in our Fields of Enthusiasm, which we take up as our life in and for faith-for, such that our "striding" toward the Godhead is nothing other than an act of fore-giving. Technology and trade are most decisively not the ways; conforming and submitting to convention are not in any way even remotely akin to the strides he envisions.

> What God has given and what God has promised to give is indeed amazing, incomprehensible, and unbelievable. This is indeed as it should be, for if these things were comprehensible and believable something would be wrong. God is in all things. The more he is in things, the more he is outside of them; the more he is within, the more he is outside. I have already said many times that God creates this entire world fully and totally in this present now. All that God created six thousand years ago and more, when he made the world, he creates right now and all together. [28]

This sensibility may be one that only a mystic could have. How do we grasp this sense? First, we experience an occurrence as faith-for and fore-giving, then we do the work to express the precept that ensues. In the terms we have developed here, we might say that the Eckhartian mystic course lays out this way: We "go forth" into our experiencing in the stance of faith-for, that is, in movement that is at least bi-directional: one direction oriented to the "World" assemblage (as described in Chapter Three) that comes, is utterly "other" and "excessive," and that also generates its affects on our beings; we are the "threshold" on which these affects take hold and generate life ways. What the life way of faith-for entails then is restraint, detachment, and also a strict denial of the luxury of any so-called ecstatic "release," which merely disperses these potentially generative energies into oblivion and futility.

We deny such fleeting pleasures of release, and also we deny our habituated notions of exchange, of cause and effect, of chains of habituated sequences (shades of Hume's eighteenth-century skepticism) in order to demand of our psyche that it do the work of discerning, learning and then expressing that accompanies the radical acts of fore-giving. Eckhart's "detachment" can be considered as one form of this fore-giving: not passively "taking" whatever comes, but actively engaging what comes in an affirming response that forms the psyche into specific ways that give right into the teeth of what is occurring. The occurring is thus enhanced and amplified thereby; and the experiencing person, the one who is fore-giving, does the work of attuning to acts that both amplify and resound right along with occurrence. This is not a matter of rapture or of dissolving into "oneness," but rather a completely responsive seeking of ways to engage in an attunement (not an "at-one-ment") with the most active, generative and formative aspects of the occurrence. What else, in Eckhart's mind (not having the notion of an aspiring mind available to him), could this exertion of fore-giving be but the way of God (as opposed to, of course, being the Godhead itself)?

HEARING THE PRECEPT. Eckhart envisioned that the work of the human endeavor, in light of this way of God, is to *hear* and then *express* the *precept* into our sensing of the scene. That precept then places before us a notion of emergent generativity, Eckhart's Godhead; that is whatever is generative in this notion has not only been produced by or emanates from the generative and lies there as an inert result (a thing or object), but is itself also generative, and so on and so on in the great surge of the generative. This is a figuration of the mystic "World," in a depiction of the Iconic Imago, the Field of Enthusiasm: generativity without reservation, all of a cosmic "giving-its-all" that from moment to moment, that in each morsel, pulsation, volume (all the words that attempt to present a substantiality without having a distinctive formation in which it comes to rest) comes forth as nothing other than all-that-it-is and more. To this immense, irrepressible and overflowing "World," the person finds it within herself (in all the ways that the Beguine mystics gloriously evoked) a way to insist that whatever formed and convinced ego there is (that actively resists just such a demand, craving its own (re)vindication) give way, fore-give to that very generativity.

> "In the kingdom of the heavens all is in all, all is one and
> all is ours. The bliss that Our Lady possesses is all mine—

when I am there—and in no way as flowing and emanating from Mary, but dwelling in me as my proper good, not as derived from elsewhere. And thus I say: what someone possesses in the beyond, another possesses equally – not as acquired from him or taken from him, but as dwelling in himself, so that the grace which is in the one is fully also in the other exactly as one's own grace. [Italics added for emphasis – MHS]. [29]

In this explosive passage, which was specifically called out and condemned by his inquisitional judges, Eckhart declares his precept: all there is, is cosmic generativity, coming to us all; and, continuing on, once it is ours it still remains of that cosmically generative nature – even as it is ours. Surpassing even "wholeness" or even One, or even "God the Father," faith-for entails a complete permeation of generative energies within and emanating out to its own generative multiplicity.

FAITH-FOR AS DETACHMENT. Eckhart's notion of detachment resonates with our notion of "faith-for."

> "...then how should I love God?" You should love God unspiritually, that is your soul should be unspiritual and stripped of all spirituality, for so long as your soul has a spirit's form it has images, and so long as it has images, it has a medium, and so long as it has a medium, it has no unity or simplicity. Therefore your soul must be unspiritual, free of all spirit, and must remain spiritless; for if you love God as he is God, as he is spirit, as he is person and as he is image – all this must go! "Then how should I love him?" You should love him as he is a non-God, a nonspirit, a nonperson, a nonimage, but as he is a pure unmixed being "One" separated from all duality; and in that One we should eternally sink down, out of "something into nothing." [30]

In our notion of faith-for, the mystic's orientation is directed toward that Field of Enthusiasm. Those things going on in the immediately experienced milieu certainly do exert their inertial forces and so pull even the mystic's attention toward the "stuff" and the "ideas" out of which we construct our "reality." But to say that the mystic's attention and concern are oriented toward faith-for the Field of Enthusiasm means that the "World" of pressing and vividly affecting saturating phenomena is literally – as flesh, face and voice – at stake in the mystic's body and soul from moment to moment. In the mystic's aspirations, there is precious little to relate to, barely trace remainders available for engaging in a living relationship in our technically, socially, economically and legally prescribed everydayness. All the partial selections and filtered exclusions that have been exercised on the multiply dimensioned saturating phenomena in order to make way for our commerce and production leave little to engage in the way of aspiration, faith-for and fore-giving.

"NOTHING" (WITH A WINK AND A NOD, THAT IS). Eckhart is thus speaking apophatically, or ironically or maybe even sarcastically, when he declaims the "nothing." This "nothing" that Eckhart refers to is hardly a blank and empty abyss that is powerless to affect us. It is certainly a "nothing" in comparison to the hard verities, instruments, money and artifacts that were starting to fill up his environment. This "nothing" announces the act of *detaching* from those things. Detaching does not mean destroying them or abandoning their use (becoming ascetic or vegan); but just letting them arise and pass away in their own manner, and not assigning any value to them whatsoever. And also, not replacing these with other "things" – even ideas or gods or even (as we will see shortly) "God". Rather, detaching entails a stance in which one opens up, opens out, so as to allow vital forces to do their work – in all their unpredictable, unknowable ways. Detachment is thus the opening salvo, the cutting edge of faith-for. Instead of attaching to all the names and prescribed formulas that carve up what occurs, the mystic opens up to what as yet has no name, as yet has not produced results or effects, and yet comes in a way that is as real and poignant as a moist morning breeze. It is thus not at all "nothing" that detachment opens on to, but rather the fullness of the powers exerted on one's being by the saturating phenomena of the "World" assemblage (described in Chapter Three).

WITHOUT A "WHY." Detachment means *cutting free,* but it also means *letting be.* What is cut, in Eckhart's view, is only what has been superfluously added (albeit productively so, in a mundane sense) to the vitality at the heart of things, and it does not affect the substance or the processing of those things. Thus, cutting is done by a "twisting free," a squiggling and wriggling action, in place, that only changes one's own status, one's own range of motion, one's own horizons of prospective movement. What is cut is only the stricture, only the binding; and it is only cutting what is amenable to being cut in the first place: all the add-ons and artifacts that weigh down our aspirations.

What do "whys" do to us? In creative moments, asking "why" spurs us to undertake deeper analytical reasoning about the causes of our states of affairs. Once our conclusions are reached, however, these rationales turn into their counterparts: they entrench us in the behaviors our reasoning has prescribed. Asking "why" becomes a rhetorical question, serving only to help us identify the validating and reinforcing signposts along the way that reward us for our sagacity, or remind us to get back to our prescribed paths, digging us deeper into the canyons of our habits.

What happens when we give up these "whys"? Without the reinforcements of these rhetorically deployed "whys" (that is, without these perpetually repeated rationales), what do we have? We have some kind of connection to what is occurring and our psychic abilities (both habituated and not) to engage.[31] And we have risk. We may change. We may not be validated. We may discover something about ourselves that is as unsettling as it is undeniable. That is why *detachment* is the core of Eckhart's ethic, and why it is so forbidding. It is not proposed as a nihilist denial of the "reality" of our state of affairs. It is a living on an edge, facing in two directions at once, a living that is at once capable of displacing the primacy of the given state of affairs, and, apophatically at the same time, of being ensconced in faith-for the open's sway. Detachment then cuts twice: it cuts *away* the presumed power of the given and then, when cultivated as a way, it cuts one's need for these prescriptions. And so, it also affirms twice (as in Derrida's "yes, yes"): it affirms that one lives without a why, and then it affirms the flesh, face and voice of what comes of that generative arising. Or, to put it in another way, detachment allows faith-for's power to rise to the fore, and enable the mystic, you or me, to say, *I choose the powers that can change me.*

What Faith-For Achieves: Breakthrough to Fore-Giving.

> While I stood in my first cause [in contact with the generative power, the godhead] I had no God, and I was my own. I willed not, I wanted not, for I was conditionless being, the knower of myself in divine thought; then I wanted myself and I wanted nothing else; what I willed I was and what I was I willed. I was free from God and all things. But when I escaped from my free will to take on my created nature, then I got me a god; for before creatures were, God was not God: he was that he was...Wherefore we pray we may be quit of God...[32]

This is the seminal passage, the explosive and still-to-be grasped precept from Eckhart's masterpiece, the sermon "Poor in Spirit."[33]

We have said that the mystic breakthrough implies neither ecstasy nor bliss. It requires total faith-for: poise and detachment in the face of what comes, totally engaging of and with the generative forces of life, until, as one Zen master puts it, we are nothing but ash.

One of Eckhart's most enduring contributions to the genealogy of the mystic way is what his conception of breaking through to wider realizations of living *does not* entail: specifically suffering and ecstatic experiences, or combinations of the two. Eckhart did appreciate suffering, as certainly it was all around him in that hard and grim medieval life. But while suffering may indeed be a royal road to the godhead, that does not mean that suffering is required. It also means, as Porete declared, release from the "virtues." The virtues are "veils," "garments," says Eckhart.[34] Virtues are simply the mirrors we put up in front of ourselves in order to give ourselves our own names. This has nothing to do with what Eckhart requires of detachment, in order to arrive at the new man, the breakthrough creative who lives as the generative. Visions and ecstasies share the same low status in Eckhart's view, as they are more productive of delusion than revelation: "Good pious souls are hindered too from their proper object by lingering with holy joy over the human form of our Lord Jesus Christ; and by the same token, over-reliance upon visions is a pitfall to some people."[35]

None of these religious touchstones are required for Eckhart's vision of faith-for because of his conception of what constitutes being human. The human state, in Eckhart's faith-for, is already a holy state; the soul is sprung from the very ground that generates, gives birth to, all occurrences, everywhere and anywhere in the cosmos. Neither does Eckhart have need for the kind of concentrating, squeezing and compressing of life's energies into a One.

The notion of there being a God who does his work "beyond" the actual states of affairs in which we live our visceral, socially productive lives amounts to being an affront. The "sources" of energies are necessarily beyond any comprehension of them as they generate the conditions for that comprehension as well. To use a spatial metaphor, the expansion of our comprehension simply marks the further expansion of the universe of comprehension that has already taken place, and that is as such beyond the already accomplished comprehension. The movement goes in reverse also: it entails aspiring to a greater humility in the face of this opening up, to a need to sustain one's detaching equilibrium and give way to that opening impetus:

Why I pray God to rid me of God [Italics mine – MHS] is because conditionless being is above God and above distinction: it was therein I was myself, therein I willed myself and knew myself to make this man and in this sense I am my own cause, both of my nature which is eternal and of my nature which is temporal. For this am I born, and as to my birth which is eternal I can never die. In my eternal mode of birth I have always been and now and shall eternally remain. That which I am in time shall die and come to naught, for it is of the day and passes with the day. In my birth all things were born, and I was the cause of mine own self and all things, and had I willed it I had never been nor any thing and if I had not been then God had not been either.

...I flowed out of God then all things said, There is a God.[36]

To "pray to God to rid oneself of God" is to move oneself, with all of the energy and might one can muster, to the very edge of what has been comprehended and to feel the energy there, to turn one's eyes to the light, to fully absorb in one's hearing the silence of that very act of generative expansion and immanent enrichment that is taking place, to let the incomprehensibility of it all wash over one's being like a canyon wind rising up with such vehemence that one feels on the verge of flight. It is to *obey* (the key element on the royal road to "Detachment"[37]) the profound upsurge of energy into the unknown that beckons to one's will to "keep going."

Its spirit never rests content until it pierces to the coil, into the primal origin where the breath has its source. This spirit knows no time nor number: number does not exist apart from the malady of time. ...This spirit, transcending number, breaks through multiplicity and is transfixed by God, and by the fact of his piercing me I pierce him in return: God leads this spirit into the desert, into the solitude of its own self, where it is simply one and is welling up in itself. This spirit has no why, for if it had a why the unity would also have its why. This spirit is in unity and freedom…

…He who abandons himself and everything, who seeks not his own in any wise but does all he does for love and without why, that man being dead to all the world is alive in God and God in him…

…A man then must be dead, must be dead indeed, devoid of any being of his own, wholly without likeness, like to none, to be really Godlike. For it is God's character, his nature, to be peerless, incomparable…[38]

FORE-GIVING: THE GIFT. And we still have one last step to take in our appreciation of Eckhart's forming of the mystic way. In our context of grasping how to collect our sense of the mystic open into a way of living, we call this stance, this way of living generatively, the mystic form of breakout creativity "fore-giving." While "faith-for" is the mystic's own construct for what his or her living entails, it is enacted as fore-giving into the world. The notion of "faith-for" envisions a literal "fore" of "giving." The faith-for the coming entails that the mystic gives *before* she is asked; and she assumes all the risk of disappointment and betrayal that such a giving entails. She gives *before* any time appears in which she is "ready" to give. She just lives, giving this way. And she gives in the *fore*, in the face of, in the presence and witness of others, in advance of any possibility of even conceiving, no less hoping for, there to be a "return" or reciprocation, no less an exchange.

In the Eckhartian mystic ethic, our task as humans is not to merely *make* a gift (and so it already assumes a stance far beyond, and long before *taking* a gift), but to *become* one, become a gift – to each other, to the earth and to this moment and locale in the universe. It is to *enact* faith-for as a *way,* and not merely as a personal orientation. If we act out of less of a moving into what comes, we are sinking back into animal life — and to retreat from such a fore-giving entails nothing other than this sinking back. How do we live the fully human life? By *fore-*giving, as giving beings rise to the fore, rise to the surface into the living world, that we are so born, so coming to the fore. Now for Eckhart, this is a possibility for all humans. This is the precept of the mystic given full blast, without reservation, and utterly apparent and real for the mystic. Eckhart is the true voice of the precept. Hear Eckhart, and you can hear the mystic.

Our response to him might be one of ambivalence (based on more than his medieval theistic language). We hear the words, feel their power, and even feel ourselves being moved. But we freeze. Few human figures could endure this ethic. Why? Because, as we see it, in the midst of the panoply of the human figures, the mystic, in distinction from all the other figures, *gives* from that pure faith-for. That is precisely and exactly the quality the mystic has in abundance and that we others have yet to develop. In living that plunge into the open, constantly, from moment to moment in faith-for, the mystic gives out to others, to nature and a living world *before* there is even a single person doing the giving.

Following Eckhart, and beyond, what we fore-give (give before we have encountered, or entered into encounter to give or die) is what impresses as irredeemably real. The "real" isn't what comes at us, is given to us, is sensed or intuited as something from "out there." The real is what faith-for opens, what impels fore-giving, what the Field of Enthusiasm has already brought to life. Eckhart, at the least, gives me the room to think this and carry it forward into a new mystic realization.

> He who gives up all things gets back a hundredfold. If he
> expects his hundredfold he shall get nothing; he is not
> giving up the things but getting more, an hundredfold...
> Anyone who looks to find anything in God, knowledge,

understanding or devotion or whatever it may be, even it he find it will not be finding God but knowledge, understanding or devotion: all things I heartily commend; but to him not lasting.

Seek nothing at all, not understanding nor gnosis nor piety nor inwardness nor peace but only God's will. The soul who is as she by rights should be, would not be satisfied even if God gave her his whole Godhead; it would no more console her than his giving her a fly. ... *Never pray for any mortal thing* [my italics]; if thou must pray for anything at all, pray for God's will and nothing else for therein thou has all...[39]

Let's pause and appreciate this statement for a moment.

Summing Up

The defining elements that Eckhart exemplifies for us are these (I use italics to highlight the terms I have proposed in the course of our study so far):

- A notion of a conceivable emanation of cosmic, *generative* energies (for him, the godhead, and for us, self-organization).

- A *Field of Enthusiasm* through which the mystic relates to the world and carries forward through devoted attention, study and/or action.

- A capacity for discernment and realization beyond practical knowledge and reason that concentrates its articulation in a *teachable precept*.

- A sense of continual birth and renewal, the life of *faith-for*.

- Envisioning a path to *faith-for* through active detachment.

- Unshakable integrity and fidelity to the saturating phenomena of the "World" assemblage given through the Field of Enthusiasm.

- The ethic of *fore-giving* as the mystic way.

Now what remains is for these elements of mystic aspirations to find their way and for them to take their places in the newly emerging scene that would succeed the Medieval Age, and in which new practices (new expressions of leader, artist and prophetic aspirations) were coming into their own.

Chapter Six

Science, Spinoza and The Twilight
of the Classical Mystic

Our mind, insofar as it knows both itself and the body under a form of eternity, necessarily has knowledge of God, and knows that it is in God and is conceived through God.

~ Spinoza [1]

If you will meditate on God, take before you the eternal darkness, which is without God; for God dwelleth in himself and the darkness cannot in its own power comprehend him; which darkness hath a great longing after the light, caused by the light's beholding itself in the darkness and shining in it. And in this longing or desiring, you find the source, and the source taketh hold of the power of virtue of the light, and the longing maketh the virtue material, and the material virtue is the enclosure of God or the heaven...All this is incomprehensible to the natural man, but not impossible to be found in the mind; for paradise standeth open in the mind of a holy soul.

Thus you may see how God creates all things out of nothing, but only out of himself; and yet the out-birth is not from his essence but it hath its original from the darkness. The source of the darkness is the first Principle, and the out-birth, generated out of the darkness by virtue

of the light is the third Principle and that is not called
God: God is only the light and the virtue of the light, and
that which goeth forth out of the light is the Holy Ghost.

~ Jacob Boehme [2]

Mystic "Science"?

Our genealogy of mystics recounts critical nodes in the stream of the
mystic life, a stream that carries this endeavor into our own times.
Indeed, with Meister Eckhart we reach an apogee in which nearly all the
elements of the mystic figure are in place. Next in the process of
establishing a mystic figuration of aspiration was not adding more
elements, but rather firming up these elements so that they would not
just be descriptions of an exceptional relation to the divine, but they
would be able to become a definitively accessible set of practices that
had value relative to other aspirational ways that were also taking shape
at that time, and subsequently.

But the process by which this work was done was not a straightforward
one. As often (or still) happens, as the mystics were opening up this
portent for the human endeavor, it came under withering institutional
attack, in the form of banning their works, executing Beguine mystics
and, in the case of Eckhart, subjecting him to inquisitional imprisonment.
As a result of this sustained assault, mystic aspirations were relegated to
relative obscurity. However, as sometimes happens, their works were so
powerful and were so nourishing to people who were eager for expression
of their aspirational energies, that when the time came, this incipient
way became not only useful, but attractive enough to be promoted and
supported by the institution that had once condemned it. A salvaging
thread was lowered to the mystic vocation as a way to counter the threat
posed by the secularizing forces that were emerging and that Church
dogma had no way of answering. The church's authority was being
assaulted on several fronts: the emerging empirical sciences (represented
by Copernicus, Kepler and Galileo), the new subjectively oriented

philosophies (epitomized later by Descartes), the rigorously materialist account of human knowledge (exemplified by Spinoza, and only tempered by Leibniz), as well as the emergence of "capital" as an expansive, universalizing and disruptive technology for assigning an "economic value" to nearly everything. Church authorities found in the mystics' precepts and preachings a way to validate the exceptionality of the divine and a vocation of pure aspiration, and thereby cement their authority in that supreme realm. And so, in order to counter or at least supplement these fast-rising power centers, the Church looked to mystic works to provide another narrative, one that suited its "expertise" on matters divine.

"MYSTIC SCIENCE"? Emulating the powerful exertions of the Enlightenment's economic, artistic, political and academic institutions, the church attempted to establish a *"mystic science,"* which would be a prescribable methodology for attaining the mystic level of discerning insight into the workings of the divine. One step in this process was to specifically name a special category of endeavor that this "science" addresses; it gave this work the name "mystic" in 1635.[3] Another step in this process was to graft onto the mystic ways of the Beguines and Eckhart the ennobling notion of "science," and show how mystics did their work according to procedures and a "methodology." This science argued that mystic ways could vouchsafe their precepts as being matters of "force" – a force that just happened to be the one whereby God related to his universe and to us. In this valiant attempt at valorizing a specifically mystic way to a "good life," Teresa of Avila and Juan de la Cruz, for example, were abetted by the church fathers so as to validate that the veracity of the church's powers, or the powers over which the church had knowledge and authority. While the secularists scrambled to certify their measurements, the plaint went, mystics would certify the place of the infinite powers of God in each person's life. The church could then, with dire gravity ask, "Which power, which certainty, do you choose?" In the Catholic context, works by Teresa of Avila, especially *The Interior Castle,* and the works of her disciple, Juan de la Cruz,[4] with his *Dark Night of the Soul,* are exemplary. Without a doubt, the literary power of these mystics' work is great, and they certainly deserve their place in the orthodox canon of mystics – as do, indeed, so many of the others our genealogy has omitted. They are paradigmatic in their blending of great poetic power with pedagogical intent.

The import of their work for us, in charting the genealogy of mystic aspirations, is that they help us to crystallize our grasp of the criteria that distinguishes mystic aspirations from the myriad of other activities that are uplifting, exciting and even generative. That, after all, was their assignment in the context of the church's confrontations with other, new ways of advancing the human endeavor. In terms of our account of the genealogy of mystic aspirations then, these people helped to identify those practices, attitudes and concerns that contributed to the formation of these aspirations into a way of life. Their contributions can be considered in light of both the firming up of the P/SS resources that give some strength of expression to these aspirations (especially the "World" assemblage and the Field of Enthusiasm), and also to assigning a value to the life ways of faith-for and fore-giving, as well as the vocation that entails the forming and teaching of the precept.

I cite Kabbalah and Jacob Boehme in what follows, even though they fall out of the Catholic fold, because they are equally as forceful in this phase of the figuration of the mystic way and the aspiring mind. Once again, these factors also forge a mystic figuration under conditions of duress and being outcasts. Kabbalah, which I call a "folk" mysticism, is no "lesser" a form of mysticism and it plays an important role in our genealogy. As a "ghettoized" mysticism emerging in the sectors of Europe that were cordoned off, this practice translated the texts of Jewish religion and commonplace numerologies into Fields of Enthusiasm that expressed precepts that sustained this outcast people and offered them futures that could not be constructed within the confines of their material states of affairs. Jacob Boehme (1575-1640) was a Protestant mystic, who as a spokesperson for pure aspiring that one person can dare to take up, forged a stream of thought that cleared the way for the

German Romantics and Idealists who kept aspirations alive and validated the power of an aspiring P/SS resource two hundred years later.

And finally in this chapter, the notion of a "mystic science" reaches a new apogee – equivalent to that of Eckhart, and just as controversial, in the works of Baruch Spinoza (1632-1677). ("Baruch" means "blessed" in Hebrew, and is the word that begins many Jewish prayers), His *Ethics* delineate a "logic" of aspiration that is tied directly to P/SS resources – as factors of mind and body. These factors only reach their full expression and capability as living beings when they embody the "intellectual love of God," which we can translate as enacting the Field of Enthusiam as a site of welcoming for the saturating phenomena that activate, energize and make supremely urgent the evocations of our aspiration's "World."

The "Science" of Mystic Rapture

TERESA OF AVILA. A "science of mysticism" seemed to be possible, if remotely so, by canonizing the diligent and conscious efforts required to attain a full and viable conversion, if one's attention and devotion could be turned from enchainment to the secular, worldly and material to enchantment by and commitment to the divine. By pointing to the rapturous releases attained by Teresa of Avila, the church could substantiate its claims that its heavenly mandate was every bit as affecting as the scientific and mercantile ways were productive. Teresa's swoons, fits and sufferings make all the more vivid and comprehensible the real psychic combat that the aspiring mind wages as it uproots the commonplace and everyday.

Even though these extreme behaviors do not typify the genealogy of the mystic figuration of aspirations, they serve the purpose of elevating to attention a domain of P/SS activities that are, indeed, separate and distinct from the capabilities and faculties that are dedicated to knowing, certifying, producing and exchanging. To the extent that the aspiring mind, and its "World" assemblage in particular, induces a never-ending sense of relationship, the intensity of which knows no bounds (except for what the body of the person can accommodate), notions of rapture serve to delineate a difference, even more vividly than does Eckhart's regimen of detachment.

> In short, the desires of these souls are no longer for consolations or favors, for they have with them the Lord Himself and it is His Majesty Who now lives in them. His life, of course, was nothing but a continual torment, and so He is making our life the same, at least as far as our desires go. In other respects, He treats us as weaklings though He has ample fortitude to give us when He sees that we need it. These souls have a marked detachment from everything and a desire to be always either alone or busy with something that is to some soul's advantage.[5]

Of course the agenda of Teresa and the church is quite different from our own. In their case the notion of a mystic science is being deployed with the presumption that the mystic way is superior to what is offered by worldly-bound states, and that everyone who takes up this method can attain this way of nearness to God. In our notion, while aspiration is a P/SS resource that is available to everyone, the mystic figuration of it is not offered as being superior to any other state. It is just a singular state that by virtue of its P/SS dynamics has certain characteristics and offers others and the mystically aspiring person herself an active role in the advancing of what is more expansive and more encompassing. And so Teresa's mission, in delineating a methodology that traverses through the chambers of the "castle" of mystic realization, speaks to a hard kernel of the genealogy we envision: beyond the "raptures," there is the work to be done. The labor of the mystic way is that of holding out as a standard of decision and action the fore-giving that one undertakes in order to enact one's faith-for, and does not consist, in the slightest, of seeking raptures. Fore-giving intensifies the detachment that faith-for opens us to. In the process there are effects that strengthen the P/SS's aspiring resource: the "World" assemblage's relational characters and manners of coming toward and enacting threshold realizations, in the

Flesh and with a Face, can rise to articulation and can then be embraced as the mind's Field of Enthusiasm.

JUAN DE LA CRUZ. Teresa's disciple, Juan de la Cruz, can be said to explore the *"via negativa"* of the mystic way.[6] The other side of the raptures of Teresa is the abyss of de la Cruz.

> Consequently, it is at the time they are going about their spiritual exercises with delight and satisfaction, when in their opinion the sun of divine favor is shining most brightly on them, that God darkens all this light and closes the door and spring of the sweet spiritual water they were tasting as often and as long as they desired... God now leaves them in such darkness that they do not know which way to turn in their discursive imaginings. They cannot advance a step in meditation, as they used to, now that the interior sense faculties are engulfed in this night. He leaves them in such dryness that they not only fail to receive satisfaction and pleasure from their spiritual exercises and works, as they formerly did, but also find these exercises distasteful and bitter...[7]

When we speak about the "outcasting" that mystics undergo and the feelings of increasing differentiation of their ways from those of the mainstream, this "dark night of the soul" looms large. Eckhart's emptying of the soul so that God can come in is intensified by de la Cruz and expounded in its experiential rigor, without reserve (a force of articulation that landed him in fatal inquisitorial imprisonment as well). This aspect of the aspiring engagement cannot be denied. The "World" assemblage's saturating phenomena do not "originate" at a source point, neither do they have a reason (a major mystic theme). They emerge as out of a darkness precisely because no consciously formed or forming resource addresses them directly: they are always strange, they always emerge out of what has not been comprehended, and so always seem to be anti-forces or dark energies that assail whatever might be taken as certain.

No faith-for, if it is this way, vouches for what is already there and given, even to the mystically aspiring person (or especially to the mystically aspiring person). The faith-for transposes the "negativity" that is implicit in all the saturating phenomena of the "World" assemblages into occasions of awe, not fear and of devoted commitment, not aversion or reversion to the commonplace. No mystic act of fore-giving is anything but affirming, but it gives nothing that can be reciprocated and so emulates the night — not the dark, befogged and closed-in night, but the "starry night" of Van Gogh that lures us and emulates in us the sense of flight, as a Field of Enthusiasm. Once again, this classical mystic's *via negativa* provides us with the imprinting of the singular and distinctive dynamic required by the forming of a resource that is specifically dedicated to aspiring.

KABBALAH. Then mysticism also becomes a folk art that is cast in terms of methodological precision. For centuries, proceeding somewhat in tandem with the development of Christian mysticism (Gnostic roots, with a great upsurge in activity in the twelfth through the seventeenth centuries), it formed a dominant strain in Jewish religious life. Then, in the nineteenth century it lost status as a mainstream component of Jewish faith. It was relegated to a cult status among mostly isolationist and radical fundamentalist and Zionist sects. Thanks to the supreme efforts of Gershom Scholem, this great tradition of visceral, speculative and intensively interpretive Jewish life was rediscovered. Since then, there have been modern efforts at revival as well.[8]

We see that it is a deeply original approach to a life based on a primary book (the Torah) and subsequent discussions of it (the Talmud). The proponents of Kabbalah are not only knowledgeable about these orthodox Jewish texts, but also incorporate into their discussions a deep grasp of the Neoplatonic and other intellectual currents prevalent at the times when great compilations were made. Still, Scholem's study of the subject, from every angle imaginable as far as I can tell, convinces me that Kabbalah is a mysticism of a people whose world had closed and, increasingly, whose very existence had to be validated and revalidated through every form and manner of confirmation available – from the most exquisite flights of metaphysical and theosophical imagination, down to the shape of the letters of its ancient alphabet.

Another strain of Kabbalah, the practical strain, mixed this interpolative technique with numerology and mystic revelation to heal and grant wishes of seekers. Kabbalistic Jews thus acquired the reputation of being great sorcerers, among other things. These magical arts were also adapted by Christians. Frances Yates tells this story with great affect in her classic, *The Occult Philosophy in the Elizabethan Age.*[9] The Kabbalah's combination of powerfully rendered cosmologies, depictions of the origins of evil, and deep and inscrutable interpretations of alphabetical formations, when translated into the Christian fold, became powerful tools of symbolically expressing the signs of God's grace and deliverance on earth. The name Henry Cornelius Agrippa is most often associated with this movement. His unique blend of Christian Kabbalah, astrology, alchemy and the budding medical mindset of his day led to the belief in a viable science of practical mysticism.

In our genealogy, Kabbalah provides an opportunity for aspiring energies to work themselves out and to enlarge the variety of expressions in which the Field of Enthusiasm is articulated. In these mythological or magical involutions of expression, the practitioner weaves an aspiring tapestry that depicts the energies of what comes and what exceeds one's given state of affairs in ways that demand the application of new thinking, imagining and conceiving of what is actually going on. One aspires, in a sense, without knowing that one is doing that. Articulations that on the surface declare a fantastic state of being are actually acting as the shuttle on the loom of aspiration, weaving a Field of Enthusiasm that can withstand the pressures of shrinking worlds, closing horizons and rejection from the flow of current events. Aspiration becomes a robust and generative force only by virtue of such weavings as these.

JACOB BOEHME. Boehme (b.1575) could be considered a folk mystic, but even so, he exerted a life-shaping force on the people who would enact the next phase of mystic work, that of the philosopher mystics, who we will consider in Chapter Seven. With the flourishing of the printing of books, and the rise of a vibrant book distribution trade, all kinds of knowledge that was once esoteric became available to a wide public. No longer dependent on preaching in the square, people could now put thoughts, words, inspirations and whole treatises on the larger market of ideas. Boehme clearly partook of those treatises with enthusiasm, insight and great individual effort. A freelance Protestant mystic (an oxymoron), he educated himself to become well versed in the "esoteric" arts of his day. He takes the ambiguities and unsettled nature of rationality, as evidenced in alchemy and numerology, as well as some Kabbalist ruminations and turns these to great advantage in crafting an individualist mysticism of knowledge by attempting to reconcile orthodoxy with empirical experimentation and formal logical processes.

His mysticism reflects the poignancy of the experience of the infinite making its way, but on a cosmological level. As the citation in our epigram shows, the picture he paints is of the infinite power of God pushing its way into a vast darkness. The impression one gets is of a swirling torrent of forces, barely sorted out among themselves, but that detect in each other what it itself lacks. These great longings, first that of the darkness for God, and second that of God for pressing out and beyond into a material creation, offers a powerful rendering of a vision. God, individual and all-powerful, craves a state of empowered individuality; dark infinity craves light, but must give up its boundlessness to have its wish. Only the spirit of God, that longing to be material, elemental (as in alchemical elements) and human (as in the Son, Jesus) offers any succor to the human being. The dream of tapping into the infinite, into pure darkness, without the reconciling power of God, is the very essence of evil.

Boehme thus articulates the surging forth of the Field of Enthusiasm into a life's way of faith-for. We might say that the Protestant impetus, in distinguishing itself from the Catholic Church, intends nothing else. In

Boehme, however, there is an energy that cannot be ritualized, but has to be enacted as faith-for, as what no body of liturgy or worship can satisfy. Boehme, possibly more than anyone before him, then offers an account of aspiration that renders it as a faculty of action, as a P/SS resource that engenders behaviors of certain kinds. Whereas his predecessors delineated practices that demarcated access to the aspiring resource, Boehme articulates the life way that this resource, once formed and accessed, entails. It is this utterly bedazzling insight that makes it possible for the likes of Fichte, Hölderlin, Schelling and Hegel, the great Idealists, to articulate a philosophy, a stable, abiding and productive logic, that envisions the human endeavor as being one that shapes its way of being from out of the raw forces of what we have called saturating phenomena, such that a "World" P/SS assemblage can be rendered and cast forth, through the logical machinations of a Field of Enthusiasm (Spirit or Self), into a living *world*.

Spinoza

In the figure of Spinoza, I find that the driving mystic vision, despite all the efforts made to repress or assimilate it, made its way into the most rigorous of philosophical works. Spinoza would most certainly deny that his work was "mystical," especially since that term had already started to accumulate its reputation as being intellectually inferior mur-murings of emotionally over-wrought religious fanatics. But as I read Spinoza in the context of the works of the great classical mystics, and the philosophically adept ones, especially Eckhart, I cannot help but highlight the way Spinoza's vision was informed by key mystic precepts (Eckhart's "detachment" to "breakthrough," for instance). It is through this "channel" of Spinoza that the German Idealists (from Kant through Fichte and then to an apotheosis in the great trio of Schelling, Hölderlin and Hegel) were forced to come to grips with the notions of the self-or-ganizing universe as an open and dynamic regime of energies that increase complexity, of which humans are a part.

Spinoza's life path also closely resembles that of the great mystics, since he too was subjected to and condemned by an inquisition by his co-religionists, and then was forced into a secular exile as well. He exhibited a mystic's deep-seated resistance to mechanical reduction, abstraction and mathematical formula (ironically expressed in the rigid format of a geometric proof), as well as his utter rejection of religious dogmas of any kind.[10] As does the work of the great mystics we have cited in our genealogy, the power of his work (specifically the parts that convey the vision of the classical mystics) resonates down to us today by shooting the demands of the mystic precept right into the heart of what purports to be the most anti-mystic of rational discourse, that of philosophy.[11]

In the work of Baruch Spinoza[12] there arose a new possibility for grasping the mystic way: a "rational mysticism."Yes, this oxymoron has a meaning. Maybe the notion of there being a "mystic science" carried over from the last century, and Spinoza's *Ethics,* written in the rigid style of geometric proof, takes up this vision; maybe, as a man deeply learned in Latin as well as Hebrew texts, he perceived how the great notions of the generativity of the universe in its self-producing and self-organizing potency, which constituted a kernel of the human soul, could be expressed in rigorously scholastic, propositional form because its very "mode" of being was also physically structured into a robustly embodied "essence." In Spinoza the very path of rational and empirical devotion to the real, natural, material world, echoed, if not emulated, the basis for a mystic ethic, that of fore-giving, in the manner, if not the specific life's way of religious devotion, of Porete and Eckhart. It takes the notion of mystic practice, as advanced by the later mystics, Teresa of Avila and Juan de la Cruz (themselves "converso" Jews, by the way), and transports them into the universal methods of giving structure and certainty to one's knowing, that Descartes, just a few years before Spinoza's authorship, had launched. In the context of our genealogical exposition then, after Spinoza, the mystic way and its figuration of aspiration became matters for human attention and effort, once and for all.

THE HUMANIST MYSTIC ON THE THRESHOLD. Still we have to be clear, Spinoza forges a distinctive path that diverges emphatically from the way of the classical mystic. Nothing more starkly sets Spinoza apart from the classical mystic than the nature of his great opus, the *Ethics.* In Spinoza we do not have the grand flourish of lyric and erotic poetry. We no longer have lush and evocative sermons that raise us up to take up our new life. The prose of the *Ethics* is drawn up in the style of mathematical proof. But the effect of the content is more like a report of a mathematically trained botanist on a great voyage of exploration: definitions mark the touchstones, the points to be used for demarcation; axioms define a territory we are exploring; propositions mark our discoveries; these are elaborated and fixed on our mapping of the conceptual space by proofs of their viability and situated identity; and these are further elaborated in the more conversational, but never casual, scholia. The tone is authoritative, but not with any intention of "convincing" the reader as would the teaching of a precept, for instance. Spinoza, a true philosopher in the Socratic tradition, realizes that readers will have to come to these places on their own and only upon arrival at the marked zones will agreement, assent, or even valid discussion be able to take place. As his going into hiding indicates, he is keenly aware of how rare such realizations will be.[13] Instead of writing a sermon or preaching, as did Eckhart, Spinoza labored to make his prose neutral, whatever the price in its "appeal" that entailed.

THE *ETHICS*. Spinoza's *Ethics* comprises four innovations, which bear on his standing in the genealogy of the breakout creative:

1. God is Substance, whose creative powers are, necessarily, exactly as they are for us in this world.

2. Infinity and eternity are dimensions of the life and world in which we exist. The "soul" is an idea of the body, not a separately created entity.

3. Salvation is a this-world affair, a matter of collective and universal concern, a matter of an "intellectual love of God," a third kind of knowledge, not a matter of individualized "miracle" or transportation to another world.

Let's look at each of these more closely.

God is Substance, and Therefore is Nature. Einstein once stated, "I believe in Spinoza's God." The most accessible way to come at Spinoza's conception of God is to conceive that the universe is as it is because it generates out of its own supreme potencies – those of God – as they are, in accordance with what that generativity renders as its own conditions (for such generation, from moment to moment, from locale to locale). At this level or moment of generation there is no "cause" at all, but rather self-engendering potency expressing into a state of materialized occurrence.[14] There is no "cause," justification, explanation nor purpose for or in that conception. It cannot be otherwise logically, physically and substantially. Why is that the case? Because the universe exists as God could only have caused it, causing it according to his nature, and according to his nature, it cannot be otherwise. (See I:13 esp.)[15]

How controversial was this claim? It obsessed Leibniz for ten years before he was able to write his opposing thesis: that a god who must create in a certain way cannot be God, because then this God would be finite. The God of Spinoza cannot be the Christian God because Spinoza's God could not choose. Spinoza's God can only produce the world as his nature compels him to. What kind of a god is that? No, the Christian God must have choice available, and must be able to choose how, when, and what will the "best of worlds," as Leibniz described it, and so create it. No less could Spinoza's god induce an ecstasy-yielding "relationship" and "revelation" or a stigmata-producing miracle. Indeed, as Spinoza makes clear, this God offers no favors, and even to his most devoted does not respond in kind with warmth and emotion (V:17, 19, 35) as Leibniz needs and claims,[16] he is no monarch of a City of God over which he rules benevolently (if incomprehensibly).[17]

In our genealogy of the mystic breakout creative, this insight marks the irreversible turn to the fullness of the actual physical universe, as it is, as a source of generativity. Einstein had more faith in the order that Spinoza's God entailed, [18] where we are more amenable to the chaos that the likes of Nietzsche and the anamystics embrace. But Spinoza marked a turning point: God could now, logically, within a "systematic theology," [19] be articulated in terms that did not require rendering him in a deistic, anthropomorphic form, with will and choices within which our world is only one option (albeit, according to Leibniz, the best). The road to God had forked: the mystic realization of God naming (inadequately and thus "apophatically") the surging relating power of generative forces (Eckhart's "godhead") could be imported into the heart of "rational" discourse.

Infinity and Eternity, Here and Now. Could a modern Buddhist be more insistent? Does Spinoza not see infinity in a dewdrop or eternity in chopping wood and carrying water? Is there something like a "beyond" to the environment in which we carry on our daily affairs? Spinoza seems to say "No," by virtue of his idea of God. Free-forming energies combine into more stable bodies that are able to sustain themselves through time (have an essence). But these entities are not dead; they take shapes, exert forces and take up roles as "modes" of God's self-generation. As constellated energies, they force relations with other energies otherwise constellated and engender a process of change, localization of influence, and dynamic openness on the margins of stability (modes can affect essences). The condition this describes is thus one of *generativity:* out of the combination of existing constellations of energy and force, new combinations are possible, and ones of greater encompassing involvement and expanding levels of realization – to infinity – are also (more rarely than micro-level mutations, but nevertheless occasionally, and sometimes consciously) engendered. [20]

The Soul is an Idea of the Body. "The object of the idea constituting the human mind is the body – a definite mode of extension actually existing, and nothing else." (See II:13) "And nothing else." There you have it: here lies a revolution.

Spinoza's formulation is at once more and less radical than the naïve dualism of "body versus soul" (as in Descartes) permits. First, Spinoza makes it clear that any ideas we have of the body from the mind are inadequate. The ideas we have of the body are from the affections the body generates, and from the ideas we derive, secondarily from those affections. "The human mind has no knowledge of the body, nor does it know it to exist, except through ideas of the affections by which the body is affected." (See II: 19) And then, let's up the ante: "The idea of the idea of any affection of the human body does not involve adequate knowledge of the human mind." (See II: 29) No wonder we call all these feelings, thoughts, imaginings and emotions a "soul." How else would we characterize such a confused concatenation of affects from this incredibly complex sensing machine that is our body?

Here I detect an Eckhartian kernel of Spinoza's mystic way: the mind encompasses and embraces an attribute of God in the form of *ideas*.[21] And it is this concatenation and assemblage of ideas that constitute Spinoza's Field of Enthusiasm, which he expresses as an *Idea* of God. The Idea of God is the direct *expression* of God's nature as a thinking being.[22] It is not a result of any action of his thinking that there is an "idea of God." The idea is not one that God "has," in the way that we have ideas about things or about how to do things. No, "of" is used intensively as a possessive particle here. It is an idea that is an intrinsic, living, ongoing aspect of God; God is the thinking being, therefore the being constituted as ideas and comprising all ideas such as they are.

Fore-Giving, Again. It is in the fact that Spinoza's great work was an "ethics," and not a treatise on the nature of Being that seals the case of his mystic core for me. Spinoza is not giving a report or a proof of something he has discovered through a microscope, nor is he discoursing on a logic of how things appear to us and thus have "being," as in a classical (metaphysical) philosophical work. Instead, because the mind and thought directly express this attribute of self-generating and self-organizing potency, *this work of thought is directly an expression of this potency* *itself.* If this work seeks an exposition of the way we are beings that act knowingly and by doing so produce effects that then entail subsequent actions, if it seeks to present what constitutes our "reality" and what it is that "truth" consists of, it cannot be a pronouncement of a revelation given from afar; if this work does so, it must be an expression of what materially exerts itself as a force right in the heart of that living.[23] This work then is, and can be nothing other than an *Ethics*, laying out, first, the terrain of this field in which the energies of all life itself come into its living conception. This work is a *precept,* pure and simple.

Conception, being a province of human mind, is also expressed other forms of life. Other creatures however, do not *think* their expression, and thus they do not have the ability to generate, within their beings, the very idea of God. It is because of this difference that humans guide and choose the modes and forms of generativity from a God-essential standpoint, while other creatures do not. The implication – the precept – is clear: such ideas, taken up (in expression and in responsibility) become the true province of the human endeavor. What Spinoza wrote was an "ethics" precisely because at the end of all the deductive reasoning, there lies *the demand for fore-giving:* that the human endeavor take upon itself the role of actively and encompassingly standing for *generativity,* of fore-giving to what comes, and doing this to the fullest extent its active and engaged (aspiring?) mind, in the stance of faith-for, permits. Determining that extent is the province of reason and then Spinoza's third kind of knowledge, his "intellectual love of God," and what others have called his "rational mysticism."

Salvation Is a This-World Affair, a Matter of an "Intellectual Love of God." If there was one thing Spinoza disdained, it was the penchant for the institutionalized religions of his time to make salvation an arbitrary affair of a remote God, and what is worse, for the salvation to occur only upon death, or at best in the form of momentary "ecstasies" from a godly intercession. Thinking of the mystic avatars of the sixteenth century, such as Teresa of Avila and Juan de la Cruz, their salvation was saturated with ecstasies and sufferings that were supposed to take one to the threshold of mystic presence.

No doubt suffering serves the useful purpose of stripping away any value from bodily, creaturely, socially given existence. And it does open one up to an awareness of the great psychic resources of resilience we can muster in the face of such deprivation. But from Spinoza's perspective, and from ours, we have to ask, does suffering lead to exercising our active strengths? Does it leave us with anything but affirmations that are given to us as antidotes to this suffering? We think not. Even the epitomes of classical mystics, Porete and Eckhart, did not give primary place to suffering as a way to the mystic. Here, on this very point, with Spinoza as our first guide, we strike out on a path of affirming mysticism, of a mysticism of what occurs, and not what our miseries induce or necessitate.

Spinoza sets down a course of living such that salvation is fully affirming of life – even its passive emotions, its confused and inadequate ideas. Salvation in his vision becomes not a matter not of grace from afar, or of a hyper-imagined relation with a mythic being. Instead, first, salvation is a quality of living as a free being, in tune with its own idea (Nietzsche's *amor fati*), and it is fully engaging with the Idea of God, or in our terminology, in the fullness of energized generativity as it pours forth among us and each other, from within us and around us in our social/historical/ecological situations. What is so amazing about Spinoza is despite his banishment, his seclusion and the furor his writings incited, the *Ethics* is one of the most thoroughly affirming works in the annals of philosophy. Spinoza lays out a disciplined and strictly this-worldly cultivation of a third kind of knowledge, which is most certainly not a matter of "miracle" or transportation to another world. (See I: 31) The human mind is an idea of the body, as we have said. Any kind of realization of a higher way must be one of the body as well. It will comprise direct affections of the body, derived from the reactions the body has to what is around it, and secondarily, ideas it forms of those affections. Now these latter affections are ideas as well and they can be good or bad, adequate or inadequate, depending on how much consideration one applies to them. Then Spinoza makes a series of strikingly obvious and yet seemingly fresh and new claims:

> "The human mind has no knowledge of the body nor does it know it to exist except through ideas of the affections by which the body is affected." (III: 19)

> "The human mind does not involve an adequate knowledge of the component parts of the body." (III: 24)

> "The idea of the idea of any affection of the human body does not involve adequate knowledge of the human mind." (III:29)

> "We have only a very inadequate knowledge of the duration of our body." (III: 30)

Surprisingly, for all the mind's inadequacy in grasping the essence of its own body, the mind is very capable at grasping "those things that are common to all things and are equally in the part as in the whole…" (III:38). What is "common," or what we might call their "essential being," (my terminology here) and, paradoxically, for all their being hidden behind the materiality of their existence, we live adequately among these "common things" and we also "know" that what is absolutely true lies in these "essences" of things, and does not lie in the attributes we assign to them for the purposes of identification or the modes we ascribe to them for the purposes of technologically manipulating them for our immediate purposes. What, then, is that "essence?" It is that of *conatus:* "Each thing, insofar as it is in itself, endeavors to persist in its own being (III: 6) and "The conatus with which each thing endeavors to persist in its own being is nothing but the actual essence of the thing itself." (III: 7) In order to do this, the conatus of every living thing is able to gather up within itself its active emotions and so assert its existence (essence) within its world. And, the strongest and most resilient resource humans have for asserting (their) conatus against the ravages of passive emotions is that of the mind. The mind that is rightly guided, that is. "The mind endeavors to *think only of the things that affirm its power of activity.*" (See III: 54)

I propose that in this notion of Idea as "conatus," we are not being presented with a static notion of "self-survival," or the assertion of one's already existent state of being against all else. Why would a "mind" be necessary for such a mechanical repetition of a status quo (and what preservation of a status quo against all else requires a "mind")? Rather the mind affirms the activities of all the forces and potencies at the site of its engagement, it has to expand and be able to encompass these dynamics that are increasing the complexity of the scene. Therefore, what qualifies as "mind" and what this "mind" does, exclusively, is to aspire to expand its activities so as to affirmatively take its place, to en-compass more competently and capably, what is occurring, surging forth and being "fore-given" there. Spinoza says: "Of that which is common and proper to the human body and to any external bodies by which the human body is customarily affected, and which is equally in the part as well as in the whole of any of these bodies, *the idea also in the mind will be adequate.* (III: 39). (Italics added for emphasis.) This vision is the formulation, in the terms of a methodological practice, of an ethic, of the case for and the need that engenders the mystic precept itself. [24]

Idea: God Thinking Himself. Thus we get to a new realization of the notion of "idea." These ideas are not "secondary" or "transcendental." [25] Those kind of merely abstract ideas — the staple of still prevalent notions as propounded by contemporary "rationalists" — are concatenations of every kind of inadequate idea, passive emotion, false impression, habituated slavishness, wild imaginings, *that fail to account for their bodily existence, their embodied generation and also their generation as God's own self-generation.* "These terms signify ideas confused in the highest degree," says Spinoza (and I agree).

Now the question comes, from where do we get these common notions? Spinoza would never allow these notions to arise from some mysterious or deistically mandated revelation (a voice of God). Clearly common notions, as Deleuze says, are *biological* in content (as is the Freudian Unconscious, we might add): they stem from the sustenance and continuation of bodily life.[26] And sure enough, right out of bodily life, common notions do emerge: by virtue of our ability to be affected, by virtue of our having passive emotions, we can discern common notions. This great realization isn't presented until Part V of Spinoza's work. The more affects of the dynamics in play at the site of its engaging the milieu the mind is able to perceive, the greater will be the force of the idea that, in a healthy person, will emerge in order to comprehend (as mind) and engage (as body) those affections (V: 8, 9). And since the mind is able to form clear and distinct ideas from affectations of the body (V: 7), it can form clear and distinct ideas from great emotions, as long as it is not overwhelmed by them. In a "just right" picture, to the extent that we can form a "mental image" of what is occurring to us, and to the extent that such an image incorporates a great many of these emotions, we can be moved to a new realization of what is occurring. *This new image engendered by great emotions and constellated into an idea by our imagination, can displace our habits and lead us to novelty.* That is, of course, provided this surge of psychic energy does not completely cripple us; or, that is, that we have become more adept at being aspiring beings.

Now comes the crucial link in the chain: "The mind can bring it about that all of the affections of the body – i.e., images of things – be related to the idea of God." (See V:14) That is, when the common notions of these vitalized images of affections are discerned, the idea of God is at hand. When we put our individual conatus within the conatus of God, his idea of himself, we are released from our individual survival into a realization of actual eternity itself. This is the third way of knowing: *rising through and ranging out far and wide among* (not ignoring or surpassing) the ideas of the common notions, energized by the active joys of the emotions asserting life for self and all, to the living Idea of

God. "The idea of this idea must also necessarily be in God and is related to God in the same way as the idea" (is in God). (See III: 43, Proof) *Thus, common notions are ideas expressed in and as ideas, as the same power of thinking that is the essence of God.* "We *have* them as God *has* them," says Deleuze. [27]

> "Our mind, insofar as it knows both itself and the body under a form of eternity, necessarily has a knowledge of God, and knows that it is in God and is conceived through God." (V:30)

And,

> "He whose body is capable of the greatest amount of activity has a mind whose greatest part is eternal." (V: 39)

And,

> "The more perfection a thing has, the more active and the less passive it is. Conversely the more active it is, the more perfect it is." (V: 40)

The Spinozan Break

And so, what do I claim as being the Spinozan brand of mystic realization? The Spinozan precept propounds no great Mechthild-like union and, for sure, Spinoza's god doesn't love us back. (See V: 19) The realization or "Idea" that will enable us to affirm our need for conatus in the course of engaging the scene of our living will not come to us as a moment of grace, granted from on high, as Leibniz would have it. [28] We have to be content, in the Spinozan fold, with a *precept* — what the body yields as an idea — that points to a vibrant sense of being alive, and the knowing faith-for that we have the means and the capability of getting there.

This is no course to a blissful release into an imagined heaven or blessedness. The standard view of mysticism is that it is an attempt to form a kind of knowledge that is beyond the reach of our usual knowledge-producing faculties and methods. This was the idea of the "mystic" of the sixteenth century as described by deCerteau and was the subject of the preceding chapter. The claim is that there is a peculiar psychological, psychic "experience" which provides a qualitatively different access to the universe – or, for those classical, pre-Spinozan mystics – a "revelation" and a rapturous miracle to be given, which transports us beyond normal knowledge and is more significant than that knowledge, is not in the offing in Spinoza's ethic.

Spinoza offers a completely different conception of the mystic endeavor. He goes to great lengths to find a way for our relatively accessible experiences to gather into a mystic life. He is totally aware that it is impossible for people to live completely in the realm of active joys discerning common notions. He is also aware that most people would not be able to grasp the Idea of God (or, in our terminology, realize their Field of Enthusiasm), and discerning common notions from out of active joys (a kind of "flow" state of heightened and concentrated attentive energy) is out of reach for most people.[29] But this organization of our psychic energies *can* be accomplished.

The Spinozan course does not require a special emotional orientation to life; it requires instead a special dedication to certain conceptual and free-spirited orientations to life. It is an orientation that does not determine who are mystics according to any religious dogma nor does it require the internalization of any course of sacraments or specialization in a sacralized language (Latin or Hebrew). It requires, in a very Poretian and Eckhartian manner, a detachment from trivial and passive emotions and discernment of the common notions that energize all life. Not easy, but not covered over in dogma and shibboleths of scriptural references or hidden behind layers of fabulous revelations and miracles.[30]

Spinoza's work thus marks the decisive turning point in our genealogy of mystics because, while he may be a rational mystic, he is, even more, a completely *humanistic* mystic, declaring the mysticism of the human to any of us who can take the decisive steps he envisions. All of Spinoza's innovations to the mystic genome are crucial and we do carry them forward into the modern era. Here is the one demand we take away as axiomatic in going forward: *the post-Spinozan mystic is defined by an earthly, psychically possible and completely human commitment to the press of the generative and the exertion of discernment.*

No thinking after Spinoza, no thinking that keys off a precept and that intends to point a way to a comprehension of the human endeavor that includes aspiration, ignores Spinoza. Although his name falls out of frequent citation in what follows, all of the thinkers we cite in the next chapter stand on his shoulders, some more explicitly than others (for some reason Heidegger does not directly study his works, while, however, never having the classical mystics, especially Eckhart, at the top of his mind). What they take forward from Spinoza is an acceptance that no "thought" can be said to encompass what is required of the human endeavor without also accounting for the "conatus," and without the aspiration that Spinoza calls "the intellectual love of God." The Idea, of Idealism and that encompasses the domain of the pure open of Idealism's successors, is, henceforth, mystic. Subsequent philosophers (which remain true to this line of discourse, that is) have as their shared standard the marker that signifies finding accord with the *mystic precept* of generative self-organization. Their concepts range from terms such as "negation" in the dialectic (Hegel), to "God before God," (Schelling), to the "transcendental" in phenomenology (Husserl), to "Dasein" in ontology (Heidegger), to "machinics" in schizoanalysis (Deleuze/Guattari) or "differance" in deconstruction (Derrida). As different as these terms are, the thinkers who articulate them share the same standard: presenting in a way that is conceptually compelling and inescapably necessary the demand that we humans take up aspiration as a focus of our concern and thought. They all stand for the mystic precept, which declares it is not knowledge and certainty that is definitive of the human endeavor., but instead, the aspiring drive to become beings that are more expansive and more encompassing in our engaging what occurs is what makes us human.

It is to these inheritors of the Spinozan figuration of mystic aspirations that we now turn. In the work of these thinkers (that term is properly applied in these cases), the mystic figuration takes on the specifically historical and humanly necessary status of being an indispensible figuration of aspiration. It is this necessity, I suggest, that the mystically aspiring mentee who sits across the table from you is striving to express. It is the mentor's work, therefore, to align the listening, questioning and comprehending with the urgency this mentee feels in her own life.

Chapter Seven

From Precept to Concept:
Mystic Aspirations as Philosophy

This dialectical movement, which consciousness exercises on its self – on its knowledge as well as its object – is, in so far as the new, true object emerges to consciousness as a result if it, precisely that which is called... experience...

...In every case the result which emerges from an untrue mode of knowledge must not be allowed to dissolve into an empty nothingness but must of necessity be grasped as the nothingness of that whose result it is, a result which contains what is true in the previous knowledge...

...And with this new object a new Shape of consciousness also makes its appearance, a Shape to which the essence is something different from that which was the essence to the preceding Shape. It is this circumstance which guides the entire succession of the Shapes of consciousness in its necessity. But it is this necessity alone – or the emergence of the new object, presenting itself to consciousness without the latter's knowing how this happens to it – which occurs for us, as it were, behind its back...

...Presenting themselves in this way, the moments of the whole are Shapes of Consciousness. And in driving itself toward its true existence, consciousness will reach a point at which it casts off the semblance of being burdened by something alien to it, something which is only for it, and which exists as an other. In other words, at that point where its appearance becomes equal to its essence, consciousness's presentation of itself will therefore converge with this very same point in the authentic science of Spirit. And, finally when consciousness itself grasps this its essence, it will indicate the nature of absolute knowledge itself.

~ Hegel [1]

We don't yet know what "Whither?" we'll be driven to, having torn ourselves from our old soil like this. But that soil itself has bred in us the force which now drives us far abroad, into adventure, which casts us out to the shoreless, the untried, the undiscovered — we have no choice but to conquer, now we no longer have a land where we're at home, where we would like to "preserve." No, you know better, my friends! The hidden Yes in you is stronger than all the Nos and Maybes with which you and your age are sickened and addicted; and if you have to go to sea, you emigrants, then what compels you is a *faith*...

~ Nietzsche [2]

But now the great turning around is necessary, which is beyond all "revaluation" of all values,' [Heidegger cites Neitzsche's precept here] that turning around in which beings are not grounded in terms of human being, but rather human being is grounded in terms of be-ing. But this requires a higher strength for creating and questioning and at the same time a deeper preparedness for suffering and setting within the whole of a complete transformation of relations to beings and to be-ing.

~ Heidegger [3]

The Rise of the "New" (Philosopher) Mystic

As a result of the intensification and turmoil of the socioeconomic, scientific and intellectual endeavors of the eighteenth century, it became clear that a new stream of conceptualization was needed in order to bring together the myriad new connections that these movements were uncovering. The feeling that something was horribly wrong with how people were regarding their own lives, the lives of other people and their communities arose with a vengeance. Whether in the form of revolution or polemical texts of literature or philosophy, the accepted comprehension of what was occurring in people's lives, their economies and social/political institutions had to be reevaluated. In a way that is analogous to the social and historical circumstances in which the classical mystic arose, the conditions were once again ripe for the potency of mystic aspirations to come to the fore.[4] This feeling was especially poignant in Europe's mid-section. The seekers for a new comprehension of the prevalent state of affairs turned to the writings of the mystic ways of aspiring.

In terms of our mystic genealogy, I see this era giving rise to what I call mystically informed prophetic thinkers who articulate a new discourse.[5] This fusion of mystic aspiration and prophetic conceptualization allows localized and delimited spheres of endeavor to be infused with mystic aspirational precepts. The mystic impetus can thus thereby proliferate, diversify and have its dynamics be specified with respect to one domain or another, while maintaining its aspirational character – opening the articulation of each present circumstance to the expansive forces that are also imminently and immanently transforming it. The discursive domain that is most amenable to such an aspirational localization is philosophy. Here is a line of discourse that is already stocked with a vocabulary that richly describes dynamics that shape the logic with which we engage occurrences. With some effort and imagination the mystic impetus translates well into this already established endeavor. Writers such as David Hume mocked classical philosophy for rigidly separating creative and originary dynamics from the categories that the understanding used to explain a "fact." These categories supposedly accounted for the factors that gave rise to and supposedly accounted for its reliable repetition, but just a moment's reflection would make clear that it was just as likely that the repetition would not transpire and the "fact" would disappear. In these classical dogmatics, notions of "energy" and "change" or even of "things in themselves" were either rendered as states that preceded existence (or God's creation) and so were beyond description, or they were attributed to the machinations of extra-mundane powers, which, as miracles, nevertheless were devoted to producing factors that were amenable to human understanding and appropriation.

The new thinkers, or these thinkers of the new situation, realized that this separation could not stand. The powers of change were in the air — from science's new competence, to revolutionary forces that were changing economic, social and political ways of being — and any thinking worth the ink it was printed in had to infuse these dynamic powers of change right into the constitution of what was known. This meant changing the comprehension of what "knowing" entailed, demanding that knowing be comprehended as a dynamic and affecting power in its own right. The revived teachings of the classical mystics, from Boehme to Eckhart, rang true in this regard. The "eye" of knowing, it seemed, was the same "eye" with which something was to be known. But how does philosophy translate such an insight into its discourse? The thinkers we cite here either take up the challenge of constructing a new conceptualization of our way of being that explicitly accounts for this self-generating dynamic. Their intent was not to make philosophy more difficult to grasp, although it did do that; the intent was rather to pick discourse up off of the cold ground, wrest it from the cold, dead hands of the dogmatists, and have it ride on currents that allowed for and even beckoned the changes that promised a more expansive and more encompassing comprehension of the human endeavor. The mystic articulations of aspiration fit this purpose to a tee.

MYSTIC PROPHET FIGURES: THE CONCEPTUAL TURN. The mystic prophetic figures, whose works we touch upon here, reassert the compelling connectedness and the surging abundance of nature's generativity. It is the combination of these generative forces, and not the power of human logic, that pulses at the very core of what it is necessary for the human endeavor to comprehend and embrace. The mystically informed prophet figures envision and articulate the kinds of lived and discerned relations (dialectical, generative, historically or cosmically expansive) that are as expansive as the precepts of the founding and classical mystics, and that, by all means and maybe even more forcefully, operate now, right in the midst of everyday life activities. Against the dogmatic and skeptical complacency codified in instrumental (sufficient) reason, the new expositions of these thinkers infused our discourses on the Aspiring Mind schema and its capabilities to engage our worlds with the powers to exceed any given mode of existence or form of expression right into the interstitial fibers of the traditional logics of substance and essence. In the works of these new thinkers, mystic aspirations are no longer relegated to the realms of the inexpressible sublime or the mumblings of ecstasies. In the works of these thinkers, the aspiring potency can be properly *conceptualized* and *articulated* for the sake of analysis. But this same conceptualizing localization could only be grasped "in truth" by also pointing to their "World"-affecting powers, those P/SS forces that irrepressibly exceed any existent, prevailing, currently present state of affairs. In their works, this potency was still called Spirit, or God, but these thinkers deploy those terms in strikingly new ways, ways that we are still grappling with.[6]

In this chapter we will discuss how philosophy earns its spurs as a successor to the apophatic discourses of classical mystics by taking the most aspirational dynamics of the classical mystic vocation and seeing these energies in play in local areas of objects, relations and processes. In terms of our genealogy, I suggest three moments in which this "turn" of mystic aspiration into diverse areas of conceptual engagement unfolds:

(1) German Absolute Idealism, (2) the radicalized articulations of Nietzsche and Heidegger; and (3) recent reintegrating work of the thinkers I call "anamystics." In German Absolute Idealism, the force of mystic precepts breaks philosophy free of the boundaries that confined it within the search for a logic of certainty and human hegemony over nature. Then, Nietzsche and Heidegger (and others at this turn of the century juncture whom we do not cite) attempt to insinuate the vast, primordial and untamable potencies of generative forces squarely (as do the Beguines) in the midst of every nook, cranny and interstice of life on this planet as well as in the human endeavor.

We will also take up the work of our contemporaries, whom I call the "anamystics," who, also in the philosophical fold, begin to articulate the dynamics of this presumed to be unintelligible realm and so bring it into the range of our concern to comprehend the depersonalizing but still driving and affecting forces that make us "aspiring" beings to begin with (and not as a matter of reacting to situations or states of affairs). Their orientation is to articulate these dynamics so that we can enter into their overflowing and exceeding dynamics with respect instead of just fear, and approach them with a sense of readiness to expand our capabilities in anticipation of what comes (as a saturating phenomenon). These figures restore and then heighten our awareness as to the actively creative or generative factors that the "World" assemblage entails, and that constitutes a "functioning" mystic Field of Enthusiasm. In the works of these anamystics the situation that humans confront is not one in which, as Wordsworth said, that "the world is too much with us," but rather one in which we just do not attend to what that world offers sufficiently, and it is time to do so.

German "Absolute" ("Mystic?") Idealism

The arrival of German "Absolute" Idealism, as post-Kantian Idealism is called, constitutes a world-shaping event in European philosophy.[7] I use the term "event" literally. Just as one conceives of an "event" as comprising a surge of unexpected activity that, beyond any anticipation, explodes into a scene at one time, in one place, so too did German Absolute Idealism explode in one place, at one time. The place is the seminary of Tübingen, and the time comprises the years between 1788 and 1793, with its ripples and ramifications extending through to 1854 (the year of the death of Schelling). This philosophical tsunami surged over the land largely as a result of the discernments, dialogues and collaboration (before it all fell apart) among "the Swabian Trio": Schelling, Hölderlin and Hegel (under the aegis of a fourth: Fichte). [8] Within the span of a lifetime, a whole new standpoint on and about the status and significance of mystic aspiration in the context of the human endeavor was put into play.

KNOWLEDGE AND ACTION UNCHAINED. At the time the Swabian trio attended Tübingen, the universities in Europe (and Germany in particular) were stirred by the thinking of Immanuel Kant. Kant's mission was to reconcile two powerful forces that were shaping people's lives at the turn of the seventeenth century. One force was reshaping how "knowledge" and "certainty" were understood. The works of two writers dominated this movement: (1) Descartes made the conscious, subjective mind, the "cogito" (of "cogito ergo sum") the center of certifying knowledge; and (2) Leibniz provided the logical grounding in the form of monadological (universal localization of all occurrences) and sufficient reason. In the meantime, another force was sweeping the continent. Europe (and the newly formed United States as well) was exploding with the fervor of notions (from Spinoza, Hobbes and Locke) that took the mystic precept of the "right" of human actions to aspire to godliness to heart, in the form of *freedom*. What was so stunning about these ideas was that they incited flesh-and-blood revolutions. The proprietors of the intellectual status quo at the time seemed at a loss to comprehend this upsurge of universality within the human fold as articulated by these politically-oriented thinkers.

The issues at hand were legion: How is certainty and truth vouched safe within the realm of human freedom? What is the status of knowledge in the "free" human endeavor? What can such an action as human "knowing" touch upon? What is the "value" of such knowledge in the face of freedom? Does knowledge produce verities worthy of (equal to the certifying power of) the sacred designations of "truth," "universal" and "good" as do theologically validated revelations? These questions burned at the quotidian level because people's lives were being determined by the "values" that the new means of production were setting down; and they burned at the "conceptual" level because a new scientific order of what allowed for there to be certainty (eternally, universally, morally good) was emerging, and new demands on socioeconomic arrangements were being pressed in flesh and blood.

KANT. Kant's contribution to this situation, as presented in his fundamental text, *The Critique of Pure Reason*[9] (also known as the "First Critique"), was both epochal and paradoxical. On the one hand, he validated the efficacy of reason in the context of freedom by limiting its range of certainty; and on the other hand, he restricted the reach of human freedom within the compass of what experiencing reason could encompass. And so, on the one hand, what can be known was rendered certain by means of well-accepted categories of realization as rendered by the reasoning faculties of the understanding. On the other hand, these categories did not by any means make all that experiencing offered in the moment of engaging available for the purposes of producing knowledge. What was knowable was limited in two crucial (to the breaking point) ways. First, knowledge was limited to what the categories of understanding could accommodate – what could, with relative ease and common sense, be perceived in a cause-effect process. Thus, the very act of knowing (as per Kant's schematism) had an undesirable side effect: it *also* produced "things in themselves." What we could know for certain rendered also that which was perennially extended out, in an ever-receding horizon, beyond what is known. Thus, in the second sense, knowledge is limited by the overflow of experiencing itself, such that no complete rendering or representation of an "object" in the faculty of Reason is ever equal to the richness of the "thing in itself." These notions of knowledge and morality, while allowing for freedom, leave a lot of experiencing out of bounds for rational understanding; and much of what we experience thus overflows what rational understanding and moral law account for.

While Kant wrestled with how to contain, restrain and legitimate human knowledge, the mystic way, to the contrary, and at a minimum, *validated* the dislocations caused by the overflowing richness of extra-categorized reasoning. [10] The mystic precept established the demand that human efficacy be considered in its most expansive and universalized way, imbuing each of the actions and relations of living with a sense of infinite capacity (if not yet capability – that was the Idealists' contribution) that could not be denied any individual, no less a whole people. The students of Kant's teachings, who were witnessing his confining rationalizations take hold in one field of endeavor after another, were unsatisfied. Witnessing the revolutionizing events in France, they completely accepted the proposition that freedom had been unleashed and like that radiating wave we mentioned earlier, was washing over humankind. Taking their cues from this and other currents of expanding the compass of human engagement (including the works of the German Romantics), the philosophers took up the task of formulating new thoughts that would enable these transformed endeavors to be accommodated in formal, moral and social thought. What really mattered to them was not how to certify knowledge or subscribe to duty, but rather taking up the project of articulating the way living power and potency came into being and spurred a welcoming sense of there being a more expansive and more encompassing way of conducting human engagements, whether those engagements take place in fields of science, art, society, philosophy or religion.

While none of the figures I discuss would claim to be a "mystic," each of them acknowledges the influence of mystic aspirations in his work. They are all philosophers, and one is also a world-class, history-making poet. What is important for us is that these greats do what mystics do: they take the mystic propensity and use it to *reshape* the worldly discourses they expound into future-generating precepts that pertain to our living here and now. What we see in their works, prominently on display, is the stuttering, stammering and obscurity that comes with the territory of expressing qualia in the Field of Enthusiasm. We summarize below what we regard as the mystic kernels of the work these people offered.

FICHTE. Fichte went right at the abysmal chasm of the "thing in itself" opened by Kant's critical philosophy, and in doing so *stepped right into* the mystic stream. The opening words of his magnum opus, *The Science of Knowledge,* present nothing less than a full-fledged mystic demand: "Attend to yourself: turn your attention away from everything that surrounds you and towards your inner life; this is the demand that philosophy makes of its disciple."[11]

This, of course, is the battle cry of Idealism as it cascades down through the ages from none other than Socrates himself. In Fichte's hands this precept turns one's attention toward the gateway in which all coming into being of what is actual, as it occurs cosmically, for all, among all, as with all, can be witnessed and comprehended within the means, practices and life ways of the human endeavor. This turning opened onto far more than knowledge alone: it opened onto the unfolding of the ways of life being lived in freedom (echoing Spinoza). It is this *act* of unfolding the details and dynamics of these forces as we strive to comprehend them from moment to moment that makes humans who we are. Human knowledge is not mostly a matter of knowing things so as to do or make stuff; rather human knowledge is a gateway for the coming into being of what can come to be at all. In Fichte, the mystic way, the precept, becomes a (prophetic) way to shape our relationships, our knowledge, ethics and faith-for.

The standpoint Fichte envisioned was that of the "I" – which stood amidst all that was "not-I." This "I" can only be understood "mystically," in the sense that we have described: the coming to speech, and decision of an act through the *act* of that which comes to be. Fichte describes his "First, Absolutely Unconditioned Principle" this way:

> Our task is to discover the primordial, absolutely unconditioned first principle of all human knowledge. This can be neither proved nor defined…if it is to be an absolutely primary principle.
>
> It is intended to express that Act which does not and cannot appear among the empirical states of our consciousness, but rather lies at the basis of all consciousness and alone makes it possible. [12]

In the world of philosophy this declaration is as bold and as revolutionary (and to positivists, absurd) as our own Declaration of Independence. It launches philosophy into a new terrain in which knowledge, self, certainty, ego and "I" are not merely static capsules with an immense capacity to absorb impressions and process them into truths. Is it any wonder that Fichte could never "finish" his magnum opus? His very definition of knowing that also co-produces its knower, forbid any closure. The Field of Enthusiasm is reconstituted, and a new act of speech, performance, decision arises. Fichte's very act of writing a science of knowledge re-constitutes the science as the act of "truing" – evoking the true into being – itself. Speaking of the philosopher, the one who formulates, expresses and defends that which "true" offers, he says:

> This self-constructing self is none other than his own. He can intuit the aforementioned act of the self in himself only…Freely and by his own choice, he brings it about in himself.
>
> But – it may be asked, and asked it has been – if this whole philosophy is erected on something brought about by an act of mere arbitrary choice, does it not thereby become a fancy of the brain, a mere fabrication?…

[Fichte's answer:] This act is by its nature objective. That I exist for myself is a fact... Now I can only have come about for myself through acting, for I am free; and through this particular act only; for by this I come about for myself at every instant, and by every other, something wholly different comes about for me. The act in question is simply the concept of the self, and the concept of the self is the concept of this act; both are exactly the same; and by means of this concept nothing else is thought, nor can be thought, save what we have referred to. It is so, because I make it so...[13]

HÖLDERLIN. Nowhere does the mystic precept have a more unadorned expression than it does in Hölderlin; nowhere does this orientation become a more unembellished salient, and nowhere more than in Hölderlin's work is there put into play a more lasting and still formative expression of the itinerary for mystic aspiration. In these passages I will cite, written before his poetic career took hold, Hölderlin is working with his Tübingen peers (with Hegel transcribing, it is thought) in response to the ferment stirred by Fichte's radicalization of the notion of an idea's "flesh." In so doing, he participates in the founding of the Absolute Idealist movement in philosophy, which culminated in the work of his friend Hegel.

First, this passage expresses the vibrancy of the Field of Enthusiasm and stands at its threshold as a host, both welcoming and offering no delusions:

It is with joy that you must understand the pure as such, man, and other beings, must receive 'everything essential and characteristic' of the former, and must recognize all relations, one after another, and repeat their constituents in their coherence so long for yourself until the living intuition again emerges more objectively from thought, from joy, before necessity sets in; the understanding which emerges merely out of necessity is always distorted towards one side.[14]

Then, in this one sentence, in a way that recalls the classic mystics' apophatic expression, Hölderlin crashes through all of the rules of syntax, grammar, subject/object correlations and bursts through to the notion of qualia: the energies that refuse, deny, defy and refute our common sense experiencing:

> Yet how is it [the act of the spirit] comprehended within this quality?...Not merely through life in general...Not merely through the unity in general...[MHS: *Here we go...*]

...for the spirit determines life insofar as it is merely conceived of as formally opposing, yet in the concept of the unity of that which is unified, so that of the harmoniously connected there exists *at the point of opposition and unification* [MS: my italics: at the "point" of "a" qualia] ...*is tangible in its infinity;* that the pure, conflicting as such with the organ, is present to itself in this very organ and only thus becomes a living one; [MHS: *Here note the breaking through of the notion of "organ" as one of having "capacity" to that of a facilitating faculty that engages by reaching out beyond its current state by virtue of its capability, and thus, and only thus, becomes "living"— a very Spinozan notion.*] ...that where it is present in different moods, the one following the basic tone is only the prolonged point which leads there, namely to the *center point* [My italics – MHS] where the harmoniously opposed modes meet one another, ...in the conflicting, onward striving acts of the spirit...that precisely there [*"there," i.e., the qualia*] the most infinite presents itself in the most *tangible*, most *negative-positive and hyperbolical manner* [MHS: My italics]; ; that through this opposition of the presentation of the infinite in the conflicting striving toward the point and its coinciding at the point, the simultaneous inwardness and differentiation of the harmoniously opposed, living and founding sentiment is replaced and at the same time is presented more distinctly and more formed, more universal, as an autonomous world with respect to form as a world within the world, and thus as *voice of the eternal directed to the eternal by the free consciousness.*[15] [MHS: My italics.]

The element of mystic aspiration in this fragment of Hölderlin's thinking is instructive for us. Not only does he begin the work of discerning the dynamics of what we call the Field of Enthusiasm, but also he labors to demarcate mystic aspirations as lying *within* the course of our living, as activating and spurring our quest for knowledge and terrestrial certainties. That is, Hölderlin articulated a *secular* precept, a course of aspiration that is set outside of the rituals, revelations and orthodoxies of religion-based ideas that seek the assurance or certainty offered by God (and this from the graduate of a conservative theological institution). Instead, Hölderlin's mystic aspiring renders the precept as a *human* way, one for which we are responsible and to which we are bound in our generative moments. His charge, "walk bare-headed in the storm..."[16] is disciplined and grounded in a thorough thinking-through of just what it is that enables the human endeavor to proceed in knowing while being free.[17] The passage we have cited gives us an indication of the anchoring and grounding thought that this declaration "founds" German Absolute Idealism. This insight is a mystic one in the firm sense that we intend it: it moves our attention to the free-flowing and generative co-emergence of all that occurs. And it is mystic because it demands the breaking out into a new regime of becoming in our world – in our living, our re-membrances and in our language.

HEGEL. In his great "genetic" works, *The Phenomenology of Spirit* and the *Science of Logic,* Hegel brings to full logical and comprehensive expression what had been submerged in strictly mystic realizations. In so doing, he let loose the dynamics by means of which the fully realized mystic age would be set on its way. The citation of Hegel in the epigram at the start of this chapter sets out what I take to be the insight in which philosophical, prophetic and mystic work comes together. A "force" or a power drives any human way of knowing out of its state of equilibrium and equanimity.[18] This being driven out of such a state is not a matter of knowing more or having better tools for ascertaining "truths," but instead proceeds to constitute new "shapes" of human "consciousness" or knowing engagement with occurrences altogether. These new "shapes" are *new ways of being human,* new ways of engaging what occurs in the course of living, knowing and deciding that become more competent as an "age" and its cutting-edge "faculty" (such as self-consciousness and reason) develop and become more fully articulated (in logic and in institutions as well). This "more" is not a matter of a "progression" that we can valorize as "improvement" or making a "better" species (like a making a better light bulb or faster computer). Rather, this "more" constitutes a more expansive and more encompassing way of engaging the human endeavor. While it is true that in his "historical" accounts, Hegel only goes as far as describing the establishment of Reason – viewing Kant's accomplishment from that larger, aspiring perspective – he does put the mystic precept into practice. What the precept specs out, the human way ventures upon – and only on this way of venturing is there what we know.

This notion of "Absolute Knowledge" then, that static and process-minded interpreters (including Marx) took to be a conceptually imperialist act of ascribing to human knowledge complete veracity, truth and justice is, instead, a mere *moment* in the process by which we come to claim that we "know," according to the "shape" of consciousness in which we, in our culture, society, economy and means of production, reside and acclimate. This is a properly mystic precept, not because it is philo-sophically consistent, but rather because within that very philosophy is an apophatic work in the extreme – the very dynamics of its propositions overcome the "truth" of exactly what is known by the means made available to that knowing person (that shape of consciousness in the act of knowing). The key to Hegel's mystic realization is his notion of "aufhebung" or self-surpassing that both negates and surpasses as it takes on a new shape. A "shape" here meaning a human who lives according to a certain knowledge, culture, or theogony, and a "new shape" marking the appearance of a new "Person" in a new mode of devising new ways of knowing and of knowing what there is to be known.

Hegel displayed how this realization was at work in shaping our comprehension of politics, art, religion, and, of course, in philosophy, and he did so by making all of these endeavors into enterprises that *struggled* (or, aspired) to produce the most complete expressions of their ideas. Hegel remains faithful to his discipline, philosophy (as it was constituted at that time), by bringing the mystic impetus into expression only up to the point where the mystic vision, in its classical (Eckhartian and Spinozan) form, was articulated. He thus also completes the Kantian mission: now the mystic vision is safe, because it encompasses and gives shape to precisely the ways of knowing that yield a "thing in itself" and also exceed and surpass such a mode of understanding one's experiencing.

SCHELLING. Schelling never abandoned his mission, as a minister's son, to take up the prophetic role of delineating the ways our relations take shape, in the midst of the mystic open (that is, that of the classical mystic, as it was interpreted by the Protestant revolution). He is the absolute idealist who realized the godhead to which Eckhart had long ago prayed had *come into view* in the processes of our philosophical explorations. So Schelling set out to articulate the mystic Field of Enthusiasm and faith-for as a precept that we can take up in our living: a fully articulated rendering of what Spinoza's "intellectual love of God" had only pointed to.

Here I highlight the insights of Schelling's latest period: the incomplete, unpublished and only newly recovered *Ages of the World*. The driving force of this work is mystic to the core: "From now on, science will present the development of an actual, living essence. In the highest science what is living can only be what is primordially alive: the essence preceded by no other, which is thus the first or oldest of essences." [19]

Schelling's vision of cosmic generativity drives beyond all the metaphysical and theological formulations of his day and arrives at a truly radical (and very post-Newtonian-feeling) expression of cosmogony.[20] How do I express to the non-philosopher what Schelling proposed? In philosophical terms, he set in motion the astounding notion that *Being is not primary* —

which means that there is no "presence" or presented notion, concept, idea or "thing" – even that of God – that is not a matter of being produced by human processes of knowing. In the terms of our premise with respect to aspiration, we might say that Schelling articulated the precept that the human endeavor rides on the "wave" of the universe's generative potency: that potency by which the cosmos drives to become more expansive and, at the same time, become enriched with increased complexity. It is also a notion that cannot be brought to the fore without employing the mystic device of apophasis, such that each term employed cancels any immediate connection with conventional notions (of things and existing) and at the same time points beyond them. The difficulty of this "hyper-apophasis" can be read in this passage, which also sets out Schelling's mystic agenda – his faith-for and precept:

> We can therefore say of *this* –…It is what-is and it is being, because there is a thing-that-is and there is being, and it could express these; or: it is what is and it is being, with respect to the expressible, to the possible. It is not what-is, nor is it being with respect to itself or in deed, because it does attend to the opposition. But if something does not attend to what it is, it is not actual.
>
> It can therefore be said without contradiction that the unconditioned is not what is and it is not being, and yet it is not what-is-not, and it is not nonbeing.
>
> The unconditioned can express itself as what-is and as being, and it can refrain from expressing itself as both…
>
> Only an immovable, divine – indeed we would be better to say supradivine – indifference is absolutely First; it is the beginning that is also at the same time the end. [21]

The import of this cryptic, inscrutable, neo-, hyper-apophatic statement for the mystic genealogy lies in this: there *can* be a conception reached in expression that can encompass and enfold all the talk of "being" and even that of "God" and so, by virtue of encompassing these notions, can also exceed them. The important insight here, the precept operating here, is that such an excessive "notion" can be expressed. Human knowing and engaging what occurs (and becomes, through psychic-somatic processes) can be expressed and so can be put into play within the working of the everyday human endeavor. What greater faith-for can there be? That Schelling was unable to complete such a discourse satisfactorily is testament to his fidelity to that vision, not a failure of it. It would fall to Heidegger and the contemporary thinkers we call the "anamystics" to take up this task, to appreciate what difficulties and challenges it poses, and to continue the struggle to render in a propositional, life-shaping text what that precept entails.

Nietzsche: The Eloquently Stammering Demand

And do you know what the "the world" is to me? Shall I show it to you in my mirror? This world: a monster of energy, without beginning, without end: a firm, iron magnitude of forces that does not grow bigger or smaller, that does not expend itself, but only transforms itself; … force throughout, as a play of forces and waves of forces, at the same time one and many, increasing here and at the same time decreasing there; a sea of forces flowing and rushing together, eternally changing, eternally flooding back with tremendous years of recurrence…out of the simplest forms striving toward the most complex, out of the stillest, most rigid, coldest forms toward the hottest, most turbulent, most self-contradictory, and then returning home to the simple out of this abundance… Still affirming itself in this uniformity of its courses and its years… This my Dionysian world of the eternally self-creating, the eternally self-destroying, this mystery world of the twofold voluptuous delight…do you want a name for this world?…—This world is the *will to power* — and

> nothing besides! And you yourselves are also this will to
> power – and nothing besides.[22] [My italics – MHS]

This paragraph succinctly sets out the mystic stance of Nietzsche's aspirations: The profound sense of what the term "over" allows us to envision – whether that be the "overman," or overflow, overturning, turning over. Finding a way to express how great forces generate what occurs, then forms, and takes shape – this is the mystic aspiration that drives Nietzsche's authorship. His whole mission is to discern and express how it might come to pass that this process of "taking shape" does not have to be one of succumbing to weakness, to convention, conformity and fear, but rather can be one that takes up these forces on their own generative terms, and so keeps the human endeavor in a state of rising "over" whatever it had already become.

HIS AUTHORSHIP: WRITING THE PRECEPT. Nietzsche's writing is incandescent. His phrases and images burst off of the page, and the unresolved character of his intentions intensifies a burning sensation to the hilt: the reader feels the heat of his own confusion.[23] One does not read Nietzsche's aphorisms, or even encounter them. Written as though he were speaking right to us, directly, in our company, one *experiences* each aphorism as a single, even isolated force, a force that has no other intent but to demand…*something* of or from us (as a precept is wont to do). And it makes its demands on us without clarification, and without feeling the need to offer a justification. Each aphorism is a perceptual invocation, or, in Nietzsche's own terms, a hammer. His text just demands. A reader has to raise his or her own energy to a different level in order to withstand, no less stand with, this energy.

In the terms of our genealogy, I suggest that we can suppose that everything Nietzsche writes emanates from his Field of Enthusiasm – as though nothing else existed; he expresses his faith-for what must be brought forth, restored to potency. His way is to form the precept, as an aphorism, as if each was a Field of Enthusiasm of its own, enveloping and encompassing a moment of emergent becoming. He took up his authorship within his abode (of his myopia and his migraines) and shouted out from it; he took (willfully and not mistakenly) the defocused shapes that roamed about him as being his responsibility, what his "paternity" calls on him to raise, nurture and offer in the mode of fore-giving.

His guiding precept is clear: people live in their daily lives as though they were in a dream. Not only are they (we?) not paying attention, but also, and possibly more disturbing, they (we?) devalue this world in favor of *another* world. This other world is completely imagined, but is spoken for, defended and promoted in forms of reasoned, glorified, power-driven dogma, from religion to science and, philosophy in the name of "truth." This make-believe world is alleged, in some strange way, to be a better one then the terrestrial one in which they walk, talk, eat, breathe and re-produce. He sees this denial of the living world as being a complete and thoroughgoing *nihilism* – as *annihilating* in advance, by means of concepts, beliefs, superstitions and ideologies, the vitality of the living world of generative forces that is right there to feel and celebrate.[24] And yet, and here we land in paradox, he writes from the standpoint not of journalistic repetitions of how great the life of the body is, but rather he writes from an equally not-existing standpoint: from his own Field of Enthusiasm – which can hardly be said to be "real" either.

But there is a difference between others' nihilism and Nietzsche's mystic Field of Enthusiasm: in advance of engaging the terrestrial life world, the nihilist mindset projects a lifeless, fabulously decorated, non-earthly realm as being superior to what our paltry senses yield up. Not only that, and here is the kicker, one has to *die* in order to get to this superior world. A doubled nihilism: not only does this nihilism project the superiority of a lifeless and dead world to the living and generative one, but it sets in motion a death wish as the price of admission to this world.[25] Pace that fabulous concoction, Nietzsche's Field of Enthusiasm pulses with overflowing energies that drive living beyond any deadened equilibrium, identity and moralistic limitation in order to get "back" to the potencies that all existence and occurrence partake of. In Nietzsche's precept, besides surging impulses and drives, there is no other world; and so for humans the only the task is that of overcoming and surpassing the nihilist man who shuns such vibrancy.

Any formation, interpretation, valuation that acts in the first mode, depleting energies, although strong, worthy, and cunning in their resentment, is subject to this mystic's wrath. Any social institution, political formation, artistic distraction, or philosophical proclamation that diminishes the free flow of strengthening energies is fodder for this mystic's attack. And this hammer-like assault that Nietzsche unleashes doesn't look pretty. Nietzsche is not writing to explain or expound, nor especially does he embellish the stark demands of his aphoristic/apophatic precepts. He does not give quarter to the reader's comfort so as to allow her to "absorb" the ideas. No, he is creating the return of an experience of a certain kind, which only certain people will be able to experience at all. And if you don't, you are among the weak, and to you he bids a not-fond "adieu." The only point is to launch the precept: How do I bring this experience of overflowing, "monster" energies into com-munication, commerce and awareness so that the human (or the "overman's") endeavor can get on with its work?

NIETZSCHE'S FAITH-FOR AND FORE-GIVING. I will admit to have surreptitiously slipped into the text my interpretation of Nietzsche's anti-nihilist precept: ***proceed with what exceeds and so choose what changes you.*** Or, at this point we can also say, ***keep your aspirations alive, and choose them.***

Will to Power. Nietzsche, like the well-mentored mystic (his mentors being writers such as Schopenhauer and Emerson, and also Richard and Cosima Wagner), condensed the workings of his Field of Enthusiasm into a diamond-like crystal of expression: the "Will to Power." First, let me say this notion intentionally carries with it all the negative connotations one takes from it. Yes, it denotes a nihilist cynicism that everything that comes about does so because of a will to exert and sustain willing in the form the originator intended. It is *Ugly*. What is "good" (read "apophatic" and mystic) about this notion, however, is it radically refuses to accept or apply any moralistic valorization of the current slavish state of affairs, thereby remaining faithful to the mystic's demand to drive toward the liveliness offered by the "World" assemblage and the Field of Enthusiasm. Instead of righteously justifying one's claims of "truth" (another form of the Will to Power), turn to the unsettling vibrancy of those distinctive, individuated nodes of occurrence that rise and fall, from moment to moment as one lives with energy, faith-for, and in order to fore-give. This precept, instead of remaining tethered and tied to conventionalized truths that accommodate productive and commercial exchanges, expresses how all of the living forces drive to bring forth a "yet to come" for which there is no value and cannot be owned or appropriated. It maintains the sense of the driving mix of multiple forces that defy simplifying and abstracting into a merely intellectual notion.

The "will" in the notion of the Will to Power refers to all the forces that are active in the cosmos; they all act in this way. It is just that in the human realm, once nihilism sets in, that Will to Power seeks to annul exactly all the ways its generative potencies bode forth. It turns that will into an "auto-immune" response, attacking exactly the forces that enable it to thrive without reservation. While the notion of "will" in this precept is not well understood, "power" is the part of the notion that is most misappropriated. Power names the occurrence in which one force exerts its affects upon another, something other than itself. In Nietzsche's formulation, whatever occurs rises above the level of a mass of undifferentiated muck by virtue of the relative strengths of these exertions; and these exertions of will transpire as instances of power incessantly, irrepressibly. In contrast to this, a person's "individuality" is formed by the exertion of a will to cancel that diversity and instead *pose* himself as a character, indeed a caricature of a living being, as a perpetually melded and abidingly material "identity." And once this process is set into motion, a person will unleash whatever ferocious means at his or her disposal to assure that static point of fervent identity.

The Eternal Return of the Same.

> "The concept of the 'individual' is false. In isolation, these beings do not exist: the centre of gravity is something changeable; the continual generation of cells, etc., produces a continual change in the number of these beings. And mere addition is no use at all..." [26]

There is nothing the mystic can tolerate less than being closed in, or tied down. Nietzsche was often ill and homebound, he had migraine headaches that rendered him solitary, and he was nearly blind. His mind, however, once freed from imprisonment in migraine incapacity, was completely freed of any strictures. In mystic aspirations there are verbs, not nouns; and so the mystically aspiring figure hears, tastes and smells all manner of things *happening* rather than things being merely *there*. The question for the mystic is not, *what is* it, but rather, "What am I really *doing?* And why am *I* doing it?" [27] Here Nietzsche's cosmology speaks loud and clear. The universe comprises teeming swarms of contending forces, a "monster of energy." This is no world for the faint of heart, not a collection of things on the shelf or not yet on the shelf:

> The new world-conception. — The world exists: it is not something that becomes, not something that passes away. Or rather: it becomes, it passes away, but it has never begun to become and never ceased from passing away — it maintains itself in both. — It lives on itself: its excrements are its food....
>
> If the world may be thought of as a certain definite quantity of force and as a certain definite number of centers of force — and every other representation remains indefinite and therefore useless — it follows that, in the great dice game of existence, it must pass through a calculable number of combinations. In infinite time, every possible combination would at some time or another be

realized; more it would be realized an infinite number of times. And since between every combination and its next recurrence all other possible combinations would have to take place, and each of these combinations conditions the entire sequence of combinations in the same series, a circular movement of absolutely identical series is thus demonstrated: the world as a circular movement that has already repeated itself infinitely often and plays its game in infinitum.[28]

Eternal Return of the Same (ER) names Nietzsche's conception of how these forces gather into individuated and singularly functioning beings.[29] It is a dynamic required only when an occurrence is in the active process of taking its *own* place, as a singularity, in the context of the irrepressible forces of diverse energies that would tear it apart. ER describes a dynamic that arises from out of this welter of forces – is just one of them, really – that we organic, living and then conscious beings have elevated to prominence as our most necessary condition (for being singular, existing beings). It signifies to us two things, one valorized and prized, the other not allowed to be thought by us at all. First, we valorize and place into our rites of worship (and philosophy as "first cause") that where before there was neither occurrence or place, now there is something. But what we do not valorize, and disdain to think, is that for there to be something, a force must return, must iterate, what had gone on before so as to generate the originary moment of that first burst of something taking place and such a return is neither necessary, anticipated, or meaningful. It just happened, by accident, by virtue of the numbers of iterations that may or may not ensue from the fact of the vast and in-calculable varieties of forces that are in play, exerting their powers. Another way of thinking about Eternal Return of the Same is to consider the notion of "rhythm." In this notion we arrive at the concrescence of Nietzsche's work: where his sense of the burgeoning forth of what occurs takes shape in the Eternal Return of the Same, and thus can find its mode of expression in the aphorism.

We can look at this abyssal notion from the standpoint of nihilism and come to the conclusion that "nothing matters." Or, in Nietzsche's precept, we can come to the dance, celebrate this one throw of the dice, and affirm that by emergently generatively living we constantly become (if we can fore-give into ER as being an occasion for our faith-for).

What appears to our consciousness is what repeatedly arises, through sensory and bodily encounter, and which then works its way through our whole organism, so as to be given credence as a necessary bodily (psychic/somatic) forming for our survival, thriving, and power. The more frequent the appearance (rapid the tempo), the more weight it is given in its psychic/somatic hierarchy of being constitutive of a situation. Socratic/moralistic "reason" misses the variation, the subtle inflexions that render these energies completely fresh. The grasping of psychic realization as aesthetic, generative, and musical supports a fuller engagement with actual occurrence — fleeting and transitory as it is. Engaging the arising and passing away is full living. It engages a rhythm, discerns a melody, and dances, sings. It is the Field of Enthusiasm played out on the earth.

This is Nietzsche at his mystical best. The notion of the Eternal Return is apophatic and mystic to the core, and we can get a sense of that energy here: lively expanses of rhythmic eddies that coalesce into forms, and these are carried along on vessels (melody) into new spaces and expanses (which are, themselves, either within the frameworks of the same rhythm or break into a new one — a new tempo and/or section of the piece).

> A concealed Yes drives us that is stronger than all our No's. Our strength itself will no longer endure us in the old decaying soil: we venture away, we venture *ourselves:* the world is still rich and undiscovered, and even to perish is better than to become half-hearted and poisonous. Our strength itself drives us to sea, where all suns have hitherto gone down: we *know* of a new world.[30]

Questioning, chance, desire, risking. By opening into faith-for we live in the bursting that we feel; by stepping into fore-giving we congeal the acts of living into ventures into the more expansive and more encompassing. Thereby we venture in what comes and the other saturating phenomena of the "World" assemblage, putting our lives on a trajectory toward energies of terrestrial life we have not yet begun to contemplate, no less engage.

> Deep disinclination to settle down comfortably once and for all in any single overall view of the world; charm of the opposite way of thinking; refusal to be robbed of the attraction of the enigmatic.[31]

Heidegger: Surveying the Promised Land

I consider Heidegger's work to be a gateway, threshold or turning point of nineteenth-century philosophy – the work of a Moses who took philosophy up to the elevated threshold that offered a new vista of conceptualizing, but who does not set foot into the land below, which was espied from that high place.[32] Heidegger is the philosopher who most directly follows upon Schelling's faith-for – that philosophy can articulate that generative impetus, identified by the mystics and carried into a human-shaping philosophical endeavor. Or, he writes out the faith-for the precept, he teaches the precept that humanity is not done with its work to engage generative occurrences more expansively and more encompassingly. His texts speak of mystic dynamics that dare to go right to that fringe where the most generative potencies, those that never can be grasped, swirl and centripetally twist into what may and can become beings.[33]

Heidegger's *Contribution to Philosophy* (From *Enowning*)[34] is a work of mystic import of the level of Eckhart and Juan de la Cruz, while remaining firmly in the tradition of systematic discourses (which the anamystics in the next chapter will disavow) of the likes of Kant, Schelling and, of course, Hegel.[35] It is uncompromising in the demand for there being a "second" or "new" beginning, which, while needed as a matter of life and death (for humans and for the earth) is not necessarily in the offing, because it can be overwhelmed by the ingrained powers of technology and "common sense." If such a beginning can come to pass, it would reconstitute the human endeavor entirely. Such a reconstituting, beyond a "revaluing," is analogous to what Eckhart called for in "praying to God to be free from God," and what Nietzsche called for as a "revaluation of all values." It is coming into the domain where the human endeavor is shaped, moment by moment with the awareness of its coming to be. Such a surpassing does not happen "behind the back" as it does in Hegel, or even in a "beyond" being as it does in Schelling and the other idealists. Instead, it happens in a rhythmic sheltering of such an emergence, in a continuous to and fro, a continuing unfolding of the time/space of engagement. Humans cannot use their vaunted technology to bring this new beginning about; humans can only prepare, and wait.

To help us on this way, mystics and mystic poets emerge onto the scene. People such as Eckhart, Nietzsche, Hölderlin, Rilke, Trekl and Silesius rise to the fore and offer their precepts.

> Only a few come to the leap, and these on various paths. They are always those who ground Dasein [MHS: *the potency of the originary, new beginning, as it forms itself, in living as the carrier of the human*] in creating-sacrificing. — Dasein, in whose time-space beings are preserved as being as with the truth of be-ing is sheltered. But be-ing is always at its utmost sheltering-concealing, is the removal-unto the incalculable and unique, unto the sharpest and highest ridge, which makes up the "alongside" for the abground.[36]

This is normal prose for Heidegger, but it is dizzying and unsettling for us. The sense and motion of the passage is clear: it is apophatic and mystical. The "sheltering" field of enthusiasm always shimmers with qualia that are taken by these people as constituting the highest of what they, in their faith, are bringing forth.

After Nietzsche and Heidegger, and in view of Hegel's accomplishment, the work goes onward: the mystic endeavor is now completely freed from any classical, religious or God-based foundations. The mystic endeavor is truly released into the "open," and the Field of Enthusiasm now comes into view as the rightful and expressible (at least perceptually) force that shapes human aspirations. The "anamystics," as I call them, take up this task of bringing this mystic resource into play and into relief as a distinctively human mode of engaging a generative universe (under the banners of self-organizing "machinics" or non-Oedipal "schizoanalysis" for example). With our presentation of these figures, the genealogy of the mystic figure will be brought up to date, and our own work can go onward.

The "Anamystic:" Precepts of the Specific

I reluctantly introduce a new term in order to discuss the way mystic aspirations are recast (once again) in the scene of contemporary philosophy. I coin the term "anamystic" because our present times have moved us with ever-greater force into a new figuration of mystic aspirations. In this new "anamystic" shape, precepts no longer deflect our attentions to generalized, abstract or transcendent forces, but instead direct us to appreciate the forces of increasing complexity and generativity in the small, local and the near-at-hand experiences we engage every day.

This new era marks out a difference between the precept of the anamystics and that of their classical forebears. The classical mystics wrote with the intent of opening up the "soul" to the divinity of life that they felt had already been given to us by God, or the godhead. The anamystic writes in a way that offers no such clear path to some prescribed endpoint. Their precepts can be "applied" or directed anywhere, to any human endeavor so as to engage situations that are increasing in complexity at increasing velocities and intensities of affecting power on more and more dimensions of our lives.

The prefix "ana" refers to this *turning* of the trajectory of mystic aspiration. In terms of our aspiring mind schema, the turning constitutes an elevation in prominence of our engaging with the saturating phenomena of the "World" assemblage. In the time of the classical mystic, the Field of Enthusiasm erupted as a new arena of expression, and the theogonic notions of Christianity fit well with what needed to be expressed. By virtue of the discerning articulating work of the prophetic mystic philosophers, the logical and P/SS dynamics that generated this Field came into view. Their work started us on the way to a clearer comprehension of and thus a strengthening of the "World" assemblage's generative force — as expressed in the forms of saturating phenomena. With this specifying capability now being available, the generalizing sweep of the Field of Enthusiasm could be deployed over vast areas of concern and at the same time be concentrated in a specific area of concern

By introducing the new term "anamystic," I propose that we are on the threshold of a new and qualitatively different era as to the way mystic aspirations are expressed in precepts. The significance of a new figuration for discourses such as philosophy is immense and is still being sorted out, and exceeds what we can ever pretend to accomplish (our Fields of Enthusiasm), but step into it we must. The import of this turn for mentors is no less monumental. With the advent of anamystic figuration of aspirations, the impetus to aspire in this way can touch upon any endeavor in which a person takes on the role of advancing mystic precepts, in a highly flexible and specifiable way, and does so without either "religious" overtones or universalizing "transcendental" conceptualizations.

In what follows I introduce two of the thinkers who, along with others, were seminal in my own formation of the notion of "anamystics." The first, Gilles Deleuze, may someday be considered the Eckhart of the anamystic endeavor.[37] His work, like Eckhart's, takes the terms and narratives that have always been regarded in "traditional" ways as static categories of understanding, and turns them into dynamic factors that actively form, constitute and construct our sense of what is occurring. I used his work in Chapter Three when I used the notion of "machinic" operations in order to describe how our aspiring mind generates a "World" assemblage and a Field of Enthusiasm. The second thinker is Luce Irigaray, who takes up the role of the modern Beguine, and articulates what must always be kept in mind as we consider the mystic and anamystic figure: the restoration of the feminine in our sense of meanings and relations. Only if this feminine sensibility is kept alive will aspirations not degenerate into possession-seeking ambition. By re-asserting the relational and generatively formative moments of our ex-periencing, Irigaray offers us a glimpse into the workings of the "World" assemblage such that we can also step into its potencies and enact more expansive and more encompassing ways of engaging our lives, each other and the earth.

GILLES DELEUZE: THE FIELD OF ENTHUSIASM, AND THE MACHINICS OF ASPIRATION. After some deep study, Deleuze can provide a mentor with a way to reflect analytically and structurally on the Field of Enthusiasm.[38] That is, he offers a way to think anew about the classical terms of philosophy, such as "sense" and "difference" and even "Being" in order to provide a schema of dynamics that shape, not objects and certainties, but aspirations. In Deleuze's work these classical dynamics no longer occur within a "container" and no longer "emanate" from any kind of transcendent, self-producing or originating creator. Deleuze's notions fall completely and rigorously within the self-organizing milieu, which activates itself according to the parameters of the energies and embodied situatedness of the person involved. His precept, which he never enunciates but that I hear (*ad*-hear) as I experience his work, is this: each of us is a fractal point of generating "sense" and constructing concepts that scales up into a plateau, a living surface that can be lived, engaged, and engendered anew as a vibrant actuality.[39] From Deleuze the mentor can construct formal images of aspirations taking shape right on the spot and can appreciate better how "real" these notions are for the mentee.[40]

Surface. I consider Deleuze to be an anamystic figure because he relocates the realm of energizing, transforming and vital dynamics from the "beyond" of the classical mystic to the "surface" of what we immediately experience in ways that account for aspiration being a part of those engagements. I can easily translate his notion of "surface" to what I have described as the P/SS resource of the "aspiring mind." This "surface" constitutes a complex, highly textured surface that rolls out into *plateaus* of continuity by means of highly nuanced processes of sense-making, machinic iteration and temporal differentiation.[41] Each surface constitutes a rule-bound milieu in which energies are organized with respect to a specific "problem" that the P/SS engages. Deleuze regards a "surface" as providing all the generative potency needed to form ideas, knowledge and make decisions about what is occurring.[42] And for us, this "surface" accords well with what constitutes the mystic's Field of Enthusiasm.

Once this field, plateau or surface is operative (by means of the machinic processes we described in Chapter Three), Deleuze goes on to describe its "contents" — *virtualities.* For us, these virtualities activate aspiration in a coherent way in the form of a surface, plateau or "plane of consistency" called the Field of Enthusiasm

These virtualities even induce a sense of "doubt" about our certainties. As *my* virtuality, a dubious "factoid" breaks apart and then other kinds of factors — factors that are different from the ones that establish "certanty" — start to pour in. The factoid "expands" in its significance, right before my "aspiring eyes." In *addition* to the given "meaning" of what this occurrence signifies, it *also* includes its more mobile and evanescent "sense." That is, instead of this being an inert "thing in itself" that I freely operate on for my own productive purposes, the site of the occurrence also includes in its rising to my attention an evocation of my *initiative* for engaging it on *different* terms and in *different* ways than have been prescribed. And this invocation to engage this site differently surrounds this "factoid" with threads and tractors that induce my powers to engage the site in new ways.

The "Machinics" of Virtualities. All of this activity transpires "non-consciously." The gathering of these "virtualities" and sorting out the ones that continue to viably engage the site of the engagement or the "problem" is not something that our "conscious" processes decide. Recall that in our schema we located the Aspiring Mind resource at the threshold between the classical "unconscious" and the conscious functioning of the productive ego. Because there is no conscious sorting out and ordering of these virtualities, there has to be another process in operation which performs this function. Here, you will recall, we invoked Deleuze/Guattari's notion of *"machinics."*[43] *Machinics* names a particular process of iteration, one that always entails "restarting" and recasting of the stream of energies that would, otherwise, simply cruise along, un-perturbed. What occurs in this plateau or plane of consistency is a constantly *iterating* process in which the virtualities generated by the energy and its composition at the site of the engagement are able to it-eratively recalibrate, restart and reconstitute in a continuing stream of variation; and then this stream of "sense making" takes on a robustness of its own. It is this "machinic" process that, in a self-organizing context of our mind's sense-making, opens our psyches to thought and aspiration, to becoming more complex, and places the anamystic mindset in play among us.[44]

That whole complex of motion, virtuality, change and difference constitutes a singular "experience," one that we call "aspiration." Nothing but *aspiring* surges of generative engagements are in play here – each moment becoming more expansive and more encompassing, iteration by iteration. To be true to the experience as a whole, to the state of being constantly energized, this field accommodates the only expression that is possible, a "perceptual" one. This picture turns the tables on our business-as-usual assumptions. From this perspective the other conscious modalities of our productively socialized existences are the remainders of aspirational forces that are primary, and that we suppress at our peril. Using Deleuze's (and Guattari's) work then, we can assert that the anamystic figuration of aspiration is the primary moment of our P/SS's engagement with occurrences, and aspiration thereby instigates all the states of mind so as to enable us to engage occurrences (as "conscious" and "knowing" beings) as being vital and generative at their cores. They are every bit as much occasions for aspirations as they are sites for our productive projects.

IRIGARAY: THE "WORLD" ASSEMBLAGE AND RESTORING THE FEMININE. Irigaray roams this world in the spirit of the Beguine: born in Belgium, writing in Italian, living in France. She restores the feminine overtly, with clarity and as a compelling demand. Where Deleuze opened up notions that can help us to articulate the Field of Enthusiasm, I see Irigaray as operating in the moment of the "World" assemblage and restoring to their full expansively relational, feminine potency, the saturating phenomena of mystic aspiration.

The feminine in Irigaray does not envision any particular woman, or even necessarily "woman" at all; and the "feminine" is not a matter of either gender or genitalia. It is a "sense" within all occurring that is other than that which constitutes the masculine; or, we might say, it is a sense that drives into the anamystic aspirational open in defiance of and refusal of reduction to certainty and power. For Irigaray, the feminine exerts its way through us, though it is not the quality of energy we take up in our institutionalized life. The feminine has been *"abjected"* (literally, the way the child abjects the mother as it individuates – that is "cast aside" as in leave behind and move on, into male-based hierarchy and production [45]) into merely being nearby, on the periphery of our most profound inner selves, and yet also the most distant, other, strange and unnamed. This abjection increases with each and every decision we take to enter into the domain of the sensible, logical and productive "selves" we can be. We retain the feminine as the sense of freshness, surprise and wistfulness of play before rules, and not what we set ourselves to do, accomplish and possess. [46]

The "Between" World. That space opened by sexual difference is more than a matter of gender; it opens up a space that is ambiguous because it is defined or generated to begin with by an absolute difference — femininity and masculinity. As this ambiguous space asserts itself — as doubt or hesitation or questioning — saturating phenomena rush in to fill the void. This space constitutes then a third dimension: one that is of neither kind, neither male nor female, that both beckons and expands even as it works to assert its singularity and specificity in taking a place amid other people, relationships and things. Then, as the complexity of a milieu increases (multiplying in diversity and density), it asserts itself more and more as an affecting power in experiencing. It opens up and establishes a *"between"* world in which notion but the *relating* between *"different"* states of being is at stake. The more this "relating" is at issue and becomes a matter of attentive concern, the more this dimension is accorded independent and self-generating status.[47] In the terms of our schema, when I act out of this "between" realm wherein relationship is elevated to primary concern, I am giving cognizance, significance and power to the "World" assemblage of the Aspiring Mind.

When I act out of either only the male dimension or only the female dimension, my role is circumscribed on the basis of either "existent" (male) or engendering (female). But when I emerge out of this third "between" and "relating" dimension, I am neither one gender or the other, but instead I am a force of *engendering of existences,* pure and simple, over and over again, moving relentlessly onward in this co-emergent process. I am engendering the ways that forces of what occurs to me offer relationship in a completely open and unprescribed way. That is, I am engaging an occurrence, in the most emphatic sense, out of that third dimension in which I am constituting a "World" that sets me into motion, as a force of living, in expansive ways, according to the terms of the saturating phenomena in play there, in terms of what comes and what I must open my flesh up to accommodate. This is aspiration in its most passionate constitution.

Feminine Restoration. So what does *restoring* the feminine to our living entail? Irigaray states the clear feminine precept, *"Get back; and* *then love."* I read this as saying, take a moment to step back out of your drive to validate productive identity; then pause; and, finally, allow the flows of energy that are affecting you, like it or not, to have their way. This is not a stiff arm to men by frigid women. It is rather a forceful declaration of the tentative nature of whatever identity one has forged for oneself. The mystic way, after all, is not just about the expansive character of living being; it is also about the fact that living singular occurrences take shape within expanding dimensions of energy, diversity and thus ever-pressing freshness (presuming a healthy milieu, of course – which in our times cannot be presumed to be in the offing). The mystic senses the most tender and tentative of the emergences engendered on our beings by these energies before any meaning has been gathered or made from or of them.

Irigaray thus calls this "in between" dimension "incarnate transcendence": the embodied opening of new expanses never before (or to be) reached, and done so bearing onward the connecting (gravitational, cosmological constant) tissues of our originary (paradoxical) bond, through faith, to what comes.

Irigaray's "feminine" opens a psychic space, *despite* the presence of the existents that resist this opening. We must recall that this feminine potency is not a matter of abstract "negation," but is carried through all the incarnations (read the "carne," the flesh) that the feminine takes up in its creaturely proliferation: it opens while also remaining flesh. This is the *"horizontal transcendence,"* and the *"incarnate transcendence"* Irigaray sees as what "the possible" opened by the feminine entails. This means *any possibility,* she implies, in an anamystic way, that is able to roil the fringes of the status quo, that is able to garner enough robustness to take its place amid all the hard-driving certainties and power-invested defenses erected and enforced by the existent creatures (especially the males) who now roam the earth. This profound vision is, of course, at odds with the vertical images that enshrine the point-by-point occupations of male-based constellating identity. This possibility is not like that driving goal or ambition that pushes any resistant matter out of its way. It is rather that "between" dimension that opens up new spaces as it spans among the earth's beings: it is not a plow furrowing the earth, it is "air," roaming over, among and through its beings:

> Air
> You the pure,
> You who make confusion vanish
> You who flow between one and the other but without
>   Destroying either's boundaries
> You who respect the skin and nourish it,
>   And who procure the medium for every contact
> You without whom we cannot touch each other,
> Who always keep yourself between us,
> whose distance allow us to approach each other.
>
> Air,
> If you are missing, which presence will look after us?
> How do we pass from nature to spirit without you? [48]

Concluding Note

These anamystic writers, and others not mentioned here, bring the genealogy of mystic aspiration up to the present. They do so by honoring the force of the classical mystic's realization, and then they carry on by providing, with great rigor, the means for engaging and expressing these forces in all the specific ways the human endeavor does its work in our contemporary setting. Once again, our notion that people who aspire in a mystic figuration do so right in the midst of our daily concerns is shown to be worthy of our attention and respect. And, then, to the point we emphasize here, by virtue of the work of the anamystic thinkers (and also by virtue of the work of the other aspiring figures who take up this work, elaborate it and communicate it to ever-wider audiences) we can envision a practice of mentoring that addresses the concrete aspirations mentees might be experiencing. The work of the anamystic thinkers allows us to formulate a regimen of support and nurturance that pertains directly to the mystic figuration of aspirations.

In Part Three, I suggest such a process for undertaking the mission of mentoring mystic aspirations. It is based on all the insights we have developed to this point, and rides on the currents offered by our anamystic teachers.

PART THREE

Mentoring Mystic Aspirations

Chapter Eight

The Story of the Mentoring Encounter
With Mystic Aspirations

...[We] may recall the fine saying of Goethe, that for the great superiorities of others there is no remedy but love.

~ Hegel[1]

Given their actual futurity, the affirming ones remain necessarily unrecognized and strange even among the likes of themselves.

~ Heidegger[2]

Orienting the Mentoring Process

We have now concluded our account of how mystic aspirations develop as a "natural" force that shapes people's lives. We now need to turn to how mentors contribute to that shaping process.

It might be helpful to share a few words about what mentoring contributes to this shaping process. Part Three outlines the course of the mentoring engagement, from start to finish. I use several different techniques, from exposition to a table format in order to suggest a course that the mentoring conversation can comprise. This concluding section of the book offers you a way to see that it is indeed possible to mentor mystic aspirations, that aspirations do have structural elements that can be addressed and so we can envision a process that has a beginning, middle and end. I hesitate to say that this outline, and the sections of the book that precede it, constitute an all-in-one "do-it-yourself" manual such that reading it will fully prepare you for taking up the role of mentoring mystic aspirations. If you wanted to take up the role of mentor for mystic aspirations (or the other figurations I have identified) I suggest that we share some time together in person. In one-on-one sessions or in group settings, we could explore these ideas and practice engagements and then you could personalize the notions presented here. And, of course, we'd generate new insights in the meantime. It would be exciting, I think. Still, at a minimum, this text will offer you a start in taking up mentoring in a way that specifically and as a matter of principle takes into account the depth and commitment to learning and exploration of aspiring ways.

My guiding image as we proceed is that the mentor is enacting a very specific relationship to the mentee. As mentors we are neither treating nor coaching nor comforting this person. As mentors we are daring to venture into the realm of mystic aspirations with our mentees, a realm in which we may or may not be "experts." We are guests in this house, and visitors in this land. Accordingly, when we venture into a strange land it behooves us to learn about the main elements of the native people's traditions and the assumptions about their lives that drive certain customs and practices. So too, when we venture into the realm of mystic aspirations, we need to behave deferentially and respectfully, attentively and with a sense of wonder.

I hope the preceding chapters have proved the case that when mystic aspirations come to be expressed in affecting precepts they stir us: these precepts are not only initially unsettling but also are necessary if our human endeavor is going to be able to open to more expansive and more encompassing ways of living. As mentors then, we cannot hope to meet these people on their own terms if we do not appreciate their differences, not only from other people, which is fairly easy to discern, but also from other figurations of aspiring. It is by appreciatively sharing the energies of this site of aspiration that we mentors can presume to have something to offer the mystically aspiring mentee. That is why we need to become familiar with the specific ways that the mystic figuration is expressed by this mentee in order to enact her aspirations. We need to translate the mentee's terms in their aspirational intent, and not reduce them to commonplace goals and ambitions. A mentor wants to be able to envision what the life of aspiring in a mystic's way will be like, so that the mentor can speak into what might be likely as that person's future.

People are well-schooled for such futures when it comes to the other figures, especially for leaders and artists (with qualifications and allowances for individual idiosyncrasies, or even industry-specific variations[3]). But envisioning futures for those of mystic figuration, as I have said, has not yet been either documented or studied, no less comprehended as the subject matter that mentors must to take into account. There are no graduate schools to attend; there are no institutes and fellowships to take advantage of. And so, with the help of this book, we mentors have to begin to conscientiously address this state of affairs. We are pioneers in this respect.

In a very important way then (and this is an importance that I place at the very top of my aspirations for our mentoring profession), we are breaking new ground in our understanding of the human endeavor by taking on this responsibility vis-à-vis any of the aspirational figurations, but most especially with that of the mystic figuration. As we will continue to emphasize, this is not a figure that is taken into account in the accepted catalogue of "creative" types; and it is not a figuration that finds any explicit support as a figure or a life's way, in even our philosophical discourse. And so there is an "advocacy" or a re-conceptualization, if not a perceptual (in the mystic sense) trajectory to this work. By sketching out a figuration of mystic aspirations, and then by engaging in actual conversations that are intended to have "real-life" consequences for people that we deeply care about, we are doing our part to set into viable practice new (but not imaginary) ways of engaging our living such that it can become generative, and become, from moment to moment, more expansive and more encompassing – loving, if you will – of other people, other creatures and the earth.

The Threshold: "Mystic Pain"

As we all know, no one seeks out a mentor when things are going well. That is especially the case with people who configure their aspirations in a mystic way. Needless to say, as you have gathered from all the descriptions in the proceeding chapters, there is ample opportunity for things to go wrong for a person of mystic figuration. As we also know, unless the person of mystic figuration is disturbed by these events and feels that some kind of rupture is taking place, the impulse to seek a mentor will not arise. And so, the situations when I have met prospective mentees have included some awareness of there being a "pain" that is generating a specific "need." In the case of prospective mentees, this a most peculiar "pain." For one thing, it is not the pain of feeling inadequate or deficient in regard to some skill; nor is it the case that the mentee is behaviorally disabled by an overriding psychic, physical or situational factor. Of course, it is no small matter to distinguish aspiration's agonies from other situational or psychological difficulties.

THE PAIN OF STRIVING: TO BE "MORE EQUAL." It is a peculiar pain that is engendered by mystic aspirations. It is the pain of wanting to be more "equal to" the energies that inspire and activate, that expand beyond what is comfortable and known. It is a pain of one part of the psyche prying and pulling at another part; it is the pain that comes from wanting to locate and strengthen her own resources (which she knows she has), so as to be "stronger" in that aspiring life's way. It is a pain, as I will describe in greater detail below, which is not marked by panic, dysfunction or disequilibrium. It is a pain marked and surrounded by calmness and poise. It is a pain that seeks to open up beyond the strictures of any competence, a way *onward*. The person seeks, and articulates this, a readiness for moving oneself, a moving that though without destination or goal, is not a flight or excursion in errancy, but one that competently seeks a way to engage concerns more expansively and more encompassingly. Only if the prospect expresses these kinds of "pains" is mentoring an appropriate approach. But it also is a pain that is not seeking "competence" or skill so as to master and control a domain. It is a pain that wants to be equal to, ready for, the reaching out that aspiration demands. This pain does not arise in a situation that calls for a skill that will then be evaluated and measured by a governing authority. It is a pain that is utterly one's own, that persists and permeates a whole life, and that no one will ever be able to appreciate, no less judge – and that includes a mentor.

CHOOSING MENTORING. Given this state of affairs that marks the outset of the engagement, we must pause to consider what that threshold moment feels like for the mentee. In that moment, the idea of entering into a mentoring engagement is merely prospective. A person is actually considering entering into a relationship with a stranger; and the prospective mentee is doing so despite the fact that she may never have conceived of such a thing as mentoring, no less speaking openly and intimately to a stranger. There is no dire compulsion to seek help; there is no incapacitating pain (according to all the standards of viable socioeconomic functioning) that requires treatment or medication in order to function normally, no less competently or with excellence. This is someone who, above all, feels a "creative" or "aspiring" quality to their pain, and so, deep down, feels healthy in the extreme. If anything, every moment of stepping towards a mentoring engagement will evoke two steps back.

And the question then comes up: what impels that next step forward? After all, such a person will have never conceived that those energies could be "aspirations" at work, that these unsettling feelings of "pain" arise because these aspirations want their proper quotient of attention – which for mystic aspirations is a large quotient, to be sure. This person may not even consider that these feelings that want to claim attention

288

are significant in the first place. It will surely never occur to this person that these energies, while being uncharted P/SS machinics, can be discerned, fleshed out, understood and be transformed into an abiding figuration. We can safely assume that this person is not likely to have ever conceived of those urges in terms of the figure of the "mystic;" or, if the notion has occurred, however fleetingly, it was probably rejected as being a pejorative accusation. How does a mentor make the bridge from a conversation that looks at a mentoring engagement from the outside to the decisions, by both parties, to begin?

There are no pat answers to that question. When I am in a professional engagement in a leader mentoring context, the transition is eased somewhat because the mentoring context has already been set by a professionally contracted engagement (for Leader Mentoring) and presumably some level of trust has been established. I will say, however, that the first step in that direction is offering this person a sense that there is such a "thing" as aspiration in the first place. Once that notion is in circulation, other aspects of that person's "pain" can explored with the buy-in of the prospect. Until a person enters a formal process however, it is not advisable to decide or announce a suspicion that a mystic figuration is indeed at issue. Maybe the suspense alone will entice this person into a mentoring engagement. We will have more to say about this pre-engagement moment later.

THE MENTOR'S ANXIETIES. What about the mentor's feelings and concerns? Once the decision to proceed has been made, the mentor might indeed harbor some anxieties and will feel the need to prepare for the engagement. In this vein I have offered some general parameters, terms and schemas that specify how the mentor can go about preparing for the engagement with mystic aspirations. Parts One and Two of this book offer the mentor some "company" — as far as a text can do so, in that regard. By having the notions presented there as "top of mind" and at the ready during the course of the conversation, mentors can have a set of filters and templates that can help to guide hearing, perception and comprehension of specifically the aspiration's powers of affect on the mentee's life at this point in his or her life. These basic orientations fortify the mentor's work against slipping into the commonplace advisement or chitchat.

The "Occasion" for Mentoring

BEING CAST OUT. When I encounter people who might harbor mystic aspirations, they are usually fully mature adults (ranging in age from the mid-thirties – at the young end of the spectrum – to late fifties or slightly older). They have already experienced significant success in their professional pursuits. What brings them to me is that, despite this lifelong track record of success and advancement, suddenly, when they feel they are at the peak of their powers, they start to pick up, from the people who speak to them, on a peculiar tone in their voices and expectations. The people I have met have already achieved professional recognition and status at a high level; at some level they are respected and valued by their peers and "superiors" in their organizations. And then, despite that appreciation, somehow, a significant, insurmountable and tellingly valid barrier to being able to act on their most pressing concerns surreptitiously intervenes, stymieing their urge to make a difference. They have been blocked, or, in some cases actually cast out; that is, in some significant way they have been rejected. The pain here is real and it cuts deep. It is not that the rejection is intentionally "inflicted," so much as it is delivered as an assertion of will that specifically rejects the value and intentions that this person's aspirations are envisioning. The "attack" of rejection is no less real, however, for being defensive or even confiscatory.

The pain is as real as what one would experience if, when speeding down a highway, a wall rose right in one's path and there was no option but to smash into it. Whether the person remains in the organization or not, he or she has been passed over, passed by, relegated to the sidelines and a "career" is over. Relegated to this real or virtual exile, the person is set wandering, and they begin their sojourn in pain. Maybe they haven't been fired yet, but now this person is either at the onset of wandering. At this point of considering a mentor, this person might either be desperately attempting to find a way back or they might feel the need to set out on a way forward – just *any* way out of the anger, sadness, and feelings of betrayal and rejection, that are now raging within.

The feeling of rejection (or rejecting) is strong, and is stirred by different kinds of situations. In one case, the mentee was hurt by the fact that the very qualities for which she had formerly, in "lower positions" in her company, been recognized and appreciated (deep questioning, seeing possibilities no one else saw, an infinite capacity for empathy and toweringly magnificent communication skills) suddenly placed her in conflict with her executive peers. She was shocked when she was fired – by someone she considered to be her mentor (and maybe he still was acting as mentor). In another case, a woman had been completely successful in her organizational endeavors, in a company and in creating a professional association – but suddenly she realized these situations were leaving her bereft of satisfaction. She longed for something else and was on a journey to find out what that was. In still another case, a highly successful contributor to an organization returned after an extended as-signment off-site to find that the organization's options were extremely limited and seemed to offer little in the way of "worthwhile" engagement. Mentoring begins by shifting attention *from* what the organizations around them offered *to* appreciating what their aspiring energies were driving them towards. This means, in the most literal sense, having the mentee listen to her "pain."

THE PECULIAR PAIN. The pain that the nascent mystic describes is, as I have mentioned, a peculiar one. When mystics confront their peculiar energies in the context of firings, rejections, self-exclusions, such events puzzle them and leave them in a double quandary. On one level, in their organizations they have been fired or passed over, and yet, at some strange level, it makes sense that this happened. They feel

291

victimized, as would anyone who has been fired; but, then that feeling, that description of being a victim doesn't quite fit – at some level, which they kept from awareness while in the job, they recognize that they didn't *want* what was being offered anyway, they didn't want to do what was being asked of them. Or they took on jobs or assignments not out of their aspiring sense, but reactively, in response to a need for validation, giving in to family demands, or just marking time while they are figuring things out. That is one level of the quandary.

And then there is another level of painful confusion. In their quietest moments, they realize that there is something really *good* about being forced to make a change. They vividly recall how they felt "inauthentic" at some level in the old situation. Or, they are totally enjoying what they are doing after being freed from that conflictual context, but feel that it is not "productive." When they stop to think about it, after the panic and anger and self-deprecation have passed, the thought arises, "Maybe I need to do things *completely differently* in my life. But what do I do? And to what end? Why *do* I feel this way?"[4]

These questions qualify the vulnerability of mystically aspiring. It is a singular vulnerability and people with mystically figured aspirations are particularly subject to depression. The depression has a quality of utter confusion about it. The mentee might say to herself, "I am bright, more competent than the people who are 'managing' me – why am I failing?" And that message, going 'round and 'round in her mind just wears her down. A depression of this kind is a malady that I hear about frequently from mystically aspiring mentees. That said, it is usually after a prospective mentee emerges from a depressed state that she will seek mentoring. When in the throes of a depression, a mentee will likely withdraw altogether, or she will seek out a therapist rather than a mentor – and that is probably the right thing to do.

Many things can happen at this point. The proclivity toward mystic figuration of aspiration can be allowed to surface. Or, it can be suppressed, at great cost and with great effort. But let's follow along on the course of someone who is allowing something of the mystic energy to do its work. In this case, as they go along in this state of rejection (probably not their first, however), something else starts to bubble up: other outlets for their talents, energies and values send them different kinds of messages than they are used to hearing, or were able to hear when they were in their stage of socializing and fitting in. They hear people saying things like, "I never thought you fit in there," and "You are such a great teacher, I wish you'd do more of that," or "Your vision is really something the world needs to hear."

These messages, while unsettling, also relieve and elevate mystic aspirational spirits. In those words, mystics hear the ring of truth. However, no matter how much mystic aspirations want to respond by taking up that charge, new questions arise for the mentee that get in the way: How can I do this? What would my life look like if I give myself to these desires? How can I make a living at this life? Would I really succeed at this? How do I think about myself in this context? Enter the mentor.

These are the questions the nascent mystics ask. The mentor's role is not to answer these questions in ways that help the mentees to be "normal," in terms of what the general society expects of its "productive" citizens and workers. It is not even necessarily to help them be liked by everyone or fit in with business, professional or social patterns and cultures. Mentoring helps the mentee to become more fully a figure of mystic aspiration, helps him or her to live as fully as possible in that supremely generative role. The mentor guides the mentee to a life and into life practices that sustain, nurture, encourage and make more competent and robust the stance of faith-for aspiration that the mystic exemplifies.

No matter how much pain the mystically inclined may be experiencing when I meet them, I always keep in mind that there are distinctive characteristics of the mystic way that give them a real head start in the process of their self-discovery.

A LATE VEERING OFF THE BEATEN TRACK. One is this: people who are affected by mystic aspirations are very conscious of the ways their development seems to veer off the beaten track; and, while that veering off-track starts to happen early, the awareness that there might be something worthwhile to explore in this state of affairs comes relatively *late* in life. By the time the urge for a mystic's way of aspiring takes shape, these people may be in their forties or even older; as such, this drive toward making a change in one's life ways coalesces at a time in life when the person has many more resources available to draw on than does the young leader or artist, for instance. When they were young, the mystically inclined may have noticed some differences on the fringes of their socialization. She may have been more conceptually oriented and/or articulate than other kids (but so are young "prophets); or she may have benefited more from time spent alone dreaming and fantasizing then did other kids; and she may have been more gangly and physically uncoordinated than other kids (as their connections to their bodies might be more diffuse than others). But by the time the mystically inclined person seeks out a mentor in order to support a role such as that of the mystic, she will likely have already developed significant intellectual, emotional and even financial resources. Setting out on a new course, no matter how welcome at one level, still seems like an strange turn to be making at this point in life.

FACE-TO-FACE WITH MYSTIC ASPIRATIONS. The "late-blooming" aspect of mystic aspirations cuts two ways. The differences arising from mystically-oriented aspirations really become obvious later in life, maybe starting as late as one's early forties, and so, as we said, the mentee has an abundance of life experiences from which to shape a new way forward. However, by that late time in life, the abundance of psychic energies, which are profusely bestowed upon us in our youths, starts to weaken. And, in fact, it may be because one's energies become dearer as we get older that the mystic's crisis emerges at all. As the sea of overflowing energy recedes, two completely different psychic constitutions face each other on the exposed shores. One is the conforming and functioning constitution that has succeeded so well so far; and the other one is this strange beckoning – it is of the vaguest quality, towards and from hardly anything at all, and just feels like a relentless and ceaselessly resounding call that refuses any rest or relief.

To my ears, this call heralds the beckoning from the mystic aspiration's Field of Enthusiasm. Once the call starts to clarify and is allowed to take up its own voice, the developing mystic realizes how these energies have been shaping the way she engages her "world" all along. At some time, if they are operative, and if they have not been utterly crushed by a life of repression and neglect (not incidental "buts" by the way), for the fortunate, mystic proclivities that had been suppressed by productive pursuits will break out and will reveal themselves in stark relief.[5] Then the questions on her mind change. Now they become, "Am I up for this? And what is this to begin with?" Another feeling roils beneath the surface: "I am afraid." If she is lucky, a mentor will be available. The responsibility of the mentor, to such a person, is to help these people be prepared for this exposure into the open.

To be prepared to answer these questions, the mentor is well-advised to become familiar with the mystic genealogy and guiding notions that provide support to how mystic aspirations approach them. But before we get to that point, we have to initiate an agreement to proceed with a mentoring engagement.

Mentoring's Promise

DEMARCATING THE MENTORING ROLE. In the case of the person who is being addressed, homilies and platitudes like "I feel your pain," or sales pitches like "I think I can help you move on to the next thing" will be scorned. And they will not be true, as far as what a mentor offers to begin with. But presenting your expertise as a "healer" won't do either. Saying, "I have worked with many people in your situation... " is a non-starter. This person rightly feels that no one has been in *her* situation. The effort to initiate a decision that will embrace the prospects of a mentoring conversation for a mystically aspiring person is of course complicated by the "aura" surrounding the mystic figure. This person does not want to be suspected of being the airhead that the term "mystic" is applied to. And, finally, the mentor, at this point, can have only a vague suspicion that just maybe, mystically figured aspirations are in play. The diagnostic process has not yet begun, and as I emphasize below, being sure of what figuration is in play for the mentee, and/or what combination of figurations are in play (and in what relative states of emergence and assertion each of these figurations exert) requires several sessions of consciously engaged mentoring. One of the tenets that I have come to rely on is this: First impressions are always wrong.

The mentor's offer therefore might comprise these elements:

- Introduce the notion of "aspiration" as being a "real thing" that has hitherto been unrecognized or has been relegated to other notions such as drives or wishes or ideals. But in mentoring it is none of those things.

- Explain that mentoring addresses aspirations alone: not goals, ambitions or life planning, as the prime concern for mentoring. Mentoring helps to clarify, nurture, articulate and shape life ways around aspiration.

- Suggest that you hear this force being in play in the prospective mentee's pain and why it is the pain that specifically comes from aspiration (no need to mention that these are pains that seem to characterize mystic figuration at this point).

- Describe "aspirations" as a deeply potent force that is shaping how this person wants to live, going forward, and how aspirations, as they take shape, have less and less tolerance for the status quo and the conventions that hold them in place. Mention that you suspect this is going on. You might mention that our work suggests that there are four figurations – leader, artist, prophet and mystic – and that this person is likely to find common ground in the life ways of one of those figurations.

- A figuration of aspirations does not "make things better" or easier or make one "happier." Having a sense of community with a figuration simply provides a way of orienting one's anticipations of how one will engage what happens as one enacts aspirations in the ways this figuration does. One is not alone, but neither is one of a "type" whose path, destiny, future and identity are limited by personality, education, socioeconomic class or even biography. A "figuration" offers a new avenue on which to chart a course of one's life, one that only relates to, valorizes and acts on concerns that pertain to aspiration.

- The process has parameters: regular meetings, exercises and expectations; a fee; and that this is a process that the mentee decides on, from moment to moment, as to its value and worthiness for continuation.

- The process does not guarantee measurable outcomes, but does strive to give the mentee strength and a new slant on self-awareness so that she can commit to enacting, specifically, those aspirations with which she wants to address her primary, driving, and life-shaping concerns.

Constant Elements of Mystic Aspirations

To guide our perceptions and discernments as to the quality and/or extent of mystic figuration the mentee has entered into, here's a list of the most prominent of the constantly recognizable elements of mystic aspirations – elements that recur in each and every mystic discourse we have included in the course of our study, and that I have seen very clearly in evidence when I work with people of mystic aspirations. They are:

ORIENTATIONS AND TRAJECTORIES

- A *strongly explicit feminine component* in which relation to vast, undetermined and insistently generative potency is beckoned but not guaranteed in any one circumstance. I cannot emphasize this strongly enough. In every case of mystic figuration that I have encountered, the father was either absent, ineffectual or so limited in relating to the family setting that feminine influence (mother, sister, aunt, grandmother, young love) was always cited as the locus of learning and guidance. This has nothing whatsoever to do with mystic figures exhibiting "effeminate" qualities, but only that their sense of aspiration is bound up in notions of fore-giving and faith-for, rather than law-giving or being loyal to notions of hierarchical ordering (of relations, institutions or concepts).

- *Anti-totalizing in any form.* At best there are "convergences," clusters, "confluences" and gatherings or assemblages that have the appearance or quality of "singularities" — utterances, acts, decisions that intensify the momentary containment of the pro-liferating multiplicity. Religiously couched mystic aspirations may carry forward a "spiritualized" notion of God, or may take on the Eckhartian notion of a supreme "energy" or godhead that overflows even itself with richness, fecundity and increasing complexity, but mystics give up any notions of fate or predestination that might imply an over-riding controlling force.

- An *"ecological" stance* in which multiple and interacting "forces," beyond individual expressions and existences, open up opportunities for new convergences, combinations or emergences. These forces are "ecological" in that they "transcend," in a very concrete way, any single person's or even institution's abilities to shape events. This is the complement to "anti-totalization," of course, in that it is not large-scale combinations that are denied, only any ability of a monolithic force to determine predictable outcomes.[6]

- *Bodily (Somatic/Psychic)* engaging. Mystically figured aspirations often generate interests in certain kinds of physical pursuits, from yoga to mountain climbing. The actions that provide for healthy restoration and that energize their life ways of fore-giving and faith-for do not usually depend on the use of elaborate mechanical devices, such as motorcycles or all-terrain vehicles, for instance. Their activities do not require extensive training and expertise in the operation of these complex entertainment devices. It is the Artist figure's aspirations that are more likely to benefit from and relish the kinds of expert iterations with such machines. Racing or competitive comparing of physical prowess is of little interest in the context of mystic aspirations. Conceptually, the conventional, body-mind dualisms of classical, Cartesian or Platonic models is disdained. Starting with Spinoza (as Deleuze, and in a different vein, Damasio, make clear[7]), any notion of mind is given shape in the living organism. This is not a matter of naïve materialism or insistence that every mind state can be traced back to a definitive body state, but rather that the workings of our P/SS resources always touch our bodily engagements in ways that offer more expansive and more encompassing kinds of engagements. The orientations of mystic aspirations offer the development of new facultative engaging (see below), enriched perceiving, and so increasingly diverse modes of expression. The question that mystic aspiring generates is always, how does an aspiration take on a voice, achieve expression and be placed in action? Another way to ask this question is, how can the "precept" be taken up in a life way and not remain isolated in the ideal, utopic realm of ideated expression?

ASPIRATIONAL CONCERNS. These constants of pre-disposition and orientation to their endeavors then bring the mystically aspiring mentee to seek ways to express their concerns, and their hopes (faith-for) about what can happen if their still-forming precept could be taken up. The following list describes the large "categories" or headings under which a mentor might qualify, locate and gather into a more concise framework what the mentee's aspirations seek to put into play.

- *Facultative Development:* Along with the acceptance of multiple modes of convergence, there is the intent to foster the emergence of new conceptual and facultative capabilities to engage these flowing nuances in all their variety, instead of winnowing or reducing them to points of knowledge. The gateway to such development is the mystic's *faith-for* — that opening to "what comes" without setting out prescriptive limitations in advance.

- *An explicit transformation / transvaluation / transgression process* that conjoins a psychic / somatic component with its inter-personal / socio-cultural-political expressions.

- This entails a *new vision of generativity* as a standard wherein each act measures its capacity for further welcoming of growth.

THE MEANS AT THEIR DISPOSAL. Given the far-reaching and far-sighted spanning of their aspirations, there are precious few ways that mystics can act on their concerns. Thus the mystically aspiring mentee, in one way or another, will be expressing actions that have these characteristics.

- *Genuine fore-giving* in which the mystic ventures a way, in her own living, such that something more expansive and more encompassing might transpire. This is *aspiration* in its highest expression.

- An articulated *perceptual position* that cannot be attained through instantaneous revelation or in genius-like isolation, but only through a deep *practice* that traverses and meanders the labyrinth of the fabrication of the human endeavor's legacy.

- *Practices for sustaining health.*

- *A determination and discipline to teach.*

- *Faith-for* that includes, identifies and takes up as a practice how it is that this person moves from being in an abstract, wistful and suddenly affected state to shaping a viable precept that can center a life way and can drive concerted efforts of teaching (and whatever kind of research, writing, organizing, presenting and gaining of adherents that this teaching requires).

We now turn to describing these regimens in greater detail, and provide an example of what one mentee offers as her own "Mystic Way." The next chapter offers you an opportunity to think through what your own mentoring will strive to accomplish.

Chapter Nine

Three Mystic Regimens

We must try to find out what dangers arise in the middle of a real experiment, and not the lack dominating a pre-established interpretation.

~ Deleuze [1]

Life has not disappointed me! On the contrary, I find it truer, more desirable and mysterious every year – ever since the day when the great liberator came over me: the idea that life might be an experiment of knowers – and not a duty, not a calamity, not trickery! And knowledge itself: let it be something else for others;...for me it is a world of dangers and victories in which heroic feelings, too, find places to dance and play.

~ Nietzsche [2]

Sit as little as possible; give no credence to any thought that was not born outdoors while one moved about freely – in which the muscles are not celebrating, a fest, too.

~ Nietzsche [3]

The Regimens: Health, the Mentee's "Mystic Way," and Role-Making

As we seek to offer a mentoring conversation that provides support for the mystic figuration of aspirations, we need to have our guiding questions at the ready — if not yet specifically formulated. Up to this point we have provided material that the mentor can use to firm up the ground of the conversation, material which provides the mentor with a map of the aspirational terrain over which the mentoring conversation roams. The material also provides the mentor with boundaries within which to remain during the course of the conversations in order to concentrate attention and inquiry within the domain of mystic aspirations. These materials never stray far afield from the questions that guide the mentoring conversation throughout its explorations, questions that are always in play as the conversation proceeds:

1. What *life practices* does this person need in order to be able to affirmingly embrace the Faith-for needed to sustain her Field of Enthusiasm, through acts of fore-giving?

2. How does this person *coalesce* what might be a mere wisp of intimation or a fleeting flash of energy into a viable aspiration that is capable of shaping a life?

3. What is it that mystic aspirations *do* in the midst of daily life situations?

In this chapter I offer a summation of what the mentoring process aims for in light of these pressing concerns. While I can't say that mentoring mystic aspirations can have measurable "goals" that might satisfy institutional measurements, there is no doubt that there are at least two basic outcomes that a mentor can use as touchstones for judging whether or not the intention of strengthening mystic aspirations has been met. The first is that the mentee establishes a regimen for improving and maintaining health — energy and enthusiasm for their life's way. The second is that the mentee implements a "practice" that consciously strengthens the faint surges of aspirational "intuition" (wishes, in Freudian terms) into viable and robust actions that project the precept into the mentee's area of concern.

As a "guardian of aspirations," the mentor does not go so far as to prescribe a preferred course of action that promises the mentee "success." That is another kind of conversation. And since the mentor is never an "expert" in the area of concern that focuses the mystic's aspirations, it would be outrageously presumptuous of the mentor to suggest such a thing. Rather, I propose that the mentor's work culminates in the mentee seeing the virtue in, indeed the necessity of, establishing three regimens or disciplines in her life going forward; and to establish a frequency, intensity and concentration on these regimes that is equal to that of her commitment to her concerns, field of enthusiasm and faith-for. Those three regimes are (1) health-making, (2) cleaving to her own "Mystic Way," and (3) taking up the work of the mystic role.

Regimen One: Health-Making

I want to emphasize this point in the strongest way possible: for the person who takes up mystic aspirations, ***health is everything.*** The mentor needs to emphasize throughout the conversations that mystic aspirations have nothing to fall back on for nurturance and support other than the mentee's own health. The structured dynamics of mystic aspirations, as all of the terms we have developed, indicate that the mystically aspiring mentee is the sole source and point of generation of her fore-giving and faith-for, and that her Field of Enthusiasm, if it is to "feel good" at all as an *enthusiasm,* needs to be plied with energy that only she, the mentee, can provide. It's up to her. In the absence of such a regimen, especially as the mystically aspiring person gets older, she becomes more and more susceptible to depression. And, in the other direction, the more the mystic is able to follow a health-making regimen, the stronger the precept and the more resilient the mystic is in his or her way.

While I can never be completely sure that all the subtleties, nuances and texts that I refer to in the course of the conversations have been completely absorbed and taken up as a life's way by the mentee, I do not let the engagement conclude unless I see some evidence that she is establishing some significant health-making life practices. These practices include diet, exercise, mental stimulation, pure relaxing enjoyment and inspiring engagements with the environments, texts and contexts that excite her.

As a rule, the mystically aspiring people who show up for mentoring are no youngsters. The excess energies of youth that allow for persisting in destructive behaviors (poor, American, addiction-based diet; sedentary habits; degrading entertainments and diversions) have diminished, and the mentee faces the overpowering demands of her aspirations with fewer reserves to compensate for or replenish her aspirations in the face of the inevitable (and sometimes debilitating) doubts. The bad habits must be pared back, and new ones, which are health-making (as best as we can determine) must be put in place. The good news on this front is that since the people who seek out mentoring do so later in life, many of then have had to come to grips with their changing health needs, and so many of them already adhere to some kind of regimen already. My work is to consider with the mentee whether or not these practices are sufficient, appropriate and fitting for that person at her stage of life and the level of the demands made on her by her mystic ways of aspiring.

The regimens they have established comprise actions, practices and manners of attention that enable a gathering in of experiences in a vigorous, alert and affirming way. The regimen entails activities that restore and revitalize their energies, and the practices reinforce and strengthen the mystic's ability to remain open to those energies, in all their intensity, immensity and irrepressibly disruptive force. The practices that bear most directly on this ability refer to diet, exercise, and often, some kind of meditation (from Buddhist sitting to hikes alone in the woods, to reading "contemplative" or "spiritual" texts at a regularly appointed time, every day). The mentees I have worked with do get it: they either have a regimen in place in order to establish and embrace the vast, wild and chaotic energies they feel, or they begin the process of experimenting with possible new practices.

Regimen Two: Forging a "Mystic Way"

The core of mentoring mystic aspirations is centered around enabling the mentee to forge a way of life that *valorizes her aspiring way* and also allows her to get through the day at the level of excellence and affirming expansiveness these aspirations inspire. The point of mentoring aspirations is not to help this person feel "normal" but rather to help her establish life ways such that all the energies that make her "different" become strong, communicative and effective. The question I take up in this section is, what does such a "way" look like? Of course, that question cannot be asked or answered in terms of universal metrics, and instead has to be asked for the sake of each mentee, for which it will be answered differently each time. Still, we must ask this question for each mentee we engage, if we are to get a sense of the effectiveness of our mentoring.

The fact that this question must have different answers for each mentee does not mean that we are taking stabs in the dark in offering our help. It does not mean that we are dilettantes and amateurs in our work. Mentors do a lot of work on their own "procedures" in order to help mentees. The mentor's actions in the face of aspirations are always intended to be attentive and appreciative. And when it comes to aspirations, to be sure, a mentor's affirming demeanor is critical. Beyond those standards against which we measure our own procedures, I am suggesting there is also distinctive content or subject matter that mentors address when they seek to support aspirations. The intent of this book is to offer the mentor another resource in their effort of supporting their mentees. I have endeavored to show, demonstrate and delineate that there are *actual practices that aspirations engender,* and for the mentor, there is actual subject matter to consider in the course of the conversation. In this section I offer a picture of what the mentor can accomplish by adding this specific subject matter to the helpful and appreciative tone the mentor offers.

The issue in mentoring is always, as we have said, how do our mentees transpose these vague and unsettling aspiring urges to engage one's life more expansively into a robust and effective life's way? The work of mentoring then, while certainty requiring attentive listening, needs to appreciate and valorize the way the structures of aspiring do their work in the P/SS, and the way that these energies, as they are gathered together in the "aspiring mind" resource," will take shape in the life choices and social actions of a mentee. To help the mentor address that question, we have provided here the background structure and genealogy that keep the conversation on track. In Part One we addressed these structures, and in Part Two we addressed the ways aspiring energies take shape in expression and practice. But so far we have not addressed transposing those factors. At this point, however, the generalities lose their power. Each mentee is different, for each one mystic aspirations will play differently, and for each process, what such a transposing might entail will differ.

Below I offer one way that one mentee transposed these structures into life practices that were in accord with the structural and genealogical factors that constituted her mystically figured aspirations. What you will read next is offered neither as a "model," nor a replicable pattern that a mentor would prescribe by rote for any mystically aspiring mentee. Rather, this is one example of how one person, on her own volition, as she reflected on the constant parameters that I offered as ways to "understand" mystic aspirations, decided to engage these and make them effective in her life.

As such, the regimen I recount here is not my creation. A mentee I'll call Alicia offered this account of her role-making regimen to me as we concluded our conversations. In the course of our conversation, we had identified all the factors I have described in Parts One and Two. She was excited to learn how mystically figured aspirations were actively formative for her: how she shaped her aspirations into factors that aligned well with the notions of the Field of Enthusiasm, faith-for and fore-giving. She enjoyed reading the works of some of the people I cited above as constituting a mystic genealogy. In the course of this wordplay, it became apparent to me that Alicia had exceptional awareness of how her Field of Enthusiasm took shape experientially in the course of her living, and also that she was exquisitely articulate about her experiencing. She appreciated the notion that her propensity to "give," and her reticence about "charging people" for her services accorded with the notion of fore-giving." She was strengthened by the idea that her work in the field of holistic health was not a Utopian idealism, but was a "faith-for" a viable life's way. Her question then, was how does she firm up the vague feelings of aspiration into the life ways these notions affirm? In our terms, she is asking, "How does my aspiring mind work? How, in my own language, as I understand this process of experiencing, do I take up and accommodate the work that the assemblages of this resource are performing?"

Alicia arrived at one of our sessions with this outline in hand, and she had prepared it without my prompting. Since that moment, I have continued to ask my mystically oriented mentees to produce such a regimen, in writing (Alicia had only notes from which she spoke), as a culminating exercise for the mentoring process. I offer below the six essential elements that regimen must comprise. These are (1) wandering, (2) "enstartlement," (3) spatiation, (4) emotional hooks, (5) media, and (6) "outcasting." Each of these elements was specifically articulated by Alicia herself, and together we came to names or "titles" of the moments in the "way." Your mentee may have different "moments" to articulate, and may see these same moments in different ways, and as leading to different expressions and ends. But I would advise the mentor to listen carefully to the mentee's account of her way in order to assure that at least the six moments cited here are accounted for.

1. ***Wandering.*** As I said, I have most often encountered mystics
   when they are in their wandering stage. There may be no other
   way to recognize that mystic aspirations are in play than to note
   the urge, or imposed necessity to wander – either to voluntarily
   leave a comfortable situation (as Dan did), or to be chased out
   (fired), as was the case with Alicia. And even then, it is not until
   we have explored the mentee's reflections on her situation do
   we know that it is in fact mystic aspirations that are in play.[4]   In
   the case of mystic aspirations, and as Alicia meant this stage, the
   mentee sets out, in the spirit of experimentation (either physically
   leaves, or strikes out intellectually into new arenas of discourse,
   for instance), in order to expand her compass of engagement.
   The old world is too set, too pat, too set in its ways to offer
   chances for aspiring energies to grab hold, take root and rise to
   expression. "Wandering" for the mystic is a Thoreau-like
   experiment in solitariness and going back to nature. (Many of
   the mystic mentees I have worked with find Thoreau's *Walden* to
   still be inspiring.) But it is not as though the nascent mystic at
   this stage says to him or herself, "I want to do an experiment in
   mystic living" – whatever that is. The wandering is more likely
   similar to that of Ishmael in *Moby Dick:* mystics set out to sea, to
   wander, when the specifics, complexities and bothers of a given
   situation are too constricting and act as a constant drain on their
   aspiring energies.[5] Indeed, as we have noted, unsuspecting
   nascent mystics are likely not to have a choice as to whether or
   not they will commence a time of wandering or setting out on
   the seas. Whether they decide to leave in order to pursue their
   "dream thing," or they have been ejected from a career and a
   prospective approach to their lives, the mystic proclivity fully
   manifests and dominates a psyche, and the wandering will
   ensue. Think of all the feelings of uncertainty, estrangement and
   anxiety these people must go through when they upset those
   close to them and strike out anew. In Alicia's case, one close
   friend accused her of "running away" from problems. And no

one, until now, would say to her, "I think you may have tendencies toward a mystic figuration, which entails wandering." Until, that is, she met a mentor who valorized those aspirations. Only now did she hear, "If you do have mystic proclivities, this is the way mystics feel; wandering is *necessarily* what happens in a mystic life. It's normal, for you."

2. ***"Enstartlement": Breakthrough to Power and Duration.***
"Enstartlement" is the word I coined as I listened to Alicia explain what came next. Alicia spoke about being knocked out of equilibrium, and not because of her firing. Rather, her firing only highlighted to her that her feelings of veering off-track and the feelings that come from being deeply impressed by new thoughts or images were more important to her than toeing the corporate line. For one thing, these little shocks of new learning cannot be denied, paved over, prevented or gone around. They happen to her, and she likes it. Second, these little shocks each enveloped her with the utter certainty that what was occurring heralded and announced that something (else) was coming, like it or not, and she *did* like it. I coined the term "enstartlement" to signify a state that envelops a person such that being awakened, of sensing with thoroughgoing clarity and without reservation that something *different* is occurring, that a new level of awareness is being triggered – all these come through loud and clear. The state is different from a "wake-up call" that is delivered by a sudden or traumatic event. Alicia did not take her being fired as an impetus to crank out a new resume and dive into the networking pool so as to resume her career as a continuation of what she had been doing, or as a matter of going where her "career path" took her. Enstartlement occurred for her because as a mystic she lived in an awakened state that was amenable to *fresh* realizations that break continuity with the commodious flow of socialized events – *and, at some level* (as we noted above), *she welcomed the break.* The mystic aspirations draw one to the fresh, the unresolved and

vibrant. Now and again, we all are startled by an event, and most of us do not necessarily welcome such surprises. The mystic, however, finds herself strangely attracted to and even enjoying the surprises, the ruptures. The mystic *greets* these awakenings with *open welcoming.* Enstartlement replaces notions such as reverie and ecstasy that have so bedeviled the notion of the mystic endeavor through the ages. Yes, there is that sense of utter freshness and surprise that a mystic welcomes; and yes she may peel off from the ongoing activities to savor what has transpired. But there is no need for shaking, quaking and speaking in tongues. Just the fact of having risen to full awareness that one is utterly alive suffices. This old notion of rapture and ecstasy may have more to do with the limited range and kinds of "experiencing" that were available in medieval times (or for those who are still ensconced in such mindsets) than it demarcates a mystic proclivity. The receptiveness, openness, and welcoming of smaller, more localized enstartlements seem appropriate for today's complex and rich varieties of experiencing.

3. ***"Spatiation": Loosen and Illuminate the Bonds.*** Enstartlement may be a "delicious" state, but it passes. It cannot be held in place. Enstartlement initiates a follow-on response of a different quality of attentiveness. Some form of what Alicia calls a "kind of meditation" is summoned. We aren't talking about sitting in lotus position here, although such a practice is certainly constructive. Rather, we are talking about encouraging the mystic to "detach" as Meister Eckhart would say, from all words or "understandings" of what the enstartlement has engendered; that is, "bracket" immediate reactions and just let the sensations move about. This is the moment of allowing the qualia in the Field of Enthusiasm to hold sway. Rather than allowing our "normal" psychic/somatic processing to lock the experience into accustomed frames of identity and sameness, spatiation forestalls such accommodation. It orients one to body sensations that do not shut down, but

instead are held in suspense and not allowed to assert their usual priority of wanting to name and order the experience in terms that "understand" it. It emphasizes body and psychic orientations that allow the fullness of *being affected* to register as completely as the intensities in play can deliver. It is a response in which the mystic forms bonds to her field of enthusiasm. It strengthens the mystic's faith-for what must be opened, and simultaneously loosens habituated reactions. This is a complex process. The spatiating we speak of here is not just a momentary pausing, a time out for taking a deep breath.[6] To learn ways to enact the spatiating operations on the enstartling occurrence may take years. To even countenance this act of spatiation takes a certain willingness to "detach" (in Eckhart's phrase), to hold back from reacting to habituated feelings that press on us to immediately understand what is going on. A young person with the pressing need to prove competence and display acumen with regard to a situation has other concerns at stake than what spatiation entails. Whatever specifics initiated the enstartlement, spatiation changes the experience into something other than what an account of facts and immediate feelings will encompass, no less "instinctual" or entrained reactions. Also, instead of treating the enstartling moment as being a mere surprise that we shake off, or as being lasting trauma that we insistently dwell on, or even an event that immediately is assigned the special, isolated status of being a life-changing revelation, spatiation allows the enstartlement to settle in, tamp down, and so be taken up into the living constitution of mystic aspiring. Rather than become a one-time event around which other things are constellated, spatiation allows the enstartlement to become a continually precipitating source of energy (a locale of qualia in the Field of Enthusiasm) that can become, in later considerations and reflections, a robust basis for one's faith-for. One thus says of such a spatiated en-startlement: "It's something I am working through. Maybe, someday, I'll get it, or not. In the meantime, is the coffee ready?"

4. ***Emotional Hooks: Rhythm of Connection.*** When it comes to spatiating her enstartlements, mystic aspirations do not allow a person the peace offered by sublimation and suppression. Enstartlement has already torn asunder the fabric of easy continuities and habits. Alicia gave the specific example of how she could be walking through a crowded airport and suddenly the sight of a person, or a snippet of conversation overheard, or a bump into an unseen obstruction triggers an initiating enstartlement and then begins the cascade of memories, words, associations, feelings and images. These don't go away, but stay on and linger as mood and narrative. They bring up certain feelings, some of which she can't pin down.; Unresolved hooks dig into her psyche and act as triggers for engendering strange, and often unwanted, connections. These "micro" hooks are spawned continually after the initiating enstartlement has roiled the waters, and they are phenomena that both release and displace the mystic from "normal" entanglement in everyday goings-on. By accepting mystically figured aspiring energies, a person is more amenable to welcoming them as occasions that enrich and expand what we take to be the "normal" state of affairs. The aspiration-elevated energies sever the person's ties with the given commonplaces as they also energize the need for and the growing plausibility of a faith-for orientation to what is occurring. Dreams (nocturnal and daydreams) seem to provide ways for mystic aspirations to sort out. Dreams of both types seem to allow the psyche the time for these emotional hooks to either fade or to coalesce into patterns that can be considered further. Like so many words from "on high" or "omens" from anther world, dreams sparkle amid dreary routines. For emerging mystic aspirations, given the vibrancy of their *waking connections* through their faiths-for and the vibrancy of their Fields of Enthusiasm, dreams actually compress and specify those energies into images and utterances that are suitable for being worked into their precepts. Dreams help to organize, consolidate and intensify the rhythms that are

formed as the qualia generated by the enstartlement coalesce in the spatiation allowed it. The mystic takes these psychic encounters as elaborations of not fully cognized immersions in their real world, and at the same time, the mystic's life thus begins to "knit" together in her own ways.[7] The mentor, of course, is no Freudian analyst or interpreter of dreams. Indeed, a retrospective, regressively oriented probing of the mystic's dreams is precisely *not* what is called for. Listening to accounts of these daydreams or night dreams, or any other way of fantasizing or expressing detached and roaming fragments of coalescing notions, is a delightful way to keep the mentoring on the footing of playfully (though seriously so) experimenting with expression, verbalization or depicting the aspirations that are taking shape. It is a way to allow and encourage the "spatiating" process. In my work, whenever the mentee offers an interpretation of the dream that levels it into equivalences with the everyday, I ask her to think of the ways that it departs from these norms as well. The sense of what the dream is activating thus, at least for a moment, gets to play once again on the field of enstartlement and not on the ground of the next job to tackle, or feeling guilt about the one that has been neglected and put aside.

5. ***Media: Construction of Language and Signs.*** Mystic aspirations forced Alicia to create her own language. The Field of Enthusiasm entails departure from what is given. What was brought to Alicia through enstartlement, dreaming, and triggers takes primacy, and these disrupting experiences do not leave many traces of readily available associations and connections. From our work with her forebears, with the mystic genealogy, Alicia grew to ap-preciate that she had to find what media she needed in order to bring her experiences into a more stable state of being. These media included "art" or attempts at "art" by the outside world. Supremely great, world-creating poems, such as those of Hölderlin, Rilke or Celan, or plastic artworks such as those by Rodin,

Michelangelo, Goya, Manet or Bacon, which are *mystic* expressions, epitomize the very cutting edge of what the arteous will take up and perfect.[8] Sometimes the form adopted has a more "structured" expression, such as that of scholarly writers or organizational and historic world creators. Their media of choice can occur in any endeavor in which seeking out and shaping modes of expression are central to the practice.

6. ***Outcasting: Keep Fresh and Constructive of New Networks.*** What distinguishes mystic creation in media is that we can never approach their work from our given standpoints, but have to relinquish our given states of mind and frames of reference and let ourselves go to sea. In the face of the great white whales of the mystic, we have to let ourselves be cast adrift, with only the hollow, mystically inscribed coffins of our old ways to cling to – as Ishmael hung on to the coffin after the demise of the Pequod. In short, what began as an initiating enstartlement becomes the way of the mystic life. And so, we encounter those who are migrants, even, or most especially, in their chosen worlds. The mystic is no longer thrust out, but leaves. "You can't fire me, I quit," she says.

Regimen Three: Taking Up the Mystic's Work and Role – Teaching the Precept

No mystic I have met or studied remains content in a state of exile, encamped within a placid, hermetically sealed residence. Even those who finally give themselves over to the demands of their respective Fields of Enthusiasm do so in the spirit of *aspiration,* with their faiths-for impelling them to situations in which their fore-giving can take hold. In Alicia's terms, they set to wandering. Of course, the idea of taking their faiths-for into worldly engagements, expressing it "professionally," so to speak — as a matter of taking up their role, striving for accomplishments that will make their aspirations operable and viable – is utterly daunting.

As well it should be. Today's mystic aspirations have to master the subject of the discipline they are in. Only when someone achieves a level of mastery in that domain will the precepts they venture be accepted; only by demonstrating their mastery in the classics of their domain will their precepts be able to pry open the lines of power that hold their chosen domain in thrall. In the manner of Eckhart's commentaries, the precept has to be expounded in fine detail, so as to forge and map out all the new connections, relationships, and associations that her sparkling Field of Enthusiasm calls for. The action that accompanies or fulfills mystic aspirations then, that articulates what the Field of Enthusiasm and its faith-for intends, is that of teaching. And so, we can say that a mentor works on helping the mentee to take up the role of teaching.

This does not mean that the mentor provides career guidance that advises finding a teaching position in established school settings. Rather, it entails helping the mentee engage her mystic aspirations in their specific qualities in "real-life" settings – families, careers, friendships – such that her intents, messages and precepts become clear to others. Blurting out pronouncements won't do; letting the anger build from the frustration of not being heard or appreciated won't help. The mentee must be conscious that her "precepts" must be conveyed with diligence and patience in a process of *teaching*. From other parts of the mentoring, those that attune her awareness to her Field of Enthusiasm, the mentee next needs to build for herself a way to form a curriculum, a method and slow-release procedure that teaches the precept, first to adherents, and then to the unsuspecting. There is no shortcut here – forming and teaching the precept is the work that mystic aspirations require.

I find that no other part of the mentoring is more difficult and even counter-intuitive than that of coaxing the aspiring mentee into the regimen of teaching. One mentee on approaching this part of the work, actually said, "Uh oh. This sounds like I have to get disciplined. Won't that stifle my spontaneity?" I think many of mystic proclivity are able to accommodate the notion of a Field of *Enthusiasm* far more than they are likely to warm up to the idea of the slow, methodical discipline that teaching entails. So this step, establishing the regimen of teaching, requires a mentor's intervention to shape.[9] It requires of the mentee an ability to *accept* these strange energies that assail her, and then, when they are accepted as what her life entails (like it or not), she must then *grasp their power* to shape not only her life, but also deeply and constructively affect the lives of those around her. This is a big and unexpected step for mentees. The assumption is that this energy of hers is just a matter of personality; the usual "life coaching" advice is for her to accept that energy and move on. Mentoring goes one step beyond that acceptance moment: by helping the mentee form her precept, she is encouraged to see that her energy has a center, a trajectory and a means to affect other people's lives. The key to making that affecting potency comes alive is to step into the role of *teaching* the precept.

Itinerant Teaching. What is it that the mentor can point to in the way of anticipations and expectations for enacting mystic anticipations? I propose to my mentees that the life they are setting out on is one of teaching the precept. The shape that such a life entails will be one of wandering: speak, teach, move on, and speak again. The wandering continues. The open remains open, as the mystic life itself attests. The mystic *teaches.* Is it a coincidence that the great universities in Europe took shape as mystics made their appearance? Is it a coincidence that the Beguines were urban teachers to the rising bourgeoisie (who had to learn new skills of thinking beyond mere repetition and rote recitation of liturgy)? Is it accidental that Meister Eckhart's great mystic precepts are "preached" (in the vernacular, no less)? The answer to all those questions is a resounding "No!" These developments were directly tied to the fact that mystic precepts were in play, and that teaching, in all its forms, various settings, and (always) its intent to reach "the people," was now active.

It takes work to arrive at expressing a precept in a way that affects people in ways that mystic aspiring intends. Depending on the strength of the mentee's Field of Enthusiasm and the power of her faith, a mystic may indeed be "out of touch," literally, with the common sense rendition of the world. But it is the intent of the precept to place something in play that can generate a new occurrence, a new story (see below). Mystic aspirations, in the form of the generative precept, want to, intend to have such an effect. Of course, gaining adherents is a huge undertaking, and one that may exceed the time available in a lifetime. But one can find a way for the precept to be clear at one point or another. An "entry point" for the precept to be felt, and maybe comprehended, can be found. This is the core work the mystic undertakes, and undergoes, in order to put what beats so vibrantly into play. This is the key act of the mystic, to *teach*.

Thus mystic life demands a rigorous discipline that pertains to articulating the precept alone: *the way of learning that has to learn*. By that I mean mystics need to learn about their Field of Enthusiasm, and, of course, this is a field of their own making that has no other purpose but to drive a new way (and thus, moment by moment, must itself be learned). They are learning about it, but in doing so they are also learning about themselves and then are actually changing their very sense of themselves in the process (since their "identities" are so bound up with the field of enthusiasm). As the field is deepened in its scope, applicability, and power of penetration, so does the mystic change. Each stage of learning requires, in its own way, a new kind of learning, with its own demands.

Now, at some point, this learning arrives at a state of sufficiency, or at least repose. At some point, the Field of Enthusiasm reaches a state of coalesced wholeness (and not necessarily the "completeness" that an "expert" claims for his or her knowledge). The Field of Enthusiasm is sufficiently detailed in specificities, historical continuity and observed or documented factuality and it is connected by its own logical clarity and flow so that the books can be written, the pedagogies outlined and the teaching can begin. Or, we can say that the mystic's psychic capacities are, in these moments, sufficiently expressed in all the dimensions that his or her field of enthusiasm can offer.

And then, there is this. The taking hold of mystic aspirations, the taking hold of a precept through teaching, transpires over decades – not semesters or a year's quarter. First are the decades it takes for the mystic's aspiring mindset to coalesce. It takes decades, maybe three, to come to grips with the exceptional energies the mystic finds assailing her. Often, in the midst of that youthful, preparatory, emergent maelstrom, the rudiments of a mystic's Field of Enthusiasm have arisen. An interest in a field, an attraction to strange expressive behaviors, loves of the offbeat, and divergent personalities are some of the hooks I've heard mystics speak of. The triggers in the role-making regimen often set loose sparks or shrapnel from the field that is trying to have its impact on the refusing (professionalizing) psyche of the young, nascent mystic. Then there are the decades involved in elaborating that Field of Enthusiasm. The learning required in order to grasp what that field in all its dimensions of history, logic, mythology, scientific discourse, etc. is trying to assemble and render coherent (if not conventionally "logical") is monumental. Then there are years of trial and error, advance and retreat, as the mystic perfects the expression of the precept.

Adherents. What are our mentees looking for as they venture out with their precepts? Mystic aspirations appreciate, crave, and need solitude, but they are not solitary. They seek to engage other. Each aspirational figure needs to have in view what constitutes a constructive response to their particular way; our mentees need to have a reasonable expectation as to what kind of *relationships* their efforts at teaching will engender. In my lexicon of aspirational figures, I see it this way: leaders have followers, artists have audiences and patrons, prophets have disciples. What about mystics? They have "adherents" (that is, "ad-*here*-ants," and variously, as a neologism, "ad-*hear*-ants") – people who come and stay with mystics in order to hearken to their precepts, maybe in silence, often in a retreating and reticent contemplation. Mystics, more than the other figures, are likely to hear deafening silences in response to their precepts – since their demands are far out in front, far in advance, of what can be assimilated into the immediate and the habituated. The mystic sends out his or her work and, as any living being, beckons for a response. Given the complexity, sometimes obscurity, always demanding characteristic of the mystic precept, however, such beckoning may not engender warm and fuzzy replies. Anger, puzzlement, and resentful silence are just as likely. And, I always keep this in mind: it took *four centuries* for Eckhart's vision to find its way into other viable breakout creative precepts.

Fore-Giving The Precept. Of course, no one of mystic aspiring would ever declare their work of learning to be completed or their knowledge being of the certified and "vouched safe" variety. Their work is to map out a course on which the precept can be taken up by others, and set on its way. At this point the mystic begins fore-giving in earnest, as the very way of life that the mystic has. It is from this moment that we see the works of the great mystics. They choose giving fields: some work in areas that attempt to instill ideas and institutions of world peace; some work in medical-related areas of healing rather than in application of techniques to symptoms. Some work in business, but also devote time, energy and money to "causes" that open horizons seemingly closed, to those who refuse these proscriptions.

Fore-giving the precept is no mushy case of putting something out there and then accepting the response, "whatever..." The mystic's *aspirations* are being given in these words. Giving from out of the Field of Enthusiasm is a hard giving. It can only be given. Thus the precept intends to deliver an *affect,* to (re)define boundaries between what is and what can be. And this is no mere "ought" or idealism. The mystic's fore-giving creates a *difference,* a divide, a before and after. Those who choose to enter into the mystic's field hardly know what will occur. They are adherents who cling to the message as to a lifeline. They do what they can to advance the message, but are strictly bound by their own stage of learning. Some may rise to the level of the founding mystics, as Eckhart did to the founding Beguine mystics, or as Nietzsche did to the founding mystic Hölderlin. But most do not. So the mystically aspiring mentee sets out once again, to a new wandering, as Alicia might say. "Mystics leave," I often find myself saying to mentees and to their friends, and to myself as a reminder of how brief our encounters with mystic aspirations, in the flesh, will always be.

Onward

We have prepared ourselves for the engagement as much as we can. Now it is time to sit down with the mentee and begin the conversation.

Chapter Ten

The Mentoring Process: A Sketch

As Nietzsche's Zarathustra proclaimed, "Behind your thoughts and feelings, my brother, there stands a mighty ruler, an unknown sage — whose name is self. In your body he dwells; he is your body." Hence, "Become who you are."

~ Askay and Farquhar [1]

Anticipations Meet

The mentoring conversation begins.

Two people sit at a table across from one another, each anticipating that a significant conversation is about to take place, even as each frames those anticipations in different ways. Both anticipate, with a sense of excitement, the surprises that are in store for each of them.

The mentee comes for a wider perspective on "who she is," and to be relieved of her own confining and constricting habits. The mentor is there to help, but not by offering prescriptions for things to do, or nostrums that treat her feelings as "symptoms" that need to be fixed. The mentee anticipates that the structured approach to aspirations that the mentor offers will open up insights to be sure; but also the mentee hopes that by means of this structured approach, her insights will build into robust tenets of a viable life's practice that delivers the precept ever more effectively. The mentor anticipates a conversation with a person of demonstrated competence, accomplishment and maturity. [2] He or she

322

anticipates conversations with a person who exudes irrepressible passion, incomparable communication skills, prescient conceptualizing abilities and the capacity for devoted commitment to what is envisioned as not only possible but also as being necessary for her to continue in this role.

The mentor sets out to embrace those qualities and raise them to a level of being worthy in and of themselves, in their own right, and therefore worthy not only of this time together, but also worthy of that need to be nurtured and cared for, first and foremost, by the mentee. In order to help the mentee to embrace this state of autonomy, the mentor wants to firm up a figuration of the mentee's aspirations so as to see these powers and potencies in a guise of personhood that has psycho/somatic resources devoted to it. The mentor also wants these resources to claim worthiness for attention, cultivation and be given (by the mentee first of all) the conditions that foster their continued emergence into a viable life's way. Finally, the mentor wants the mentee's aspirations to be supported also by the figuration of its genealogy, by the precursors and predecessors who carved out a way for mystic aspirations to be sufficiently enduring, even in hostile conditions, to take root like that lone tree that grows on the windswept mountainside's rocky ledge.

Whatever the differences between the two sets of expectations, both parties know that conversation revolves around this premise: a process of shared learning is about to transpire. While the respective professions or life circumstances of the mentor and mentee may not jibe, so as to permit a "been there, done that" repartee, the mentee can rightly anticipate that the mentor grasps the notion of *aspiration* and can guide a person into a greater appreciation of that state of being. She can rightfully anticipate that her energies will be restored, refreshed, freed from outmoded constraints, and she can get on with her life with renewed vigor. The mentor, appreciating aspiration, can anticipate with no small measure of excitement the chance to see how the mentee's energies, discernments and articulations promise the endeavor into the more expansive and more encompassing – a restoratively generative vitality.

All of this has been prepared for in the ground we've covered so far in this book, and it has all led up to this moment.

This chapter outlines the course of mentoring mystic aspirations that my own work has settled into. In order to offer the reader/mentor a condensed presentation of this process, I have oriented this final chapter around Table 10.1. In that table I present the overview of the sessions and phases of the process (Column One), the specific mentoring intention in that session (Column Two) and then I offer suggestions as to assignments, approaches and supporting materials that help to make a session or phase of the work more effective. I also stress how to calibrate expectations as to the timing and extension of the process, and discuss the fee conundrum. I also collect in one place orienting elaborations (not quite definitions) of the key terms around which mentoring mystic aspirations are centered. The text outside of that table in this chapter offers supporting commentary for that course.

That said, I want to be completely clear: What follows here is not intended to be a definitive curriculum for a mentoring process. More important to me than any course procedure is the essential tenet of mentoring that, when it comes to mentoring aspirations, there can be no cookie-cutter curriculum. While this book offers the mentor an itinerary that comprises the "subject matter" of the mystic figuration of aspirations, it is no substitute for the process of heightened listening and attuned empathy that mentors practice in each moment of their engaging mentees. What the curriculum, so to speak, ensures is that certain touchstones of the mentoring process are covered, that the process at least (in different proportions and in different orders of presentation, explication and practice) provides the following:

- An orientation that can sustain her emerging figuration and potency of her aspirations by offering a figurative shape to those aspirations;

- Terms of understanding and recognition that pertain specifically to those aspirations;

- An outline as to what specific role (to the exclusion or de-emphasizing of other roles) enacts these aspirations; and

- Suggestions that guide the mentee's attention to the kind of relationships these aspirations engender (to the exclusion or de-emphasizing of other, even more desired, relationships).

Setting Parameters: Discerning Aspirations

MENTORING VERSUS COACHING OR THERAPY. Among the many ways the mentor has to "collect" himself and set his mind to the specifics of mentoring, one crucial orienting concentration is worth singling out: how what transpires in the mentoring that is about to commence constitutes a distinctive helping practice. In the current mix of services that are available to people seeking support, keeping in mind the ways this service is different from coaching and therapy will go a long way toward assuring that the mentee is getting the support being asked for. There may be many ways that mentoring overlaps with coaching and therapy, and many coaches and therapists do indeed provide incidental mentoring in the course of their conversations. But I want to make clear that in my view, *only mentoring addresses aspirations,* treats aspirational figurations as being worthy of stand-alone valorization and support, and only a mentoring regimen addresses the pre-psychological assemblages and operations of the P/SS resource of aspiration and its aspiring mind. What does this mean in terms of the mentoring engagement and practice?

It means that a mentor is able to hear, through all the noise, that it is *aspiration,* and not other factors (illness, failed ambitions, lacks of initiative, drive or empathy) that is "disturbing" a person's life's way. In preliminary conversations, the prospective mentee has already expressed concerns and blockages that the mentor feels are at least *worthy* of exploring, in light of what can legitimately *suspected,* as being generated by the affects of mystically figured aspirations. Once the formal sessions have begun, a more detailed diagnostic process has to be undertaken —

just to determine whether or not mentoring is the supporting service that will really help this prospective mentee. Specifically, the mentor has to discern that *streak of aspiration* that courses through all the ways that the mentee feels in need of a conversation. The mentee comes to the occasion with many aspects of her life in some state of turmoil: aspirations keep her from feeling easily satisfied; aspirations do not allow her to easily accept the commonplace and common sense ways that people all around her do things in ways that accord with "normalcy" and "good sense"; aspirations have knocked this person off the beaten paths of ambition and success; aspirations may have disrupted, disturbed or even rupture important relationships. Any of these factors could be grounds for treatment by coaches or therapists; and in some cases they should be. But if mentoring is appropriate here, it is the mentor's job to discern in these situations how they are instigated and result from *aspirations* being at work.

DISCERNING ASPIRATIONS. What are some of the ways this discerning distinction is made? First and foremost, the mentor perceives a level of the innate strength and health of this person. It is likely that this person already has strong health-giving practices, or is on the verge of establishing such practices on her own. Second, the mentor perceives that the motivation of this person is not a matter of being stronger in order to succeed or "have" success, but rather, is primarily motivated by this person wanting, specifically, to give something of value to others. Finally, the mentor discerns whether or not this person seeks to engage with others, with knowledge and with skill, *in more expansive and more encompassing ways,* rather than in ways that will, again, be more likely to assure success.[3] When my suspicions indicate that aspiration is indeed at stake for this person, I then begin to introduce that idea to the mentee to see if, in describing the factors we traced in the Preface and Introduction of this book concerning the "phenomenology" of aspiration, a spark of recognition occurs (and to test how well I can adapt my language to the mentee's frames of reference). The intention of all of this testing and feeling out is just to see if this person really does have as her primary concern, in our conversation at least, the question of how she can set out to sustain a life's way that honors that aspiration.[4]

The mentor will have to expect that when the mentee comes into the first session, the only model of professional support she will have will be that of either coaching or therapy. I have never had a case in which that expectation was not in play. Since these terms are well defined and the processes these modalities employ are well known, what else, after all, might a prospective mentee expect? These are the institutionalized modalities of supporting conversations that are currently available. The mentor has to distinguish the work about to be undertaken if it is not to disappoint, frustrate (or even distractingly fascinate) the mentee. I suggest that this clarification be done in a meeting or over a series of meetings that take place *before the formal "mentoring" process is begun.*

As a shorthand way of at least addressing those expectations, I make clear to the mentee that I am not interested in how they are "normal" as employees (even when I do leader mentoring inside an institution), family members or friends, and so I am not interested in judging her be-haviors against the very standards that her aspirations seek to exceed. The key term that is operative in this context is "normal." I emphasize that there are many resources to help with those aspects of their lives — many of which I am sure this person has consulted. As a supplement to that, I am seeking to be one person who pays attention to one aspect of their lives that may not be fully appreciated, the part that aspires to put something more expansive and more encompassing into play in the human endeavor. I will be the little gremlin on the shoulder that advocates for those aspirations being given their due.

And then, I mention how aspirations are not well-treated in our literature or culture (although ambitions and career goals are glorified to the hilt), so we will have to learn some new terms. We will be recasting the stories they typically tell for their indications of those aspirations and as harbingers of a role (such as the mystic, in this case) that it might be beneficial to clarify and activate.

Setting the Scene

The mentoring should take place in a professional setting, not in a restaurant, for example. Set a first meeting date and place.

THE FEE. This is not a "chat" between friends. You may never see this person again. The fee concentrates the effort and establishes a frame of mutual commitment. It gives each party the right to expect respective levels of effort and professional conduct, concentration and regularity. The mentee has "skin in the game" and the fee obligates her to participate. She also gets to expect that the mentor will give professional and appropriate attention to the process. The mentor has accepted an obligation, in advance, that is always subject to the mentee's evaluation.

MENTEE PREPARATION. The mentee is advised to dedicate a notebook to this process.

The mentor might also, in the exploratory, pre-mentoring session (paid or free), outline his suspicions as to mystic figurations and give a very generally qualifying statement as to what this means. That is, mystic, not as an absent-minded airhead spouting non-sequiturs, but a discerningly generative figure that places new notions of an "open" future, toward engaging our worlds more expansively and more encompassingly – and who pays the price for that.

The mentor needs to make clear that *aspirations,* not behaviors, are the concern of the mentoring. Refer to the Preface, and Introduction, as well as Chapter Eight in order to help prepare such a presentation. Distinguish, for example, between aspiration and ambition, aspiration and succeeding, etc.

The Mentoring Process: Overview

Table 10. 1 Mentoring the Mystic Aspirational Figuration		
Session/Phase Objective*	**Actions**	**Mentoring Mystic Aspirations**
Preparation for the Engagement Commentary: Fee.	Mentee has new notebook. Mentor has Keirsey Sorter (KS) questions and answer sheet ready. ** Set the fee arrangements. *** Set the location	
I. Characterizing Temperament		
May extend over several sessions. *See Below:* Using the Keirsey Sorter (KS).	Do KS right away. 20 minutes to do. Use as a guide for initial discussion.	Use of Keirsey Sorter – See Below. Mystic Orientations: three Xs (equal scores) out of the four measured factors. Validate comments and biographical support for what figuration is in play.
See Below: Validate figuration (mystic or other) *See Below:* Mentoring versus coaching in the case of mystic figuration.	Calibrate strength, resistance, and openness to mentoring intervention. Resilience and desire; firmness and commitment to the role. Sincerity in the process; realistic about effort and prospect for outcomes. Proper orientation, expectations toward *mentoring* (vs coaching, therapy) as a distinctive supporting conversation.	Read attitude body language, challenge when doubtful. Note how the mentee "fore-gives," teaches, has "faith-for" a "Field of Enthusiasm." Note the possibility of a strong feminine presence or influence, positive or negative, in the mentee's childhood.
See Below: Terms.	Establishing Trust: Affirm those aspects of the mentee's stories that resonate with the key terms (e.g. Fore-giving, Faith-for, Field of Enthusiasm, etc.). Start to introduce this vocabulary.	Mentor shares stories of other mystics' ways, in genealogy.

329

Table 10. 1: Continued Mentoring the Mystic Aspirational Figuration		
Session/Phase Objective*	**Actions**	**Mentoring Mystic Aspirations**
Celebrating Aspiration. *See Below:* Celebrating.	Acknowledge the uncertainty and indefiniteness that aspiration entails: if you can name it, it is not aspiration, but something else. Why do you (mentor) value aspiration?	Mentee may resist story telling. This is not a strong suit of the mystic.
	Comprehension of aspirational "situation," role, context, genealogy that is specific to the mystic figuration.	Mentee's impression of the term. Give some examples of mystics' stories (from the genealogy).
	What learning processes are in place to match aspirations? Reading, writing? Teaching "spiritual," holistic or healing processes might be a clue.	Mystics are hungry learners. And they find ways to teach, as we will see below.
	State of mentee's self-awareness. Some indications of awareness of his or her "different" way and its affects.	Mentee's self-assessment of the situation that spurred the request for mentoring.
See Below: Figurations of mystic aspirations versus other figurations.	State of being amenable to figuration or role as mystic. Always check as to whether other roles are in play	
	Session/Phase Evaluation: The session/phase was "productive" if the mentee's "way" of approaching situations is clarified and the notion of a "mystic" figuration of aspiration is understood.	Assignment: Respond to the Keirsey Sorter and note supporting stories. Pick up on stories of teaching, of fore-giving, Field of Enthusiasm, open spaces and ask for more detailed recollections.

Table 10. 1: Continued Mentoring the Mystic Aspirational Figuration		
Session/Phase Objective*	**Actions**	**Mentoring Mystic Aspirations**
* " Session/Phase" indicates a block of discussions that may require several meetings to accomplish. Phases may also overlap into sessions, and may even occur out of the order presented here. The first two phases, however are likely to maintain this sequence. In the case of the mystic figuration, the sessions may not even transpire as part of a continuous series of meetings, and may transpire over several disparate and long-separated conversations. Also, **"Assignments"** sections denote suggestions, but the mentoring process may suggest other options as well.		
** I use the simple, one-sheet version, and specifically do not refer to the "Types." *See the commentary* below for the use of this instrument in this mentoring regimen.		
*** The fee is optional. However, I recommend it. *See Commentary* below.		
II. Identify Wedge-Tension/Block		
This may extend over several sessions. Sift through deflection and concealment to find what they are hiding.	Constrained by… Mystics are constrained**** by a pattern of serial institutional rejections and by confining their actions of "fore-giving"* into contexts of exchanges and of assigning expectations. Fore-giving exceeds those contexts.	Self-constructed barriers: self or others (be wary of blame). See Below: Terms, "Fore-giving."
Anticipations: situations, responses, outcomes. Do these specifically require a notion of fore-giving so as to relieve expectations of exchange, reciprocity or return?	Calibrate: proclivity, urge, and energy toward "breakout" or acceptance of mystic type aspirations. Learn the mentee's modes of resistance, hiding, avoidance, and what are the ways the mentee now has available to break through these. How do the "breakout" behaviors match up with the factors of mystic aspirations?	Begin to use the terms of mystic aspiration in discussing the resistances/ blocks. Describe mystic proclivities and their genealogical "heritage" (Part Two) and connect these to your "hearing" of the mentee's concerns.

Table 10. 1: Continued Mentoring the Mystic Aspirational Figuration		
Session/Phase Objective*	**Actions**	**Mentoring Mystic Aspirations**
Gauge appropriateness of mystic figuration: gauge what aspect of this role this person has already accepted, and how he or she responds to the demands of that role.	Review assignment. Note key metaphors, shaping incidents, difficulty expressing some key ideas. Note how or whether factors in mystic figuration might provide relief or open up avenues that had been foreclosed, constricted or even denied as this block was taking shape.	Start to note repeated stories. Match to role icon: e.g., Mystic "Field of Enthusiasm." *See Chapter Three.* How "fore-giving" sets up failures, and learning from this – for purposes of subsequent teaching.
	Evaluation: The session/phase is productive if the process can distinguish specific mystic proclivities and can also see how these proclivities conflict with "common sense" expectations. The mentor can begin to affirm and name the proclivities in effect and validate them.	**Assignment:** Answer: "How do you fore-give?" Give or repeat examples. What do you have "faith-for"? When are you in touch with your "Field of Enthusiasm"?
****The key element here is to listen for the self-imposed constraints the mentee places on his/her proclivity to fore-giving. *See Below:* Terms. Also, *see below:* on distinguishing mystic figuration from other roles.		

Top Level Elements of the Process

PLACES TO PAUSE. The mentoring process that addresses mystic aspirations is necessarily a fluid one. It requires that the mentor listen acutely for the "signposts" of the emergent mystic figuration, especially factors such as:

- The feminine influence during childhood (mother, aunt, grand mother, and an absent or ineffectual father or male figure).

- An attraction to and affinity with large open spaces, such as the sea, desert expanses or mountains.

- Resolving of situations by giving.

- Inclination to teach.

- Attraction to conceptualizing viable futures.

- Impatience and frustration when others do not understand.

The mentor should note each and every mention of such factors and the contexts/meanings/emotional complexes in which they are embedded. Even pause the conversation and ask for further elaboration of these reports – stories, descriptions, explicating narrations and wording.

THE COURSE OF THE MENTORING. The arc of the mentoring process goes from the precipitation situation – block or expulsion, as I explained in Chapter Eleven – to the articulation of a precept and a "Mystic Way." The process proceeds by means of the gradual exposing of the use of the complexes named by the terms we have elaborated on (i.e., fore-giving, faith-for, field of enthusiasm, precept) and the demonstration of them being operative for the mentee, or in their absence, how considering the complexes named by these terms might help the mentee's mystic aspirations become more potent.

Although a mentoring engagement will require many sessions spread over several months (attempting a regimen of one session per month), I recommend that the mentor envision no more than eight sessions total; and that the mentor countenance and expect continuing queries to come from the mentee after a consolidated process has been completed. I do not ask for a fee for follow-on sessions, or for incidental conversation. The fee thus also helps to distinguish when a "formal" process is being conducted, from the informal queries that pop up subsequent to the formal process. A formal process may well need to resume, going further into depth on the key tenets of the work, especially the articulation of a precept (a never-ending process for the mystically aspiring ones). During these informal follow-ups, the mentor can check in on the reading and health practices that the mentee is pursuing.

HEALTH PRACTICES. Always of concern throughout the conversation is that the mentee establish a regimen of healthy practices. Enhancing and nourishing the energies that feed mystic aspirations is essential. If nothing else happens, getting this point across is worth the fee. In this regard, the mentor needs to model good health practices as well.

ASSIGNMENTS. "Homework" assignments are necessary so as to initiate practices that are oriented toward clarifying and strengthening aspirations, and also to help the mentee develop a regimen that becomes proficient at teaching the precept. Each session can begin with a review of the assignment, and often will remain within the subject material the assignment has brought to the fore. The assignments listed in Table 10.1 offer suggestions and can be repeated or broken down, or departed from, according to the needs of the mentee.

READING. The mentoring should be accompanied by reading. Since the mystic way is relatively new, and is obscured by the derogatory way the term is deployed, or the idiotic behaviors that are called "mystical," it is essential that the mentee (and mentor) have familiarity with the concrete and historical development of this P/SS resource. A reading list is difficult to suggest because, on the one hand the religious embedding of this figuration's founding requires a translating effort, and, on the other hand, the philosophical and literary expressions are, necessarily, difficult texts. Also making a selection difficult is that, aside possibly from Eckhart (and possibly Nietzsche), none of these authors would have considered themselves or their works in line with specifically mystic aspirations. This selection then, is mine (with the exception of Eckhart) and might even be controversial. That said, I am quite comfortable in recommending these works as being substantially resonant with *mystic* aspirations, above all (as compared to other genres of discourse, such as religious, literary, philosophical, etc.)

As a baseline, assuming the high-performing intelligence, and often advanced educational level (formal schooling or not) of the people who exhibit this mystic figuration, I suggest the following:

- **Meister Eckhart,** *Teacher and Preacher* (Marist Press). Eckhart is the epitome of the founding mystics. His works are medieval, theological and classically oriented to the "One." His works are highly academic and intricate. Although paradigmatically unassailed as mystic texts, I would recommend his corpus only to people who are inclined toward interpreting and independently musing about such things.

- **Kierkegaard,** *Fear and Trembling* (Princeton University Press). His account of the Abraham incident and his pointing to the "knight of faith" closely resemble the quandary the mentee might be experiencing.

- **Nietzsche:** *The Gay Science, Genealogy of Morals,* **and/or** *Late Notebooks.* These late works represent mystic writing (without knowing that they are) and present multiple precepts that, while difficult to grasp, might help the mentee to feel the urgency of mystic aspirations. His works have paved the way for the contemporary "anamystics" to envision the mystic mission of our time. His works are just that significant.

- **Melville,** *Moby Dick* **and/or** *"Bartleby the Scrivener."* We began this book with a reference to *Moby Dick* (in the Introduction) since it is, in my estimation, the epitome of mystic expression (the "white whale" as the field of enthusiasm) and mystic endeavor gone wrong (Captain Ahab's obsession). Bartleby just might be a character that fulfills Kierkegaard's image of the "knight of faith" – or not – and the ambiguity is the point.

- **Deleuze,** *Nietzsche and Philosophy.* Although this book is difficult, it offers, in my estimation a kind of depiction of a discourse that employs a mystic view of the unfolding of occurrences and our relation to them – truly in the spirit of Nietzsche.

OTHER TEXTS:

Many of the poems of Hölderlin (*Friedrich Hölderlin: Selected Poems and Fragments;* Hamburger, Tr.) are accessible and uplifting in a way that appeals to mystic aspirations. The poems "As on a Holiday," "Bread and Wine," "The Rhine," and "Remembrance" immediately come to mind.

Schelling's *Ages of the World* provides a mystic entrée as to how God emerged from a field of enthusiasm.

Jean-Luc Nancy's *Adoration* might be of interest to people of a philosophical bent who also have ties to religious sensibilities.

Of course, any of the texts cited in the genealogy in Part Two are worthy of being studied, but the ones listed here are most accessible to most readers without philosophical training.

Articulating *Mystic* Aspirations

No one comes to the conversation wearing a tag saying, "I aspire in the figuration of a mystic." And, especially in the case of the mystic, no mentee will expect that the mentor will characterize her aspirations in this way. Given the strangeness of such a figuration, never mind how strange it is to envision a project that supports the mentee in adopting such a figuration, the mentor has refrain from jumping too quickly to conclusions about the figuration of the mentee's aspirations. I adhere strictly to the premise that my first impressions are always wrong, and I continually test whatever conclusions I have come to in this regard. I continually ask: How can one be sure that it is mystic aspirations, and not aspirations of another figuration that are in play? Or, how can one be sure that even if a mystic aspirational figuration is in play, that other figurations are not in play also? Might we not even assume that given the newness and abstraction of the mystic figuration, other figurations might be asserting themselves as well?

All of these questions *must be considered* as the mentoring process takes shape over the course of several sessions.

BEGIN WITH FORE-GIVING. In an ideal world, a world of well-prepared aspirational mentors, all the figures would have been studied, and through internships and supervised engagements, people would have learned how to pick up on the subtle signs that allow for such a distinction. In the absence of that, this book provides a mentor with three different contexts, settings, and narratives that indicate mystic aspirations being in play. I key on fore-giving (see below) as an indicator of the predominance if not the singular assertion, of a mystic figuration. No other figure is put in a situation where fore-giving is required in order to express aspirations. Hearing of the frustrations and sadness that the non-reciprocating world engenders, and how this non-responsiveness, or even outright (even violent) rejection leaves the person speechless and drained of her "natural" energy and enthusiasm, indicates that a mystic figuration is in play.

DETECT A FIELD OF ENTHUSIASM. Then I go about testing whether or not other aspects of the mystic figuration are in play, such as I listed in Chapter Eight (the subsection entitled, "Constant Elements of Mystic Aspiration") and that I repeat below (in the subsection "Mentoring Process Overview"). Once it is established that fore-giving is in play for this person, it is important to discern whether or not that behavior is engendered by a devotion to and concern with a demarcated Field of Enthusiasm (possibly associated with a professional or career path). That is, the mentee operates in the way of fore-giving out of a coherent stance and set of generative parameters that this person at least intuits, if not envisions, with some level of concreteness. Fore-giving as a matter of mystic aspiration is not a "what the hell" proposition of "whatever...doing it anyway," and most assuredly does not radiate from a scatter-shot inability to focus concern, interest or attention. A person who has no orientation, no focusing enthusiasm, no oriented trajectory as an intended locus of action, speech and decision, is not aspiring as a mystic, but is, rather, either lost or has a focus that has not yet "matured" into a concentrating field. Such people are not good prospects for mentoring, and might require different kinds of supporting resources at this point.

Operating out of a Field of Enthusiasm is expressed in the behaviors associated with faith-for – with a sense that some great force that offers something more expansive and more encompassing – is in play already. The mystically aspiring mentee is devoted, in advance, to bringing those factors to light, requiring a precept; and the mystically aspiring mentee is willing to devote time an energy to this ("virtually" existent potency) and so is amenable to doing the work that teaching demands.

Keirsey Sorter (or MBTI Temperament Characterizing Instruments)

OVERVIEW. As we begin the engagement with our mentee, we as mentors seek to validate our impressions that guiding her along the path of mystically figured aspirations will offer a constructive orientation. Make no mistake: there is no substitute for the attentive listening that can detect whether or not there are present and operative the factors we listed above. However, citing those factors as "determining" of a mystic figuration of aspiration, with no preparatory or corroborating (or at least counter-pointing) orienting material might steer the conversation into being too much of a "psychoanalytical" framework, and an over-emphasis on biographically derived criteria. To address those issues, I use an inexpensive, readily available "instrument" that helps to characterize the mentee's "temperament," or approach to decisions, action and speech in interesting ways. The instrument I use is the Keirsey Sorter, which is a well-tested and validated, streamlined adaptation of the Meyers-Briggs Temperament Inventory (MBTI).[5]

For the purposes of mentoring the aspiring figurations, including that of the mystic's, I do not use the "Types" as identified by the conventional use of this instrument (that is the four letter designation, ESTJ, for instance; or the "roles" cited as corresponding to these types such as "Guardian," or "Architect," or even "Leader"). I take this composite of characterizations as depicting what the P/SS does to the energies that impress upon it, and from which we take our "experiences," as bases for speech, actions and making decisions. The energies flow through each of these four stations (I/E, S/N, T/F, J/P — from which the selection of four letters are made, i.e. INTP), where they are "translated" and then "transformed" into psychosomatic complexes that, as more or less intelligible experiences, then subsequently render these energies in the forms of decisions, actions and speech. What is of primary interest in orienting the mentoring process to the figuration of aspirations that are in play for the mentee, is to note the stations in which there are Xs (or scores that are close to an X) rather than clear dominance of one factor in the station over another (an extreme dominance of one factor over another also raises flags for me, but that is another story.

Let's step back a bit and consider this scene in greater detail. I interpret the "stations" as indicating operations the psyche performs on the flow of energies, prior to their being applied. In this very "early" forming of "energies" or impressions from engaging occurrences in the active milieu (both external and internal to the P/SS), only the occurrence's givenness, its presence, "what is happening," is at issue. The Keirsey Sorter (KS) traces energies as they pass through these operations. (See Figure 10.1)

Understanding our Temperament Through our Energy
The Flow From Information to Decision

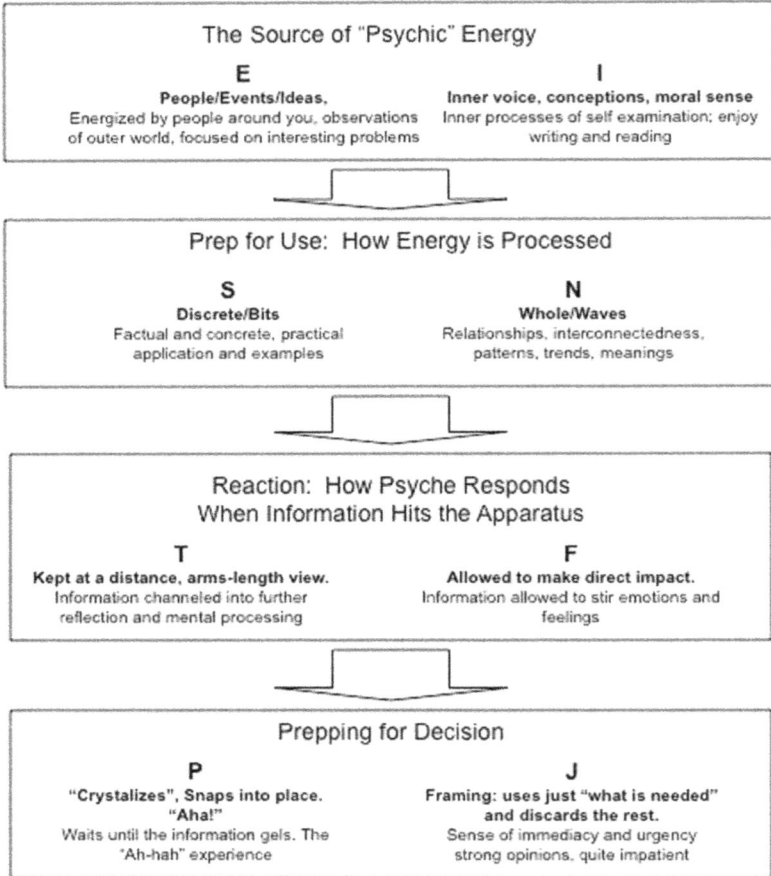

The Source of "Psychic" Energy

E	**I**
People/Events/Ideas.	**Inner voice, conceptions, moral sense**
Energized by people around you, observations of outer world, focused on interesting problems	Inner processes of self examination; enjoy writing and reading

---

Prep for Use: How Energy is Processed

S	**N**
Discrete/Bits	**Whole/Waves**
Factual and concrete, practical application and examples	Relationships, interconnectedness, patterns, trends, meanings

---

Reaction: How Psyche Responds
When Information Hits the Apparatus

T	**F**
Kept at a distance, arms-length view.	**Allowed to make direct impact.**
Information channeled into further reflection and mental processing	Information allowed to stir emotions and feelings

---

Prepping for Decision

P	**J**
"Crystalizes", Snaps into place.	**Framing: uses just "what is needed"**
"Aha!"	**and discards the rest.**
Waits until the information gels. The "Ah-hah" experience	Sense of immediacy and urgency strong opinions, quite impatient

---

We derive information from our primary energy source. We then transform that energy and convert it into information through a series of filters that can then be used as a basis for behavior, actions and decisions.

Figure 10.1

The course of energy through the "stations" of the KS model. [6]

- E/I: the P/SS gathers energies predominantly from either an external or internal (to the P/SS) source.

- S/N: energies are parsed in to being factors of sense that are either of a factical, "molecular" reach or are "molar" and more expansively composite.

- F/T: the cognizing faculty reacts to these energies either in the form of "fight" (holding close), or "flight" (pushing them away and at a greater distance).

- J/P: in one last shot, the P/SS either forms decisions by framing and eliminating data, or by allowing all the energy to have its due, until a crystallization process (an "aha" experience) pulls them into a composite state of sufficient unity.

For our purposes, these readings get interesting when one or more of these "stations" of formation does not channel energies in a way that prioritizes one response over another, and do not establish for the P/SS any clarity of operation – as far as this instrument, which operates within a range of choices that are socially recognized and communicable. Lack of clarity is indicated when the two numbers in a station are equal or close to it (4 or 5 for each factor in E/I and 9 or 10 for each factor in the other three stations). We highlight this state of affairs by designating that station with an *X*. To us, an X signifies that with respect to this operation of sense-making, the experiencing person has to construct, seemingly out of nothing, his or her own way to sort out, translate and transform these energies, if this factor is going to play its proper role in forming states of mind suited to speech, actions and making decisions. Not surprisingly, because this person has to work hard all his or her life to consciously establish viable ways of making sense, the operations at this site – in all their idiosyncrasy – become areas of concentrated attention. We might say that this X indicates a "leak" in the prevalently and conventionally available superstructure of this moment in psychological experiencing. For us, and more importantly, for the experiencing person, this "leak" provides an opening through which to exert highly individualized ways of performing the operation that this conventional "translator" does not do. Those who have the energy and the will, and the support of mentors along the way, take on aspirational figurations that shape energies into their specific creative activities.

In the context of mentoring in support of aspirational figurations, the Xs therefore do not mean that the person is somehow deficient in this area of temperament formation, nor that this person is "balanced" or even in "conflict" as to this aspect of temperament formation. In our reading of this instrument, in the context of the aspirational figures we are dealing with, the Xs indicate the openings through which this person "passes" in order to have to rely on his or her own idiosyncratic way of engaging occurrences. Depending on which "station" registers an X, a person will be open to developing idiosyncratic ways that address the factors registered by that station. An artist figuration will possibly develop when an X is registered in the I/N station, a prophet in the T/F and a leader in the E/I (or in some exceptional cases in the J/T) station.

Why are these energies, which "leak" through the opening, aspirational? In some cases, frankly, they are not. Instead of aspirational energies, confusion and conflicts do arise, and are resolved in other ways – by the formation of personality rigidities, or by the inflation of selected factors of experiences, which entail their own kinds of either deeply avowed conformity (of fundamentalist or at least orthodox intensities), or delusive compensations altogether. But this is not the case with the people who enter into our mentoring processes. *By the way, our mentoring process are specifically unqualified for dealing with these personality disturbances.* In the cases of the people we are dealing with, the energies that "leak" through the opening are aspirational because, by force of one's own energies, by upbringing, by contact with other mentors, by virtue of a favorable milieu in general (or this person's interpreting of the milieu as being nurturing and affirming, even if it does not appear so to an outsider), they were also, in addition to being vulnerable in this aspect of their personalities, able to allow for the self-organization and development of what we have called the "Aspiring Mind," or aspiring P/SS resource (see Chapter Three). As a result of this fortunate course of growth and development (at the present time in our human endeavor), an aspirational impetus of some significant intensity, status and magnitude is able to assert itself – albeit in a still (pre-mentoring) nascent and developing state.

MYSTIC ASPIRATIONS. The mystic registers *three* Xs. Three Xs means that in most ways, this mystic mentee has had to find very unique ways indeed, and has had to find many of them.[7]

We might say mystic aspirations are maximally disturbing of socialized means of sense-making. We can say that mystic aspirations gather up the creative exigencies of several figures, and yet none of these figurations will do because they are not supported by other strengths. So, the completely novel ways that the mystically aspiring person has to construct her own sense of what is occurring in her experiencing is set on its way. Mentees with mystic aspirations often describe their multiple attractions to creative forms – from poetry and music-making to crafting new concepts for scientific or social applications, to leading organizations that advocate new ideas, ways, technologies and relationships. And many also cite their inability to "stick" with one or another or combinations of these.

But the KS tool provides only one clue as to whether or not mystic aspirations are the dominating force in this person's life. There isn't much to say about this profile, after all. Instead, it offers the mentor an opportunity to inquire about how this person experiences her "world," and what she takes away from these experiences. This line of questioning might have as a backdrop the kinds of observations that Alice provided about her "mystic way" (see Chapter One).

Key Terms in Mystic Figuration of Aspiration

Since mystic aspirations have only recently formed into a recognizable figure (more so than the other figures, which have been in circulation for millennia), a significant barrier to a mentee's feeling strong and viable in their mystic figuration is that her dominant ways of experiencing, expressing and enacting her aspirations are, for the most part, invisible. As a result of this invisibility, the very orientations that are necessary for mystic aspirations to take shape seem either aberrant or even destructive to the person herself, and certainly are not comprehended in any kind of appreciative way by those around her.

Thus, far more than with the other figures, mentoring mystic aspirations requires the introduction of "specialized" terms – terms that characterize, if not name, the inevitable and irrepressible ways mystic aspirations show up as this person's inclinations and preferences for speech, actions and decisions. Another problem the mentor confronts in articulating how mystic aspirations rise to the surface is that they have been either swept up into traditional religious language, or they have been denigrated in all the ways we have described above – being rendered into the "new age, la-di-dah" regime of personalities.

In this book, I have suggested terminology that applies to mystic aspirations, at least in the mentoring context. That is, in non-sectarian, generally referential ways (that the mentee can translate according to her current situation – being religiously oriented, for instance, or not), the moments of characteristically mystically aspiring ways, can be laid out, discussed and elaborated upon, in their own right.

Happily there are not many of these terms. Each points to a "moment" of the aspiration's emergence into the scenes of the person's life. "Faith-for" shows up as the basis for this person's devotion to the aspiration's power. "Fore-giving" shows up as the only way mystic aspirations can be offered at all. The "Field of Enthusiasm" describes the way these aspirations anticipate and shape the mentee's sense of living (in resonance with her faith-for). The "Precept" opens up the specific lines of expression that the mentee's aspirations delineate. "Adherents" name the kinds of relationships mystic aspirations engender.

More detailed "definitions" of these terms are offered below. The mentor does not need to be an "expert" in these terms, such as an instructor in physics has to be an expert in explaining that discipline's technical terms (such as "quantum gravity," for instance!). It is rather that by having these terms in mind, a mentor can recognize when a mystically aspiring dynamic is at issue, and can open a discussion on what the mentee is experiencing, and then offer this term as a way of conceiving this dynamic as being a "normal" and necessary moment of mystically figured aspirations' emergence.

FORE-GIVING: The key barrier to passing through the threshold of the mystic's aspirational figuration is realizing that the usual "exchange" models of giving and return, of proposing and responding, even of offering and acknowledging do not work for mystic aspirations. There is no voice or even hint at conceptions of this notion in common parlance. We are immersed in the "exchange" and "transactional" models of engaging. Even gifts are "exchanged," and every good deed is put in a ledger somewhere – on earth or in heaven.

Often a story I have heard from mystic aspiring people is a problem of anger and rage when they were young. This is not so strange a response when what one gives is placed in a frame of exchange and reciprocation fails to materialize.

Since this notion is neither discussed nor elaborated in any applicable way, the mentee will hardly be able to recognize that he or she is behaving in this way. Instead of realizing that she is offering her work in the spirit of fore-giving, in which there is no possibility of an adequate response, she thinks she is engaging in a process of "exchange," of one sort or another. As a result of this misinterpretation of her own acts, the mentee sets up expectations that will always be frustrated and that are always doomed to fail. At some level, the mystics that I have worked with know that their expectations for reciprocity are somehow inappropriate, and express their action in terms such as "long-term exchange" or "sacrifice," or "for the other's own good." The lingering sense of there being a forthcoming "return" are also immediately set off into an indefinitely postponed future. This postponement thus acts like a tethering of her giving to a return, which, acknowledged as being ultimately not forthcoming, only produces the sense of disappointment, melancholy, and/or impotent idealism.

The notion of fore-giving is intended to be liberating by freeing the mentee from any sense that a "return," no less a comprehending response, is in the offing. And, according to the dynamic of a true "gift," it will never even be taken up by someone else as something that was given at all.[8] This frees mystic aspirations from ties to existent conditions, expectations and especially from constrictive, ideological, or religiously motivated mores. It then frees the mystic from tethers to the moments of giving, frees up the requirements of possessive reflections on the giving, and allows the mystic to move on, detached, light, into the onwarding energies of the precept.

FAITH-FOR: Mystic aspirations "hold out" for there being a concept of a state of affairs that awaits attention, commitment and action, and that fore-given, these factors can come into being. This state of affairs precludes oppression, demagoguery, greed and ignorance to the extent that they require of a person more expansive and more encompassing engagement with occurrences – other people, the earth and its creatures.

FIELD OF ENTHUSIASM: Mystic aspirations do not "come together" in either the concreteness of an artist's work, a leader's vision or even a prophet's provoking concept. These aspirations generalize and flow through and around the mystic P/SS in a way that disrupts, dislocates and fragments the usual materials, rubrics and laws that constitute "reality" for others. It is, however, a *coherent* force none the less; it is coherent in that it opens out with enthusiasm to a sense of new and fresh connections, and connections that keep opening out so as to remain fresh and imbued with enthusiasm. The best image for this "field" is that of the infinitely expanding rhizome (as Deleuze / Guattari suggest), that also continually increases its connectivity intensively as well as extensively. It is also (exactly) the way that the brain's neurons, when nourished, become more intensely and extensively connected and so are able to engender a greater variety of notions, each of them with greater depth, than a "mind" left idle, bereft or enchained to given conventions.

PRECEPT: The mystic's aspirations point to a greater openness of engagement and endeavor, not to different or more "things." The precept articulates this pointing – offering a horizon that can be reached by means of also suggested modes of endeavor, effort and striving. The precept implies that engaging by means of what awaits one on this now-horizonal destination will consist of new demands that portend engaging occurrences in ways that are more expansive and more encompassing than we can now accommodate in our present state of living.

TEACHING: Teaching is the "work" required of a person by mystic aspirations. Teaching is what a "mystic" *does* (see Chapter Four). Teaching entails articulating and clarifying the precept in each of the states of affairs to which it pertains, and then doing the work to help others gain a sense of the precept's portent and potency. Teaching might be a matter of writing and publishing; but it might also be a matter of organizing those who "get it," at least adherents (see below), into a continuing effort to do this ongoing work of teaching – including demonstrating what the precept promises.

ADHERENTS: Mystic aspirations engender the specific relationship of "adherents." Each of the aspirational figures engenders a specific kind of relationship (leader: followers; artist: audience; prophet: disciple), and the mystically figured person cannot expect any other kind of relationship to ensue from his work of teaching. An "adherent" is a person who is able to "hear" (thus also ad-*hear*-ant) the precept and spends time (in person or as a reader / studier, or even an organization member) in seriously enriching his or her understanding of the implications and nuances that the precept intends. Once that person's contemplation reaches a state of confluence with his or her own aspirational figuration, that person will likely move on (beyond that "here" of the "ad-*here*-ant") to take up the call in his or her own aspirationally figured terms.

The Closing Exercise: Celebrating "My Mystic Way"

The mystic needs to be able to express the precept, teach it, and also to have a firm idea of her "practice" if she is to do this work. She also needs to pay keen attention to the state of her health, above all.

The mentor needs to have a sense that in concluding the mentoring engagement, that such a "way" is at least clearly in view for the mentee.

As a concluding project, the mentor and mentee can work out what aspect of the way the mentee is ready to clarify and express, and so also put into practice a concrete moment of expression of that aspect. For instance, Alice was ready, by the conclusion of the mentoring, to appreciate and delineate those moments in which her aspirations rose to the surface and claimed her attention. She was, at the time of our mentoring engagement, already quite articulate about her precept, and was already adept at organizing larger-scale efforts in advancing that precept. She had no reservations about fore-giving. So, her articulation of her way of heeding and then taking up the energies that emerged from her Field of Enthusiasm was an appropriate concluding exercise.

Celebrating certainly warrants a hug as a mutually appreciated moment of how mentoring has set on a way of robust health one person who can, in some way, offer to us more expansive and more encompassing ways to envision, enact and carry onward a viable, generative human endeavor – for other humans, creatures and the earth.

۞

Bibliography

Askay and Farquhar, *Apprehending the Inaccessible: Freudian Psychoanalysis and Existential Phenomenology*. Evanston, IL: Northwestern University Press, 2006.

Badiou, Alain, *Being and Event*. New York: Bloomsbury Publishing, 2005.

_____, *Logics of Worlds*. New York: Bloomsbury Publishing, 2013.

_____, (2003), *Saint Paul: The Foundations of Universalism*. Stanford, CA: Stanford University Press.

Beiser, Frederick C., *German Idealism: The Struggle Against Subjectivism, 1781-1801*. Cambridge, MA: Harvard University Press, 2008.

Benjamin, Walter, *The Arcades Project*. Cambridge, MA: Harvard University Press, 1999.

Caputo, John D., *The Mystic Element in Heidegger's Thought*. New York: Fordham University Press, 1986.

Cottret, Bernard, *Calvin: A Biography*. Grand Rapids, MI: William B. Eerdmans Publishing Co., 2000

Damasio, Antonio, *Descartes' Error: Emotion, Reason, and the Human Brain*. New York: Penguin Classics, 2005.

_____, *Looking for Spinoza: Joy, Sorrow and the Feeling Brain*. New York: Houghton, Mifflin, Harcourt, 2003.

De Certeau, Michel, *The Mythic Fable: The Sixteenth and Seventeenth Centuries*. Chicago: University of Chicago Press, 1992.

Deleuze, Gilles, and Felix Guattari, *The Anti-Oedipus*. Minneapolis, MN: University of Minnesota Press, 1983.

Deleuze, Gilles, *Bergsonism.* New York: Zone Books, 1991.

_____, and Claire Parnet, *Dialogues II.* New York: Bloomsbury Academic, 2006.

_____, *Difference and Repetition.* New York: Columbia University Press, 1994.

_____, *The Logic of Sense.* New York: Columbia University Press, 1990.

_____, *A Thousand Plateaus.* Minneapolis, MN: University of Minnesota Press, 1987.

_____, *Nietzsche and Philosophy.* New York: Columbia University Press, 1983.

_____, *What is Philosophy?* New York: Columbia University Press, 1994.

Derrida, Jacques, *Parages.* Stanford, CA: University of California Press, 2011.

Dieter, Henrich, *The Course of Remembrance and Other Essays on Hölderlin.* CA: Stanford University Press, 1997.

_____, *Between Kant and Hegel, "The Allure of Mysticism."* Cambridge, MA: Harvard University Press, 2003.

Donald, Merlin, *Origins of the Modern Mind: Three Stages in the Evolution of Culture and Cognition.* Cambridge, MA: Harvard University Press, 1991.

Dostoyevsky, F., *The Brothers Karamazov.* New York: Penguin Books, 2003.

Edelman, Gerald M., *Bright Air, Brilliant Fire: On the Matter of the Mind.* New York: Basic Books, 1992.

Emerson, *Ralph Waldo, Emerson: Essays and Lectures.* New York: Library of America, 1983.

_____, *Topobiology: An Introduction to Molecular Embryology*. New York: Basic Books, 1988.

Fichte, J. G., *The Science of Knowing*. Albany, NY: SUNY Press, 2005.

Freud, S., "Beyond the Pleasure Principle" in *The Freud Reader,* Peter Gay, ed. New York: W. W. Norton & Co., 1989.

Gasché, Rodolphe, *Georges Bataille: Phenomenology and Phantasmatology*. Stanford, CA: Stanford University Press, 2012.

Hadewijch, *Hadewijch: The Complete Works*. Mahwah, NJ: The Paulist Press, 1980.

Hegel, G. W. F., *The Encyclopedia Logic*. Indianapolis, IN: Indiana University Press, 1991.

_____, *The Phenomenology of Spirit*. A. V. Miller, Tr. New York: Oxford University Press, 1976.

Heidegger Martin, *Contribution to Philosophy (From Enowning)*. Bloomington, IN: Indiana University Press, 1999.

_____, *The Principle of Reason*. Tr. Reginald Lilly. Bloomington, IN: Indiana University Press, 1996.

_____, *Hegel's Concept of Experience*. Kenley Dove, Tr. New York: Basic Books, 1970.

_____, *Mindfulness*. New York: Continuum International Publishing Group, 2006.

Hölderlin, Friedrich, *Selected Poems and Fragments*. Michael Hamburger, Tr. New York: Penguin Books, 1998.

_____, *Friedrich Hölderlin: Essays and Letters on Theory*. Pfau, Tr. and Ed., Albany, NY: SUNY Press, 1988.

_____, *Hyperion and Selected Poems*. New York: Bloomsbury Academic, 1990.

Irigary, Luce, *I Love to You*. New York: Routledge, 1996.

_____, *The Irigaray Reader*. Margaret Whitford, ed. Cambridge, MA: Blackwell Publishers, 1995.

_____, *Sexes and Genealogies*. New York: Columbia University Press, 1993.

_____, *Speculum of the Other Woman*. Ithaca, NY: Cornell University Press, 1985.

_____, *To Be Two*. New York: Routledge, 2001.

Kant, Immanuel, *The Critique of Judgment*. J.H. Bernard, Tr. New York: Prometheus Press, 2000.

_____, *The Critique of Pure Reason*. Norman Kemp Smith, Tr. New York: St. Martin's Press, 1970.

_____, *The Critique of Practical Reason*. Mary Gregor, Tr. New York: Cambridge University Press, 2006.

Kaehner, R. C., *Mysticism Sacred and Profane*. New York: Oxford University Press, 1961.

Kafka, Franz, *The Complete Stories*. New York: Schocken Books Inc., 1971.

Kauffman, Stuart, *Investigations*. New York: Oxford University Press, 2000.

_____, *Reinventing the Sacred: A New View of Science, Reason and Religion*. New York: Basic Books, 2008.

Kelso, J. A. Scott, *Dynamic Patterns: The Self-Organization of Brain and Behavior*. Cambridge, MA: The MIT Press, 1995.

Kierkegaard, Soren, *Fear and Trembling*. Princeton, NJ: Princeton University Press, 2013.

———, *The Essential Kierkegaard*. Princeton, NJ: Princeton University Press, 2013.

Klossowski, Pierre, *Nietzsche and the Vicious Circle*. Chicago: University of Chicago Press, 1998.

Lacan, Jacques, *Écrits*. New York: Norton & Company, 2007.

Laclau, Ernesto, *Emancipation(s)*. New York: Verso, 1996.

———, *New Reflections on the Revolution of Our Time*. New York: Verso, 1990.

Marion, Jean-Luc, *In Excess*. New York: Fordham University Press, 2002.

Marechal, J, *The Psychology of the Mystics*. Mineola, NY: Dover Publications, Inc., 2004

Melville, Herman, *Moby Dick*. New York: Signet Classics, 1998.

McGinn, Bernard, *The Flowering of Mysticism: Men and Women in the New Mysticism: 1200 - 1350*. New York: The Crossroads Publishing Company, 1998.

Mechthild, *The Flowing Light of the Godhead*. Mahwah, NJ: The Paulist Press, 1998.

Meister Eckhart, *Meister Eckhart: The Essential Sermons, Commentaries, Treatises and Defense*. New York: The Paulist Press, 1981.

———, *Meister Eckhart: Teacher and Preacher*. New York: The Paulist Press, 1986.

Montag, Warren, *Bodies, Masses, Power: Spinoza and his Contemporaries*. New York: Verso, 1999.

Newman, Barbara, *From Virile Woman to Woman Christ*. Philadelphia, PA: University of Pennsylvania Press, 1995.

Nietzsche, *Daybreak: Thoughts on the Prejudices of Morality*. New York: Cambridge University Press, 1997.

_____, *The Gay Science*. Walter Kaufmann, Tr. New York: Vintage, 1974.

_____, *Writings from the Late Notebooks*. New York: Cambridge University Press, 2003.

_____, *The Will to Power*. Walter Kaufmann, Tr. New York: Vintage, 1968.

Pfeiffer ("Copyrighted Material"), "The Sermons" and *Collations of Meister Eckhart*.

Pseudo-Dionysus: the Aeropagite, *Pseudo-Dionysus: The Complete Works*. Mahwah, NJ: The Paulist Press, 1987.

Porete, Marguerite, *The Mirror of Simple Souls*. Mahwah, NJ: The Paulist Press, 1993.

Sallis, John, *Force of Imagination*. Bloomington, IN: Indiana University Press, 2000.

Schelling, F. W. J., *Ages of the World*. Albany New York: SUNY Press, 2000.

_____, *Historical-Critical Introduction to the Philosophy of Mythology*. Albany, NY: SUNY Press, 2007.

_____, *Philosophical Investigations into the Essence of Human Freedom*. Albany, NY: SUNY Press, 2007.

Schürmann, Reiner, *Wandering Joy: Meister Eckhart's Mystical Philosophy*. Great Barrington, MA: Lindisfarne Books, 2001.

Shenkman, Michael, *The Arch and the Path: The Life of Leading Greatly.* Albuquerque, NM: Sandia Heights Media, 2005.

_____, *The Aspiring Mind: A Philosophical Inquiry into the Urge to Create.* As of 2014, unpublished; available on request.

_____, *Leader Mentoring: Find, Inspire and Cultivate Great Leaders.* Franklin Lakes, NJ: Career Press, 2008.

_____, *The Strategic Heart: Using the New Science to Lead Growing Organizations.* Westport, CT: Quorum Books, 1998.

Simons, Walter, *Cities of Ladies: Beguine Communities in the Medieval Low Countries, 1200 - 1565.* Philadelphia, PA: University of Pennsylvania Press, 2001.

Spinoza, Baruch, *The Essential Spinoza: Ethics and Related Writings.* Michael L. Morgan, ed. Indianapolis, IN: Hackett Publishing Co., Inc., 2006.

Thelen and Smith, *A Dynamic Systems Approach to the Development of Cognition and Action.* Cambridge, MA: The MIT Press, 2002.

Thoreau, Henry David, *Collected Essays and Poems.* New York: Library of America, 2001.

Waldrop, M. Mitchell, *Complexity: The Emerging Science at the Edge of Order and Chaos.* New York: Simon and Schuster, 1992.

Zizek Slavoj, *The Abyss of Freedom: Ages of the World (F.W.J. von Schelling).* Ann Arbor, MI: University of Michigan Press, 1997.

_____, *Interrogating the Real.* New York: Continuum, 2005.

NOTES

PAGE		NOTE

2   [1]   Quoted by Reiner Schürmann, *Heidegger on Being and Acting: From Principles to Anarchy* (1990). Indiana University Press; p. 43.

Preface

12   [1]   In Henrich, Dieter (1997), *The Course of Remembrance and Other Essays on Holderlin.* Stanford University Press: Stanford, CA; p. 253.

            [2]   Quoted by Deleuze (2006) in *Dialogues II* (Bloomsbury Academic: New York; p. 5. Certainly mystic aspirations, with which Nietzsche (and Deleuze) abounds, belong in this company of artists and philosophers (prophetic aspiring figurations).

19   [3]   I use the term "occurrence" throughout this book (and in the project as a whole) advisedly, and accepting of the fact that it is vague (and thus a ripe target for the materialist and positivistic analysts). The vagueness is a necessary consequence of dealing with a moment of engagement in which the terms of exactly what is taking place and what one's stance in that pressing of energies is specifically kept open and out of the clutches of the terms, habits, conventions, and hierarchies of "knowing" reason and technological prowess. The term reflects a conscious and very deliberate (methodological) distancing and holding in abeyance given formulations of what is happening at the site of the "experience." The instants of the surging are thereby allowed room for the free play of exper imental affiliations; and the "presence" at or of the site (the time/place/occasion of the engaging) is not rendered into a "substance" or an "object" that is presumed to be amenable to a subject's machinations.

20   [4]   The expanse of time is not the only factor that differentiates the notion of "change" that this work of aspirational figurations attunes to. In fact, one of the reasons the work of mentoring

aspirational figures has become not only feasible but important is that all the ways social changes have been solidified over the course of our history are now actively in play, simultaneously, in our current state of social, economic and cultural life. And, given the ferocity of all these currents of change affecting so many facets of our lives all at once, it is also certain that the creation of new modes of social change is underway already, as we speak, whether we notice them now or not.

There is also then a different level of conceptualization of the process of social change that is at work here. To be sure, and to be clear, no classical model of change, Marxist, liberal, Hegelian or Machiavellian approaches what we envision here. We can only begin to fathom the forces in play and the dimensions of engaging occurrences that are being invoked by considering what we demand of ourselves when we undertake to shape our own individuation and work out among ourselves what the terms of becoming a more expansive and more encompassing being on this earth entail. This requires of us an ability to deconstruct our hardened impressions of the "real" and to open our sense-making faculties to the dynamics of forming the concepts, myths, imaginaries and scenarios that will vie for actualization in the course of social engagements.

That such work has begun in earnest is the most encouraging thing I have take away from my studies. Beginning with the work of the likes of Derrida and Deleuze/Guattari (more than that of Foucault), of Jameson (more than that of Rawls or Rorty), and of Laclau and Mouffe (more than that of Badiou or Zizek), a way of engaging social change in a generative and prophetically promising way is being adumbrated. My contribution, if it can be considered that, is to envision a way to tap into the forming of an individual's sense-making faculties that take up this generative work as a commitment to these life-changing ways.

22   [5]   The reader might respond, at this point, "Such a self-yielding way is not realistic in this world." And I fully admit, this

notion runs counter to our prescriptions to "be strong" in the face of adversity, or to "be a rock" when it comes to leading people through challenging situations. But I would push back and say, actually the greatest of our aspirational (and inspiring) figures do nothing but enter into situation in which they know they will have to become different, will have to give way and give up their beliefs about themselves in order to meet the situation as it demands. Mystics are certainly figurations of aspirations that give way without reserve; and even our great leaders, Lincoln for example, take on challenges that they fully know will change them, or might even kill them, as the situation unfolds.

On a theoretical level, Ernesto Laclau describes processes of social change, antagonisms, which demand of the actors just such a realization: that ambiguity and contingency so permeate any structural solution that it will have to bootstrap its responses, and change itself along the way. (See *New Reflections on the Revolution of Our Time* (Verso: New York; 1990); Part I) Although flying in the face of the classical notion of the "subject" acting on an inert "object," this notion that we are presenting perfectly accords with models of self-organizing "autocatalysis" and increasing complexity – which, of course, is our standpoint to begin with.

26   [6]   Deleuze applies this phrase to what he calls a "style." But given the degradation of that term into being affective personality traits, I am diverting his elaborative phrase to the term "role." By "role" I refer to the way a person expresses his or her figuration within an area of concern (or vocation, profession, et. al.) over an extended period of time and seeks to enhance his or her ability to express aspirations in ever more affecting ways.

28   [7]   It may seem that I am open to the accusation that I am proposing a whole process of supporting people in need with a purely speculative approach. To some that will certainly be the case, and those people are certainly entitled to stop reading

(that is why I present this thesis in the "Preface," to spare them the trouble) or, they can continue reading with the intent of demolishing this premise. There will be others, however, to whom this text is addressed, who will appreciate all the ways that this approach "rings true," (and much of this text is devoted to pointing out those ringing ways), and so will consider taking up the work of advancing what we offer here.

For those of us in the "dialectical" frame of thought (the term is used in the strong sense here), we realize that it is only by beginning to take up the signs of an emergence, to give our aspirations over to what comes to the fore, that we can, iteratively, bring something like an endeavor, or a "science" or a body of subject matter into view (symbolized, textualized, narrated and lexically constrained) for examination. We have to begin with a pre-disposition toward having our living be a process of making way for what might emerge there. There is no substitute for this "decision" or for acting on this "aspiration" in a way that allows it the best expression we can bring to it.

This "presupposition," this aspiring stance that articulates a way of aspiring and holds out for its becoming a facultative resource, is unsurpassable as a starting point. So was the stance of reason that brought about reasoning, and so was the insistence on the viability of language as a domain for active engagement. This is the essence of what, in the human arena, self-organization offers us. For a well-developed philosophical narrative of this "bootstrapping" of what we can come to "know," see Zizek (2005); pp. 38ff. He notes, using a transposed Hegelian framework, "Initially, the 'thesis' arrives by definition too soon to attain is proper identity, and it can only realize 'itself,' become 'itself,' after the fact, retroactively, by means of its repetition in the 'synthesis' (p. 46).

30   8   This is a "technical" term in Deleuze/Guattari's consideration of generatively formative operations that take place throughout nature, and are most especially the primary mode of operating for "mental" or "psychic" or, as I call them "psycho/somatic

system" (P/SS) operations. The term "machinic" (see *A Thousand Plateaus*, and also Deleuze's *Dialogues II*) refers to a process that *iterates* a dynamic engagement with occurrences in a way that retains a *single continued form or mode of operability*, and yet does so while it also incorporates changing conditions, as the occurrence unfolds through time. The operation thus "flexes," expands or enriches itself ("supplements," to use Derrida's term) as the operation being performed (by the organism, or the "mind," for instance) moves from a former iteration to the current one, and then also *anticipates* (the conditions it will find at the site of the occurrence) in the next iteration. There is thus nothing "mechanical" or statically repetitive about machinic iteration; a *mechanical* operation asserts its static process regardless of the nuances of difference that affect the site of engaging and overpowers those differences in order to assert its own way. "Machinic" operation is iteration of a distinctive engaging of "occurrence" that remains *attuned to difference,* while also having its *integral singularity take its place as a viable engaging force* at the site of the occurrence.

30   9   Although I do provide an in-depth treatment of this proposition in my work, *The Aspiring Mind: A Philosophical Inquiry into the Urge to Create* (as of this date, unpublished; available on request).

32   10   That is why all of the works of the aspiring figures involve language: from the mystic's precept to the prophet's provoking concept, to the artist's work, to the statement of a leader's "brand" in offering new organizational possibilities.

33   11   There are two volumes to this work: *The Anti-Oedipus* (University of Minnesota Press, Minneapolis, MN; 1983) and *A Thousand Plateaus* (University of Minnesota Press. Minneapolis, MN; 1987). For an intensified compression of some of the seminal notions presented in this work I recommend the essay "Dead Psychoanalysis. Analyse," in Deleuze, *Dialogues II* (Op. Cit.).

35   [12]   In a more "analytical" frame, the precept is also distinct from either a "proposition" or a "statement." Whereas the latter two forms work on a template of "proposition-test-revise," the "precept" operates on the schema, "concern-express-become." Both of the latter linguistic forms pertain to given situations around which presumed parameters of "existence," for instance, or "possibility" can be either asserted or tested. The "precept" makes no presumptions as to what is "given," nor as to what its own "prowess" will bring about – it anticipates only that its way of living will "become" (assuming it continues in living) again as the expressing engagement unfolds.

The precept operates within a range of "concerns," and sets out tasks to be undertaken with respect to that concern. This concern is not an "object" on which a separate and distinct sensory faculty operates; and the "task" is not a set of procedures that are methodically executed on that object. The precepts' "concerns" activate the senses and awareness to which the person relates at all; and the tasks are "expressions" (not activated "intentions") of that person's sense being ventured and fore-given into the milieu. Thus the precept is not a proposition that is "tested" via procedures that are then modified according to the "feedback" data. The precept engages as a way that is, just as it is – as a "sign" and "signifier" (to use linguistic terms) that are intrinsically bound up together in its expression. The engagement does not spur a modification of the procedure, but rather instigates the "becoming" of the concern itself.

As a verbalization, as an expression, the precept operates as a value sign, of a way onward (aspiration) for that person, into what is already existing, a way that is set out by this living person (and only by this person) as worthy (having significance by virtue of being this person's own sign, signature and way – think of Nietzsche's *Ecce Homo*) for what can (might) come (be on the way, be-coming) forth. It also only "signs" or bears a signature of this person, as a venturing into guiding what values might offer something more expansive and more encompassing – therefore different values than are now allowed at the sites of engagement – such that occurrences can be iteratively engaged in the attitude of being attuned to difference.

Now we can say that the characterizing expressions of the other figures bear this "concern-expression-becoming" structure that we have laid out for the mystic figuration's expression. The difference between them pertains to the regime of energy, or to the concreteness of the state of affairs to which their discerning concerns are addressed. The mystic's regime of concerns are directed toward energies that are in their least "formed" or concrete states, and so their "precepts" are also the most intensely energizing and fluid of any of the expressions that the "breakout creative" schema envisions.

43   [13] In the case of leader mentoring there have been disappointments, not only with prospective mentors, as my story conveyed, but with mentees as well. I feel, in general, that these frustrations (failures?) come out of the near proximity of leading to managing and to the way that the management development industry, including, if not especially the coaching/consulting juggernaut (to which I once belonged), has confused the two. Prospective leader mentees *universally* come into the mentoring engagement expecting to be coached about how to perform better and be more "successful," and never expect the turn that the process takes as we explore aspirational notions such as "self-trust" and one's commitment to followers, no less to the notion of "creating followers." In the case of the other figures, the proximity to performance and a managerial presumption is not involved and so the notion of "aspiration" emerges in some degree of clarity much sooner.

[14] I also advocate that mentoring, as a professional endeavor, define itself as being a support resource that is devoted to aspirations. See my papers, "Mentoring and Aspiration: Two

Ideas in Search of One Another" (2013) and "Questions Concerning the 'Essence' of Mentoring" (2012). Available on request.

44   [15] *Adoration: The Deconstruction of Christianity II* (New York; 2013) p. 17. Nancy is among those contemporary figures who I classify (reluctantly) as an "ana-mystic," as I present later.

Introduction

45   [1] Melville, Herman (1998); p. 21.

        [2] Hölderlin, Hyperion; p. 1.

        [3] Ibid. pp. 189ff.

59   [4] In order to characterize these aspirations that we call "mystic," I am admittedly taking over a name that originates in a decidedly tainted history. Clearly, the mystic aspirations that operate in today's world have to be conceived of differently than the classic medieval expressions of the "presence of God." In the contemporary conception, mystic aspirations are receptive to and accepting of a "presence" all right (which I name, below, the "field of enthusiasm"), but now these energies remain unnamed, are not unified, and are not specifically designated as pertaining to humans alone; they are cosmic energies and forces of the most numerous, un specifiable, energetic, continuous, unfiltered encounters with what has not yet even been dreamed of. Mystics let these energies into their lives in the most undiluted, unsystematized and not-yet-abstractly-conceptualized manner.

They then allow themselves to persist in the discontinuity opened up by these energies so as to allow new forms of realization to take shape. That is, and this is the key that allows for a notion of "aspiration" at all, these energies tend to gather and organize, in a completely spontaneous and aleatory way, into structures that are capable of becoming *more complex*.

59   5   Kaehner, R. C. (1961), *Mysticism Sacred and Profane.*

60   6   Marechal, J. (2004), *The Psychology of the Mystics*, p. 50 and again, this time in quotes, on p. 117.

            7   We have to consider this issue in relation to all of the aspiring figures.

65   8   Nietzsche, *Daybreak* (1997). New York: Cambridge University Press; p. 449.

Chapter One

68   1   2005; p. 194.

            2   #82; 1991; p. 133.

69   3   1990; p. 3.

72   4   As I make clear in my work with aspiring leader figurations, there is little support or encouragement for their contributions either. In highly managed, return on investment-based organizations that crank out the goods at the lowest possible costs of production, the creative impetus of a breakout leader can hardly catch hold either. Aspiring leading is different from the life that mystic aspirations will engender, but the former is no easy fit in institutionalized life either; aspiring leaders also struggle to maintain their ethic of attentive responsibility against the crush of pressures to conform and get the prescribed results on time, under budget, all the time. People with mystic aspirations just experience and exhibit different tensions.

            This fact goes to another factor that contributes to my encountering mystics in corporate business settings: I am only hired to begin with by creative leaders who value, recognize, foster and invest in creative energies and talents. The leaders who hire me might very well hire a mystically aspiring person, not because they are recognized as mystics, but because these creative leaders recognize the breakout energies that radiate without reservation from mystic aspiring energies.

79   5   (Klossowski, Pierre, *Nietzsche and the Vicious Circle* (Chicago; 1997) p. 218ff. In coining this term I admit that I am attracted not only to the way the term sets out the completely giving nature of the mystic's way, but also how the term contrasts with the word "forgive." To forgive means, of course that we let pass a wrong that was done without further expectation of recompense. We thus *for*give in the dual senses that we are giving for the sake of someone who has put something in play; and it is for*giving* in the sense that we are giving up our claim in advance of anything else being offered as recompense.

In contrast to this whole exchange, the notion of fore-giving connotes a giving to and for an Other, whatever one has, and not what has already been done to a person and so can enter into some kind of calculated exchange. It is *fore*-giving in that it is prior to it having ever been received, and so it is a giving that does not even bear with it an awareness of exactly what it is that will be received, or what it will be when it is received. The giving thus, in a way, takes place in such a way that no expectations, recompense or exchange can even be envisioned.

81   6   Even in cases where the mystic's raptures are celebrated, I suspect a defense mechanism is at work. Emblematic of this, sixteenth century mystics were paraded before the public by the Catholic Church as it vied with the forces of Protestant rejection of priestly intermediaries. The venerable clerical fathers ennobled the rapturous experiences of some of its selected believers as proof that the church's intermediating function was no barrier to true union with God. Of course, such experiences, if validly "mystic," and therefore revelatory of God, were rare and only came with great exertion of effort and usually were related to and authenticated by a church confessor; but still, behold, the church, in its "societies" and "orders" could claim that it actually fostered such practices

(that resulted in the affirmation of its dogma) and protected the vulnerable people who had them.

At the height of their need to prove that the church validated individual "mystic" experiences of God, it chose to mercilessly persecute Juan de la Cruz (John of the Cross) for his depiction of the way to faith coming through a "dark night of the soul." Protection and defense of dogma tops validation of the mystic every time in the institutionalized setting.

88   7   Deleuze, Gilles. *Nietzsche and Philosophy* (1983); first quote, p. 17; second quote, p. 23.

Chapter Two

89   1   *Nietzsche and Philosophy* (1983), pp 71-2.

           2   *Friedrich Hölderlin: Essays and Letters on Theory* (1988), "Becoming in Dissolution," p. 97.

90   3   *Phenomenology of Mind* (1976).

94   4   I certainly respect all the efforts that are made to show similarities and affinities between the West and the East (to use a most sweeping and crude distinction, for the moment). However, in the larger schema of the breakout creatives project, I will show that the Western mystic arises in response to a very specific set of circumstances, to very specific states of Western religion (Christianity, in particular) and to other ways Western social and economic institutions were locked in rigid oppressions. The aspirations of Western mystics, therefore, were conceptually and historically oriented from the start (especially since, in the form of Greek and Christian/Roman institutions and texts). The historical world was what deemed to be problematic and was deemed to be in a state that required the restoration of a fresh, transcending, more cosmically attuned state of being.

One difference between the two traditions will be most helpful in situating our work with Western mystics. That is,

Eastern thinking, the thinking that is most compared to the Western mystical tradition, has little or no concern for such a "split." The Eastern practices that are compared to those of the Western mystic ("religious" practices, chants, texts and rites) are immersed in a sense of a "oneness" of all aspects of life, such that the mundane/transcendent or sacred/profane split is not effectively operative. Also, there is little sense that these practices will change "the world" (as in Western mystic notions) and reconstruct the way humans per se engage occurrences; instead there is a drive toward proper discernment, expression and then individual action in a world that is essentially static, in which nothing is new under the sun.

There are other differences as well, and these stem from what I hypothesize as differently developed machinics of aspiration (different modes of how the assemblages of the aspiring mind work). And these psychic differences drive the formations of different figurations, psychic constructions and ethical stances as well. (See: Shenkman, *The Aspiring Mind: A Philosophical Inquiry into the Urge to Create* (Unpublished; In Progress; Available on request) And so, we restrict our attention here to the Western tradition.

95   5 In pointing to the notion of "energy," I literally refer here and throughout the text to findings of contemporary science that derive matter from energy ($E=MC^2$) and to the thermodynamics of self-organizing systems that institute temporary anentropic processes within the general entropic state of the universe's energetic expansion. Freud's psychic model is also one of a filtering and condensation of psychic energies. So in no way do we need to resort to fuzzy-headed unities or pre-scientific religious monstrosities in order to speak of a mystic or any of us experiencing energy. A mystic, or any of us, experiences energy in a way that is at least analogous to the way plants create chlorophyll from sunlight. No one accuses a botanist of being muddleheaded for citing this process as essential and empirically validated. It is important to remember this

location of our sense of "energy" whenever we invoke the term as being a source of vitality for the mystic.

One way that our use of the term might seem strange is that our view does entail a shift of perspective on the relation between an individual's mind and the rest of nature. We consider the mythological-empirical-metaphysical (I relish the screams of the empirical-rationalist-positivists at this juxtaposition) view of singular and isolated human minds existing (indeed "created" separately) from "the rest" of nature to be the utmost primitive fiction, par excellence. Our view is that our minds, lives, beings, are phenomena emergent from the great energies of the cosmos (or chaosmos – to dispel any notion of there being a pre-existing order). While certain aspects of that emergence allow for differentiation of certain kinds of individualized processes, the differentiation is never so complete as to extricate the human endeavor from its "natural" milieu. I do not want this evocation of "energy" to be conflated with a monistic view of universal oneness or divine emanations from a shining godhead.

Thus, when I say that the mystic aspirations expose this person to the experiencing of "raw energies" I am referring to the notion that these people are attuned to certain moments of psychic/somatic translation and formation that are less differentiated than are other aspects of our psychic/somatically constituted factors.

This work comes out of the Hegelian, Heideggarian, Nancyan, and Deleuzian self-organizing disciplines rather than psychological or neuroanatomical discourses that are concerned with brain cartography or neurological scanning. By that nomenclature I am leaning into this notion: what we take as our living milieu comprises constellations of "pure energy made manifest". It is a constellating efficacy that presses itself onward out of whatever existed into adjacent locales, as far as it can go, until it meets an insurmountable obstruction or resistance. Our notion of "energy" then means this: a sense of pushing out to the limit, without reservation or even awareness that anything but such a pushing out is what is called for.

We are thus saying that the "Aspiring Mind" comprises those psychic/somatic resources that specifically do not close off the connection between nature-energy and the involutedly torsioned mind energy, the energy that is eventually taken up by other resources in order to form objects, certainties and knowledge. For all of these reasons, our term "energy" is vague, but is such intentionally, advisedly and with logical, and even some empirical, concreteness.

97   6   In the *Aspiring Mind* book I make the case that the mystic arises when certain psychic assemblages become robust and competent enough to stand on their own. These structures began to emerge around 6,000 – 10,000 years ago, in the Fertile Crescent (as the Abrahamic Intercession) and were further developed into a specific form of operation (and dis course) by the Greeks (as philosophy) in the last millennium BC. These resources become competent (a Sense-Making Field, an Egoic Transducing Array and "World" comprising "saturating phenomena" are gathered in a mega-assemblage called the Ego Structure) with the emergence of the mystic figure, in the thirteenth century AD, and enter into diverse and large-scale practices of science, technology, economics and law in the Enlightenment period.

7   Ernesto Laclau is one of the social thinkers who envision change on the social plane in ways that make room for the work of the mystic aspirations we describe here. I refer here to Laclau's description (see especially *New Reflections on the Revolution of Our Time,* 1990, pp. 60 ff) of external "myths" of social possibilities forming into "horizons" of possibility for actual change, by means of articulating "social imaginaries," which can become hegemonic formations of social agents' actions which are incarnated and enacted by the "subject positions" these agents articulate. A question he does not ask is, "What human capabilities make it possible for such "myths" to

be formed and articulated?" These myths, as Laclau describes them, are articulated notions that while ambiguous, tendentious and provisional, are able to make their way into becoming possibilities. I can easily (too easily?) suggest that it is mystic aspiration that generates precepts as articulations of one or another aspect of such myths; and then it is the work of prophetic aspirations to translate and transpose such myths into those possibilities that might just form concrete horizons (by means of the work of artist aspirations) and then into new social forms by means of leader aspirations. Prophetic aspirations span the process of enactment from envisioning specific social imaginaries up to the formation of regions and logics (such as Badiou envisions in *Logic of Worlds* (2009)?) into "subject positions," which can take up the figurations of prophets of demarcated endeavors to artist and leader aspirations.

In other words, Laclau's formulation of the process of social change is one that envisions and accommodates, and even points to, just such aspirational figurations as we propose here. The contribution the aspirational figuration model offers is thus twofold: (1) The aspirational figuration model envisions the sharing, communicating and transporting of the work of change among several different life ways of very complex and devoted figurations, *over time* and as transpiring in ways that are increasingly appropriate for the circumstances they address (obviating the need for violence or mechanistically totalizing – totalitarian, ideological – upheavals); and (2) the model provides a resource for educating people to accommodating aspiring energies in ways that make such engagements matters of concerted effort, but not anomalously fearful extremism, that it makes such construction of social horizons and social imaginaries a matter of facultative capability rather than willful assertion after the fact.

Laclau thus envisions a stage of engagement which he describes as that of "the age of democratic revolution," or a state of affairs in which "the mere temporality and incompletion of something that has become essentially unrepresentable (1990, p. 75). The term "something" here stands for any and every mode and factor that would claim to have an "objective" presence or reality – everything from "natural objects" (which are now completely under the sway of human efficacy) to technological and cultural artifacts (epitomized by the frantic pace of digital innovations and their effects), and then on to social relations (which are now overturned and dislocated on ever more-frequent bases in all of their governmental, economic and nationalist forms). What we and Laclau and our coterie of observers discern as a state of revolution is the dire need for a new spurt of individuation, a new exertion of aspiration to set into play ways of engaging that continuously expand and persistently labor to encompass our "world" with greater generative comprehension. And we are far from achieving such a facultative capability.

99   8   As I survey the art and literature offered by the breakout creatives, there is continuity to what is emerging in their highly individualized works. It centers on the notion of the co-generation of all occurrence (mind and world being one such co-generation). It is not that these figures meet at a world summit and decide these things. Rather, the process of epoch-producing symmetry-breaking offers a region of openness, a margin, an envelope of possibility. These figures are sensing what that margin offers, not merely propounding their own fantasies of utopias.

Yes, the Buddhist might say, we have pointed to this for millennia. But, the Western mystic might say, "What good did that pointing do? Grant a few privileged souls enlightenment? We as Western breakout creatives have our own baggage to deal with, unfortunately. We might well have taken a wrong turn when we did not pay heed to your precept – and went with the Hebrew prophets and Plato instead. But now we are ready, and maybe we have learned some valuable lessons in guiding the human endeavor in the meantime."

100   [9]   Laclau (1990, p. 67) describes this state of affairs in our socioeconomic/cultural lives in more concrete terms, "The combined effects of commodification, of bureaucratic rationalization and of the increasingly complex form of division of labor – all require constant creativity and the continuous construction of spaces of collective operation that can rest less and less on inherited objective, institutional forms. But this means that in contemporary societies the (mythical) space of the subject is widened at the expense of structural objectivity."

[10]   Derrida (2011). This essay, "*Pace* Not(s)," in *Parages* exemplifies this thinking, as does, of course, his notion of "difference."

101   [11]   For this kind of dissecting analysis I refer the avid reader to Henrich's *Between Kent and Hegel* ((2003, Ch. 16) for an exquisite rendering of Fichte's notion of "reflection". It is clear that Hölderlin's effort here is to dynamically and immanently describe the process Fichte works through in coming to grips with our creative engagement with life as self-conscious, generative beings.

[12]   Hölderlin is one of the forebears of the contemporary anamystic figure. When he, Hegel and Schelling were writing, during the dawning of the nineteenth century, mysticism had been in a state of eclipse, and the texts of Meister Eckhart were just being rediscovered. The thrust of idealism at that time was to grasp hold of the sense of promise that exceeded every synthesis of knowledge and certainty and sufficiency (of the Kantian and Leibnizian kind) and recovered the sense of purely overflowing generativity, more akin to what Spinoza had conceived. In every sense, these true *thinkers* succeeded in that they outlined the parameters of the aspiring mind that contemporary anamystics have continued to extend, map out and bring to expression.

102   [13]   Pfau, (1988), pp. 97-98.

105   [14]   (1998); "From the Abyss;" p. 313.

Chapter Three

106   ¹   *The Science of Knowing* (2005), p.128.

            ²   *The Arcades Project* (1999), p. 456.

108   ³   This is not a matter of a person facing a "mid-life crisis." Rather it is an "ontogenic" factor in the development of the aspiring mind – a subject to which we will be turning our attention momentarily. In the spirit of foreshadowing I can point out that each of the four assemblages of the aspiring mind (see Diagram 3.1) have emerged as the human endeavor encountered states of affairs of increasing complexity – they developed historically, that is.

The complexity of the aspiring mind's collection of assemblages increased by new modes of organizing engagements *inserting themselves between* the primal Destinational Comprehension (DC) assemblage and its immediate formation of the Iconic Imago, that of the Leader figure's "arch." (I consider the assemblage of the Iconic Imago to be a possible variant or offshoot of Lacan's "mirror stage" formation of the ego – see *Ecrits* [2007], "The Mirror Stage as Formative of the I Function as Revealed in Psychoanalytic Experience," p. 75).

The assemblage that engenders and sustains mystic aspirations, that of the "World" assemblage, asserted its way into configuring aspiration only late in this evolution (in the thirteenth century – in its European incarnation), and was preceded by the insertion of the Arteous assemblage (which arose after the establishment of the first permanent human urban (centers) and then the Ego Structure (which arose about 6,000 years ago in Mesopotamia), respectively. Each insertion entails a different formation of the Iconic Imago and thereby generates aspirations that have different modes of relating, different life priorities and proximities and different ways of generating their aspirational actualities.

The mystic's figuration is the latest and most of these Imagoes to be generated. Accordingly (in the spirit of "ontogeny recapitulates phylogeny"), the Imago of mystic aspirations also takes shape late in life – after all the other assemblages of the aspiring mind are up and running.

109   4   Each figuration of aspiration emphasizes different machinic operations of the whole aspiring mind complex. For a complete and general account of the aspiring mind resource, I will make my as yet unpublished manuscript of the *Aspiring Mind: A Philosophical Inquiry into the Urge to Create* available upon request.

111   5   When undertaken with logical rigor and philosophical ardor, this move clearly resembles that of Husserl's "epoché," or "bracketing" of everyday assumptions. Only in this case, the "bracketing" is even more radical, closer to that of a deconstructive operation, that also suspends the primacy we give to our "objects" of scientific verity (which Husserl was at great pains to validate).

         6   I do want to offer the reader a few caveats as we begin this sketching operation. First, I know of no other depiction of such a thing as an "aspiring mind;" I know of no claim that there is a "region of the brain" that is dedicated to aspiration (as there is supposedly a region that is dedicated to language, for instance), and so, our depiction is somewhat "speculative," in that regard. However, in the philosophical arena (the arena in which philosophy is being *done* and not merely imitated or its trappings of discursive style being layered upon gross trivialities, as in analytical positivist "philosophies) such notions of pre-conceptual energies taking on shapes and characters that generate aspiring affects are considered quasi-systematically, in coherent (if still exploratory) narratives. Also, in "scientific" circles, the notion of psychic self-organization and emergent development is gaining traction. See Thelen and Smith, *A Dynamic Systems Approach to the Development of Cognition and Action* (2002); also Kelso *Dynamic Patterns: The Self-Organization of Brain and Behavior* (1995).

Our work builds on these two streams of explorative thinking. Our proposal therefore is experimental and "hypothetical," or propositional, but it is neither fanciful nor purely an exercise of the imagination. It is a philosophical speculation in the sense that it undertakes the work of philosophizing as described by Deleuze and Guattari in their masterwork, *What is Philosophy* (1994). That work is devoted to creating concepts within which further explorations (conceptual, experimental, law-making) can be pursued, even to the point of correcting the provisional, precursor "perceptual" concept. The notion of the "aspiring mind" is such a concept. (In this regard, the brute mechanics offered by linguistically oriented logical positivists and analysts does have a place – as a mechanic has a place in the chain of experts needed to maintain an automobile, after it has been conceived, designed, produced and sold. That work is necessary and can even be constructive, and could be helpful in clarifying the work I offer here. But first, as is always the case, a concept must be constructed, contextualized and placed in an operative hypothesis, as we are doing here.)

Second, the "aspiring mind" comprises a notion of a psychic resource that is still very much in the process of developing; and so, it is not surprising that it is not yet subject matter for "empirical," clinical or experimental research (although Thelen and Smith (2002), and Kelso (1995) are leading the way in devising methodologies and logical frameworks for such study). The aspiring mind is an expression in the human arena for the larger, self-organizing impetus toward individuation: toward self-organization tending to achieve complex levels of organization that, in turn, engenders further increasing complexity (rather than remaining in the state of rock, or in a static condition of organic functionality).

And so, third, in the strongest sense I can aver, the whole notion of the "aspirational figure" is that of how self-organizing increasing complexity in it own right, as a matter of study and as a locus for intentional development, has become the focus of the human endeavor. In depicting the aspiring ways of the mystic, we are thus describing how self-organizing increasing complexity becomes subject matter for our attention and operates at the highest levels of our values. The mystic figuration, in this proposed thesis, elevates this individuating/aspiration to being something that can be grasped (in faith-for), articulated (in an act of fore-giving), acted upon (as a precept), and taught and developed as a life way on its own terms, for its own sake.

114   7   This nuance of the conscious and unconscious effects on the aspiring resource forms a key "constraint" on what aspiration intends. Right from the start, and in every fractal instance of its operations, the aspiring mind is permeated by (contaminated with) the factors that have already been assigned values and have been given shape by other P/SS resources that are already prominently in use, already lend significant (and signifying weight and value) to ongoing life ways. Aspirational figures, accordingly, in their health (and it is the role of mentors to support this healthy state) establish expansive and more encompassing links and passages into new states of engaging.

These are not the fanatical figures that codify notions into actions of totalitarian terror or that use the lever of power in order elevate their notions to false grandeur or righteous certitude. As long as aspirations retain their expansively transitive and generative constitution, their effects are ones of concern and attentively mindful engagement; and, as we know, maintaining this generative state for aspirations is not something the human endeavor has in any way mastered. Again, it is the role of mentors, at this point in time, to support aspiring people in their aspiring ways, so that it might become possible to learn how this is done on a broader and more sustainable (and socially organized) basis.

115   8   A subtext to this hypothesis is that the human endeavor has now reached a state of affairs in which this resource does stand alone and has become an as-still-not-acknowledged

driver of ever more of the decisions, events and happenings shaping our times. In this view, aspiration and its aspiring mind is worthy of being subject matter for study and "treatment" as the unconscious and neurosis was for Freud. This suspicion is not offered lightly, and it offers the field of mentoring the opportunity to become a professional practice in its own right.

116   9   To state this musing in a more appropriately forceful way, I would say that the process of human P/SS development includes this "artist figured" state of articulation – the development of images and metaphors – as marking out a distinguished and differentiated cluster of criteria that, later, are worked on by "prophetic" conceptualizations that are turned into articulations of robust Ideas and then objects, forces and laws. Our envisioning a "schema" in advance of there being a fully articulated and existent "object" of an "aspiring mind," is thus a step offered in the effort to have such a resource emerge in its own right.

117   10   See Deleuze/Guattari, the two-volume *Capitalism and Schizophrenia,* and especially Volume II, *A Thousand Plateaus* (1987). Other writings of Deleuze are helpful as well, especially, *Nietzsche and Philosophy* (1983), which is fairly well accessible to lay readers. On a more technical level, see Deleuze's *Difference and Repetition* (1994) and *Logic of Sense* (1990). For an intense, cryptic, but brief deployment of these notions, see the essay "Dead Psychoanalysis. Analyze," in *Dialogues II* (2006).

    11   It is the branches of philosophy that "deconstructively" approach the generation of stances, positions, insights and new ways of living that I refer to here – with precursors in the mystic literature (that we consider in Part Two of this book), German Idealism, Hegel, Nietzsche, phenomenological discourses (Husserl, Heidegger, Merleau-Ponty, et. al.) and then the currently working "anamystics," such as Derrida, Deleuze, Nancy, Lyotard and others (some of whom are also considered in Part Two).

Also, it is exactly the work in bringing such "metaphorical" infrastructures to fruition, through facultative development and even brain development, that mystics and the other breakout creative figures are dedicated to doing. The aspiring mind, in essence, intends no other activity but generating exactly the kind of account and discourse (metaphorical, perceptual, experimental) that we are employing here.

121   12   In this regard, I would suggest that every creature that relies on "consciousness" or "intelligence" (a very rough designation) is born with a P/SS that exerts a measure of reserved dehiscence with respect to decisions and actions so as to generate a range of options as to what to do next. Humans are able to generate a wide range of choices because of the establishment of language as an independent locale that absorbs situational factors and provides a medium in which to analyze them into being "objective" options. As ubiquitous and essential as this "infantic," aspiring resource is in the lives of "intelligent" creatures, it can be *crushed* as a generative factor. When this occurs (in old dogs and adult humans?) conscious creatures are left to rely on habits, instincts, rules and conventions; to a lesser or greater extent, this leaves them disabled in terms of generating appropriate variations in decision making because of the complexity or strangeness of new situations. This "crushing" takes place in the human scene by oppressive upbringing, impoverished circumstances, brain and mental impairments or malformations as well as by over-submission to given norms, rules, texts or prevailing ideologies. Laziness and lassitude in the face of the need to learn also crushes the delicately gossamer matrices that this resource is wont to engender as well.

122   13   This discussion applies the self-organizing model to the notion of "machinic" processes as described by Deleuze and Guattari in *A Thousand Plateaus*.

124   14   We touch on matters that have to be given "technical" attention. The logic of formation we are using here is that of "autocatalysis" and "symmetry breaking" rather than one of "cause and effect."

Autocatalytic logic envisions a temporality that presupposes an "existent" state being perturbed by another factor; and this is a strange factor: it is a factor that does not (yet?) have an existence that is either equal to or opposite of the existent (as is presupposed by the classical causal model). The "other" referred to in the autocatalytic process is not even formally a part of the "reaction" that is under consideration as undergoing autocatalysis. This factor is completely estranged from, external to the reactant site, and so exerts forces that are indeterminate and outside of the factors that had constituted the "existent," and so comprise, for the existent, what is inexplicably more expansive and more encompassing than its current state of being comprises. Still, however, this outside "other" is necessary: it provides the conditions (an energizing state) under which an autocatalysis can transpire at all. The result of the engagement is a different state of being than had existed prior to the exertion, and also the continuing and even enhanced capability of the exerting impetus to continue.

What about the happenings right "in" the site of the autocatalysis itself – doesn't the catalyst "cause" a certain reaction and produce its specific effects? It is true that one can analyze the happening in such a way as to find correlations between occurrences that proceed in the way of the cause and effect chain, but such a conclusion would constitute putting on blinkers as to the larger frame of the expanse that the occurrence encompasses, and in fact, gives the occurrences its specific character. This same "blinkered" approach, such as we might call Newtonian physics, when compared to the more vast landscapes of Relativity or Quantum Mechanics. The "thermodynamic," self-organizing models of occurrence, which rely on catalytic and autocatalytic processes, are another in that vein of more expansive, encompassing and inclusively integrating approaches to occurrences. The "causal" approaches can be productive and effective: Newtonian physics get us to the moon and back, for instance. But they are not descriptive of the generative states that we know to produce even more generative states, and these generative states are what concern us here.

So, for us, what is the crux of the matter that imposes this autocatalytic and symmetry-breaking logic upon us? It is this: a machinic iteration of the aspiring mind's operation takes whole and as a momentarily constituted state the global reconfiguration of its site of engaging as it has changed, from one iteration to the next. A machinic iteration is not concerned with causality, but is most concerned about the change in the global state which its engaging, its aspiring, has to account for and in some measure accommodate. The machinic operation thus has to encompass processes that change not in the manner of being an effect, but rather has to change in the manner of arriving at a different state of being, a different constituted and constituting site of encompassment. At most, the succeeding state of affairs that a machinic iteration generates retains mere traces of its prior states, but these traces do not any longer act as affecting agents that organize the new configuration in a coherent manner in the same way, with the same influence and with the same power as they did in the "old" state of affairs. The traces of the prior state no longer persist in such a manner that there is any "causing" agency remaining as attributable to them.

As pertains to the P/SS context, this expansive and diversifying process takes place in a constrained and organized way such that while increasing the machinic scale and complexity of operation of the aspiring resource, it does not obliterate any of its factors. This autocatalytic, symmetry breaking process can continue to expand, proliferate and organize as long as there is energy of some kind to sustain the perturbations, and also that there is a sufficiently elastic and plastic existing milieu to absorb, accommodate and accept the ensuing perturbations. This is no "ex nihilo" process, since there are always predecessor states within which any one such process transpires; and any one autocatalytic and symmetry breaking process always has taking its (own) place in this milieu at stake (Spinoza' "conatus"?). Chains of causes and effects can be isolated out in any local transaction of a "taking place" among reactants that project their ongoing operations. But in the case of machinic operations, no such established and iso-morphically repeatable processes are in play. Machinic processes always are defined as anticipatory proceedings that accommodate the increasing complexities that await its efficacies and constitute its horizons.

124   [15]   Autocatalysis and symmetry breaking allow for the scaling up of these factors in ways that are not merely repetitious but, instead, as the autocatalysis proceeds, allow the machinic processes to iterate or self-generate amid and upon conditions which are slightly different, slightly more expansive than what the previous iteration had engaged. The autocatalysis results in both an expanding "scaling up" of the process and an increased capacity to encompass the expanded (and different) conditions the next iteration will encounter. Changes occur by a logic not of continuously chained effects, but by periodic eruptions of "symmetry breaks" that, on a continuum of the minute to the macro, allow for the emergence of new configurations that differ in mode and character from their predecessor states.

A "machinic assemblage" (possibly) takes shape when the au-tocatalytic machinic process continues on in engendering "emergences" of succeeding machinically iterable configurations that continue to autocatalytically generate conditions for sub-sequent symmetry breaks (on its continuum of scale from the minute and momentary to the molar and momentous). In this way the dynamic that allows for emergences within a certain range of formation and deformation stabilizes and iterates in a more constrained, but never mechanically repetitious way. This "emergence" of an iterable machinic dynamic becomes a force in its own right. When these effects are noted and registered and rendered into accounts as matters of attention and concern, they become available for other P/SS resources to act upon, guide and conceptualize, as aspiration, for example.

125   [16]   *The Aspiring Mind: Philosophical Reflections on the Urge to Create* (op. cit.)

             [17]   That means, of course, that the other assemblages play dominant roles in constituting the other figurations. The DC and Iconic Imago dominate in configuring leader aspirations; the Arteous and Sense-Making Field dominate in the artist figure; and the transducing assemblage and the self-stream components of the Sense-Making Field dominate in the prophet figuration. These shifts in dominance between different operations of the aspiring mind's assemblages then result in the different configurations of each figure's Iconic Imagoes.

126   [18]   I put this term in quotation marks in order to indicate that we are considering the assemblage of the aspiring mind and we are not using the term generically. The quotation marks also serve to indicate that the aspiring mind has specifically and idiosyncratically cordoned off its engagements with oc currences from the machinations of the other resources of the productive, acquisitive and knowing mind.

             [19]   Note in Figure 3.1 that the "World" assemblage has its originating impetus firmly ensconced in the fourth ("anomalous") orbit of the Arteous (categorially ordering) assemblage. The contents of the other "orbits" do affect the generation of the "World" assemblage. These more stable factors comprise a "base" or a "milieu" which provides a point of "orientation" for what the "World" assemblage takes up (the wild and anomalous factors of the occurrence), but do not "determine" or "characterize" what the "World" assemblage takes up as its content.

             [20]   This notion extends and modifies what the phenomenologist theologian Jean-Luc Marion describes as "saturated phenomena." See *In Excess* (2002), pp. 112ff. His discernment of these specific agents that permeate the sense of there being a "world" that is in the process of being engaged offers an important avenue for continued philosophical (and then even psychoanalytical?) consideration. What he (as is typical of the

theological enterprise, and of the classical metaphysical/scientific enterprise as well) identifies as results and as having independent standing as factors in an experiencing matrix, I take as energetically affecting potencies that precisely and exactly prevent any such formation of named appearances.

At best, we can characterize affecting energies (as phenomena, proper), which, in the mode of self-organizing thermodynamics, permeate or saturate the engagement we call "experiencing" – of situating our attentions to the immediacies of being affected (which can include either occurrences that are either external to or interior to our own bodies). As philosophers will surely recognize, I am shamelessly recapitulating here Spinozan operation.

126   [21]   Each aspiring figure we consider in this work is most affected by one or another of the aspiring mind's assemblages. Mystic aspirations are most oriented toward this "World" assemblage. Prophetic aspirations are most concerned with the machinics of the Sense-Making Field, again in the Ego Structure. Leader aspirations focus on the Iconic Imago, while the Artist figure focuses on the Arteous assemblage. Each figuration was (historically and developmentally) "responsible" for the emergence of the structure that focuses its concerns, and subsequent to the emergence of later assemblages' interventions (for example, the "World" assemblage is the most recent intervening assemblage), each takes up the task of adjusting the machinics of its centering assemblage to the new dynamics that aspiration now comprises.

134   [22]   Similarities between this notion and that of the classical "soul" come to mind. While that notion gets the mentor's orientation going in the right direction (away from instrumental behaviors and motivations), it also short-circuits the thought process we are proposing. The classical notion of "soul" is tied to a transcendent force, in a way that is somewhat analogous to the way that saturating phenomena affect the psyche. But "soul" refers to static and defended (to the point of seeking

its salvation) layers of one's "self" — that means of psychic nomination that gives rise to classical "identity."

The II, on the other hand, relates to affects of a "world" that is set in motion by aspiration, and thus the impetus to engage occurrences differently the next time, and so also entails that any static aspect of one's "identity" be amenable to change. The II is not "defended," but instead is placed under scrutiny, examined, judged and destined for change. There is thus nothing "there" to save, there is only a "role" vis-à-vis one's "world," to be strong enough to engage in a more expansive and more encompassing way, next time.

I cannot but think here of how, just as in the case of the mystic, forgiving is transformed into *"fore-giving,"* I think that forgetting is translated by aspiration into "fore-getting:" the II coalesces energies into a state such that the aspiring mind is ready in advance, and anticipates, a way of taking up its way differently than it had. It fore-gets its own construction, such that it sets in motion the process by which the ego cogito of knowing and production will forget what had gone before.

135   [23]   This "open" factor might be a historical reflection of how new the mystic figuration is. It may be that mystics have not yet found a figuration of their aspirations in ways that are reliably viable for charting ways. It might well be the case that after a few eons of articulation and expression, the precepts will form into defining and organizing faculties that render architectural structures.

Or, it might be that as the figures arise in response to the increasing complexity of their milieus, the figurations of the icons also become less architecturally specific, and so instead of developing more definitive structure, the mystic will become more adept at deploying its non-specific figuration into life ways that we do not yet comprehend, and so will teach us new modes of discernment that are currently beyond the pale of our currently available and operative concepts.

136   [24]   This last category of energies pertain most of all to what I call "transversals." These are energies that are produced by the very fact of the II consolidating and organizing, and as such are *excluded* from that organization. They cannot be "known" by the II for that reason. And, even more, as byproducts of the II's own organizing, they are *specifically unknowable* by the II, from moment to moment. I see these unknowable factors as being noticed and then even accounted for, at least in their effects, by notions such as Hegel's "negation," or Schelling's *"katabole,"* or Derrida's "arché-traces" and "differance." In these prescient discourses, these factors are named so as to assure any that discourse remains open and available to further engagement, i.e., to aspiration/individuation. These factors are considered explicitly and in detail, and from several different angles in *The Aspiring Mind*.

137   [25]   I have not read any literature from neurobiology that documents specialized regions of the brain lighting up in EEGs as the mystic thinks. And so I cannot claim that this "Field of Enthusiasm" is (as yet) demarcated as being a dedicated region of the brain. Of course, to do so such a study would have to begin with an accepted way to designate a psychographic population called "mystics."

But, I do think, if such a population were identified, these mystics might show a noticeable rise in right brain (non-rational) activity. This activity would be indicative of faith-for the immediate connectedness with primal flows of our dynamic milieu. Maybe the so-called "right-brain" activities would be more definitively delineated. This defining of right brain energy would keep specific things from being suffused in rational, reified, linguistically determined (left brain) forms on a one-on-one basis (maybe the way Derrida's "de-construction" engages one notion of one author at a time). However, this heightened right brain activity would then ne-cessitate heightened activity as required for making sense of pure, unassimilated and "processed" right brain flows. There would be a much greater dependence on images, metaphors and analogies, as opposed to analytical structures. And this brain might well have a richly connected network to limbic, emotive, affective centers.

This heightened capability of formulating and coalescing right brain flows prior to and in preference to left brain processing might evolve into a distinctive brain specialty – as did the whole right brain and frontal lobe capabilities. But I speculate (and await the data, not to mention the evolution). For now, we are left with a speculative and projected notion of tentative and proscriptive formations in image, language and gesture, the field of enthusiasm.

Chapter Four

141   [1]   "Heidelberg." In Dieter Henrich, *The Course of Remembrance and Other Essays on Hölderlin,* 1997; p. 257.

142   [2]   *Bergonism* (1991), p. 111-112.

         [3]   *Nietzsche & Philosophy* (1983). p. 101.

         [4]   *Wandering Joy: Meister Eckhart's Mystical Philosophy* (2001) p. xx – xxi.

143   [5]   Wikipedia opens its entry on this item this way, "The theory of recapitulation, also called the biogenetic law or embryological parallelism— often expressed in Ernst Haeckel's phrase as "ontogeny recapitulates phylogeny"—is a largely discredited hypothesis that in developing from embryo to adult, animals go through stages resembling or representing successive stages in the evolution of their remote ancestors." Haekel coined this phrase in a work published in 1899, and that was translated into English in 1901 as *The Riddle of Life.*

For the record, I am not claiming any "scientific" validity to the notion. However, I have noticed in my work the conjunction of two patterns: the late historical development of the mystic figuration (analogous to the reference to phylogeny), and the late coalescing of this figuration in individuals' lives (c.f., the reference to ontogeny). It's a catchy phrase that, rhetorically at least, sheds light on a hypothesis offered in the work on the emergence and development of the aspiring mind and its figurations.

143   6   Or, as we discussed in the last chapter, under the heading of the "infantic," maybe it is more proper to say, all infants express nothing else but the way of groping, searching and expanding one's sense of being in a world, and these are the very potencies that, if they survive into adulthood, are shaped into mystic – type aspirations.

149   7   Bernard Cottret, in *Calvin: A Biography* (2000) makes the important point that in the times of the classical mystics, if a person held heretical views, the body religious could not tolerate this affront, and that person had to be dispensed with, cut out, like a cancer. There was no such idea as "tolerance" (pp. 206-8). Today, there are executives in companies who do look for ways to tolerate their "aberrant" employees up to a point. But when Dan left the executive fold of the company, the reaction was reminiscent of ancient banishment. No one spoke of him anymore. Or if they did, a man once praised for his creativity and open managerial style suddenly became the CFO who didn't connect the dots and didn't sweat the details (a kind of sweating most CFOs do profusely). The mystic often generates such a response. The utter strangeness of their motivations and the fact that they do work at high levels of corporate and organizational responsibility generates intense feelings of resentment, maybe even fear.

150   8   As with all distortions of vitally coherent energies, the behaviors of the broken mystics are innumerably diverse. Still, I submit, there is a way to characterize in a general way what this phenomenon looks like. I suggest there are two forms this "broken" aspiration takes.

The first form comprises people whose own expansive energies as engendered by their "World" assemblages have not consolidated (into their own Iconic Imagoes) and they end up channeling their energies into atavistic, fetishized and ideologically concretized mythico-religious form or practices (which need not be tied to a religion, but can also be expressed by rigid, often hateful political stances). They are people whose ways are all about ritual, idolizing worship and cultic dogma.

The second form produces behaviors that suppress their lives beneath the radar of recognition and/or even the most basic acknowledgement of their existences. In this mode of being broken, such people are hardly visible at all. Some become so dispirited that they lapse into what we call "psychological illnesses." Depression, I think, is one of the forms mystic failure takes. Drugs can relieve the symptoms sufficiently so the person can function "normally," but drugs do not restore the strength necessary to fully engage the mystic aspirations.

The "broken" mystic figure is also different from what I mentioned earlier as "crushed" aspirations. The "broken" state is one in which the aspiring energies are still pulsing and generating affects, but do so in ways that only express the anger and rage that comes from these energies constantly hitting walls, and there not being sufficient avenues for elaborating alternatives or new experiments in expression such that the energies are channeled into given and prefabricated forms of anger. The "crushed" state refers to a condition in which aspirations do not any longer have the potency to generate affects. The crushed state is one that pertains to aspirations in general in that no specific figuration has been allowed to form at all. While most conscious creatures retain traces of the aspiring capability in their range of being able to adapt to novel circumstances, people whose aspirations are crushed make no attempt to generate such responses on their own. The still active ones with crushed aspirations imitate the behavior (a vestigial echo) by reducing their strivings to accumulating more of what is already generally available. The ones that have been rendered inactive in this regard self-medicate the wound of the crushed resource by consuming and seeking out mere novelties for "enjoyment" and the "pursuit of happiness" (a plebian and banal pursuit when viewed from the perspective of aspiration).

152   9   It is not the case that an absent father and strong, supportive and socially constructive feminine influence will "result" or "cause" the formation of a mystic proclivity; it is rather, as a confirming notation, when a mystic proclivity takes shape, these conditions prevailed during the childhood of the adult. Other factors in the childhood situation are commonly in play as well: good health of the child, a modicum of financial security and a literary, expansive, challenging and highly articulate regimen of education. I have neither seen nor read of any accounts of mystic aspirations developing where these factors are absent.

While such a background can be thought of as being "privileged" and so even the designation of mystic aspirations being an "elitist" one, we have to point out that the notion of self-organization depends on the health and robustness of the factors that precipitate new organization. That is, the premise of symmetry breaking depends on there being a healthy, robust, vastly and intricately capable force being in play so as allow for new and more expansive dynamics being installed after the dissolution of the old. In the absence of that strength and encompassing robustness, changes would either degenerate into chaos, or would disaggregate – dissipate or explode.

We have more than an ample number of instances where changes in our lives occurred in exactly those ways wherein the organizing vigor was not in effect. And so we can also note that it is rare that the changes that surge to the fore are gathered and are offered a measure of coherence– which is the forte of mystic aspirations. What accounts for that rarity?

Might it not be that certain kinds of "fortunate" or "favored" circumstances allow for the flourishing of the aspirations that are capable of providing that capability? In our society, growing up without a father figure in the picture can hardly said to present easy circumstances for the families involved. Finally, that mystic aspirations by no means necessarily result from these circumstances indicates that it is also the values in play in that household that validate the child's "infantic" ways and allow it to mature into mystic figuration. Given the "outlier" and "outcast" life path that this figuration entails, it is unlikely that an "elitist" ethic was ever in play in that household. Indeed, it turns out that all of the mystically inclined people I have mentored come from very humble circumstances, ones in which the women in the household worked hard and long in order to make that place healthy for the child.

153   10   Dispelling some of the high drama here, it is important to note that not all of the mystic's life is so fraught with these entanglements. The mystic propensity expresses itself in "slivers" of a person's life. Many aspects of the mystic's life can be conducted quite normally. It is just in the areas by which the mystic defines what her place, her most driving way and aspirations are that the mystic entanglements show.

155   11   Badiou's notion of the "subject" gathering, holding, articulating certain *points* of contention and choice in situations so as to engender consequences comes to mind here. The consequences that a subject engenders can only occur by the configured embodiments of actions/articulations/sayings that a subject puts into play as being an "exception" to the existing state of affairs. This figuration is realized only as a reflection on those consequences, and not in advance in some kind of speculatively propositional form. In light of Badiou's formulation, which has merit for us, each of our figures then forms their Iconic Imago not to claim an "identity" in a fictively abstract mode of a pose or a personality type, but rather forms this assemblage in order to act according to the points that are held therein, according to certain proximities, which then entail and

presage a certain mode, type, character and constancy of action. In the case of the mystically aspiring person, that action is composing, articulating, working on and standing for the precept. See Badiou, *Logics of Worlds* (2012), pp. 50ff.

Spinoza's dogged insistence that any "idea" only produces effects when it is *embodied* also resonates here. See, for instance, Montag, *Bodies, Masses, Power: Spinoza and his Contemporaries* (1999).

155 [12] The diagnostic process will be elaborated on in Part Three.

156 [13] In Part Two we will cover some of the people who constitute the genealogy of the mystic figuration of aspirations and have done so in written, linguistic texts. However, mystic-figured "language" is deployed in other media as well. I think of Beethoven and Messiaen as musical composers of mystic bent, and Cezanne, Rodin and Picasso as painters with that orientation.

157 [14] In terms of the assemblages as depicted in Figure 3.1, the mystic figuration swallows the workings of the Sense-Making Field whole, but in mystic aspirations, only the fact of there being a dynamic constitution of sense, only the sense-*making that goes on,* rather than any specific concept or sense-image, is what matters. Mystic aspirations then, strongly interposing saturating phenomena and firming up a "World" assemblage, operate back on sense-making in order to keep that operation on its toes, so to speak, and does not allow our "sense" of things to become hardened into "things," facts and certainties.

161 [15] Her sponsor, who already had the title and position such as she was being encouraged to apply for, responded in a correspondingly aspiring way. He asked for some time to consider an answer and over the next few days wrote a response to her. He was moved, in other words, to respond not to a challenge of skepticism about the organization's hierarchy, but chose to respond to the precept, which this question put into play.

161   [16]   That said, all of the aspiring figures have a language component in their formation. This follows from our thesis that aspiration enacts the decision to guide the course of the human endeavor as it becomes more complex. The establishment of a distinctive domain of language allows for a "detachment" from the course of immediate engagement or reliance on multigenerational genetic adaptation for considerations as to how to engage oc currences in more expansive and more encompassing ways to be articulated and be enacted as corporeal and or P/SS choices for developmental action. However, it is the mystic role that specifically and solely employs the resources opened by the domain of language(s) – including symbols, metaphor and metonymy – to open up new ways out of which new concepts might be developed (by prophetically-aspiring figures) to be offered as means to enact that individuating/ aspiring decision.

Chapter Five

172   [1]   Pseudo-Dionysus: the Aeropagite, *Pseudo-Dionysus: The Complete Works* (1987), p. 135

       [2]   *Hadewijch: The Complete Works* (1980), p. 298.

173   [3]   *The Flowing Light of the Godhead* (1998),. IV12; p 152.

       [4]   *The Mirror of Simple Souls* (1993); Chapter 134

177   [5]   Badiou, Alain, *Saint Paul: The Foundations of Universalism* (Stanford, CA; 2003); p 51.

179   [6]   ...to use Michael Sells' formulation: *Mystical Languages of Unsaying* (Chicago; 1994).

180   [7]   Pseudo-Dionysus: the Aeropagite, *Pseudo-Dionysus: The Complete Works* (1987), p. 135

181   [8]   The phrase used by Bernard McGinn: *The Flowering of Mysticism* is the title of the third volume of his *Presence of God*

series. This is an essential survey of (mostly authorized) Christian mysticism.

9   Simons, Walter, *Cities of Ladies: Beguine Communities in the Medieval Low Countries, 1200-1565.* (2001); p. 4.

182   10   Ibid; p. 6.

184   11   This statement telescopes four hundred years of our epoch's development. While the Beguine mystics initiated the process, Meister Eckhart (yes, an officiating male) gave irrepressible and epoch- forming voice to this image (for which he was roundly condemned). The insight spawned new art and science, and then new thought, beginning with Spinoza and then the nineteenth-century Idealists. All of these greats brought forth into active engagement the generative, feminine potencies of creative engagement (even as they so ardently attempted to restore the viability of the male god notion. This notion, however, collapsed of its own improbability and logical convolutions. That's my story, and I'm sticking with it!

12   Certainly no small part of why this event is so little appreciated is due to the conscious efforts of male authorities to expunge this episode from the self-image propagated through histories and liturgies. It is not only the fact of how capable and successful these women were in carving out a distinctive way of living that the cover-up hides, but also, maybe even more so, the murderous means applied in order to bring this episode to an end. The burning at the stake of Marguerite Porete marked the beginning of that oppression that extended into witch-hunts and other purging activities well into the sixteenth century.

185   13   This is another controversial element in the literature. I tend to agree with Simons who relates the etymology of the term with the old French term *beguer* which means to stammer. In other citations as to the source of the term, we can also mention that in French, "beguin" now means, variously "flirtation" or infatuation/"crush," also a child's bonnet or

nun's headdress. Also, Lambert le Begue was a priest who helped get the Beguines founded, according to one reference I found. Interesting linguistic puzzles.

Whatever its etymology, the term "Beguine" ties in well with other words applied in other languages that were applied to this phenomenon going on in their midst. All of these terms refer to some kind of stammering or unintelligible speech. The implication is that of hypocrisy: that these women mumble about spirituality, but are, in their conduct something else, i.e., prostitutes, connivers or worse. This also fits as an inverted projection of the dominant way of male medieval life, where the men profess great chivalry, gallantry or piety while actually living lives of schemers, cheats and misogynist oppressors, or even rapists. Inverting projections is a potent weapon of oppression by the ignorant of the *avante garde* in any social change.

186   [14] I see very similar moves oppressive to women and in direct combat with contemporary feminism in the Right to Life movement and home schooling, not to mention the vilification of female power figures. Burkas can be bigger than a body-covering garment; they can also consist of homes into which women are relegated out of sight, out of mind and most decidedly out of influence.

[15] Simons (2001); p. 125.

187   [16] In all fairness to the Church of the day, they too recognized the enlivening influence holy women brought to their institution. Caroline Bynum points out that "women were 50 percent of the laity canonized in the thirteenth century and 71 percent after 1305. By the later Middle Ages, the male saint was usually a cleric or a friar; the ideal layperson was female." Bynum, Caroline W., *Fragmentation and Redemption* (New York; 1992); p. 137.

187   [17] Newman, Barbara, *From Virile Woman to Woman Christ* (1995); p.129.

18   McGinn, Bernard, *The Flowering of Mysticism* (1998), p. 200.

19   The volume *Hadewijch: The Complete Works* (Mahwah, NJ: 1980), part of the Classics of Western Spirituality Series, features sturdy and reliable introductory material on Hadewijch and the Beguine movement.

190   20   *Hadewijch* (1980); pp. 171ff.

195   21   All text references are made to *The Mirror of Simple Souls* (1993).

197   22   As we have noted, this prodigy of Dominican Masters was sent to several "troubled Beguine communities" including Paris, Strasbourg and Cologne. He obviously absorbed a great deal of learning from preaching to these highly developed women spirituals. His sermons, mostly delivered to them, carry the markers of the kinds of Beguine spirituality we have outlined and connect these Beguine writings to the highest levels of learning of his day.

198   23   This is a supremely difficult notion to grasp, as it is truly one that is "impossible" according to our conventional understandings of how such communicative experiences occur: a voice indicates a presence that is in proximity and so invites a connection that is presumably within our reach. But this is not what she is depicting here. The difficulty must remain un explained. That said, this notion forms a seminal dynamic in Maurice Blanchot's writings and this dynamic in Blanchot's writings is the subject of one of Derrida's most challenging essays Pace Not(s)" in *Parages* (2011). For instance: The almost, the proximity of the almost does not simply keep at a distance; it crosses over, and 'the wild statement that has no rights' takes place there, a place that cannot be situated in a topography that would only receive it or would have preceded it." (p. 46). The point of mentioning this difficult "anamystic" text at this juncture is to highlight how the seeds for the most salient of mystic work now underway, at this very moment in

the early twenty-first century were planted by this mystic master in the fourteenth century.

202   [24]   Pfeiffer, *The Sermons and Collations of Meister Eckhart* (Copyrighted Material) #58; also in *Meister Eckhart: The Essential Sermons, Commentaries, Treatises and Defense* (1981); #52; p. 199.

203   [25]   Pfeiffer; p. 221.

204   [26]   Pfeiffer, p. 136.

206   [27]   Eckhart assumed the chair and position that had been occupied by Saint Thomas Aquinas. In intellectual and philosophical circles, that name resonates with the cornerstones of "Scholasticism" by which a discourse of philosophy was marked off as having its own character, in distinction from the discourses of technology, trade and law that were also being crystallized at this time. The fact that Eckhart was not only not sainted, but was condemned (and died in confinement, awaiting inquisition) indicates how iconoclastic he truly was.

Eckhart was radically conservative, philosophically speaking, in that he resisted the Scholastic compartmentalization of philosophical work, and, like Socrates, preached to the common folk (although I don't know how an uneducated populace could ever comprehend those sermons) that the human way was to take up the Godhead in them (the Greek "en-thu-siasm"), as a life's way, and nothing else. He was, also, however, radically "creative," in the mold of the breakout figure, in that pronouncement. The role of the human, we can translate him as saying, is to take up the life of aspiration, the way that acts on the energy and impulsion of the Godhead "in us" so as to engage in ways that, like the generative forces of the universe itself, are more expansive and more encompassing.

207   [28]   *Meister Eckhart: Teacher and Preacher* (1986), Sermon #30, p. 292ff. Also in Pfeiffer,: LXVI; p. 164.

209	29	*Teacher Preacher* (1986). 76; pp. 327ff; Pfeiffer: VII, p. 31.
	30	*Meister Eckhart: The Essential Sermons, Commentaries, Treatises and Defense* (1981): #83 p. 208
211	31	The mystic opened this question anew in the context of the rising Western bourgeois culture. This question is the one that founded philosophy, but early on, soon after the collapse of the classical Athenian schools, this question was swept up into the imperial and Christological formations of the Roman era. The mystic's contribution, we can say, was to restore this question to salience and power even within those parameters by promising that there was a way to both express this question in flesh and blood, and to mark out a life's way that remained open to this question as its primary guide. They promised, and delivered, the way of aspiration.

In the onslaught of institutional rejection of this notion, the seventeenth and eighteenth centuries in particular (of which Leibniz is the apotheosis) were dedicated to re-establishing the hegemony of positivist logic and causal models of nature. Spinoza, as we will see, posed nasty objections to this model, and then, fortunately, the likes of Hume and Kant did not allow that proposed hegemony free reign. The struggle continues.

212	32	Pfeiffer: LXXXVII: p. 219.
	33	This sermon was written and delivered after his summons before the inquisitional authorities. It is thought to be a statement of his steadfast solidarity with the condemned and burned mystic Porete.
213	34	*Meister Eckhart: Teacher and Preacher* (1986): 9, p. 255. See also, Pfeiffer: LXXXIV, p. 213.
	35	Pfeiffer: LXXXVI, p. 187.
214	36	Ibid; p. 221.

	[37]	See Eckhart's "Treatise on Detachment" in *Meister Eckhart: The Essential Sermons, Commentaries, Treatises and Defense* (1981), p. 285.

215   [38]   Pfeiffer: LXXIV, p. 180-2.

217   [39]   Pfeiffer: LV; p. 140.

Chapter Six

219   [1]   *The Ethics in Meister Eckhart: The Essential Sermons, Commentaries, Treatises and Defense* (2006)); V: 30; p. 155.

220   [2]   *Jacob Boehme,* Robin Waterfield, ed. (2001); p. 112.

221   [3]   This according to Michel. de Certeau, *The Mythic Fable: The Sixteenth and Seventeenth Centuries* (1992); p 76.

        [4]   I prefer to use the name he would use in his Spanish homeland, to the translation, John of the Cross. The intent Juan himself would want to convey is still maintained, but we also keep this great figure in his own context by keeping the Spanish.

224   [5]   Ibid; p. 224.

225   [6]   This line of mystic articulation transposes the "apophasis" set in play by Pseudo-Dionysus into their experiential sensibilities. The mix of the "unsaying" expression that apophasis entails and the experience of the onslaught of incomprehensible but palpably affecting saturating phenomena are conflated in the contemporary works of the "deconstructionist" philosophers. The directly mystic formation of this contemporary strain is advanced by Georges Bataille, for instance, while the prophetic figuration, in an operable, provoking concept, is articulated most notably by Jacques Derrida.

        [7]   *John of the Cross: Selected Writings,* Kieran Kavanaugh, O.C.C., ed. (1987); pp. 179-80.

226   [8]   A reader reminds me that such a revival is advocated by a personage no less esteemed than the pop idol Madonna.

227   9   (1979).

230   10   His theological writings were so explosive that he had to hide them. They were released posthumously. His political writings were no less heretical.

         11   Giles Deleuze's early work, *Expressionism in Philosophy: Spinoza* (1992), and his follow-on manual on Spinoza's terms, Spinoza: Practical Philosophy (1988), sifts out the self-organizing impetus that drives Spinoza's notion of the self-production of God/Universe in line with a Nietzschean vision of the surging of generative forces that become "beings" through the Eternal Return of the Same. In Spinoza, these loci of singularizing gather as "attributes" and combine into subsequently generative forces of a more local and definitively differentiating nature, as "modes."

         12   Spinoza also used the name "Benedict," and this name is used in many accounts of his work. I keep the Jewish name, meaning "blessing," in order to stress the ties Spinoza maintains to deep, prophetic currents in the Jewish fold. We will address those in a later book. Here, and in the next chapter, we concentrate on his epochal contribution to the figure of the mystic breakout creative.

231   13   Socrates, of course, steadfastly remained in Athens, and accepted the death sentence his peers imposed on him.

232   14   This observation accords with every mystic notion about the "existence" or "essence" of what is most real, and is poetically intensified by Silesius's phrase (parsed by Heidegger in *The Principle of Reason* (1960), "the Rose is without why;" p. 35.

         15   While Spinoza's conception marks a turning point in the Western philosophical canon around the idea of God, Spinoza himself may have, in his own mind, simply been cleaning up some of the messier aspects of Kabbalistic notions of God's emanative creation. Though I have not seen any scholarship proving what versions of Kabbalist notions Spinoza was

exposed to, it is most likely that given his extensive knowledge of Scripture and Maimonides (both of which were the objects of his critique in his *Theologico-Politico Treatise*), he is likely to have been familiarized with Kabbalist interpretations and intensifications of scriptural components as well. One of these is the current of literature that denies a Neoplatonist type of emanation and insists that God's "personality" is to express his manifestations in his very attributes. This is not a temporal process and does not "necessitate any change in God Himself; it is simply the emergence from potentiality into actuality of that which was concealed within the power of the Creator." (Scholem, G. *Kabbalah* (New York; 1978); p. 103). This was one view among many conflicting Kabbalistic accounts Spinoza may have heard, and one toward which he tended, and then rendered in a "scientific" and mathematical proof manner.

232   [16]   See for example, Leibniz, "Principles of Nature and Grace," #18, how God's love, though "disinterested," allows for our own contentment. Einstein once said that our most important question is, "Is the universe a friendly place?" Spinoza is agnostic on the answer. Leibniz, on the other hand desperately wants the answer to be yes.

[17]   See, for example, Leibniz, "Discourse on Metaphysics" 35-36; and "Monadology" 85ff.

233   [18]   Einstein is alleged to have said, "My God is Spinoza's God." If he didn't actually recite those words, he might have said something exactly like that.

[19]   I don't think Tillich would object to my allusion to his great work in this context.

[20]   Thus we disagree with both Badiou's label "Spinoza's Closed Ontology" (*Briefings on Existence* (pp. 73ff) and in *Being and Event,* "Spinoza" (pp. 112ff.) and Hegel's complaint that Spinoza has no negation. I once believed the latter, but closer

reading, especially from the standpoint of the mystic register of interpretation, has changed my mind. Spinoza does not foreclose on event, as Badiou claims. It is rather that events are not of the grand, once-and-for-all, Maoist quality Badiou craves. Rather, events occur continually on the microscopic scale (Spinoza ground lenses for microscopes, perhaps because he wanted to see his "subjects" in action?), as modes constellate into essences. As for negation, each mode is the condition for its own dissolution by a contrasting, invasive and completely other mode. The negation is biological and viral rather than conceptual, but it occurs and the concept of the essence is thus set in motion as well. Is this dialectical? Certainly not to Hegel's satisfaction; but then Hegel's dialectic is not satisfactory to the empirically-minded either (Marx or Kierkegaard, for example). But Spinoza meets Hegel's main mystic requirement: that the absolute arises from the realization out of the flux of what actually occurs, and is not a fiat of the deity (Leibniz's figuration). Both Spinoza's substance and Hegel's absolute only have their moment: infinite in its depth, eternal in its fullness of actualization. But a moment, nevertheless.

234 21 And this idea is also Platonic. This coincidence does not make this notion less of an ingredient of the mystic's way. Western mysticism, and Pauline Christianity for that matter, as we have said, begins with the Platonic expression of the Ideas as living factors set into play by the (Platonic) "good," or the generative force, which, without cause, engenders occurrences that can be taken up into expressed experiences.

22 "Expression" is an important notion in the prophetic register or figure. It envisions an active agent's pure and unmediated externalization, its essence as immediately existing (the crucial thought here being the inextricable tie between agent and externalization, and the simultaneity of the agent's being and that externalization – essence being completely co-originary with existence). This is a way of thinking that intends to counter Neo-Platonic ideas emanation (as we saw with

Plotinus and Pseudo-Dionysus) in which energy self-generates from a stable, abiding, and itself unchanged locus or being.

Spinoza's "Idea of God" is *expressive* in that these ideas are of God, that is to say, they are not merely spoken attributes that are attached to something else (that is God), but rather they are *God's own ideas and thus bear him in their very existences / essence and occurrence, simultaneously as they appear.* They are far from being ideas that we have about God. We can thus clearly see that Spinoza's Idea of God is certainly mystic for its time. It goes farther than any other conception of God in a generative direction. It approaches our criterion of the mystic as opening out onto new constellations of energy that compel us to resituate ourselves within our own experience and within the universe itself. We consider these notions in greater detail in the text below.

235   [23]   I am sure that it is this aspect of Spinoza's work that inspired Nietzsche to write this testimonial (on a postcard to his friend Overbeck, from Sils-Maria on 30 July 1881): "I am utterly amazed, utterly enchanted! I have a precursor, and what a precursor! I hardly knew Spinoza: that I should have turned to him just now, was inspired by 'instinct.' Not only is his over-tendency like mine—namely to make all knowledge the most powerful affect — but in five main points of his doctrine I recognize myself; this most unusual and loneliest thinker is closest to me precisely in these matters: he denies the freedom of the will, teleology, the moral world-order, the unegoistic, and evil. Even though the divergencies are admittedly tremendous, they are due more to the difference in time, culture, and science. In summa: my lonesomeness, which, as on very high mountains, often made it hard for me to breathe and make my blood rush out, is now at least a twosomeness..."

238   [24]   I cannot but think of Nietzsche's notion of "will to power" here. I consider this notion mystic and perceptual to the core (see the section on Nietzsche in the next chapter). That is, as a precept of affirmation, the "will to power" is the exertion

one extends, in aspiring, to take oneself, to *will* oneself to a state of being that is able to exert *power*, or the ability to do the work of taking one's place, in conditions that, in the absence of such explicit and intentful wiling, will demolish one's very being. Transposing back to Spinoza, the "conatus" is an expression of a way of being that must affirm its own effort, aspiring, to take its place, from moment to moment. The "conatus" can be thought of as the condition of the human endeavor that has as its very basis of possibility, and has as a necessity for its affirmation, to aspire.

[25] I use the term "new" advisedly. Spinoza's rendering of the notion of "idea" is new relative to how empiricists had deployed notion. They portrayed the "idea" as a quasi-phantom generated in the human mind alone, and that required the certainty of God's imprimatur (as Descartes and Leibniz account for it), which requires the full subscription to the belief that God would only create a world that is able to (sufficiently) produce truths. Spinoza's notion of the Idea is actually closer to Plato's, especially as an account of this term is rendered by Heidegger (in *Essence of Truth*) or Derrida (in "Khora").

239   [26] Deleuze, (op. cit.); p. 278.

240   [27] Ibid. p. 281.

[28] Leibniz, G. W. "New System of the Nature of the Substances and their Communication, and of the Union Which Exists between the Soul and The Body," *G. W. Leibniz, Philosophical Texts,* R. S. Woolhouse and Richard Francks, Ed., Tr. (1998), p. 150.

241   [29] In his *Theologico-Politico Treatise* he makes a clear division between the masses and the active citizenry. The presentation of the Ethics itself seems to actively draw a line between those who can follow complex and high-level conceptual connections and those who have no such ability. This immediately limits for whom his rational mysticism would be available.

241   [30]   I detect here an influence on the Jewish Spinoza of the Jewish Kabbalah. This great body of Jewish mysticism, formulated from the same Gnostic and Neo-Platonic roots as our own mystic genealogy, was tightly bound to Jewish scholarship, ritual and belief by the time of Spinoza's education. One of the great centers for Jewish learning after the expulsion from Spain in 1492 was Venice, where Spinoza's primary teacher (and eventual accuser), Rabbi Mortiera received his education. This austere and authoritarian man cannot but have been in fluenced by Kabbalah since, according to Gershom Scholem, Kabbalah was the main driving force for shaping Jewish life, emphasizing prayer, custom and ethics during this time (Scholem, G., *Kabbalah* (New York, 1978); pp196ff).

Certainly Spinoza is hardly writing a covert Kabbalah for the wider world. However, it must be remembered how we cited just such a movement in the Christian fold – to use the Jewish Kabbalah as a means for further validating the truth of the Christian story. Indeed Spinoza's *Ethics* is an "anti-theology" – with it no "theology" is necessary. Still, lurking deep in Spinoza's psyche, his intent bears traces of that Kabbalistic mode. I see this, first, in his ethical and prophetic intent. The Kabbalah is intended to render every single letter of Jewish scripture and law into a lesson for living in the Jewish way. The attributes of God as revealed in the texts of the tradition (Kabbalah means "tradition") are transported into the very fiber of Jewish language, word and practice. Second, it is exactly this kind of spirited "immanence" which Spinoza's depiction of God as substance, essence as existence and mode necessitates. Finally, Kabbalists carry forward a profound faith that the word of God, no matter how ineffable, can be written and in its intellectual comprehension can have salvational effect. Spinoza's very culminating realization affirms the same faith.

Spinoza may have been excommunicated from the Jewish community, but his life was profoundly linked to its most essential ways of being in the world.

Chapter Seven

245   [1]   In, Heidegger Martin, *Hegel's Concept of Experience* (1970); pp. 23-26.

    [2]   *Writings from the Late Notebooks* (2003); (2/207) p. 100. A variant, and more frequently cited rendition of this thought can be found in *The Gay Science;* Walter Kaufmann, Tr. (1974); Book V; #378; p. 340.

    [3]   *Contribution to Philosophy (From Enowning)* (1999); p. 129.

246   [4]   Indeed, we can say that it is a "law" that the aspirational figures and their roles rise to the fore when social, economic, historical and intellectual ferment reach a certain level of complexity and intensity. In the language of self-organization, this law translates "symmetry breaking": a regime of thermo dynamic conditions in which the once-effective means of providing organization and continuity (the exiting symmetry) is exceeded by energies in play; the old system breaks apart and a new "system" reorganizes in such a way as to encompass the old regime in a new and more expansive mode of organizing. This new mode is not a matter of reshuffling the deck chairs on the Titanic, but constitutes a mode of organization not anticipated as being effective at all in the old regime. Some of the old ways pass out of existence, but many are preserved and carried on, but in a new, displaced and now dependent status. Philosophers will recognize this as being analogous, at least, to the Hegelian "aufhebung."

    [5]   The term "Prophetic" refers to the Breakout Creative Aspiring Figurations schema and the prophet figuration of aspiration. This is a specific figuration that concentrates on translating the aspirational energies (which exceed those that can be enacted by terrestrial activities such as production, commerce or law making) into *concepts* and texts or other compositions that, in response to the dynamics in a specified situation, delineate new ways (faculties) by means of which the "world" these dynamics are elevated into comes into view, are able to

makes sense and conveys meaning. One of the major vocations or roles in which this aspirational figuration was taken up as a specifically human way was in the discipline of "philosophy." Although this form of discourse declined into rule-making and assertion of dogma, or into demeaning skepticism, some philosophers, certainly the ones we cite here, remain true to the prophetic mission of philosophy. And, I suggest they did so by contemplating and incorporating into their work the insights that the classical mystics had advanced.

248   6   It is this localization that also, in the deployment of terms and syntax, that makes their works "prophetic." The work of prophetic aspiration is to articulate a "provoking concept," in comparison to the work of mystic aspirations being the articulation of the "precept." The provoking concept is a localized generalization, on the level of a logical discourse that conflates the sense of the current state of affairs with a notion of its being surpassed. Hegel's provoking concept of the "aufhebung," the surpassing that dislocates, relieves and preserves, is a prime example. We can say, in the most com pressed way, that a concept that encompasses a precept (as does Hegel's notion), is intrinsically "provoking."

249   7   This movement occurred in Germany, as we will note, even though counterparts of Idealism as a whole had proponents elsewhere – Bishop Berkeley in Great Britain, for example. I employ the term "Absolute" in order to separate the post-Kantian Idealists from others who worked in this vein and since all philosophy can be considered an "Idealism" to the extent that it is in pursuit of undertaken language, concepts and notions that express ideas.

I place the word "absolute" in quotes for the time being in order to designate that the use of that term is controversial. It is a term that is used derisively in some circles to designate an alleged philosophical hubris for expounding a formula or logic that offers truth and certainty once and for all. In other circles, ones that benefit from further reflection, the notion of "absolute" is taken to designate the encompassingly affective power of the *moment's* "presence"(and the certainty of its passing, in its presently engaged composition) as constitutive of a *commitment* to engaging an occurrence at a specific site, temporally and with the expectation of its surpassing.

This latter interpretation, to which I subscribe, incorporates the mystic perceptual inflections of our particular and local engagements bearing the intimations of a universality that overtakes specificity and shapes the ways of viably and competently engaging a site that is potentially dynamic and changing. It thus takes into account the "dialectical movement" that impels a being to aspire to become more expansive and more encompassing even as an engagement unfolds in the "present" before us.

250   8   This moment was as brief in the lives of these thinkers as it was in its eventuation. After their attendance at the seminary, they briefly remained friends. Hegel and Hölderlin collaborated in founding the basic tenets of Absolute German Idealism (Hölderlin reciting, Hegel transcribing), and Hegel collaborated with Schelling on the publication of a journal. But Hegel seems to have lost touch with his friend Hölderlin, and Schelling came to regard Hegel as a mortal rival later in his career (when he wrote the works we cite here).

251   9   1970 edition.

252   10   To see how mysticism hovered over and around the orientations within German Idealism, see Dieter Heinrich, *Between Kant and Hegel,* "The Allure of Mysticism" (2003).

253   11   Fichte, J. G., *The Science of Knowledge* (1982); p. 6.

254   12   Fichte, *Science of Knowledge* (op. cit.); p. 93.

255   13   Ibid. p. 35-6. (On a frivolous note, it seems that Captain Jean-Luc Picard of the "Next Generation" of Starfleet commanders was a Fichtean, as he issued an order in the form of "make it so.")

256   [14]   *Friedrich Hölderlin: Essays and Letters of Theory,* Thomas Pfau, Tr. and ed. (1988); p. 47.

257   [15]   Ibid. pp. 69 – 70. Of course we have to note here the "meta physics" of presence that Hölderlin calls upon in this exposition. The idealists, after all, were working to make what was taken to be "represented" and held as concept in presence as truth. The issue for Hölderlin, remember, is not to dispute the metaphysical, but to ground it in mystic dynamics, and thus have it be alive in the Fichtean sense of reciprocally, continually and generatively mutual generation. Also, as a poet, Hölderlin also comes to grips with the artist mindset, which is one of deploying symbol/word formations through which viable, true and actual engagements ensue.

[16]   "Patmos," *Selected Poems and Fragments* (1998).

[17]   According to Beiser, Hölderlin is the intellectual father of Absolute Idealism, the progenitor of the friendship of Schelling and Hegel that germinated its philosophical masterpieces, and the one who most unreservedly makes the mystic way a viable life demand. See Beiser, *German Idealism* (2008); pp. 375ff.

[18]   In the opinion of Bataille, the major influences that moved Hegel to his "dialectic" of negativity stems not from philosophical sources such as Heraclitus, Plato or Fichte, "...but much rather," says Gasché, "from Gnosticism, and Neoplatonic and German mysticism..." Georges Bataille (2012); p 252. At least Bataille acknowledges this element in Hegel's thinking, which is more astute than most com mentators on Hegel have been.

259   [19]   Zizek Slavoj, *The Abyss of Freedom; Ages of the World (F. W.J. von Schelling)* (1997); p. 113. This is a translation of the 1813 draft of Schelling's essay. Other drafts preceded it. See Schelling, *Ages of the World* (2000).

[20]   There is no doubt that Schelling's reaction to Hegel's successful (to a degree still only being comprehended) "completion of

metaphysics" – especially in his *Phenomenology of Mind* and in his *Science of Logic* – egged him on to formulate notions that could begin to surpass and exceed whatever Hegel had claimed. It is to Schelling's credit, and to his cleaving to his mystic way, that his efforts took him into a vision that presaged the kind of generative astrophysics now being developed, as well as the whole range of "deconstructive" practices being forged in the work of the "anamystics" I describe in the next chapter. Also in this pace-setting work is his *Historical-Critical Introduction to the Philosophy of Mythology* (2007) (from which Freud would have benefitted) and then his mind-shattering (Hegelian "mind" that is) shattering work (and a core of Heidegger's work), *Philosophical Investigations into the Essence of Human Freedom* (2007).

260   [21]   Ibid; pp. 131-2.

262   [22]   #1067; *The Will to Power,* Walter Kaufmann, ed. (1967).

[23]   As Klossowski points out, as an author, Nietzsche sought to perfect a mode of writing that would "intensify without interpretation."That is, from the standpoint of mystic expression, he sought to do the "un-saying" of apophasis without pointing to a resolution in a state of being or "meaning" in a "beyond" of the text. The text, for Nietzsche, is all there is; and also, that text, when exploded, leaves us in just the open, just at the threshold of our own Fields of Enthusiasms, and then we get to choose whether or not to take that next step…It is then the province of Nietzsche's successors, the anamystics such as Maurice Blanchot, to complete the sentence so that it reads, "…we get to choose whether or not to take that next step *(not) beyond*."

263   [24]   See also *The Will to Power* #586 and #595.

[25]   I cannot help but read Kafka's *The Trial* as an account of someone, K, who has not yet succumbed to this death wish, and is at an utter loss as to why he has been condemned in its court. Also, the *Metamorphosis* I read as an account of the

mind of Gregor Samsa (was Kafka aware of the Buddhist notion of Samsara? – the illusion in which our daily living is ensconced?) being consumed and transformed by this death wish, in a manner that, once again, totally exceeds the ability of the protagonist to understand what is happening to him, while, at the same time, strangely succumbing to it.

266   26 #34 [124]; *Writings from the Late Notebooks* (2003); p. 8

27 Nietzsche, *Daybreak* (1997), #196.

267   28 #1066, (also, #1888); *The Will to Power* (1968).

29 The notion of the "Eternal Return of the Same" acts like a conceptual Rorschach Test in the corpus of philosophy. It is taken to indicate Nietzsche's deterministic fatalism, or even an atavistic tribal streak in his thinking. My reading of the notion of the Eternal Return of the Same benefits from Deleuze's superb work, *Nietzsche and Philosophy* (1983).

268   30 # 405; Ibid.

269   31 2/155; *Writings from the Late Notebooks* (2003).

32 His not-disavowed affiliation with Nazis in the 1930s is well known. (Rudiger Safransky offers a satisfying and fair accounting of this era in Heidegger's life in *Martin Heidegger: Between Good and Evil* (2002). And, in my estimation, there are good reasons embedded in his thinking that could result (combined with youth, narrowness, provinciality of maturation, and raw academic ambition) in such an atrocious decision. And yet, his dedication to that seam between oblivion and coming to life that we call "mystic" is astounding and profoundly revelatory of the minute steps, jerks, leaps and stumbles that occur in that tortured "swaying" of be-ing.

I cannot help but think that it is precisely because of Heidegger's "conservative" penchant for upholding the classical philosophical forms of expression (such as Being and "presence") that he "missed" the reactionary and racist dynamics of Nazism (and he was not alone among philosophers who missed these elements – Schmidt and Leo Strauss come to mind), mistaking them for a primal and mythic restoration of "vitality" of some kind. I do not believe that Heidegger was either racist or anti-Semitic, and it might have been because he did not subscribe to these policies that he came under suspicion by the Nazi regime. I take Heidegger's silence on the subject to be one of a fidelity to his finitude, to the futility of such "ownings up," the impossibility of repentance-based salvation (in the press, no less) and the more pressing need to get on with the work, such as he could do it.

269   [33]   Heidegger invents words out of our existing vocabularies in order to (at least) deprive our conceiving (to "unsay" our cause-effect, subject-object formations), and insist that we give ourselves over to forces that unfold and have no regard for our "take" on what is happening. He also transposes a noun into a verb-form, and thereby deprives our understanding of any pre-maturely fetishized assigning of the term to a specific thing, entity or concept.

For a detailed commentary on Heidegger's relation to Meister Eckhart, see Caputo, *The Mystic Element in Heidegger's Thought* (1986).

[34]   (Bloomington, IN; 1999)

[35]   As I have mentioned, Heidegger is strangely silent about Spinoza, and yet this work in particular has a flavor of Spinozan rigor and progression of exposition.

270   [36]   Ibid. p. 167. "Abground" names the site where, as the co-emergence of Dasein (the human mode of being) and the living that ensues from such emergence, any former mode is surpassed.

272   [37]   In opening his essay, "Theatrum Philosophicum" (in *Language, Counter-Memory, Practice* (1980; p. 165), Michel Foucault

famously wondered whether "perhaps one day this century will be known as Deleuzian."

273   [38]   The next few paragraphs will be, admittedly, difficult to absorb – even more difficult than the notions presented in Chapter Three (which were, by the way, thought through in dialogue with Deleuze). I urge the reader to be patient and to approach this text with as much of a sense of openness as you can muster. Of course, I ultimately recommend that the reader consider undertaking a serious study of Deleuze (and Irigaray). But in the absence of that, I present this difficult material in the belief that these texts do offer a way of thinking about aspiration as being a distinct but integrally operating aspect of our engagements with the events and oc currences in our lives.

[39]   This is how I take the intent of especially his later work that replaces the term "psychoanalysis" with his (and Guattari's) neologism, "schizoanalysis." The former term refers to a state of mind in which an abnormal disintegration sets up along side of a "normal" one – implying that there is a "normal" formation. This "normality" presumes all the habituated and socially sanctioned forms of relations that support conventional existence. The alternative implies that while there may be more healthful ways of living than others, no formation of psychic/somatic energies can be presumed to be a "normal" standard. Instead, the notion of the "schizo," which had once been cast as deviant, becomes a starting point for a plurality of formations that operate alongside of one another in a complex psychosomatic set. All of these active and generative forces (constituting a veritable Field of Enthusiasm) self-organize in the living being according to the ensemble of factors the person is able to set into motion.

273   [40]   Of course, what I am presenting here is a delimiting (directed and reduced) interpretation of Deleuze's work, which has a much wider intent than we do. The translations I make of his

terms focus in on those aspects that relate to the mystic figuration of *aspirations* – and I do not take into account all the other factors that pertain to our ways of knowing in general (and the other classical philosophical problems this subject evokes). This translation in one way then simplifies Deleuze's notions (and assumes all the risks that such a distillation entail); but then, in another way, this translation requires that the reader make a leap from one difficult notion (Deleuze's concern with "knowledge") into our schematization of mystic aspirations. While this operation is challenging, I suggest that it is no more challenging than what a mentor has to do, on the spot, in translating the mentee's articulations into the terms that the mentor can use in order to clarify the aspirations that are at stake. At a minimum then, the difficulties presented here can be considered *practice*. You, the mentor/reader are translating my articulations into ways that aspirations can be discerned in them.

274   [41]   See, Deleuze and Guattari, *A Thousand Plateaus: Capitalism and Schizophrenia* (2005).

[42]   By advancing the term "surface" he is protesting against the traditional notions (Platonic) of a distinct, super-sensible world of Ideas lying beyond this terrestrial world of copies and shadows. Because of what Deleuze designates as constituting the "surface," there is no need for "metaphysics" or "transcendental" ideas to underpin our experiencing. He endeavors to reject anything like a "phenomenological" acting of appearances "behind the back" of what we take to be "present" or as having "meaning." He also rejects any hint of a Hegelian "deep" and/or "hidden" negating process. He verges on positivism in this respect, but escapes this ideologically inclined intellectual intransigence because of one aspect of his thinking – what I call the *generativity of the actual* (which, in my reading aligns him with the mystics and places him at the apex of the "anamystics").

415

I am not so sure that Deleuze totally escapes the logic of these also great mystically informed thinkers, Plato and Hegel; but he does succeed in relocating the dynamics in question to that terrestrial surface on which actual, flesh and blood living occurs. He thus makes the anamystic mission possible.

275   43   The concept of "Machinics" was used as a crucial dynamic in our depiction of the "Aspiring Mind" in Chapter Three.

44   One way to think of this moment and make it more "real" is to think of what thermodynamic scientists call a "phase shift." In this moment insurgent forces act on existing formations in a continuous way, and then, suddenly, in a flash that defies analysis or perceptual sequencing, the formation changes shape. One of the simpler examples of such a shift is "crystallization," which we commonly observe when water either freezes into ice or ice melts into water.

276   45   The term "abject" itself arises in the feminine frame, as the term given by Melanie Klein to the infant's pre-oedipal separation from the mother's breast. To stitch the narrative of the anamystic together, and to reassert my claim of the resurgence of the feminine in the anamystic figure, I cite this passage from Bataille (cited by Gasché), "The incandescent reality of the Earth's womb [*one way of "mythologizing" of the feminine* – MHS] cannot be touched and possessed by those who misunderstand it. It is the misunderstanding of the Earth, the forgetting of the star on which he lives, the ignorance of the nature of riches, in other words of the incandescence that is enclosed within this star that has made for man an existence at the mercy of the merchandise he produces, the largest part of which is devoted to death." Gasché elaborates: "The constitution of the society of exchange, the restricted economy of accumulation, the perpetuation of phallic genealogy rest upon the concealment, the forgetting, the misrecognition, the repression [*the abjection* – MHS] of the feminine. Its elimination is the necessary precondition of patriarchal and phallic domination." Gasché, *Georges Bataille* (op. cit.); p. 203.

276   [46]   I take up this theme of the "abjection" of the mother in the context of describing the Prophetic figuration of aspiration. In the biographical background of this decidedly male figure there lurks the loss of the mother, either through death, illness or other kinds of social or mental instabilities. In the biographical background of the mystic figuration, however, we find a diminishing of the father figure (for instance, in Nietzsche's case, the death of the father) and the dominance of a strong feminine influence (in Nietzsche's case being brought up by his mother and his aunts).

277   [47]   *To Be Two* (2001); p. 35.

279   [48]   *To Be Two* (2001); p. 111.

Chapter Eight

282   [1]   *The Encyclopedia of Logic* (1991); p. 212.

          [2]   *Mindfulness* (2006); p. 100.

284   [3]   In the case of the prophet figuration, of course there is no "prophet academy" in which these people can learn the ways pertaining to prophetic aspiration. However, so much of our culture is influenced by and translates (or degrades) prophetic practices that we know about this figuration without "knowing" it specifically or thematically as being aspirational. Academic careers, consulting, leading evangelical religions or protests and even novel-writing are all "careers" into which the prophetic figuration has been absorbed.

290   [4]   This quandary, spurred by mystic aspirations, is different from those taken on by other aspirational figures. The quandary, for instance, arises at a different time in the mystic's life, as we have said. It arises much later than it does for the artist or leader, especially. And while the other figures have almost no recourse within themselves with which to "answer" their doubts, the mystic does have such recourse. While the leader's "confidence" may be shaken, and the artist and prophet figures

suffer from feelings of "nothingness" and despair, the mystic knows something is there and then decides how to treat that beckoning potency.

293　　　5　　It may seem that there is a "class bias" in plain view here. Any speaking into this problem will only aggravate that situation. Knowing that full well, I will charge right into the teeth of this monster. It is true that the people I have met, who have formed my notion of the mystic figure, are people who are in roles and positions that offer them certain economic and social advantages and choices. In my research on the genealogy of mystics, all of them also either come from backgrounds of some wealth, or they are part of institutions that provide shelter from having to be preoccupied with financial or social security.

But there are larger issues involved in this "bias" than ones of class. That is, an aspirational mind-set can only flourish when a living being's mind capabilities are not completely absorbed in survival, and when every perception, stimulus, occurrence and event is not anticipated as being life-threatening. An aspiring mind requires some measure of safety so that one's psychic/somatic, cognitive/emotional capabilities are able to welcome and affirm the experiences that bode forth in "aspiring" or venturing living. Thus, the aspiring mind only became a factor in its own right when stationary, protected and abiding communities were constituted (in the form of Arteous discernments and celebrations of what human aspirations – in the form of projected gods – could accomplish). The aspiring mind was only in a position to find its own voice (in the Prophetic figure), when it could be "promised" that a future would have Yahweh in it, and so a still-living "blessedness" could be anticipated. And finally, the aspiring mind could only take shape as a singular force that humans could engage when there was evidence that a faith-for what aspirations could engender would be a source of vitality, not certain death.

And so, without a doubt, there is this: the mystic mindset arises in response to plentitude and abundance that is in play in such measures as to exceed the limitations of existing forms of interaction. And then, this expansive and encompassing response to that plentitude, as we have seen in the descriptions of the machinic self-organization of the mystically aspiring mindset, is certainly the most tentative and fragile of aspiration's figurations. It operates only on the whims, wisps, airs and surging intensities of pure "enthusiasms" that only go so far as to establish a "*Field* of Enthusiasm." And so, I am left with what seems to me to be an unavoidable conclusion, for the moment, that some kind of sheltering and baseline of well-being has to be in place for the mystic mindset to take shape. In our Western, European/American culture that necessity has implications in the form of one's socioeconomic position and "class." It is a mystic (e.g., Jean-Luc Nancy, Luce Irigaray) or prophetic (e.g., Jacques Derrida or Walther Benjamin) aspiration, at its highest, "messianistic" expression to alleviate this stricture, or whatever form (racial, gender, political) such strictures take.

296   [6]   With these two "constants" it may seem that I am sorting out mystic aspirations based on ideological criteria. To the extent that I would own up to having a personal ideological orientation, I would say that, of course, I am guilty of having such criteria in play. That said, in mentoring aspiration we are neutral as to the areas of concern to which a person applies these aspirations. I admit to not accepting the notion that any mystic aspiration, no matter how tethered to a political, social or religious institution, can aim at being more competent at imposing a repressive, totalitarian and/or sectarian regime.

It is an explicit tenet of mentoring aspirations that its intent is to prevent the likelihood of there being another Hitler, or Ku Klux Klan or the repression/enslavement of women, gays or people of color, for example. Our definition of aspiration, our mentoring, seeks to support people in their efforts to engender *more expansive and more encompassing ways* to engage others, other creatures and the earth. To the extent that mystics open new prospects for this way of living, they would, it seems to me, to be the last aspirational person who would be oriented to these despicable repressions and their representative organizations. I do not see how mystic aspirations, as expressed and enacted by its forebears and exemplars, could be sympathetic to ritualized degradation, institutionalized ignorance, conceptual rigidity and allegiance to prevailing norms, or confinement within logical strictures that wrench vitality out of our living.

I am not alone in this orientation. In my chosen field of philosophy there are only certain strains of work, those that I would characterize as specifically non-positivistic, non-analytical, and even non-pragmatic, that even countenance, no less comprehend, works of aspirational expression. Even the most retrograde of these thinkers, Heidegger, who totally misread what aspirations required of thought (and became involved with the Nazis for a time), extricated himself from the comforting temptations of classical formulations that tethered thinking to technology, ideology and positivist scientism. There is no way but to open acceptance of difference, moderated only by what a person's life can accommodate, in the mystic's aspiring way into the open.

297   7   Deleuze's pioneering conceptual work is often cited in this book; while Damasio, in works such as *Descartes' Error* (2005) and *Looking for Spinoza* (2003), remaining within the confines of classical psycho/biological rubrics of accepted experiences, does not quite reach the horizons of aspiration, but he certainly dispels facile notions of mind and spirit versus body. For this his work merits citation and might provide mentors with a start in making the kinds of distinctions that open up to notions such as the aspiring mind and its figurations.

Chapter Nine

300   1   *Dialogues II* (2002); p. 82.

         2   Quoted in Derrida's essay, "Interpreting Signatures," in *Looking After Nietzsche* (1990). Quoted from Nietzsche's *Gay Science,* # 324.

         3   Quoted in Gasché's essay, "*Ecce Homo* or The Written Body," in *Looking After Nietzsche* (op. cit.); p. 122. Gasché outlines Nietzsche's regimen for health in this essay. Considering that Nietzsche was a mystic figure who avowedly based his work on rising out of illness into health, this essay might be worth a look by some adventuresome mentors.

307   4   For instance, the prophet role is a nomadic one, and so leaving situations is also endemic to that figure. However, the prophet figure exhibits a certain "animus" with regard to the leaving, and leaves for no particular reason other than "it is time." Leaders leave when there is nothing more to do in order to act on aspirations – we see this in "serial entrepreneurs," for instance. Artists are often expelled from organizations and groups because of their inability to compensate for the ways their combative personalities irritate other people, or because they are kept from expressing their aspirations in the projects they want to take up.

         5   Melville is a contemporary of Emerson and Thoreau, as well as Poe – the American literary greats, in my opinion (and in the opinion of the contemporary philosophers who are shaping our notions of the aspiring mind). Emerson inspired Nietzsche, for instance. Melville's classic, by the way, along with his story "Bartleby, the Scrivener," epitomizes mystic expression in American literature. Ishmael declares that when things get tough, he sets out to sea. The sea is one of the great mystic metaphors or locales. For a purely mystic text in modern literature, nothing I know of surpasses the chapter, "The Whiteness of the Whale." This is also a metaphor favored and often employed by Nietzsche.

310   6   In the context of the aspiring mind resource, this spatiating work takes place in the assemblage I call the "Sense-Making Field." See Figure 3.1. I did not emphasize the workings of this complex system because it is not the primary driver in the forming of the mystic figuration, as are the "World" assemblage and the Field of Enthusiasm. This is the area of expertise of the prophet figure. In sum, the saturating phenomena from the "World" assemblage are ensnared in the "streams" that flow through this "delta"-like formation, and are enriched and stabilized with concepts and language that can be reflected upon and deployed as affecting agents in their own right. I detail this process in the work, *The Aspiring Mind: Philosophical Reflections on the Urge to Create* (a rough draft of this work is available upon request), and I relate it specifically to my work in progress on the prophet figuration of aspiration.

312   7   In this scheme then, the mystic's dreaming fully expresses the late Freud's realizations about the movement of psychic flows from that great inorganic cosmos into the organic fold. The dream represents a "death instinct" in the mystic fold precisely because it does directly translate from great and incorporeal, inorganic energies into a living, specific, mortal form. It is not that Freud's later realizations pertain only to mystics. It is rather, as we see it, Freud's later schema rises to the level of full mystic realizations of life energies. Most people do not experience dreams this way. But we would argue, maybe along with Freud, that the mystic rendering of the encounter with dreams is the most encompassing and complete realization of the encounter and the more "psychologistic" renderings are derivative of this. So Freud's earlier *Interpretation of Dreams* still fits, but is now an elaboration and specification of a larger cosmic/mystic/psychic encounter.

313   8   It is not easy task for us to delineate the boundary between the mystic and the other breakout forms. The highest level of any of the breakout forms, the level at which what is accomplished in these forms is entirely beyond the pale of

imagining within the forms of action the breakout creative adopts, bears the stamp of the mystic. Celan and Hölderlin are mystic poets, Manet and Bacon are mystic painters; St. Paul, Freud are mystic prophets; Gandhi is a mystic leader. Even falling out of the regime of the breakout creative, we have indicated that Hegel is a mystic philosopher. Nietzsche is another case entirely, as a mystic artist and prophet.

315   [9]   This is a major responsibility in the process of mentoring mystic aspirations. If a mentor does not help this person shape the role of teaching, that which expresses these mystically figured aspirations, another resource's influences will shape them, and not for the better of anyone concerned. Gershom Scholem, for instance, refers to the "conservative" aspect of the mystic's way. He is highlighting how often (and in the case of the Kabbalah mystics he covers, this is absolutely, exclusively the case) mystics tie their wish to open up new dimensions of living to traditional texts and institutions (the classical mystics all desired to have the church be the primary beneficiary of their visions). As I envision the role of the "professional" mentor, this work would proceed in a way that at least eased the sense of isolation that arises when the mentee is not being institutionally supported or employed.

Chapter Ten

320   [1]   *Apprehending the Inaccessible: Freudian Psychoanalysis and Existential Phenomenology* (2006).

320   [2]   Mentoring, let me be clear, is not a substitute for other support modalities that are geared to address issues on the level of personality disorders, chronic depression or other psychic disturbances that prevent basic functioning in complex and demanding social and production-oriented situations. Mentoring is a support for nascent and developing aspirations that are seeking ways to be expressed and that can do so only with an aware acceptance of the exigencies of roles that enact generative aspirations – in this case, mystically figured aspirations.

3   I use the phrase "more expansive and more encompassing" as a benchmark in my listening to determine whether it is aspiration or some other "drive" or "ambition" that is at issue for a prospective mentee. While this person's words might be chained to the conventional language of ambition, getting ahead, attaining status and rank, the "more expansive and more encompassing" dynamic can be detected when, for instance, the intent of all this "climbing" behavior is not intended for the embellishment of that person's own ego needs. There is, in this case, always included a clear statement of resignation that these steps are "necessary" in order to do something else, something "more" important, "more of a contribution," and enables "more giving," not less.

The notion of "power," implicit or explicit, is also put out of play – either one's own power, or acting in ways that either lead to or result in increased power of one group becoming privileged over another. Being "more expansive" cancels out working or sacrificing so one group, one family, one party or class has power over another. Acting in a way that is "more encompassing" rules out the imposition of external laws or enforcing of conventions, and envisions a liberating of others' ways into a larger, more harmonious whole.

I use the term "great" to describe this orientation. By "great" I refer to a willingness of a person to venture into a situation knowing full well that she will not emerge from that situation with the same "identity" or "self" with which she entered it. The term conveys a sense that this person "fore-gives" rather than calibrates, and has "faith-for" rather than assumes and assesses the "risk/reward" ratio.

The standard this term applies is what I call *"generativity"*: the state of being in which whatever is existent exerts its energies and competencies so as to make way for new ways of engaging the milieu – in this case, other humans, other creatures and the earth.

325   [4]   This is a major philosophical, methodological, professional and operational distinction that I am needs to be made. I cannot provide all of the supporting material and arguments that sustain this claim here. For more a thorough approach to making a case I refer the reader to these works of mine, which are available on request: Articles (published in the proceedings of the Mentoring Conference of the University of New Mexico, "Questions Concerning the 'Essence' of Mentoring" (2012) and "Mentoring and Aspiration: Two Ideas in Search of One Another" (2013); and a book-length study, *The Aspiring Mind: A Philosophical Reflections into the Urge to Create.*

337   [5]   I use the "Keirsey Temperament Sorter II" publication, (About $.50, with steep volume discounts, from Matrix Books (http://matrixbooksinc.com/index.php?main_page=index&cPath=3&zenid=8e09abf2c929f2350f2690cf50849f8e). I use only the "self-scoring questionnaire," and not the booklet, since I do not refer *at all* to the "types." For an online version of the instrument that individuals can take (recording the numerical results, two for each category, would be sufficient), go to www.keirsey.com.

338   [6]   Bonny Gorbaty (2004). *Inner Resources.*

341   [7]   My thanks to Bonnie Gorbaty, my colleague and partner in mentoring for more than twenty years, for preparing this figure.

Xs in different locales give rise to different modes of creative exigencies: E/I: leader; S/N: Artist; F/T: Prophet; J/P: an elevation of some sort of decision-making necessity (usually one of the mystic's Xs in this sector).

Four Xs indicates to me that the person has not been willing to make distinctions according to the binary choices the instrument provides. I don't consider the instrument of any use in that case. Three Xs indicates that this person does have some track of experiential engagement that transpires in socialized ways so as to have a foothold or orientation to those engagements.

344   [8]   See Derrida, *Given Time: I. Counterfeit Money* (1992). "So as
not to take over the other, the overtaking by surprise of the
pure gift should have the generosity to give nothing that
surprises and appears as gift, nothing that presents itself as
present, nothing that is; it should therefore be surprising
enough and so thoroughly made up of a surprise that it is not
even a question of getting over it, thus of a surprise surprising
enough to let itself be forgotten without delay...the gift as
remaining without memory, without permanence and
consistency, without substance of subsistence...The secret of
that about which one cannot speak, but which one can no
longer silence." (Italics in the text; p. 147.) Also, *The Gift of
Death* (1995).

About the Author

Michael Shenkman has more than forty years of experience in first coaching and then mentoring executives, mostly in technical, creative and entrepreneurial fields. He currently works with aspiring mentees across many fields and stages of life in his private practice, Desert Sky Mentoring (www.desertskymentoring.net). He has personally mentored more than 300 aspiring mentees and has trained more than 50 mentors in this work. He has published books and articles on this subject, and has presented his findings on mentoring aspirations at academic and professional conferences. Shenkman earned a BA from Dickinson College and a PhD in Philosophy from Boston College (1977).

A gateway and overview of his work is available at

www.breakoutcreatives.net.

www.ingramcontent.com/pod-product-compliance
Lightning Source LLC
Chambersburg PA
CBHW022345280326
41935CB00007B/85